-From one traveler to

3.

MW01123099

*A*dventure Guide™ to
Idaho

Genevieve Rowles

HUNTER

Hunter Publishing, Inc.
130 Campus Drive, Edison NJ 08818
(732) 225 1900, (800) 255 0343, Fax (732) 417 0482
e-mail: hunterpub@emi.net

In Canada
1220 Nicholson Rd., Newmarket, Ontario
Canada L3Y 7V1, (800) 399 6858

ISBN 1-55650-7789-5

© 1998 Genevieve Rowles

Maps by Kim André
All photographs by author, unless otherwise indicated.
Cover photo: Superstock

For complete information about the hundreds of other travel guides and language courses offered by Hunter Publishing, visit our Web site at:

www.hunterpublishing.com

1 2 3 4 5

Contents

About the Author

Genevieve Rowles here shares her fascination with the Gem State's fabulous adventure opportunities, its gold and silver mining history, its colorful cultures and interesting people, its strikingly beautiful mountains and river valleys, wildlife and wilderness.

In 1989, Genevieve made her first trip to Idaho, running the gnarly South Fork of the Payette River, exploring portions of the Main Salmon and Hells Canyon and generally getting acquainted. The following year, she returned to check out several Idaho Centennial events, including a recreation of Salmon River sweepboat days and Cataldo Mission's Return of the Black Robes.

Idaho beckoned again. And again. Every year, numerous magazines and newspapers published Genevieve's Idaho stories. These icovered river running, B&B inns, exploring historic gold mines, jetboating into Hells Canyon, hiking the backcountry, mucking for garnets, a couple's losing battle to preserve a cabin on the Salmon River Road, RVing through Idaho with a 10-year-old. And much more.

In 1996, Genevieve and her two daughters and baby granddaughter moved from Utah to the Oregon Coast. But Idaho is still next door; close enough to return to again and again.

Home is a barn-red house on two forested acres. Neighbors include black bears and the coyotes that keep a predatory eye on the family chickens. A "pooddly kind of dog" and two cats help Genevieve and daughters Heather and Amy to tend the wood stove in winter and raise a year-round organic vegetable garden. Recycling and composting contribute to the family's self-sufficient lifestyle.

Genevieve's professional life includes membership in the Society of American Travel Writers and articles published in dozens of periodicals, including *National Geographic Traveler* and *Sunset*.

Help Us Keep This Book Up To Date

We need your input to keep the information in this guide current and accurate! Please send your comments and corrections to Hunter Publishing, 130 Campus Drive, Edison NJ 08818. Or e-mail us at hunterpub@emi.net.

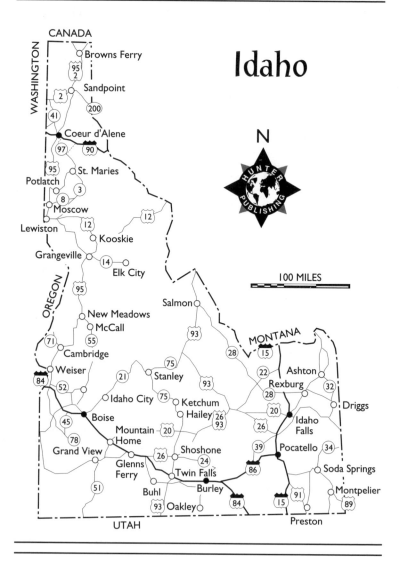

Idaho

Introduction

A dventure assumes many shapes in the sprawling, complex state of Idaho. It can be as mild as an hour spent in one of the numerous small town museums celebrating potatoes, birds of prey, or a facet of the historical mix that shaped the Gem State.

Adventure, Idaho-style, can be as white-knuckle exciting as plunging through the rapids of one of the nine rivers that make Idaho synonymous with river running for thousands of river rats who come back for more every year.

Or it can fall somewhere between these extremes: perhaps an afternoon mucking for gem-quality garnets in the Emerald Creek Ranger District, a day or two hiking one of literally hundreds of US Forest Service trails, a week's stay at a guest ranch, a ski vacation, or a road trip through country so heart-wrenchingly beautiful that staying on the road is a challenge.

No matter what shape your idea of adventure assumes, it awaits in Idaho. This book encourages you to get out and do things, to track your personal course through this many-faceted land, to get a fix in advance on where and how to experience the highs that will make your spirit soar. While it was written with first-time visitors in mind, repeat visitors will read of places and adventures that will set them to planning another trip. And yet another.

It is strongly suggested that you read this book through before deciding on the form that your Idaho adventure will take, and what emergency and other items you will need. Many caveats and suggestions mentioned in one regional chapter will apply to other regions, as well.

Idaho's vast Frank Church-River of No Return Wilderness Area and the Boise, Caribou, Challis, Clearwater, Nez Perce, Bitterroot, Payette, Salmon, Sawtooth, Targhee and Panhandle National Forests more than make up for the state's lack of national parks. Few parks can approach the grandeur of these areas' soaring peaks, deep azure lakes aleap with fish, rollicking rivers, thick forests, fanciful rock formations, and endless adventure opportunities. Ditto, Idaho's excellent state parks, many of which offer great fishing and miles of hiking and snowmobiling trails.

Outside of Boise and Idaho's few other cities, resort towns such as Coeur d'Alene, McCall and Ketchum/Sun Valley, and a handful of popular tourist attractions like Silverwood Theme Park have few crowds. In more remote areas of the state, you and your companions could well be the only humans within miles. This book will help you to avoid or seek out other people, as your mood indicates.

This is an adventure guide. It is not a whistle-stop restaurant and accommodations guide. Lodgings and eateries of special interest and/or historical value are included in this book on the premise that they belong under the "adventure" heading. Others, especially bed and breakfast inns and some chain motels, are listed for your convenience. The area contacts given under each region can be used as sources for complete accommodation and dining options.

There is no way you can take in all of Idaho in one gulp. Even if you narrow your trip to a single adventure, say backpacking, informed choices are vital. This book will set you on the right track toward making those choices. Informed choices will make the difference between a so-so visit and one enriched by insight into the people, history and wildlife of the terrain you have chosen to traverse. Anyone with a pair of hiking boots and a backpack can tromp a trail. Not just anyone might know, for example, that this particular trail parallels a segment of the Mullan Road, built circa 1859-62 to link Fort Benton, Montana with Fort Walla Walla, Washington. This book will either provide that kind of information or direct you to sources for it in a given area.

Idaho lends itself to do-it-yourself adventuring. To a point. Beyond that point, it's advisable to seek out the services of an experienced outfitter or guide. For example, you might float the Boise River or kayak a portion of the Main Payette River on your own, but unless you are an experienced river runner with the required permits, you must join a guided trip to raft the Salmon River or the Snake River through Hells Canyon. This book offers valuable, even potentially life-saving, advice on what to attempt on your own, and what you will need help with. Included are listings of licensed guides and the trips that they offer.

For many, Idaho is a great unknown. Its neighbors are Washington, Oregon, Nevada, Utah, Wyoming, Montana and Alberta, Canada. Yet, it is distinct unto itself. Idaho's rugged and beautiful terrain encompasses the struggles and aspirations, the history and traditions, of the diverse peoples who call this place home. You're sure to brush shoulders with some of them: Blackfoot, Finn, Shoshone, Basque, Nez Perce, Mormon, Coeur d'Alene, Anglo-Saxon.

Take your time studying this guide. Through its pages, Idaho and its people will become a bit less of an unknown. Map out your trip with care, so that your core adventure may be enriched with insight into the rich history and culture that underlies this exhilaratingly beautiful state.

Then, come and enjoy!

History, Geography & Background

Idaho is alive with a spirit of adventure as fresh as a glistening mountain lake at dawn, as exhilarating as shooting Class IV rapids on the River of No Return. One of the Lower 48's last wild outposts, Idaho projects a sense of discovery whose edge shows no sign of wearing thin, despite a recent spate of media hype and the resultant increase in visitation.

Idaho harbors no pretensions, with no interest in appearing to be something it's not. It doesn't need to. Idaho doesn't swagger; doesn't need to do that, either. Maybe that accounts for the state's low profile. Maybe, too, that accounts for Idahoans' ability to poke fun at themselves. Case in point: Stinker Service Stations, at least one of which occupies a prominent spot in almost every town.

Few folks had even heard of Idaho until the 1930s, when railway potentate W. Averell Harriman went ga-ga over the Wood River Valley and set about developing the area into the Sun Valley of winter sports fame. For the next 50 years or so, Sun Valley was synonymous with Idaho and that was that. It took then-President Jimmy Carter's highly publicized 1979 float down the Middle Fork of the Salmon, followed a decade later by the hoop-la surrounding the Gem State's Centennial celebration, to wake flatlanders up to Idaho's literally endless opportunities for adventure.

Idaho's welcome mat has gained texture and some pretty plush pile since Harriman's pre-Sun Valley days. Accommodations no longer run to seedy motels. Idaho's sudden popularity has spawned a rash of new B&Bs. An example is tiny Almo, gateway to the City of Rocks, also known as rock climbers' heaven. Idaho's bed and breakfast inns range from a couple of spiffed-up spare bedrooms in someone's home to luxury digs. Breakfasts vary from continental to downhome hearty to Western gourmet (an oxymoron, perhaps).

Idaho boasts few luxury resorts. Most accommodations are B&Bs, motels/hotels built within the last decade, or rustic cabins. A few historic hotels are stand-outs. Prices vary widely. High season lodgings can be pricey in popular Coeur d'Alene and trendy Ketchum/Sun Valley.

Camping and RVing are popular. Idaho's splendid state parks offer luscious dollops of nature in safe surroundings. Forest Service and Bureau of Land Management (BLM) campgrounds are numerous and well-spaced, particularly in high traffic areas such as Hwy 75 along the Salmon River.

Dining options are spotty. You can buy a burger in every crossroads hamlet. Sometimes very good burgers. Potatoes? You bet! Vegetables? Maybe, maybe not. Most larger towns/resorts, especially those popular with the summer sun-and-swim crowd, offer one or more eateries serving up sophisticated Southwestern, continental or California cuisine. Even predominantly Mormon Snake River Plain towns, long known for bland fare, are exhibiting a cautious culinary creativity.

Idaho's comfort quotient is on the upswing as more travelers discover its beauty and opportunities for adventure. It hasn't always been thus. Idaho is proud to be a state where history shakes hands with the present.

In the mid-19th century, folks regarded Idaho as a corridor to someplace else. California, Oregon and Utah were the big draws. Idaho was left to a scattering of fur trappers and a clutch of Native American tribes living out their last peaceful years on ancestral land. Since time out of mind, the Nez Perce, Shoshone-Bannock, Coeur d'Alene, Kootenai, Kalispell and Paiute tribes had called this place home. Their descendants still live here, weaving vital, colorful threads through Idaho's many-textured tapestry of peoples.

Lewis & Clark were Idaho's first adventure travelers. In 1805, the intrepid pair, guided by a young Shoshone woman named Sacajawea, trekked across the state en route to the mouth of the Columbia River.

A few gold-bedazzled 1840s prospectors slogged through the Idaho Panhandle on the Mullan Road, a forest track extending west from the end of Missouri River navigation at Fort Benton, Montana. Others cut across a corner of southeast Idaho. Neither group thought of Idaho in gold mine terms. Ironically, gold and silver lay near to hand. It's a wonder they didn't fall over it. It was only decades later, after the bright promises of California and Yukon gold had lost their luster, that prospectors trickled back into Idaho and hit pay dirt. In remote places like Murray, they're still at it.

Meanwhile, Oregon-bound wagon trains wended their weary way across the Snake River Plain, making perilous river crossings, resting briefly at Fort Boise before tackling Oregon's formidable Blue Mountains. They little guessed that the parched sage brush lands over which they labored hid agricultural gold. That discovery was left to 1860s-era Mormons seeking to extend their territory north from Salt Lake City.

At about the same time, Confederate sympathizers from Missouri, on the run from harassment (or worse) by Civil War-era bushwhackers, were finding a haven, and gold, in Idaho's soon-to-boom gold towns. The Indian-US Cavalry skirmishes that followed spelled an end to life as the state's Native Americans had known it. The Nez Perce War ended in 1877 with the capture of Chief Joseph and 100 of his followers just short of reaching a safe haven across the Canadian border. That put the cap on what Whites perceived as "Indian uprisings." Chief Joseph's poignant speech started his people on the long road to peaceful co-existence with Whites: "I am tired of fighting... the old men are all dead... it is cold, and we have no blankets. The little children are freezing to death. My heart is sick and sad. From where the sun now stands, I will fight no more forever."

Idaho Territory was created in 1863 as a kind of holding facility for lands, comprising parts of present-day Idaho, Wyoming and Montana, that no one wanted. Take a good look at a map of Idaho. Except for a straight line bordering Utah, all those illogical looking zigs and zags reflect the borders that remained after Congress "squared up" Wyoming, Montana, Washington and Oregon. That "step-child" mentality still held sway in 1890, when Idaho achieved statehood. Idaho was admitted to the Union as the 43rd state, but it was perceived as being so remote and inconsequential that no one much cared. Even today, 42% of Idaho is designated a frontier under the less than two-people-per-square-mile Federal guideline for such matters.

Even Idaho's name fits this "step-child" perception. Seems that the name was dreamed up by a 19th-century mining lobbyist who palmed it off on Congress as meaning "gem of the mountains" in some conveniently unidentified Indian language. But the name was only plastered on the territory that became Idaho after being tried on for size by several other Western locales. So Idaho became Idaho. It came by the "Gem State" designation honestly, Idaho being the only place in the world outside India where star garnets are found.

As recently as 10 years ago, most folks driving across Idaho on Interstates 15, 86 and 84 hadn't an inkling of the wonders awaiting discovery beyond the cultivated and/or desert belt.

I discovered Idaho in 1989, while researching a travel article for publication during Idaho's centennial year. My friends were mystified by my enthusiasm over a state synonymous, in their minds, with potato fields. I countered their disbelief with rapturous accounts of a doe and her fawn ambling just feet away while I breakfasted beside the frolicking Middle Fork of the Salmon River; of hiking through a thick fir forest to an abandoned gold mine shaft penetrating deep into a mountainside.

That romance has long since settled into an enduring relationship, but the wonder remains fresh. I still gasp in surprise at the sight of jagged Sawtooth peaks flamed by the setting sun; at a cold water drenching as our raft plunges down yet another stairstep rapid on the South Fork of the Payette.

Rumor has it that, next to the Dakotas and maybe Kansas, Idaho is one of the last states that travelers get around to visiting. It took awhile, but flatlanders are discovering, as I did, that Idaho serves up no end of adventures amid an astonishing variety of natural and geographical features.

It's a toss-up whether to define Idaho geography by its magnificent mountains and lakes. Or by the rivers that many consider to be synonymous with the state, making Idaho one of the top river-running states in the country. But there's much, much more. Most visitors identify Idaho with their favorite activity, be it backpacking, horseback riding, fishing, boating, camping, wildlife-watching. Or just chasing the scenery on roads that are reasonably good, considering all the mountainous terrain and rugged backcountry.

Idaho is wide across the bottom, narrowing northward to a chimney-like panhandle. Plunk in the center is the largest wilderness in the contiguous 48 states. In 1980, Congress set aside this 2.3-million-acre, roadless, mountainous tract known as the Frank Church-River of No Return and Selway-Bitterroot Wilderness. You explore here by foot, horseback, watercraft or airplane. Except for a scattering of grandfathered guest ranches and lodges, these lands, once the domain of prospectors, hermits and a few homesteaders, are totally primitive.

This is more than okay if you're hiking or rafting, less so if you want to drive from here to there. For example, you're in Salmon (the town, not the river) and want to drive to Coeur d'Alene. You either head north through a chunk of Montana to Missoula and then into the Idaho Panhandle, or you head south, then west, before wending your way north. By any route, the scenery is knockout fabulous.

The **Teton Range**, straddling the Idaho-Wyoming border, lords it over the slice of Idaho east of I-15. Some say the hiking and skiing are better on the Idaho side than on the heavily hyped Wyoming side. And you can count on more solitude. Potato fields blanket the area around Idaho Falls; sheep graze to the north. A pocket of undulating hills in the southeast corner of the state provides a study in contrasts: neat Mormon agricultural towns, funky Lava Hot Springs, Bear Lake with its windsurfers and waterskiers, Fort Hall Indian Reservation's tax-free shops.

West of I-15, the topography echoes the high deserts and rocky outcroppings of Utah and Nevada. Craters of the Moon National Monument seduces in jumbled, jagged splendor north of the Snake River Plain and south of where the Central Idaho mountains get serious. The lavafield is a maze of tubes and crevices waiting to be explored. To the south, the Snake River cuts a deep channel in the tableland, creating 60-story volcanic rock monoliths and sheer canyon walls. To the south and west, the desert gets real with sand dunes and wind-sculpted rock formations. The ghost town of Silver City recalls Idaho's gold rush backlash. The

Bruneau/Jarbridge and Owyhee, hang-on-tight river systems plunging between incised canyons, slice the dry desert.

The **Sawtooth Range**, arguably the most spectacular of the 80 mountain ranges that make Idaho the most mountainous of the Rocky Mountain states, soars skyward to the north of Sun Valley. It is scored by the Salmon River and its equally fabulous Middle Fork, encompassing the wilderness areas, studded with hot springs, miners' shacks leaning that-a-way, and more feisty characters than you'd meet in a lifetime anywhere else. Central Idaho defines adventure.

Boise, Idaho's rapidly growing capital city, is the gateway to a north country of forests, lakes and rivers. North of New Meadows, US 95 meanders across the sun-soaked Palouse and Camas Prairies, in summer awave with acres upon acres of ripening grain. The Camas is Nez Perce country, studded with reminders of Chief Joseph's valiant stand against the US Cavalry. On the west, the prairie drops off into Hells Canyon, the deepest canyon in North America.

The Panhandle may be relatively small, but it's big on fir-fringed lakes: the Coeur d'Alene, the Pend D'Oreille, the pristine Priest. Rivers, too. Not roistering rivers like the Snake plunging through Hells Canyon, but lazy canoe-friendly rivers. This is silver and logging country, home to crusty miners and fun-loving descendants of Finnish loggers.

Idaho is too big, too varied, to digest in a single foray. Add the you-can't-get-there-from-here situation caused by the wilderness areas, and it's best to savor it in bites.

Choose your bite for the adventures that appeal, according to the people and/or history that spark your curiosity, and for scenery that sends your spirit soaring.

You'll yearn to come back for more. I guarantee it. Idaho exerts that kind of irresistible, magical pull.

How to Use this Book

Idaho is a spacious state that defies a logical regional breakdown. Unlike the Idaho State Tourism Department, this guide uses principle access routes, rather than geographical features or zones, to divide the state into five manageable chapters. However, I hope that you will find the following regional breakdown easy to work with.

Chapters are arranged in a sequence reflecting gateway cities. Beginning with Boise, the state capital, this book describes a circle that swings northward through the Panhandle, dips southward through the vast

Central Region, curves to take in eastern Idaho, then travels through southern Idaho and back to Boise.

- Region 1 includes Boise, Idaho's largest city, and an hourglass-shaped area defined by the Interstate 84 corridor on the south, the Idaho-Oregon state line/Hells Canyon on the west, ID 55 and US 95 on the east, and a stretch of US 12 on the north. **Airline gateways**: Boise, Lewiston and Spokane, WA.

- Region 2 includes the Idaho Panhandle from US 12 on the south to the Canadian border. **Airline gateways**: Spokane, WA and Moscow.

- Region 3 covers Central Idaho and encompasses the vast Frank Church-River of No Return Wilderness Area. It is defined by Regions 1 and 2 on the north and west, the Montana state line and I-15 on the east, and I-86 and I-84 on the south. **Airline gateways**: Boise, Sun Valley/Hailey and Idaho Falls.

- Region 4 covers the territory east of I-15 and butts up against Montana on the north, Wyoming on the east, and Utah on the south. **Airline gateways**: Pocatello, Idaho Falls.

- Region 5 takes in Idaho's high desert west of I-15 and south of I-84. This region's geographic features merge seamlessly with those of Utah, Nevada and eastern Oregon. **Airline gateways**: Boise and Twin Falls.

Each chapter begins with an introduction and a run-down on the region's history, culture, climate, topography, points of interest and activities. Next comes *Getting Around,* a brief section designed to fix in your mind the basics of traveling through each region. This section also describes designated scenic highways and byways and things to look for (or to watch out for) along the way. It also includes useful information sources and contact numbers for chambers of commerce, and US Department of Agriculture Forest Service ranger district offices.

The *Touring* sections highlight museums and other points of interest.

Separate sections detail specific adventure categories within each region. These include options for independent travelers and for those seeking guided trips. This book lists State of Idaho licensed and bonded outfitters and guides offering trips in specific categories. It is against the law to outfit or guide professionally in Idaho without a license. The licensing protocol is rigorous. Most of the outfitters listed in this book are members of Idaho Outfitters and Guides Association (IOGA). IOGA

Introduction

members adhere to a rigid code of ethics, believe in promoting the preservation and conservation of Idaho's natural resources, and enjoy a positive working relationship with state and federal land management agencies.

The following are brief descriptions of these adventure categories and what they may include.

This book does not pretend to be a definitive guide to Idaho's every remote corner and every adventure opportunity. That would be virtually impossible. Idaho's vast wildernesses and adventurous activities offer literally endless chances to discover your own fun. This guide will get you started.

On Foot

Hiking/Backpacking/Rock Climbing

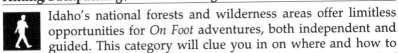 Idaho's national forests and wilderness areas offer limitless opportunities for *On Foot* adventures, both independent and guided. This category will clue you in on where and how to locate trails that suit your interests and abilities. Idaho has no end of hiking trails, and every one leads to a surprise: a sparkling hidden lake, an abandoned gold mine, a walk in the footsteps of historic trekkers, fields of wildflowers, bald eagle nests, skittish mountain goats, hot springs, silver streams, and always a come-hither vista of mountains, sky and forest. No doubt that Idaho is a hiker's dream come true.

Idaho's hundreds upon hundreds of miles of trails range from easy paths of a mile or two to strenuous multi-day wilderness adventures requiring specialized rock climbing equipment and finely-honed skills. Trails for every hiking level fall between these extremes. It is impossible to list them all, but you will find trails for all ability levels, plus information on where to find helpful brochures, purchase topographical and/or trail maps, information on specific trail ratings, and updates on current trail conditions. Forest Service personnel are there to help you. Make use of them. No question or concern about backcountry travel is too minor.

- Some trails or portions thereof may be closed or impassable due to floods, landslides or other natural causes, particularly in spring and early summer. Ask questions, no matter how hesitant you may be to display your ignorance in backcountry matters. Make sure to match your abilities to the trail, then stay on it and take no chances. Never hike alone.

- Be sure to advise someone of your hiking plan and when you expect to return so that you can be found if something goes wrong. While most US Forest Service offices and ranger stations do not offer this service, someone there may agree to note your name and planned route. An important caveat: be sure to contact the person you left your itinerary with upon your return. Setting a search party in motion when all the while you are happily hefting a beer in a local watering hole is a serious no-no. And you could be stuck with the search and rescue bill.

- Even though most short trails are boot-worn and well marked, it's easy to get lost. Becoming lost on longer backcountry trails stretches possibility to probability. It's essential that you make careful preparations before heading into the wilderness.

- Respect the altitude. Altitude sickness is no joke. If you live below 500 feet, take a day or two to get used to Idaho's 2,500-9,500-foot altitudes before even thinking about strenuous activity. And remember that Idaho is a mountainous state where hiking and uphill slogs often combine. Make sure your physical condition matches the activity you have in mind.

- Wear sturdy, waterproof, well-broken-in hiking boots with lug soles. A blister is the last thing you need. I've seen people on the trail in sneakers, even sandals. They're the ones who get carried off the mountain on stretchers. Even if you're heading off on a day hike on a sunny mid-summer morn, be sure to put a rain poncho and cold weather gear in your backpack. You could become lost and stranded. Nights are cold in the mountains, sometimes dipping to freezing even in summer.

- Never venture out without water: a gallon per day per person. Remember that even though that mountain stream or spring appears to be sparkling clean, it may contain nasty microscopic critters that cause *giardia*, an intestinal illness that packs a bear-size wallop and lingers long after you return home. Pack food for a couple of days longer than you expect to be out.

- Only experienced backcountry hikers with solid orienteering and survival skills should attempt independent backpacking into the Frank Church-River of No Return Wilderness. It is strongly recommended that you hire a guide licensed to lead treks into these areas. Failing that, don't overestimate your backcountry skills.

Trails of the Frank Church-River of No Return Wilderness by Margaret Fuller, published by Signpost Books, is an excellent reference for hikers wishing to venture on their own. It costs $14.95 and is available in most Idaho book outlets, or from Signpost Books, 8912 192nd St. W., Edmonds, WA 98020.

On Horseback & Travel with Pack Animals

Horses and pack animals, usually mules or burros, have taken Westerners where they want to go since pioneer times. These sturdy, surefooted animals are still the best bet for trekking into Idaho's national forests and wilderness areas. You can save your feet by riding into the backcountry on horseback, or save your back by stowing your gear on the backs of mules, burros, or even llamas.

Horses are available for rent in some areas. Guides offer horseback and/or pack-supported multi-day wilderness trips reflecting a variety of interests, even camping in wolf country. Licensed outfitters and their specialties are listed by region.

Guest ranches offering horseback riding are listed under accommodations.

On Wheels

Jeeps, Bicycles, Wagons

Jeeps or other sturdy high clearance 4WD vehicles are musts in negotiating many of Idaho's unimproved backcountry roads even in dry weather, let alone in spring and fall. Idaho has hundreds of miles of minimal roads which may include numerous switchbacks and steep grades climbing into some of the state's most remote areas. Most are marked on the Official Idaho Road Map. Watch for "Warning: Suitable for 4-Wheel Drive Vehicles Only" signs at some points of entry.

Unimproved and private farm or ranch roads may look similar. Be careful to stay off private land and on the road. Off-road country is often ecologically fragile. Wheel marks can take decades to erase in some ecologies, especially deserts, if they are erasible at all.

Some Forest Service trails are open to mountain biking. This guide lists some, but not all trails. Before setting out, stop at the applicable Ranger District office to purchase a travel map and obtain updated trail information. Guided mountain biking trips are available, some over historic trails. Many include soaks in one or more of Idaho's hundreds of hot springs.

If you prefer more sedate bicycling, you can enjoy numerous Idaho State Park trails, city greenways and paths in and around Sun Valley, Coeur d'Alene and other resort areas. Check this guide's regional listings for bicycle trail suggestions.

The Oregon Trail's 1993 sesquicentennial celebration spawned an interest in covered wagon and other trips over historic trails. Idaho was criss-crossed by the Oregon Trail and several cut-offs, so it's not surprising that revisiting the Oregon Trail is on the state's adventure menu. This book lists both guided and self-generated trips.

On Water

Whitewater Rafting, Kayaking, Canoeing, Jet Boat & Lake Excursions, Sailing, Fishing & Diving

 With few exceptions, if you can do it on water, you can do it in Idaho. It may seem a stretch for a land-locked state to make that claim, but it's a fact.

Idaho has 3,100 river miles, more than any other state. These rivers, and the canyons through which they course, are legendary. Some have been designated Wild and Scenic Rivers. Many test the mettle and skills of rafters and kayakers. Rapids are rated on a I through VI scale. **Class I** offers relaxed floating. **Class II** has gentle waves that a kid can negotiate. **Class III** rapids are considered intermediate, with thrilling get-wet waves. **Class IV** rapids get serious, requiring a knowledge of river dynamics. **Class V** rapids are dead serious, often requiring advance scouting by expert river runners. **Class VI** rapids are unrunnable. A given river's rapids and character may change according to weather conditions and time of year. Flows are heightened in spring, when runoff is high. Trips suitable for young children are usually scheduled for late summer, when flows are low.

Choose a guided trip unless you or a generous friend owns a whitewater raft or dory, plus the mountain of gear needed for several days on the river – and unless you are willing to take your chances on obtaining a coveted permit allowing you to put into a particular river on a specified day. Many outfits offer theme trips such as history, ecology, even wine tasting floats. Floats designed for specialized groups, such as seniors, families, women, recovering alcoholics, are also available. Many outfitters bring along inflatable kayaks, a fun way to get a feel for the river without committing yourself to serious kayaking. Kids love these.

Take your time selecting an outfitter. This guide lists whitewater river outfitters and guides of proven reliability who are licensed to operate in Idaho and are members of the Idaho Outfitters & Guides Association. Contact several: request brochures, ask questions about price, insurance, cancellation policies and what is included (first night in a motel, transportation, what kinds of gear, fishing tackle, inflatable kayaks, dinner wines). You may wish to request client references.

Decide which river pushes your buttons for scenery, climate (yes, much of Idaho lies above the 45th Parallel, but deep canyons like Hells are hot as Hades in summer), wave action, history, wildlife watching, surrounding terrain. How long a trip do you have in mind? Do you want a rustic sleep-on-the-ground trip, a "luxury" float with tents and gourmet cuisine, or one on which guests overnight at riverside lodges? Do you want to paddle or let someone else do the paddling? Some trips offer both options. The smaller the raft, the bigger the ride. Ask the outfitter under consideration how many people his/her rafts carry. Carefully match the trip with your abilities. Don't take on more whitewater than you can handle.

Some outfitters offer half-day or one-day river trips, often with plenty of thrills. This might be an option if you aren't sure whether everyone in your group will get into shooting rapids. These trips don't usually require advance reservations. This guide will clue you in on where to locate such spur-of-the-moment trips.

Jetboating the Snake into Hells Canyon is an adventure everyone can enjoy.

Not all Idaho rivers boast the high profiles of whitewater rivers like the Salmon and Lochsa. Numerous quieter rivers, notably the shadowy St. Joe and Coeur d'Alene, offer pleasant canoeing. Jetboating trips on the Snake into Hells Canyon, and on some segments of the Salmon, are big draws for those who want to experience these rivers, but haven't the time or the inclination to go the whitewater route. This guide lists jetboat operators.

Idaho's natural lakes include Coeur d'Alene, Pend Oreille and Priest in the Panhandle, Payette Lake north of Boise, and Bear Lake in southeast Idaho. These are the quintessential north country summer playgrounds. Boats and a variety of aquatic toys are available for rent. Tour boat excursions operate on some lakes. This guide includes tips on where to find the fun.

Retreating glaciers, ancient volcanoes and earthquakes left gem-like lakes of azure blue in the high mountain reaches. If you happen upon one of these secret lakes, you will know the exhilaration that mountain man John Colter must have felt back in 1808, when he stumbled onto Yellowstone's geysers. See *On Foot* for tips on finding these hidden gems.

Man-made lakes backed up behind dams cozy into seemingly every fold in the hills below the 44th Parallel. These multi-purpose reservoirs were designed for storing water to irrigate Idaho's bountiful fields of potatoes, sugar beets, alfalfa and other crops. Most aren't much to look at, having sagebrush and native grass shorelines. Nevertheless, they are popular with local boaters. Boat ramps are available. Some, such as Cascade Reservoir, offer excellent fishing. Others, such as sprawling Dworshak Dam and Reservoir on the North Fork of the Clearwater River, support hydro-electric plants. Every reservoir does not warrant a mention. This guide describes those affording the best boating and fishing.

Two cautionary notes: alcohol and water can be a lethal mixture. Every year, numerous water-related injuries and deaths are directly attributed to alcohol consumption. Wait for down time in camp to quaff that beer. And always, no matter how calm the water appears, wear a life jacket; it won't do you any good if left in the boat while you're floundering in the water.

On Snow

Skiing, Snowmobiling, Dog Sledding, Ice Climbing, Ice Fishing, Winter Festivals

Snow begins to shawl Idaho's mountains and plains in late October or early November, transforming autumn's golden aspens and arid hillsides into a hushed white landscape.

Idaho is snow country, as surely as it is mountain and river country. And posh Sun Valley is far from being the only star in Idaho's winter galaxy. The resort that railroad dollars built and Ernest Hemingway made trendy is justly famous for Alpine and Nordic skiing, ice skating and ski tours. But a proliferation of new ski resorts offers plenty of challenging downhill fun. Some, such as the Panhandle's Schweitzer Mountain, boast the shortest lift lines in the West. Brundage Mountain at McCall, whose winter sports tradition goes back farther than Sun Valley's, and Bogus Basin in the hills north of Boise, are adding new lifts and facilities. Grand Targhee affords a Tetons high in a less crowded setting than Jackson Hole on the east side of Teton Pass.

This guide lists Idaho's ski resorts, plus the information you'll need to make an informed choice.

You may think of Idaho as being all mountains (Idaho has more peaks over 10,000 feet than any other Rocky Mountain state), but it's not so. Large areas such as the mesa (actually a large volcanic caldera from the Pleistoscene age) in the extreme northeast corner, the Lava deposits on the Snake River Plain, the Panhandle in the Coeur d'Alene/Sandpoint region, are virtually table-top level. These and numerous other areas lend themselves uncommonly well to cross-country skiing over miles of groomed trails.

Park N' Ski, an Idaho Department of Parks and Recreation program, utilizes 18 separate trail systems and four State Park Ski Areas throughout the state. Permit decals can be purchased at sports shops, State Park offices, US Forest Ranger Stations and chambers of commerce.

Not all trails are level and not all are near populated areas. Some are hilly, some penetrate the backcountry, where snow conditions are often unstable, with avalanches a possibility in certain areas. It is strongly recommended that you check with a regional information source before heading into the backcountry. And it's always a good idea to apprise someone left behind of your plans. Weather conditions can, and do, change rapidly. Be sure to dress warmly and carry high energy foods. Don't wear cotton, which retains moisture. Do wear waterproof outerwear. Be realistic about matching your abilities to the proposed route.

This guide lists Nordic ski areas and the safest backcountry touring, trekking and hut-to-hut skiing terrain, plus where to go for instruction and rentals. Cross-country, yurt-to-yurt and dog sledding guides and tours are also listed.

Idaho has more groomed snowmobile trails than any other Western state; more than 5,000 miles of them over every imaginable kind of terrain. These include private and public lands with many interconnecting mazes. A map showing these snowmobile areas and including important information about snowmobiling in Idaho can be obtained by contacting the Idaho Department of Parks and Recreation, Attn: Snowmobiling, 2177 Warm Springs Ave., Boise, ID 83702. ☎ 208-334-2284.

Numerous resorts and guest ranches cater to the sport, with guided snowmobile trips on offer. This guide lists the principle snowmobile areas, guest lodges, resorts and licensed guides.

Dog sledding trips are an option in some areas. Ice climbing is the ultimate winter high. This book will steer you in the right direction for these and other winter adventures.

Several Idaho lakes offer super ice fishing. Bear Lake is famous for its Bonneville cisco, claimed to be found nowhere else in the world.

In the Air

Backcountry Flying & Flightseeing

 If you sign on for a float down the Middle Fork of the Salmon, or a stay in a guest ranch in the Frank Church-River of No Return Wilderness Area, chances are that getting there will involve putting your life in the capable hands of an Idaho bush pilot. These four- to eight-seater bush planes resemble toy airplanes propelled by a tightly wound rubber band – scary, considering that's all there is between you and eternity. But not to worry. These and similar aircraft have been safely flying over the Idaho wilderness for decades. So relax and enjoy the views.

Idaho's mountainous wilderness looks much different from the air than from the ground. To the east, the rising sun tips the Sawtooths with irridescent pinks and golds. A gem of a mountain lake, a day's hike from a trailhead, sparkles below. You fancy that you see a fish rippling the water.

From the air, you can see more of Idaho, in bigger chunks. You begin to appreciate the immensity of this place, to get a handle on its complexity. How did Lewis & Clark and the trappers, explorers, prospectors and settlers who followed even begin to find their way through this enormous maze of mountains, valleys, rivers, and canyons? How did Native Americans range over this land for untold centuries without losing their way? It looks so untrackable. Now you understand why the best advice is to enjoy Idaho in small bites, then come back for more.

You needn't be heading into the wilderness to flightsee over Idaho. Many licensed pilots offer flightseeing trips. This Adventure Guide will put you in touch with the best.

Wildlife Watching

Where to See Birds, Animals, Flora

 From the Snake River Birds of Prey Area in southwest Idaho to Grays Lake National Wildlife Refuge in northeast Idaho, to the expansive wildlife habitats in the wilderness areas and national forests, Idaho rivals Alaska in the numbers and varieties of birds and animals supported by varied ecologies. Trumpeting swans, black bears, mountain goats, peregrine falcons, song birds, deer, elk, moose. Whatever your interest, you'll find sighting areas and guided wildlife watching trips in this book.

If you are serious about spotting wildlife, you would do well to have in hand Leslie Benjamin Carpenter's *Idaho Wildlife Viewing Guide*. To obtain a copy, send a check for $6.95 to Viewing Guide, c/o Idaho Fish & Game Dept., PO Box 25, Boise, ID 83707.

Wildflowers begin popping up in early spring in Idaho's lower elevations, spreading into the higher elevations as the season progresses. High mountain hikers may come upon color displays as late as September. Certain meadows, like the one bordering the access road to Stanley Lake, are famous for their rich wildflower tapestries. The largest wildflower displays follow snowy winters and wet springs.

The showiest and most evocative "wildflower" displays began as shrubs and bulbs planted by settlers yearning for a familiar sight of home in what must have seemed a wild and alien place. Their cabins have long since crumbled away, but here and there a riotously blooming purple lilac bush, a patch of yellow daffodils, tells their silent story. While it's impossible to list every spot in which wildflowers bloom, this book mentions some highlights. Keep your eyes open for unexpected pleasures.

Kid Stuff

Adventures for Eight-to-Teens

 This Adventure Guide covers few adventures unsuitable for eight-to-teens (Class V river rafting and rock climbing come to mind). Kids' definition of adventure may not always mesh with their parents' (the umpty-ninth historical museum, for example). Sometimes doing kid stuff is a must, if only to counter boredom. Some of this may not appeal to parents, but you want to expose your tagalongs to every mind- and body-expanding adventure possible, don't you?

We pick up on especially-for-kids stuff and present it here for parental perusal. Not only can you offer your tagalongs some of these cool adventures on your own, but you can enroll them in a tailored-for-kids course and/or join a river trip designed for families. Some include kids younger than this book's admittedly arbitrary cut-off age of eight.

Eco-Travel & Other Adventures

 In Idaho, placing eco-travel in a separate category seems redundant. The ecology is as jealously guarded as a medieval maiden. Strict regulations are in force, especially on rivers and in wilderness areas, regarding the disposal of trash and personal refuse. But a few guided trips are designed to heighten guests' appreciation of a given area's ecological and cultural heritage. You will find them listed herein.

Idaho is a grab bag full of adventures that defy classification. Gleanings from that bag are also listed.

Festivals & Special Events

 Idahoans are big on festivals. Some of the most colorful are staged by Native American tribes. Oregon Trail trekkers are duly remembered with commemorative doings. Others include tribal celebrations, summer arts and crafts festivals, music festivals, Mountain Man rendezvous and, of course, Western-style celebrations complete with rodeos. This guide will clue you in on established annual events throughout the state.

Where to Stay & Eat

 In many ways, Idaho is but a blink removed from the frontier. The colorful characters you'll meet hanging out at equally colorful watering holes in some areas of the state could be crusty mountain men or prospectors reincarnated. In other places, especially agricultural areas, bland is in.

Many listings under this heading reflect this book's raison d'être: adventure. "Adventure" is not a synonym for "cool." This book will try to steer you toward positive lodging and dining adventures. A meal in a restaurant can be an adventure, as can a night's lodging in a bed and breakfast inn. Meeting the people who own and manage these establishments can be a real adventure. This guide lists places offering a unique experience, as well as those offering home comforts. Wherever possible, listings reflect B&B tastes, not motel tastes.

The US Forest Service has cabins and former fire lookout towers available for rent in the Bitterroot, Nez Perce, Caribou and Panhandle

National Forests. Most are primitive furnished accommodations with wood stoves. Expect to bring your own bedding, cooking utensils and possibly water. Some require minimum or maximum stays. Contact a Forest Service office to request a copy of the US Forest Service's *Northern Region Recreational Cabin and Lookout Directory*, to obtain a cabin permit, and for information on what to bring. Look for National Forest contacts under *Information Sources* at the end of each chapter.

Guest ranches offering horseback riding and numerous other activities are listed by region. By definition, guest ranches offer horseback riding and lots of it. They may also offer fishing, hiking, river rafting, cross-country skiing and/or other outdoors activities. Most of the ranches listed in this book include a range of services in their prices; they do not simply rent cabins. These ranches are situated in the midst of unimaginable natural splendor.

When contacting a guest ranch, be sure to ask plenty of questions. Does the ranch concentrate on horseback riding to the exclusion of other activities? Some do. If not, what other activities are on offer? What kind of horseback instruction is available, and how much? Is this instruction/orientation mandatory before guests may go on trail rides? Is there a children's program? If so, for what ages? You'll think of a raft of other questions. Don't be bashful.

Idaho folks are becoming visitor-savvy, in even the smallest towns. You can find a bed and a meal in every corner of the state, save the wilderness areas. Local chambers of commerce and tourist information offices are good resources. A phone call will get you a blizzard of lodging and other local information.

Camping

This section includes state parks, US Forest Service and Bureau of Land Management (BLM) campgrounds and some commercial campgrounds. Wilderness camping is included in *On Foot* sections within each region.

Travel Strategies & Helpful Facts

Idaho is a big state. Reaching some areas can be awkward because of that big chunk of wilderness in the center of it all. Unless you have a couple of weeks to savor more than one or two regions, you'd best decide which section of the state suits your adventurous spirit and plan on returning for more at a later time. If you book a multi-day outfitted trip, the outfitter may arrange to meet you at the airport. Otherwise, you'll need a car. Consider renting a high-clearance 4-wheel-drive vehicle if you plan to drive in remote areas or on unimproved Forest Service roads. Major car rental agencies serve gateway cities.

Touring Idaho in a recreational vehicle is feasible. A plus is the state's numerous RV parks. A drawback is that some unpaved roads are not recommended for RVs. These are usually unimproved roads requiring 4-wheel-drive vehicles. I've covered all but the remotest parts of Idaho in my 24-foot motorhome.

Boise is served by Delta, Northwest, United and Southwest airlines. Horizon and Skywest fly into Boise from regional destinations. The Panhandle is served by Air Canada, Alaska Airlines, Delta, Northwest, Southwest and United flying into Spokane, Washington, a 30-minute drive from Coeur d'Alene. Delta serves Idaho Falls. Skywest and Horizon Airlines link Lewiston, Pocatello, Sun Valley/Hailey and Twin Falls with Boise, Spokane and other Western cities.

As this book goes to press, Amtrak's Empire Builder stops at Sandpoint in the Panhandle and the Pioneer stops at Pocatello and Boise. Amtrak seems to put trains on and off routes as easily as a child moves toy trains, so be sure to contact Amtrak at ☎ 800/872-7245 for current route information before considering traveling to Idaho by train.

With the exception of a few high-profile summer and winter playgrounds, Idaho remains surprisingly uncrowded. You can hike for days without seeing another human. River floaters may pass other outfits, but they never share campsites. Some adventures must be enjoyed in summer, but consider visiting in late spring or early fall when schools are in session, families have yet to hit the road, and the weather is crisp, with clear cold nights and sunny days.

Ski resorts, especially Idaho's lower-profile resorts, offer uncrowded conditions virtually all season long. Experienced skiers know that spring offers some skiing with warmer temperatures than January and February. Before you go, contact the resort you are considering to request current snow conditions.

Climate

On a given summer day, Idaho's temperatures can range from 60° on a Sawtooths trail above Redfish Lake, to 95 in Boise. Hells Canyon may be a baking 105°. The higher you go, the cooler it is. The lower you go, the hotter it gets. Factor in summer temperatures when deciding which adventure to choose and when to do it. You might want to save that Hells Canyon or Owyhee Badlands hike for spring or fall. Hike the Sawtooths in mid-summer.

Winter temperatures also vary widely. On a given mid-winter day, Boise could be basking in a sunny 45° while at Grand Targhee Ski Resort the thermometer registers a frigid -10°.

While the Snake River Plain, Boise, Lewiston, deep river canyons and Idaho's other lower-lying pockets might enjoy as many as eight snow-free months, higher elevations can receive snow in any month, with the possible exception of July.

Idaho is mostly a semi-arid state. The Panhandle gets more rain than the southwestern desert; the mountains receive the most, in the form of thunder storms. Snows can be fickle, deluging the slopes in some years, merely dusting them in others. But, in most years, Idaho ski resorts receive at least 500 inches of snow.

Plan your Idaho adventure with weather conditions in mind. You'll be glad you did.

Clothing & Gear

Casual clothing fits the Idaho lifestyle. T-shirts or sweatshirts and shorts or jeans are okay everywhere except for dining in Boise's upscale restaurants and the tonier resorts. Here, men might don a sport jacket in winter, shirt and tie in summer; women a skirt or dressy pants and top. Match your clothing to your activity and you can't go wrong.

Packing tons of clothing can seem like overkill, especially if you don't end up wearing it. However, it's essential to take along warm clothing, even in summer. Layered clothing is a must for high-sweat, quick-cool-off activities such as hiking, biking and cross-country skiing. Planning for the severest conditions is the key to comfort and to deriving the most pleasure from your adventure. You can shed layers as the day warms up and your activity level rises, or add a layer if the shivers strike.

On the flip side, be sure to pack a swimsuit and beach towel, even in winter. If you were to poke holes on a map, designating all of Idaho's hot springs, the map would resemble Swiss cheese. I doubt that every hot spring has even yet been discovered.

Sneakers and sandals are okay for touring, but not for activities more adventurous than museum-visiting and shop-hopping. Stout hiking boots and a pair of rubber-soled sandals with woven straps held in place by Velcro do me just fine in summer. Take along a pair of broken-in cowboy boots if your plans include more than a few hours of horseback riding. Hiking boots with heels will do for short rides. Rubber sandals are indispensable on river trips. Substitute snow boots in winter. You can hardly pack too many socks; wool for hiking, lighter socks for nippy weather.

Pack rain gear. A light poncho will do for summer rainstorms. You might substitute a slicker for spring or fall hiking or biking. A wetsuit may be needed for spring kayaking and rafting. Many sports shops rent kayaks and wetsuits. River outfitters usually provide these and other gear such as life jackets and tents.

Before leaving home, ask your outfitter what gear is included, and what you'll need to bring.

If you will be adventuring on your own, find out in advance everything you can about your destination from local US Forest Service ranger stations and/or other sources. What about water supplies, firewood availability, restrooms or waste disposal practices? What are the restrictions on camping, group sizes, wood cutting, fires? Ask lots of questions.

Be sure to match your skis to the type of skiing that figures in your plans. New designs in skis and related equipment seem to pop up every winter. Research the market before making an expensive purchase. Ski rentals are widely available.

Always carry extra food and water when venturing into the backcountry. Don't forget sunscreen. And wear a hat and sunglasses. This is mountain country. The closer you are to the sun, the more intense the ultra violet rays. And "dazzling" understates snow glare. You may wish to pack insect repellent, especially if you'll be on a lake or in wet terrain. Idaho's state bird may be the mountain bluebird, but sometimes I'd have sworn it was the mosquito.

Driving

You cannot savor Idaho without a car. Interstate highways and main arteries are unavoidable at times, but do get off them whenever possible. You will gain a feel for the real Idaho and its friendly people along the byways and in the small towns. Idaho's Scenic Byways meander through some of the Lower 48's most beautiful terrain, racking up one fabulous vista after another. US Forest Service and BLM roads, many old logging roads, track some gorgeous chunks of backcountry.

Southern and Southeastern Idaho are well-endowed with interstate highways and other national and major state highways. A single artery,

US 95, connects Boise with Lewiston and the Panhandle. It enters the state at the Canada line, exits at Jordan Valley, Oregon. Idaho 55, the Payette River Scenic Byway, heads north from Boise through McCall, ending at the US 95 junction in New Meadows. Central Idaho's Frank Church-River of No Return Wilderness and the Selway Bitterroot Wilderness sit in the center of the state, hugging the eastern border and thus blocking north-south travel within Idaho.

From time to time, Panhandle residents get into a snit over what they perceive as their "step-child" relationship with the rest of the state, fulminating about secession movements that never go anywhere. Long northern winters breed deep memories. It happened well over a hundred years ago, in 1864, but Lewiston has never quite forgiven Boise for "stealing" its territorial capital status. Boise became the state capital 27 years later. Accusations of chicanery are still bandied about.

Idaho's paved roads and highways are well maintained, but suburbia it's not. Be alert for deer, moose, cattle and other animals on the road, particularly at night. You might happen on a cattle or sheep drive, especially in spring and fall when stock is moved to or from high country BLM grazing lands. Should you find yourself approaching a stock drive, stop and reach for your camera. The drovers on horseback will appreciate your patience and courtesy. If you're going their way, a drover will signal when it's safe to drive through at slow (very slow) speed. If the drive is headed for you, he'll likely try to move the animals to the side of the road before waving you on. Be alert for a confused calf darting into the road or an ornery cow determined to do it her way.

Idahoans take their history seriously. **Historical markers** are placed along the state's highways and byways to denote significant historical events and geological points of interest. These handsome signs include an explanatory paragraph alongside a map of Idaho pin-pointing the site.

The Idaho Transportation Department has put together a nifty guide to the state's historical markers that includes dozens of old-time photos. To order a copy, send $3.50 and a request for the *Idaho Highway Historical Marker Guide* to: Idaho Transportation Department, Public Information Section, PO Box 7129, Boise, ID 83707. Allow two weeks for delivery.

If you plan on driving over unimproved and/or US Forest Service or BLM roads, do take along **survival gear** for both yourself and your vehicle (extra fuel, spare tire and jack, water for your radiator). Most small towns have at least one gas station, but in remote areas you might top off your tank whenever the opportunity arises. Be prepared for muddy conditions in the spring and after rainstorms. Proceed with caution if the road seems to be petering out. Attempting to turn around

Scenic Byways

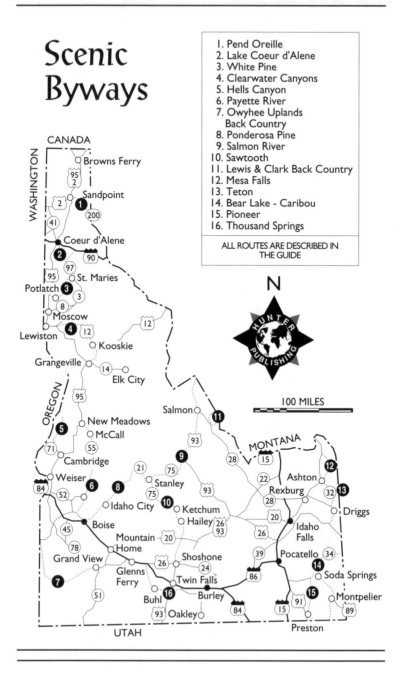

1. Pend Oreille
2. Lake Coeur d'Alene
3. White Pine
4. Clearwater Canyons
5. Hells Canyon
6. Payette River
7. Owyhee Uplands
   Back Country
8. Ponderosa Pine
9. Salmon River
10. Sawtooth
11. Lewis & Clark Back Country
12. Mesa Falls
13. Teton
14. Bear Lake - Caribou
15. Pioneer
16. Thousand Springs

ALL ROUTES ARE DESCRIBED IN
THE GUIDE

N

100 MILES

in a mudhole is no fun. A CB radio or cellular phone could be a good idea, but mountains can obstruct cellular phones' range.

An **up-to-date map** may be your best friend. The *Idaho Transportation Map* is one of the most detailed state maps I've seen. Unimproved roads are clearly marked, as are historic trails and Scenic Byways. Topographical and Forest Service travel maps are available at Forest Service offices.

Winter driving is a whole other game. Always check with local state patrol offices for current information before setting out. And remember that conditions may change in a wink. Forget unimproved roads unless you're driving a snowmobile. Paved roads are generally well plowed, but road clearing can take awhile in sudden and/or heavy snowstorms. Always expect the worst. Don't go anywhere without snow tires or chains, a snow shovel, an old rug or mat and kitty litter for traction, plus a flashlight with fresh batteries or a lantern. Stow blankets, food and water. You may be glad you did.

Special Concerns

- **Idaho is one of the most ecologically responsible states in the Union, and folks here want to keep it that way0.** Observing basic rules will keep Idaho clean and green. Backcountry rules of etiquette are strictly enforced in wilderness areas. Taking only photographs and leaving only footprints is advice everyone can, and should, live by. Everything packed into designated wilderness areas must be packed out. That means everything. In non-designated wilderness areas, human waste can be buried 100 feet or more from any water source and away from any possible campsites.

- **Black bears** and the occasional grizzly roam much of Idaho's forest land. Most bears want as little to do with you as you want to do with them. Grizzlies are the touchiest, but a black bear sow can get pretty riled up if she thinks you're going to come between her and her cub. Be alert; an encounter can happen before you know it. It happened to me one day as I walked with head down, looking at flowers. Hearing a snuffling sound, I looked up to see twin cubs climbing a nearby tree, and mom snorting a warning below. It took courage to walk away without appearing to flee. Bear-proof your camp by bringing enough rope to hang all food high in a tree and well away from camp. Bury garbage (dig it up to pack out in wilderness areas) away from camp.

■ **Fire danger** is often high in Idaho forests, especially in late summer. Hard-to-control forest fires, some of legendary proportions, hit Idaho every year. Most are caused by dry lightning, but careless use of campfires and disposal of cigarette butts cause far too many preventable fires. Check with a local ranger station regarding current fire regulations before setting out. An extreme fire hazard alert will prohibit all camp fires. Fire hazard road markers offer quick information on fire danger. A camp stove is preferable to building a fire. If you must build one, use a fire ring if available. Otherwise, build it in the open, away from combustible materials. Burn only small sticks; forage for dead wood and don't ever cut a tree. Before leaving, make sure your fire is dead out, then scatter the ashes and cover the site with sod or organic materials.

■ Take care **choosing a campsite**, if you are not in a designated camping area. Select an already impacted campsite whenever possible. Failing that, choose one at least 200 feet from trails, lakes, streams and wet meadows. Hide the campsite from view, and don't dig ditches around tents.

■ Don't even think about **drinking river, stream or lake water** unless you have boiled it for 20 minutes! You can't see the giardia lamblia protozoans waiting to lay you low with stomach cramps and diarrhea, but you can bet they're there. Pack in water or bring along a water purifier designed for camp use. Use naturally occurring water sources for a swim or for washing, but it's best to wash in a bucket or in running water if possible. Use only biodegradable soap.

■ **Respect private property.** If, for some very good reason, you must cross private land (some snowmobile trails are on private land), be careful to close any gate you open. Open range is often not fenced, though some ranchers place metal cattle guards across roads to keep animals in. Don't approach cattle. Cows are curious creatures and they might follow you at a distance; just ignore them. Bulls are seldom put out on open range, but be alert anyhow. These guys have been known to take umbrage, with uncomfortable results.

Introduction

Information Sources

The US Department of Agriculture Forest Service administers Idaho's 11 national forests with their network of trails, unimproved roads and campgrounds. US Department of the Interior Bureau of Land Management (BLM) lands include maintained trails, several Idaho rivers, including designated Wild and Scenic Rivers, and numerous primitive campgrounds, many in wilderness areas. Some campsites are on BLM grazing lands. These public lands sprawl across 32,614,363 acres of Idaho's total of 52,933,120 acres, representing 61.6% of the state's land. That's one hefty playground. These areas are divided into forests and regions. Regional Forest Service, BLM and State Parks headquarters are listed below and in regional sections of this book. Ranger District offices are listed in regional sections of this book.

Many of the following information sources are included in the regional chapters, but these sources can help you get started. Most contacts provide lots of free information on what to do and see, where to stay and eat, tours, rental car services, special permits and regulations. Some National Forest maps may require purchase for nominal sums.

Idaho Travel Council, Idaho Dept. of Commerce, 700 West State St., Boise, ID 83720-0093. ☎ 800-635-7820 or 208-334-2470. Fax 208-334-2631. Web site www.visitid.org.

North Idaho Travel Assn., Greater Sandpoint Chamber of Commerce, Box 928 (Hwy 95 N.), Sandpoint, ID 83864. ☎ 208-263-2161 or 800-800-2106. Fax 208-265-5289. E-mail: chamber@netw.com.

Coeur d'Alene Convention & Visitors Bureau, Box 1088, (202 Sherman Ave.), Coeur d'Alene, ID 83814. ☎ 208-664-3194. Fax 208-667-9338. E-mail: cdacc@coeurdalene.org.

Greater Kellogg Area Chamber, 608 Bunker Ave., Kellogg, ID 83837. ☎ 208-784-0821. Fax 208-783-4343. E-mail: kellogg@rand.nidlink.com.

Kootenai County Convention & Visitors Bureau, Box 908 (510 E. 6th Ave.), Post Falls, ID 83854. ☎ 208-773-4080. Fax 208-773-3843.

Wallace Visitor Information Center, Box 1167 (#10 River St., Exit 61), Wallace, ID 83873. ☎ 208-753-7151. Fax 208-753-5072. E-mail: rand.nidlink.com.

North Central Idaho Travel Assn., Lewiston Chamber of Commerce, 2207 E. Main St., Lewiston, ID 83501. ☎ 208-743-3531 or 800-473-3543. Fax 208-743-2176. E-mail: lewcoc@valley-internet.net.

Grangeville Chamber of Commerce, Box 212 (Hwy 95 at Pine), Grangeville, ID 83530. ☎ 208-983-0460. Fax 208-983-9188.

Moscow Chamber of Commerce, Box 8936 (411 S. Main), Moscow, ID 83843. ☎ 208-882-1800. Fax 208-882-6186. E-mail: chamber@moscow.com.

Introduction

Bureau of Land Management, Idaho State Office, 1387 S. Vinnell Way, Boise, ID 83709. ☎ 208-373-4015.

Bureau of Land Management, Boise District, 3948 Development Ave., Boise, ID 83705. ☎ 208-384-3300.

Bureau of Land Management, Burley District, Route 3, Box 1, Burley, ID 83318. ☎ 208-677-6641.

Bureau of Land Management, Coeur d'Alene District, 1808 North Third Street, Coeur d'Alene, ID 83814. ☎ 208-769-5000.

Bureau of Land Management, Cottonwood Resource Area, Route 3, Box 181, Cottonwood, ID 83522. ☎ 208-962-3245.

Bureau of Land Management, Idaho Falls District, 940 Lincoln Road, Idaho Falls, ID 83401. ☎ 208-524-7500.

Bureau of Land Management, Deep Creek Resource Area, 138 S. Main, Malad City, ID 83252. ☎ 208-320-4766.

Bureau of Land Management, Pocatello Resource Area, Federal Building, 250 S. 4th Ave., Suite 172, Pocatello, ID 83201. ☎ 208-236-6860.

Bureau of Land Management, Salmon District, Route 2, Box 610, Salmon, ID 83467. ☎ 208-756-5400.

Bureau of Land Management, Shoshone District, PO Box 2-B (400 West F Street), Shoshone, ID 83352. ☎ 208-886-2206.

Bureau of Land Management, Jarbridge Resource Area, 2620 Kimberly Road, Twin Falls, ID 83301. ☎ 208-736-2350.

❧

Idaho Dept. of Fish & Game, 600 S. Walnut, Boise, ID 83707. ☎ 208-334-3700. Fax 208-334-2114. E-mail: idfginfo@state.id.us.

Idaho Outfitters and Guides Assn., Box 95, Boise, ID 83701. ☎ 208-342-1438. Fax 208-338-7830. E-mail: outfitt@aol.com.

Idaho Guest and Dude Ranch Assn., c/o John Muir, 7600 E. Blue Lake Road, Harrison, ID 83833. ☎ 208-689-3295. Fax 208-689-9115.

Idaho Department of Parks and Recreation, Box 83720, Boise, ID 83720-0065. ☎ 208-334-4199. Fax 208-334-3741.

Hells Canyon National Recreation Area Headquarters, 2535 Riverside, Clarkston, WA 99403. ☎ 509-758-0616. Fax 509-758-1963.

Sawtooth National Recreation Area, Sawtooth National Forest, 2647 Kimberly Rd., Twin Falls, ID 83301. ☎ 208-737-3200. Fax 208-737-3236.

Genessee

95

Clarkston
Lewiston
Asoton

12 Spalding

Lenore

■ Dworshak Dam

Orofino

11

Nez Perce
Hist. Park

Hell's Gate
State Park

Nezperce

Kamiah

WASHINGTON

Craigmont

Winchester
Lake

95

Kooskia

12

129

Salmon River

NEZ PERCE NATIONAL FOREST

Snake River

Anatone

OREGON

Grangeville

To
Elk
City

White Bird

14

West-Central
Idaho

Hells Canyon

SEVEN DEVILS MTNS

Lucile
Riggins

Salmon River

95

IDAHO

Homestead

■ Oxbow Dam

New Meadows
Payette Lake

To Baker City

McCall

Richland

71

Council

Donnelly

Cascade
Reservoir

55

Cambridge

Cascade

Crane Creek
Reservoir

To Pendleton

95

Smiths Ferry

Weiser

84

Ontario

Payette

Crouch

Vale

New Plymouth

Banks

Payette River (Scenic Route)

To Sawtooth

Nyssa

52

N

16

Horseshoe Bend

Wilder

Emmett

21

201

Caldwell

Eagle

Boise

Marsing

Nampa

Meridian

84

HUNTER
PUBLISHING

45

78

Lucky Peak
Reservoir

20 MILES

95

To Twin Falls

West-Central Idaho - Boise to Lewiston

This hour glass-shaped slice of western Idaho is anchored by bustling **Boise** and the Treasure Valley cities of **Nampa** and **Caldwell** on the south, by the inland seaport city of Lewiston on the north. In-between, the fertile fields of the **Treasure Valley**, named for the earthly treasures growing there in irrigated abundance, give way to an intriguing jumble of mountains sliced by deep valleys. On the west, the **Snake River** lazes through pungent onion fields and widens to create Brownlee Reservoir before plunging over Hells Canyon Dam into 5,500-foot-deep **Hells Canyon**, the deepest river gorge in North America. Across the Seven Devils Mountains and 9,393-foot He Devil Mountain lies **Riggins**, at 1,800 feet above sea level. North of Riggins is the beautiful **Camas Prairie**, ancestral home of the Nez Perce. On the region's eastern edge, the arid foothills above Boise give way to the conifer-forested slopes of the **Payette National Forest**. McCall, doing triple duty as year-round resort town, Smokejumper Base and air gateway to the Frank Church-River of No Return Wilderness Area, poses at the foot of gem-like **Payette Lake**. This region, like much of Idaho, bears the scars of a gold mining boom-bust period that continued well into this century. Folks still pan for gold hereabouts.

Auto touring here is so spectacular that you may never get around to more active adventuring. The Payette Rivers, Hells Canyon and Clearwater Canyons Scenic Byways fall within this area. Each trails through country rich in human history and abounding in natural beauty. Here, perhaps more than in other sections of the state, you can lollygag along at a leisurely pace, taking your fun where you find it. Advance planning is usually not necessary for a Salmon River day float from Riggins or for a hike in the Payette or Boise National Forest. You can decide on a whim to soak in a thermal hot spring, cast a line into Cascade Reservoir, plop a tube into the Boise River, or visit a museum showcasing the history and culture of Idaho's diverse peoples. Many wayside towns maintain museums related to the history, agriculture or other special features that make townsfolks' bosoms swell with pride.

Except in isolated Hells Canyon, the conveniences of modern life are seldom far away. Boise and other I-84 corridor cities offer amenities that are often longer on comfort than on atmosphere. Elsewhere, the restaurants, lodgings, shops and such assume a resort-flavored rusticity that fits the river-running, hiking, fishing and backpacking ethos. Here, the workaday pick-up trucks of the Treasure Valley give way to 4WD vehicles sporting kayaks and truck campers packed with fishing gear. Shorts, T-shirts and river sandals assume the status of uniforms.

Geography & History

This area's jumbled mix of mountains, valleys, rivers and lakes creates vistas of breath-catching drama. Spring and summer are clothed in hues of green and blue. The deep green of pine-clad slopes, the softer green of valley pastures, the sparkling blue of lakes, the whitewater-splashed blue of rivers are all topped by a hard blue sky that Idahoans insist is the world's biggest. (No offense to Montana intended.) As summer progresses, the greens of the valleys and lower slopes fade to a soft brown. The threat of fire always shadows this idyllic scene. You can trace past wildfires by blackened pines stretching bare limbs to the sky, and by lush re-vegetation hugging the ground below.

You'd never guess it to see Boise's present-day sprawl, but time was when it was a very remote place. By 1824, French Canadian trappers had discovered the wooded river they named Boissie, meaning "wooded." Around 1860, one Tom Davis homesteaded a riverside plot, now a park named for his wife, Julia. In 1863, a fort was established to replace an earlier one on the Snake River and a townsite was laid out between the Davis homestead and the fort. Boise soon replaced Lewiston as Territorial capital. The new city took off in fine style, increasing in size and influence. The growing population included a vibrant mix of politicians, miners, Eastern emigrants with fancy ways, Basque sheepherders, merchants and just plain folks.

The territory between Boise and the Camas Prairie was left to miners of various stripes until well into this century. These prospectors, and the methods by which they extracted the glittering gold, assumed many shapes. Many were crusty types hardened by disappointment in the California gold mines. Others were Civil War veterans. Still others were Chinese, with a knack for making good on claims others had given up. Many Chinese were set upon and killed for their gold. Hydraulic mining scarred many a river bank. Mountainsides are honeycombed with the shafts of failed or played-out claims. Only panning for placer deposits left no trace. It wasn't until 1938 that a paved highway, US 95, was built to link the state's northern and southern halves. Previously, penetrating this area had been an adventure in itself.

Today, most of the Camas Prairie, the bitterly fought-over ancestral lands of the Nez Perce, is under cultivation. But the Nez Perce Tribe still is a vital presence. Their reservation occupies the prairie's northern half. Historical markers along US 95 and other cross-reservation routes identify Nez Perce historical landmarks. Markers have also been placed on White Bird Hill overlooking the White Bird Canyon Battlefield, where 70 Nez Perce warriors routed two US Cavalry companies on June 17, 1877.

Lewiston, Idaho's lowest lying community, is an inland seaport 470 miles from the Pacific. The Clearwater River empties into the Snake at Lewiston, swelling and deepening the river before its journey across Washington to the Columbia. Ships and barges line the Lewiston levee.

Lewiston began as a shantytown thrown up at the river's confluence in 1860 when Elias Pierce found gold in Clearwater country, 75 miles to the east. Located at the head of Columbia River system steamboat navigation, the shantytown boomed with gold seekers and other colorful characters. Lewiston, the first Idaho city to be incorporated, prospered despite the Territorial capital's 1863 removal to Boise. The history of the peoples of this western slice of Idaho reflect a gritty, on-the-edge hardiness. Native Americans, Chinese, explorers, miners, Basques and settlers from numerous other backgrounds demonstrated high courage and determination. It follows that this place of rumpled mountains, valleys, lakes and rivers continues to attract adventurers mesmerized by its great beauty and spurred by its challenges.

West-Central Idaho

Getting Around

Boise, served by several major airlines and situated on east-west I-84, is the logical starting place for touring this western region. Northbound US 95 and Idaho 55 form a loop that meets at New Meadows. You can drive the loop, ending up at Boise, where you started. Or take one route or another north to Lewiston and the Panhandle.

Pick up US 95 some 35 miles west of Boise just before I-84 crosses into Oregon. This route will take you through the heart of the Treasure Valley to **Weiser**, famed for its annual Old Time Fiddlers' Contest and Festival. After Weiser, the highway traverses mountain valleys before entering New Meadows. This route sees more heavy north-south truck traffic than often narrow, twisting Idaho 55. The advantage: getting onto Idaho 71 at Cambridge for the spectacular drive to **Hells Canyon Dam**.

Idaho 55 takes the scenic route sweepstakes. Heading due north from Boise, it tops the Boise Ridge over a splendid sweep of roadway built to replace an arduous climb over a narrow, often congested twist of road. That accomplished, Idaho 55 becomes the **Payette River Scenic Byway,** following the rollicking Payette upriver for 60 miles to **Cascade** and Cascade Reservoir. The Scenic Byway continues through McCall to **New Meadows,** where Idaho 55 ends. At this crossroads hamlet, you'll pick up US 95 for the run through Riggins to **White Bird Hill.** Here, the highway climbs 3,000 feet in 7.2 miles before coming out on the **Camas Prairie.** I always pull off here to gaze at the Prairie's splendid top-of-the-world sweep of fields and sky. If I'm lucky, the canola is in brilliant yellow bloom – a color palette that Gauguin would have coveted.

At **Grangeville,** you must make another choice: go straight on US 95 or bear right to Idaho 13, which crosses a corner of the Prairie before merging with US 12 at Kooskia. From there, the route, now the **Clearwater Canyons Scenic Byway,** follows the wide Clearwater River beneath prairie-top bluffs.

Both routes offer fascinating insight into Nez Perce history by way of historical markers placed along the roadway and the occasional interpretive turnoff. US 95 slices straight across the Prairie, running through several small agricultural towns before joining US 12 for the downhill run to Lewiston. The region's paved side roads are relatively few, but rewarding. The more plentiful unimproved Forest Service and BLM roads are equally rewarding. A 4WD vehicle is recommended for some of these roads, indispensable for most.

There's no end to the fun things to do. Hiking or biking can be as casual as a half-day foray on Ponderosa State Park's wooded trails, or as strenuous as a multi-day hike in Hells Canyon. Whitewater rafting/kayaking can mean a half-day run on the Salmon River from Riggins, or a Class IV to V plunge down the South Fork of the Payette. You can fish Cascade Reservoir for lake trout, cast a fly for brook trout in the Little Salmon River. Thermal hot springs are conveniently placed, as though by some benevolent deity. Museums and historical sites are as varied as Boise's Basque Cultural Center and Museum and the Nez Perce Historical Site near Lewiston.

Information Sources

Idaho Winter Road Report: ☎ 208-336-6600.

Highway Accident/Emergencies: ☎ 800-632-8000.

Bureau of Land Management, Idaho State Office, 1387 S. Vinnell Way, Boise, ID 83709. ☎ 208-373-4015.

Bureau of Land Management, Boise District, 3948 Development Ave., Boise, ID 83705. ☎ 208-384-3300.

Bureau of Land Management, Cottonwood Resource Area, Route 5, Box 181, Cottonwood, ID 83522. ☎ 208-962-3245.

Idaho Dept. of Fish & Game, 600 S. Walnut, Boise, ID 83707. ☎ 208-334-3700. Fax 208-334-2114. E-mail: idfginfo@state.id.us

Idaho Outfitters and Guides Assn., Box 95, Boise, ID 83701. ☎ 208-342-1438. Fax 208-338-7830. E-mail: outfitt@aol.com.

Idaho Department of Parks and Recreation, Box 83720, Boise, ID 83720-0065. ☎ 208-334-4199. Fax 208-334-3741.

Hells Canyon National Recreation Area Headquarters, 2535 Riverside, Clarkeston, WA 99403. ☎ 508-758-0616. Fax 509-758-1963.

Hells Canyon National Recreation Area, Riggins Administrative Site, Box 832, Riggins, ID 83549. ☎ 208-628-3916.

≥ఉ

Nez Perce National Forest, Box 475, Grangeville, ID 83530. ☎ 208-983-1950. Fax 208-983-4099.

Nez Perce National Forest, Clearwater Ranger District, Rt. 2, Box 475, Grangeville, ID 83540. ☎ 208-983-1963.

Payette National Forest, Box 1026, 800 W. Lakeside Ave., McCall, ID 83638. ☎ 208-634-0700. Fax 208-634-0744.

Payette National Forest, Weiser Ranger District, 275 East Seventh, Weiser, ID 83672. ☎ 208-549-2420.

Payette National Forest, McCall Ranger District, 202 W. Lake St., McCall, ID 83638. ☎ 208-634-1600.

Payette National Forest, Council Ranger District, PO Box 567, Council, ID 83612. ☎ 208-253-4215.

Payette National Forest, New Meadows Ranger District, Hwy 55, Box J, New Meadows, ID 83654. ☎ 208-347-2141.

Payette National Forest, Big Creek/Krassel Ranger District, PO Box 1026, McCall, ID 83638. ☎ 208-634-1700.

≥ఉ

Idaho Travel Council, Idaho Dept. of Commerce, 700 West State St., Boise, ID 83720-0093. ☎ 800-635-7820 or 208-334-2470. Fax 208-334-2631. Web site: www.visitid.org.

North Central Idaho Travel Assn., Lewiston Chamber of Commerce, 2207 E. Main St., Lewiston, ID 83501. ☎ 208-743-3531 or 800-473-3543. Fax 208-743-2176. E-mail: lewcoc@valley-internet.net.

Grangeville Chamber of Commerce, Box 212 (Hwy 95 at Pine), Grangeville, ID 83530. ☎ 208-983-0460. Fax 208-983-9188.

Boise Convention & Visitors Bureau, Box 2106 (168 N. 9th, Suite 200), Boise, ID 83701. ☎ 800-635-5240 or 208-344-7777. Fax 208-344-6236. E-mail: admin@boisecvb.org.

West-Central Idaho

McCall Chamber of Commerce, Box D (1001 State St.), McCall, ID 83638. ☎ 208-634-7631. Fax 208-634-7631.

☙

Ponderosa State Park, PO Box A, McCall, ID 83638. ☎ 208-634-2164.

Salmon River Chamber of Commerce, PO Box 289, Riggins, ID 83549. Chamber Office, ☎ 208-628-3778. Visitor Center, ☎ 208-628-3440.

Winchester State Park, PO Box 186, Winchester, ID 83555. ☎ 208-924-7563.

Hells Gate State Park, 3620A Snake River Ave., Lewiston, ID 83501. ☎ 208-799-5015.

Dworshak State Park, PO Box 2028, Orofino, ID 83544. ☎ 208-476-5994.

Touring

Boise

Boise is a sprawling city with a heart of green. The population, including gobbled-up bedroom communities, numbers some 220,000 and counting. Boise may be headed for big city status, but residents' comfortable friendliness reflects their small town roots.

Considering Boise's situation on the eastern edge of the Treasure Valley agricultural region, it follows that the city's most prominent industries revolve around food: Ore-Ida Foods, Inc., the Albertson's super market chain and others. The headquarters of Micron Technology, Inc. is at the apex of Boise's growing computer industry presence. Not that you, bound on a vacation adventure, care about those things. But these underwhelming facts serve to illustrate that Boise is a real city whose businesses, hospitals, etc., can fill any needs that may arise.

Most attractions are centered in the downtown area, easily accessible from I-84 and the Boise Municipal Airport.

Time was when Boise was a hick town, a slightly scruffy city plunked in a leafy-green bowl surrounded by arid hills. It had little going for it save the Boise River, and that was hidden among warehouses and other grunge. Sure, Boise had an interesting history, but even the past's more respectable remnants presented a tarnished appearance.

Then, before Urban Renewal got a bad press, Boise's movers and shakers set the gears of change in motion. First to go were those scruffy warehouses down by the river. A hodge-podge of down-at-heel structures followed. In their place rose shops and eateries, gleaming hotels,

Boise

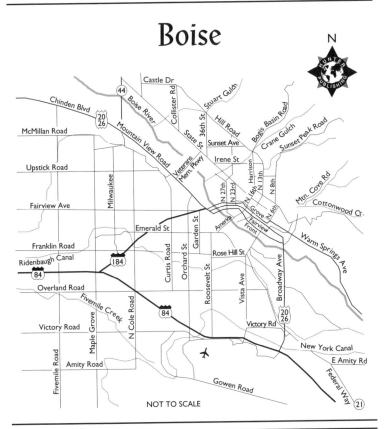

West-Central Idaho

NOT TO SCALE

a handsome convention center; all anchored by spacious plazas. An extensive parks system encompassing a sweep of river bisecting the city became the feather in Boise's cap. The turreted Hotel Idanha led a parade of interesting refurbished historic buildings, interjecting an intriguing flip side to Boise's new look. Architectural elements of historic buildings that could not be saved were incorporated into the vest-pocket C.W. Moore Park at 5th and Grove Streets. A focal point is a waterwheel that once lifted water from the river to Boise's gardens.

Today's walkable downtown – defined by the domed Idaho Capitol on the north, the river greenbelt on the south and historic Warm Springs Avenue and the Old Idaho Penitentiary on the east – is as pleasant a city core as you'll find anywhere. Fine homes built by Boise's political and commercial elite in the late 19th and early 20th centuries line **Warm Springs Avenue**, named for the thermal springs that supply these houses with hot water.

The **Old Penitentiary**'s austere stone buildings, glooming over the end of Warm Springs Avenue, offer a grim reminder of 100 years of frontier justice, Idaho-style. "The pen" looks as it did when the last prisoner walked out in 1973, right down to iron cots, refuse pails and clanging doors. Not only can you tour the pen, but you can chat with a former prisoner and a one-time guard.

Cary Harrison, life-buffeted lean and hard, replied openly when I asked him how he landed in the pen. "Armed robbery," said he, drawing hard on a cigarette cupped in his hand. He regards volunteering at the pen as a way of repaying society.

Jim Reddick represents the other side of prison life. Just for kicks, he "locked me down" in #5 House. Gut panic clawed at my throat even though I knew he'd let me out in a trice. Jim left no doubt that a guard's life in that primitive pen was not much better than an inmate's lot.

The Old Penitentiary is open daily 10-5, Memorial Day-Labor Day, 12-5 the rest of the year. It's closed on state holidays. Nominal admission fee.

The **Museum of Mining & Geology** is nearby at 2455 Old Penitentiary Road. Exhibits include photographs and artifacts from early Idaho mining days. Other exhibits depict the state's varied geologic features. Open weekends (☎ 208-368-9876 for hours). Nominal admission fee.

The **Idaho Botanical Garden**, up the pike at 2355 Old Penitentiary Road, has seven gardens abloom from late April through mid-October. A brick plaza boasts a cascading fountain. A three-quarter-mile trail leads through a nature garden. Open April 15-Oct 15, Tues-Thurs, 10-5, Fri-Sun, 12-8. Nominal admission fee.

The 20-mile **greenbelt** straddling the lazy Boise River is a magnet for locals and visitors alike. Paved biking/walking paths wind along the greenbelt and through adjacent **Julia Davis Park**. Julia and Tom Davis planted 7,000 fruit trees on their riverside land just a year after claiming the Boise Valley's first homestead. The fruit trees have long since been replaced by a cooling canopy of mature trees. A series of pedestrian bridges connects the park with the Boise State University campus across the river. Tubing down this mellow river on a hot day, with kids and coolers in tow, is splashing good fun.

You can easily spend a day or more enjoying Julia Davis Park and the adjacent stretch of greenbelt. The park is the site of a small **zoo**, a children's **amusement park**, the **Boise Art Museum** and the **Idaho Historical Museum**. The latter is an excellent resource if you wish to get a fix on the lives of Boise's early inhabitants, from Indians to Chinese, from oldtime prospectors to the settlers who put down roots and made Boise hum. The Art Museum is open Tues-Fri, 10-5, Sat-Sun, 12-5. The Historical Museum is open Mon-Sat, 9-5, Sun, 1-5. Free admission.

The bright red **Boise Tour Train** departs from the Historical Museum for hour-long narrated city tours. The schedule varies seasonally. ☎ 208-342-4796 for current times. Adults pay $5.50, seniors, $5, kids 3-12, $3.

The **Morrison Knutsen Nature Center**, at 600 S. Walnut Street (on the eastern edge of the park block behind the Idaho Department of Fish & Game offices), packs a microcosm of Idaho wildlife into a mere 4½ acres. This fascinating interpretive center offers a valuable introduction to the state's wildlife and habitats. View fish through underwater windows, see the rainbow trout life cycle from eggs to sizeable adults, get a close-up look at a beaver dam. An interactive salmon video provides information on some of the primary issues affecting fish and wildlife management in Idaho and the Columbia drainage system. Kids enjoy the Touch and Feel Gallery, featuring animal skulls, hides and a life-size bear den. The outside Nature Walk is open daily, sunrise to sunset. Free admission. The Visitor Center observes seasonal hours and is closed Mondays. ☎ 208-368-6060 for current hours. Nominal admission fee.

Few cultures are as synonymous with Southwest Idaho as that of the Basques, who came in the 1890s to herd sheep and work in the mines, staying on to carve a strong presence. Boise's Oinkari Basque Dancers are world-famous. The **Basque Museum and Cultural Center**, in the 1864 Jacobs-Uberauga House at 607 Grove St., offers a rewarding glimpse into the lives of this proud people and their place in Idaho today. The Jacobs-Uberauga House once served as a boarding house for Basque sheepherders during their infrequent visits to town. Open Tues-Fri, 10-4, Sat, 11-3. Donations appreciated.

If you're interested in matters military, you might enjoy visiting the **Idaho Museum of Military History** at Gowan Field, adjacent to the Boise Municipal Airport. Open Wed-Sun, 9-5 in summer, Fri-Sun, 1-5 in winter. Donation.

The **World Center for Birds of Prey** is south of Boise. You'll reap a panoramic view of the Boise River Valley from the Center's perch high in the hills above the Snake River. A guided tour of the Center includes an introductory video exploring birds of prey and their world, demonstrations using live birds, and viewings of live peregrine falcons and some of the world's largest eagles. The Center was established for the rehabilitation of injured birds of prey, and to educate the public about these birds and other endangered species. Breeding and release techniques are practiced. Take Exit 50 off I-84 to S. Cole Road, six miles south. The Center is at 5666 W. Flying Hawk Lane. Summer hours are Tues-Sun, 9-5; Nov-Feb, 10-4. Donation.

Boise shopping is less than world-class, but several antiques shops and galleries are worth a browse if you are into those kinds of things. **Made**

in Idaho, at Boise Towne Square, adjacent to the Convention Center, offers an astonishing variety of Idaho products. Most are foods gussied up in fancy packaging: wines, huckleberry candies and jams, dry beans. Potato products include big bakers bearing big prices and chocolate-covered potato chips. Kids go for Idaho Spuds, plump chocolate-covered marshmallows resembling... you know what.

Caldwell & the Treasure Valley

Caldwell, situated plunk in the middle of the Treasure Valley, is surrounded by orchards, truck farms and fields of potatoes and other crops. Irrigated farmland covers 96% of the land in the Boise and Snake River Valleys, a figure that's declining due to an influx of residents and the resulting sprawl of bedroom communities.

Get off I-84 and wander the Treasure Valley's country roads. From mid-summer to late fall, you'll happen on you-pick-it orchards and roadside produce stands. Agricultural towns, such as Middleton, Emmett and Fruitland, are microcosms of small town America.

The Oregon Trail passed south of present-day Boise before taking a sharp northerly turn, following the Boise River to the future site of Caldwell, where it tracked the Snake River along present-day US 95 before crossing into Oregon. The trail's route parallels I-84 for a short distance, but no trace of it remains.

Caldwell, the hub of western Idaho's food processing industry, sprouts a thicket of grain elevators, potato storage warehouses and other less-than-scenic structures. Except for the Warhawk Air Museum, which may be of interest to some, Caldwell is forgettable.

The **Warhawk Air Museum,** located at the Caldwell Industrial Airport adjacent to I-84 (take Exit 29), is a treasure trove of World War II military aircraft, artifacts and memorabilia. Hours vary throughout the year. ☎ 208-454-2854 for current hours. $2 donation requested.

Weiser

Though Weiser boasts some of the state's most remarkable 19th- and early 20th-century architecture, the town might today snooze among memories of its whiskey mill days and attendant shoot-'em-up mayhem, had not a fiddler named Blaine Stubblefield catapulted it to fame. Since 1963, the **Old Time Fiddlers Contest and Festival** that Stubblefield jump-started has placed Weiser squarely in the center of the nation's folk music map.

The third week in June, fiddlers and fiddler groupies descend on Weiser like flies to shoo-fly pie on a hot day. Then Weiser goes to sleep until the following June. Several historic structures, most notably the circa 1904 turreted sandstone **Pythian Castle**, make a look-see tour of the town worth your while.

Visit the **National Old Time Fiddlers Hall of Fame** for a reassuring glimpse of Americana. The rogues' gallery is lined with contest winners and other fiddlin' greats, but I was captivated by the photos of local youngsters enjoying their 15 minutes of fiddle music glory. The museum is adjacent to the Weiser Chamber of Commerce office at 8 E. Idaho Street. Open during business hours. Free admission.

Cambridge & Hells Canyon Dam

Northbound US 95 rambles through Weiser Canyon to Cambridge, site of an interesting small-town museum showcasing local historical artifacts. The **Cambridge Museum**, at the junction of Highways 95 and 71, is open May 15-Sept 15, Wed-Sat, 10-4, Sun, 1-4. Idaho 71, the scenic route to Hells Canyon Dam, meets US 95 at Cambridge. Below the dam, rafting parties put in for Hells Canyon floats down 80 wild and scenic miles of the Snake River.

Hells Canyon Scenic Byway

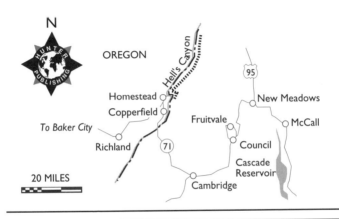

West-Central Idaho

The 62-mile paved road looks in on three dams: the Brownlee, the Oxbow, and the famed Hells Canyon Dam. The road crosses the Brownlee Dam into Oregon, then rims the Snake for 10 miles before crossing back into Idaho at the Oxbow Dam, where the Hells Canyon Scenic Byway begins. To state that the road above the east side of this deep declivity in the earth is narrow and winding, with steep grades, is to understate the case by a country mile. The scenery is so spectacular that you won't know whether to look up or down. Better keep your eyes on the road.

Depending on your personal bias, the effects of these three dams and their resulting reservoirs can be viewed as either positive or negative.

- **Positives**: dams generating about a million kilowatts of electricity provide jobs; downstream areas are protected from flooding; the reservoirs' 95 linear miles of slackwater offer boating and prime bass and rainbow trout fishing.

- **Negatives**: dams taming the turbulent Snake's plunge to meet the Columbia have put the quietus on upriver salmon and steelhead spawning migrations; the dams trap sand coming downriver, destroying spawning habitat below the dams; thousands of acres of farmland and wildlife habitat have been destroyed by rising waters.

Whatever your stand may be regarding the damming of rivers in general, and the Snake through Hells Canyon in particular, there it is and you might as well enjoy the scenery. Had it not been for dam construction, you would not be taking this spectacular drive above North America's deepest and narrowest canyon. Statistically, the Grand Canyon pales by comparison to 5,500-foot-deep Hells Canyon.

From Council, 20 miles north of Cambridge on US 95, you can point your 4WD vehicle onto the steep, winding, unimproved Hornet Creek Road over the Seven Devils Mountains into Hells Canyon via the steep and infamous **Kleinschmidt Grade**. Forest Road 112 accesses the southern end of the Seven Devils Range at Black Lake. Trails head into the Seven Devils from here. These remote and rugged mountains conceal 36 lakes and relics of circa 1890-1930 Placer Basin and Black Lake area mining operations.

The Payette River Scenic Byway

Horseshoe Bend to McCall

US 95 meets Idaho 55 at New Meadows, a crossroads village occupying the lower end of a postcard-pretty meadow. More about New Meadows later. For now, we'll crow-fly it to the south, picking up Idaho 55 at the North Fork of the Payette River hamlet of Horseshoe Bend. For 50 miles, from here to Cascade, the highway and a set of railroad tracks flirt with the rollicking rock-garden river. The upper: a beauty that makes you yearn to get out onto the river. The downer: this narrow, twisting stretch of highway is often thronged with mammoth logging trucks, lollygagging RVs the size of small houses, cars dwarfed by roof-top kayaks, vans towing raft-laden trailers, and you. For all of that, the Payette River Scenic Byway, with the mountains of the Boise National Forest rising on both sides, shouldn't be missed. The route is punctuated by rafting outfitters, a chainsaw sculpture workshop, assorted touristy shops and the inevitable rustic

West-Central Idaho

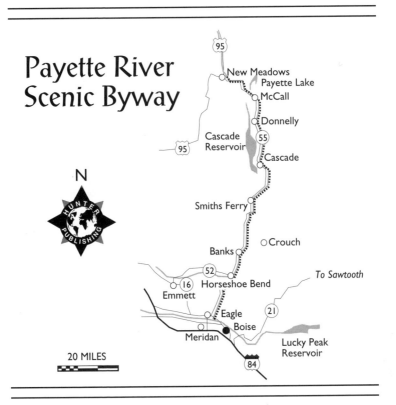

Payette River
Scenic Byway

Long Valley near McCall provides lush grazing for cattle.

watering holes. Far from being intrusive, these modest establishments interject a laid-back ambience.

Laid-back only begins to describe the hill community of **Crouch**, a few miles from Banks off Idaho 21. Referred to locally as the Lowman Road, the 23-mile route linking Banks and Lowman skirts a deep gorge containing the plunging South Fork of the Payette River, one of North America's gnarliest stairstep Class V rivers. Reminiscent of a hippy commune with aspirations, Crouch is the kind of off-beat place where chatting-up is an art form. Crouch still aspires, having recently planted an RV park sign on the Lowman Road.

Cascade, at the foot of grassy Long Valley and edging Cascade Reservoir, couldn't provide more of a contrast. This Boise-Cascade lumber mill town is all business, providing basic services and plenty of hometown ambience. A produce stand just off the main drag offers fresh fruit, corn and such in season.

From Cascade, a paved Forest Service road climbs 26 miles to **Warm Lake**, wherein Mackinaw (lake trout) swim. From there, a network of unimproved Forest Service roads as curvy as a tangle of horseshoes in a barrel meanders through the Boise National Forest. Like much of Idaho, this was mining country; still is. Beyond Warm Lake, the roads become gravel or dirt tracks. Two roads loop to McCall. The road heading north from Warm Lake parallels the South Fork of the Salmon River. The other parallels

Johnson Creek into Yellow Pine Basin. The hamlet of **Yellow Pine** is evocative of the mining towns of 100 years ago.

Three primitive hot springs can be reached from Cascade via Forest Service Roads (FS Roads) #22 and #474. **Trail Creek Hot Springs** is off #22, and Molly's and **Vulcan Hot Springs** are off #474 (take #22 to #474).

Long Valley, once the summer pasture for Boise-area livestock, is a lovely high mountain valley that is, for better or worse, sprouting second home farmlets. As you travel through this valley to McCall, you'll pass through (blink and you miss 'em) Donnelly and Lake Fork.

A gaggle of late 19th-century buildings on the abandoned Finnish townsite of Roseberry, 1½ miles east of Donnelly, comprises the **Valley County Museum**, open May 15-Sept 15, Wed-Sat, 10-4; June-Aug, Sat & Sun, 1-5, or by appointment (☎ 208-325-8871 or 345-1905).

Lake Fork was settled by Finnish farmers in the early 20th century. A picturesque Finnish church tops a hill east of the village. Spot distinctive Finnish barns along the Town to Market Road, linking Lake Fork with McCall. The road runs parallel to Idaho 55.

At Donnelly, take FS Road #186 to **White Lick Hot Springs**, located at a Payette National Forest picnic area and campground. Bathhouses are fed by several thermal springs.

McCall

McCall was once a lumber town on the skids. Its picturesque location at the foot of sparkling Payette Lake rescued it from said skids. Today, McCall embraces tourism with zeal and panache. Somehow, the town has managed to avoid the pseudo-north country tackiness that affects many north country resort towns. With commendable adroitness, McCall juggles summer and winter vacationers, summer residents, tanned backpacker types, a dead-serious Smokejumper base, and air taxis flying recreationists into the Frank Church-River of No Return Wilderness. McCall's annual Winter Carnival has been drawing big crowds since 1924.

The ambience of a simple lake town survives all this busyness. Sure, there's congestion, especially at the stoplight, vying with the first glimpse of the lake for your attention, at the bottom of 3rd Street. Here, you must decide whether to make a right turn around Hotel McCall, or take a sharp left onto McCall's single block of tourist kitsch.

A right turn will take you through a woodsy residential district to **Ponderosa State Park**. Turn left to reach the sprawling **Payette National Forest** headquarters. Knowledgeable rangers are on hand to dispense information about hiking and backpacking in the Forest, which meets

West-Central Idaho

the Seven Devils Mountains on the west and the Frank Church-River of No Return Wilderness on the west.

McCall is a good place to stock up on groceries, fishing supplies and other gear. The new modern shopping center south of town puts me in mind of a poodle at a rodeo, but the parking lot is more convenient than those of in-town markets if you're driving an RV or pulling a trailer.

McCall boasts a fair number of trendy eateries, even a brew pub. A bid to attract summer people has resulted in a condo complex on the lake east of town, but it's unobtrusive enough.

In the summer and fall wildfire season, some 80 smokejumpers live at the **McCall Smokejumper Base**, one of a nationwide network of smoke-jumper bases. The program began in 1939 as a fire-fighting experiment. Today, smokejumpers are the elite of Western wildfire fighters. They live for adrenalin-rushing calls to gear up, take to the sky and parachute into forests to put out wildfires before they grow into conflagrations that can devastate thousands of acres of forest and threaten entire communities. When not fighting fires, smokejumpers keep busy building trails and repairing parachutes.

Unless a fire emergency is in force, you can tour the Smokejumper Base. ☎ 208-634-0390 to arrange a free tour.

The **Central Idaho Museum and Visitor Center**, at the corner of State and Lake Streets, showcases McCall's history, utilizing several log structures built in the 1930s by the Civilian Conservation Corps (CCC). ☎ 208-634-4497 for tour hours.

Idaho 55 continues through McCall to New Meadows, but first we'll take a detour on the historic Warren Wagon Road, looking in at Upper Payette Lake, Burgdorf Hot Springs, and the (more or less) ghost town of Warren.

Upper Payette Lake is a mosquito-infested puddle aleap with native brook trout. Tenting there one mid-summer night, we watched a brace of curious elk approach within 100 feet of our camp. In the morning, moose tracks scored the muddy bank.

After you've rub-a-dubbed old miners' style in a clawfoot bathtub under the runoff from a steaming swim-size pool, or grappled a floating log in said pool, the hot tub at home will seem mighty tame. It's all in a day's fun at Burgdorf, the thermal hot springs where miners from up the road at Warren loved to recreate. Some still do.

Burgdorf is romantically situated in a wildflower-strewn mountain-ringed meadow. The thermally heated pool is surrounded by a straggle of shacks leaning that-away and a big old log hotel that must have been something in its day. You can flop down for the night in one of the shacks for a nominal fee, but the hotel has been condemned (admire the fabulous log furnishings through the windows). Burgdorf is open year-round and charges nominal soaking and flopping fees.

Warren, a mishmash of frame structures in various stages of disrepair, at the end of the road and the edge of the wilderness, is home to a bevy of mining-era ghosts and about a dozen free-spirited 'live residents. They (the 'live ones) won't intrude on your reveries as you poke among mining relics, but do observe Private Residence signs.

You can pick up a *Warren Historic Walking* tour guide and borrow an audio cassette relating tales of this once-rip-roaring town at the McCall Ranger District office.

What's a ghost town without a saloon? Warren's is suitably dark and dank. Early one morning, a bush plane deposited us at the Warren Landing Field. We explored Warren while the pilot returned to a Salmon River guest ranch to pick up other passengers. The saloon's regulars were already in place, languidly discussing the fire situation (good) and the political situation (scary).

The splendor of the short stretch of Idaho 55 leading to New Meadows, the Payette River Scenic Byway's last lap, begs description. The road, twisty as a pink pig's tail, plunges between high granite cliffs before meeting up with the chortling Little Salmon River.

New Meadows

The junction of US 95 and Idaho 55 has caused the old cattle ranching community of New Meadows to expand, but not to put on airs. That may come later, as California developers have their way with this idyllically beautiful setting. For now, New Meadows consists of a gaggle of service stations, an eatery or two, a tidy bed and breakfast inn that looks as though Grandma might still be rocking in the parlor, and a big sign advising truckers where to obtain their permits.

Up US 95 a piece, you'll find **Zim's Hot Springs** tucked against the mountains in a pasture full of grazing cows. The Nez Perce once camped at the springs. Homesteaders used the 149° water to scald hogs. In fits and starts, a series of owners developed the springs for recreational use. The swimming pool and RV campground we enjoy today is a family affair owned by Linda and Al Dixon. The circa 1926 "plunge" pool, cooled to 96°, has been used for church baptisms, scuba diving lessons and smokejumper survival training.

West-Central Idaho

Riggins

From New Meadows to Riggins, US 95 follows the Little Salmon River gorge for 34 miles. The Seven Devils Mountains rise precipitously to the west. The occasional rustic riverside cabin dozes fetchingly beside a vegetable garden. Like many other deep declivities in Idaho's crinkled landscape, this pocket-size valley enjoys a mild climate conducive to raising vegetables and fruit trees. Hells Canyon, a brief crow-fly over the Seven Devils from here, shares this salubrious climate.

Riggins takes full advantage of its location at the confluence of the Little Salmon and Main Salmon Rivers. Riggins is on a roll, having abrogated its livestock town status in favor of the twin seductions of the Hells Canyon National Recreation Area (HCNRA) beyond the Seven Devils Mountain Range and Salmon River rafting fame. Occupying a sliver of land wedged between mountains and river, Riggins' single street is chock-a-block with river outfitters, eateries, lodgings. Each sports a sign bolder than the last. Riggins is wide-awake in summer, but dozes in winter. All of Idaho's direct north-south traffic, from ancient Volkswagon Bugs to tractor trailers, is compelled to thread Riggins' narrow, congested street.

If you stop anywhere in Riggins, make it the HCNRA office south of town. Knowledgeable rangers will be happy to provide information on the Payette and Nez Perce National Forests, BLM lands, local services, the Seven Devils Mountains and the Hells Canyon Wilderness.

Forest Service Road 517 heads into the Seven Devils from the south edge of Riggins, rising 5,400 feet in 17 miles and terminating at Heavens Gate Lookout. This landmark provides an eagle's-eye look into Hells Canyon. Two Forest Service campgrounds and the Windy Saddle trailhead are just down the road, near Seven Devils Lake.

FS Road 241, the gravel/dirt Race Creek Road, meanders into the Hells Canyon Wilderness from the north edge of Riggins, climbing over Bean Creek Saddle before connecting with a tangle of roads running along the ridgeline. At Iron Phone Junction, the road swings north to meet FS Road 242, which follows Cow Creek up from Lucile. Many of these tracks were, and still are, used by ranchers moving stock into Hells Canyon in the fall and out in the spring. A trail leads to the Kirkwood Historic Ranch in Hells Canyon. The ranch is also accessible by boat from Pittsburg Landing.

*Kirkwood Ranch in Hells Canyon remains as it was
when the Jordan family lived there in the 1930s.*

Kirkwood Historic Ranch

Owned by the US Forest Service and preserved to recall a vanished way
of life, Kirkwood Ranch was memorialized by Grace Jordan's **Home
Below Hells Canyon**, a gripping account of the 11 years that she and
her sheep rancher husband Len (later, a US senator and governor of
Idaho) and their three young children lived at the ranch in the 1930s.
Settled around 1880 by J.W. Kirkwood, the ranch was one of Hells
Canyon's earliest homesteads. Copies of Jordan's book are available
locally.

The house and bunkhouse look much as they did when the Jordans
lived there. The furnishings reflect the spareness of their lives. The
family was self-sufficient, raising much of their food and home-teaching
the children. Ranch families visited back and forth via rowboat and on
horseback and made do with what came to hand.

I've visited Kirkwood Ranch several times, always exploring with a
sense of awe – and of wonder at the magnificent scenery that the Jordans
woke up to every morning.

West-Central Idaho

Riggins to Grangeville

Northbound, US 95 slicks alongside the Salmon River for 29 miles. From Riggins, the Salmon takes a northerly course to White Bird Hill, then cuts a westerly swath, emptying into the Snake below Pittsburg Landing. Wide and lightly riffled, the stretch of Salmon paralleling US 95 once reverberated to large-scale hydraulic gold mining. Today, historic markers recalls those days of boom and inevitable bust.

I always stop at **Fiddle Creek Produce Stand**, tucked against a hill a few miles north of Riggins. In an area where market offerings of fresh produce are scarce as hair on a rooster, this cornucopia of home-grown fruit and vegetables is a welcome sight. Home baked pies, jams and such are also on offer.

A few miles farther on, in the mini-community of Lucile, the aptly named **Riverfront Gardens RV Park** is an inviting sight. I have often intended to stop here at least overnight, but have never managed to work it into my schedule. Someday.

White Bird Hill climbs 3,000 radiator-busting feet in 7.2 miles, topping out on the Camas Prairie. Completed in 1975, the road replaced a scary switchbacking road that, in 1921, replaced an even scarier rutted wagon track. The saga of White Bird Hill's roads emphasizes the historic division between the northern and southern halves of Idaho.

The nondescript community of White Bird nestles in a deep canyon at the foot of the infamous hill. An unimproved road leads from White Bird to the foot of Gospel Peak, crowning the Gospel Hump Wilderness (more about this area in the chapter on *Region 3*, Central Idaho). Forest Road 493 crosses White Bird Bridge, climbs over 4,200-foot Pittsburg Saddle, and comes out below Hells Canyon at Upper Pittsburg Landing, the trailhead for the Snake River National Recreation Trail. FR 493 is a steep, well-maintained gravel road suitable for passenger cars in summer, but chains are required in winter.

About halfway up White Bird Hill, a wide pullover affords a sweeping view of **White Bird Battlefield**. Signs in the interpretive shelter pinpoint the positions of participants in the June 17, 1877 battle, which played a key role in the Nez Perce War. ("White Bird" is an eponym for a Nez Perce chief). Look for White Bird Battlefield auto and walking tour guides inside the shelter.

Several small towns are scattered across the Camas Prairie, some on, some off the Nez Perce Reservation. The largest is Grangeville, heralded by grain elevators saluting smartly beside a railroad siding. The Nez Perce National Forest maintains an office and a visitors center on Idaho 13, just outside town.

The Camas Prairie

The 200,000-acre Camas Prairie is named for the delicate blue-flowered camas bulb. The spring-dug bulbs once provided the Nez Perce with food to sustain life in the period between depleted winter food supplies and the abundance of summer. Partly for that reason, the Prairie occupies a sacred place in Nez Perce culture and religion. No wonder that the Nez Perce were determined not to relinquish it. The tribe ended up with the northern half of the Prairie, much of it leased to non-Indian farmers.

The Prairie, bisected by US 95, is bordered by the Snake River on the west and Clearwater Canyon on the east. Secondary roads link small towns and farms. Historical markers identify sites that figured in Nez Perce history. To understand the full impact of the Nez Perce presence on the Camas Prairie, drive the entire US 95-Clearwater Canyons loop, anchored by Grangeville on the south and the Nez Perce National Historical Park at Spalding on the north. On the way, take a side-trip to Nezperce and other Prairie towns.

West-Central Idaho

Across the Camas Prairie Via US 95

It mystifies me why the State of Idaho neglected to give Scenic Byway status to this route across the Camas Prairie. The drive over this gently undulating prairie, vibrant with healthy crops of wheat, canola and other grains, is surely one of Idaho's finest. Looking in on towns where tractors and harvesters hold sway, the road passes tidy farmsteads that Norman Rockwell, had he ventured here, would have loved to paint. Most of the route weaves through the Nez Perce Reservation.

Two miles southwest of Cottonwood, on the Keuterville Road, you will find **St. Gertrude's Museum**, a respository for an eclectic assortment of local historical artifacts, Oriental art and religious mementos. Open daily by appointment. ☎ 208-962-3224 or 962-7123.

Perhaps **Winchester Lake State Park** is the reason why I never seem to work in a stay at Riverside Gardens RV Park. I find the thickly wooded lakeside park irresistibly peaceful. While Winchester Lake has the appearance of a natural lake, it was created by the Craig Mountain Lumber Co. when it dammed Lapwai Creek to form a mill pond. The state took over the lake when the lumber company decamped. Nearby Winchester began as a company town.

The Nez Perce Tribal Office is in the historic town of Lapwai. Traces of Fort Lapwai, Idaho's first military fort, are visible a mile from town.

Not much remains of **Spalding** – just an old store, a Nez Perce cemetery containing the remains of missionaries Henry and Eliza Spalding, and the park-like site of the couple's mission to the Nez Perce. Spalding founded the Presbyterian mission on the banks of the Clearwater River in 1836. The mission lasted, sometimes amid considerable un-Christian contention, until Henry Spalding's death in 1874.

The **Nez Perce National Historical Park Visitor Center and Museum,** a dramatic structure topping a hill above Spalding, contains a wealth of Nez Perce artifacts and historical information. Operated jointly by the National Park Service and the Nez Perce Nation, the museum celebrates the saga of the Nez Perce with rare sensitivity. *Nez Perce Country*, an Official National Park Handbook, is well worth the nominal price if you wish to gain a deeper knowledge of the Nez Perce and their history.

Clearwater Canyons Scenic Byway

The easterly half of the loop begins on Idaho 13 at Grangeville, meets US 12 at Kooskia and continues on to the top of Lewiston Hill. This, the designated Clearwater Canyons Scenic Byway, travels beside the broad Clearwater River through a deep cleft dividing the Camas Prairie on the south and the equally fertile Palouse on the north.

Clearwater Canyons Scenic Byway

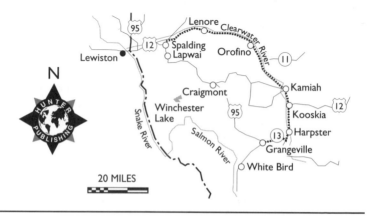

If you have an extra day or two, explore **Idaho 14, The Elk City Wagon Road**, side-tripping on the **Gold Rush Loop Tour** south of Elk City. From the hamlet of Mount Idaho, Idaho 14 follows the Clearwater River to Elk City, a gold strike-cum-homesteaders' town plagued again and again by forest fires. From here, the Loop Tour over FS Roads 233, 311 and 222 looks in on numerous old minesites and townsites. Check out the pools at **Red River Hot Springs**. These once-promising places hold little promise today, save for a memorable wilderness experience. This heroically rumpled country is the land of the historic Nez Perce Trail, of miners and bandits whose legends live in the telling.

Back on the Scenic Byway, watch for a **Nez Perce National Historical Site** turnoff between Kooskia and Kamiah. A short walk will take you to a volcanic outcropping. Here, an audio tape relates the Nez Perce Creation Legend, "The Heart of the Monster."

Tiny **Kooskia** and **Kamiah**, near where Lewis & Clark camped on their way back east in 1806, offer hospitality to a different breed: retirees attracted by sheltered Clearwater Canyon's mild climate. Kooskia characterizes itself as "The Gateway to the Idaho Wilderness." There are few Idaho towns that cannot make that claim.

Orofino, which translates as "fine gold," has been on a roll since its founding in 1898. Boom-or-bust gold mining and lumbering enterprises preceded Orofino's most enduring strike: the recreation boom created by the **Dworshak Dam** project. Constructed between 1963 and 1973, the world's largest straight axis dam backs up the North Fork of the Clearwater for 54 miles, creating a big aquatic playground for boaters and fisherfolk. The US Army Corps of Engineers maintains a visitor center at the dam featuring audio-visual programs and natural history, archaeological and historical displays. Dam tours are offered daily from 10-4 in summer. ☎ 208-476-1255 for current visitor center hours. Dworshak State Park and several other campgrounds and day use areas are situated on the Dworshak Reservoir shoreline.

The US Fish and Wildlife Service operates the **Dworshak National Fish Hatchery**, three miles west of Orofino at the confluence of the North Fork and Main Clearwater Rivers. The hatchery claims to be the world's largest combination producer of steelhead trout and spring chinook salmon. Daily self-guided tours are offered during daylight hours.

The **Clearwater Historical Museum**, at 315 College Way in Orofino, is worth a visit. Open daily 1:30-4, Tues-Sat. Free admission.

Clearwater National Forest information is available at the US Forest Supervisor's office on Hwy 12, north of Orofino.

Several hamlets, tucking vivid pages of Idaho history into their collective memory, line US 12 between Orofino and Lewiston Hill.

West-Central Idaho

Lewiston

Lewiston, the erstwhile capital of Idaho at the confluence of the Snake and Clearwater Rivers, has done pretty well since losing out to Boise. Sure, Boise beats it for size. But can Boise boast of being the Western inland port most distant from the Pacific Ocean? Serving as the northern gateway to Hells Canyon is no mean deal, either. At 739 feet above sea level, Lewiston shares banana belt status with Kamiah and Kooskia. This is great in winter, when folks sometimes go about in shirtsleeves. But in summer, it often feels as hot as the namesake of that canyon up the Snake.

Lewiston's downtown area has been gussied up with attractive shops and eateries. What you can't find in Lewiston, you may find in Clarkston, Washington, across the Snake. Lewiston owes its prosperity to the shipping terminus for lumber products and grains from the Camas and Palouse Prairies. And to the Potlatch Corporation's pulp mill on the US 12 approach to town. When the wind is right, and that's most times, an unmistakable *eau de pulp mill* aroma wafts over the city. Offenses to your olfactory senses aside, Lewiston is an interesting place to visit. The city's heritage includes an Oriental presence derived from Chinese miners who streamed through Lewiston on their way to the gold fields up the Clearwater and Snake Rivers.

You can view exhibits related to Lewiston's Chinese culture in the **Lewis & Clark Center for Arts & History** at the corner of Fifth and Main. The museum also has rotating art and history exhibits. Open daily, 10-4.

Luna House Museum, at 306 3rd Street, has rotating and permanent exhibits depicting pioneer and Nez Perce artifacts. Open year-round, except for two weeks at Christmas. Tues-Sat, 9-5.

Most Lewiston visitors come in response to the irresistible lure of Hells Canyon. Several Lewiston-based jetboat operators conduct trips up the Snake, bucking whitewater to just below Hells Canyon. More about them in *On Water*, below.

Adventures

On Foot

In this slice of Western Idaho, "on foot" can range from a tame walk along the Boise River Greenbelt to a strenuous multi-day hike over the Seven Devils Mountains into Hells Canyon. One

constant: high altitude. Most visitors can handle altitudes in the 1,500-
to 2,500-foot range, common in river valleys and basins. Flatlanders
would do well to take this into consideration when contemplating high
altitude hikes.

Altitude sickness *usually begins with a headache and
nausea. Vomiting, disorientation and loss of
consciousness may follow. Death is not out of the
question. The best remedy: descend to a lower altitude as
quickly as possible. The best preventative: become
acclimated by planning a couple of low-activity days at
high altitudes before engaging in strenuous high-altitude
activity.*

*Don't drink stream, lake or spring water. Giardia may
well lurk therein.*

Be prepared for **rapid weather changes,** *even in
mid-summer. Severe mountain thunderstorms come up
quickly. Snow is found year-round at high elevations.*

Keep your distance from **wildlife.** *Wild animals will
usually avoid you. If you scare or surprise an animal, its
response may be unpredictable, even dangerous. Don't
tempt animals by leaving food about your campsite.*

Before setting out, stop at a local Forest Service **ranger
station** *for trail updates. Weather and other conditions
can result in closed or restricted trails.*

The following listings are by no means complete. You could spend a
lifetime exploring the Idaho wilderness and still not cover it all.

The Boise Front

The **Boise River Greenbelt paths** are great muscle-toners, should you
remain in Boise for a couple of days.

The **Ridge to Rivers Trail System** in the hills directly north of Boise has
several multi-use trails. Three are pedestrian-only trails. The 3½-mile
Hulls Gulch Interpretive Trail has signs highlighting area wildlife,
history, vegetation, soils and ecology. Trailheads are 3½ miles and five
miles, respectively, and start up the 8th Street Extension. The short,
steep **Tram Trail** is to the east of the Old Penitentiary. The easy **Cottonwood Creek Trail** runs through the Military Reserve adjacent to the Old
Penitentiary. A network of multi-use non-motorized trails (foot, bicycle,
horseback) meander farther into the hills, culminating in the approximately five-mile **Shingle Creek Ridge Trail**, climbing to 5,348 feet at

the base of 6,625-foot Boise Peak. Contact the BLM, Boise District, for a Rivers to Ridge System trail map.

McCall, Krassel & New Meadows Ranger Districts of the Payette National Forest

These ranger districts maintain numerous trails of varying lengths and degrees of difficulty in the McCall-New Meadows areas. Many are short half-day hikes. Contact the Payette National Forest office in McCall for specific directions and trail updates. The following descriptions should get you started.

These five hikes branch off the Warren Wagon Road

You may encounter horses on the **Twenty Mile Trail**. The first three miles are easy going. A longer, steeper hike will take you to the high lakes area. Good trail for wildlife viewing.

The **Victor Creek Trail** is 12½ miles long, but a hike of just over a mile will take you through the area of the 1994 Blackwell fire to a large meadow offering a splendid view of the mountains across the Payette River.

Josephine Lake Trail is only a half-mile, but steep. It leads to a 13-acre lake tucked into a granite cirque that's a favorite with fly fishermen.

The fairly flat 10-mile round-trip **Loon Lake Trail** is popular with people on horses, llamas, dirt bikes, mountain bikes.

The 15-mile **Secesh to Loon Lake Trail** is bracketed by Ponderosa and Chinook Campgrounds. The scenic trail follows the Secesh River.

The following four trails branch off the Lick Creek Road

The **Box Lake Trail** is only 3½ miles, but it's steep. You might wish to make this an overnight hike, especially if you want to fish or swim.

The rugged two-mile **Snowslide Lake Trail** is steep and rocky, but you'll be rewarded by a view of a lake seemingly set at the edge of the Earth. It's necessary to ford Lake Fork Creek to get onto the trail, so this hike is not recommended for early spring.

The **Duck Lake Trail** is a pleasant two-mile ramble. After a mild climb, the trail levels out, making it ideal for most ages and abilities. Longer hiking trails lead off it.

The **Hum Lake Trail** takes off from just below Duck Lake, climbing nearly 1,000 feet to a ridge, then dropping another 1,000 feet to Hum Lake. Great views of both lakes.

The following two trails branch from the Elow Road

The **Louie Lake Trail** is only a little over a mile long, but it's a steady uphill walk. It leads to a good fishing lake and offers a pretty view of Long Valley far below.

The **Boulder Lake Trail** is only two miles long, but accesses longer backpacking trails at the lake. **Anderson, Maloney, Summit, Rapid, Fogg** and the **Kennally Lakes trails** are accessible from this trail.

The following six trails, branching off the Brundage Mountain Road, are suitable for families with young children

The one-mile **Powerline Trail** leads to Goose Creek Falls. It starts by going downhill and ends with an uphill climb.

The one-mile **Twin Lakes Trail** climbs steadily, but is not steep. The lake is subject to draw-down in late summer. Good fishing.

The **Big Hazard Lake Trail** extends about a half-mile through the Corral fire area and is suitable for most abilities.

The **Upper Hazard Lake Trail** is two miles long and gains about 360 feet in elevation. This pleasant trail passes through meadows before reaching the lake.

The **Scribner Lake Trail** offers a short hike after a long drive. The trail climbs through boulders and the 1994 Corral fire area.

You can spend a couple of days enjoying the **Grassy Mountain Twin Lakes Trail** and connecting trails to Serene, Coffee Cup, Frog, Disappointment and Morgan Lakes.

Last Chance Spring is at the end of a half-mile walk along **Goose Creek**. Turn off Idaho 55 two miles beyond the Brundage Mountain exit. Mineral water of 102° is piped into a rock pool.

Ponderosa State Park, fetchingly situated on a 1,000-acre peninsula jutting into Payette Lake, has trails leading to a point overlooking a dreamscape of lake and pines.

Hells Canyon National Recreation Area Trails

Hells Canyon and the Seven Devils Mountains have some 900 miles of annually maintained trails. The **Snake River National Recreation Trail** is open year-round. Pets are not allowed in the backcountry. Fair warning: this country is extremely rugged. All backcountry safety measures should be taken. Some trails leading from the Snake River to sub-alpine country have very steep pitches. It is strongly recommended that you prepare for the difficulty of the trail you are considering by

West-Central Idaho

first contacting a Hells Canyon National Recreation Area (HCNRA) office. The HCNRA offers literature covering every condition that you might encounter. There's a lot to read, but don't slough off. The part you skim over might save your skin.

There are three main trailheads on the Idaho side of Hells Canyon Wilderness. Campgrounds are at each trailhead, but don't count on their having potable water.

Windy Saddle is reached via Forest Road 517, off US 95 just south of Riggins. The trailhead (at 7,200 feet) is the main access point for the Seven Devils' high elevation country.

Black Lake trail provides access to the southern end of the Seven Devils. Consult a map of the Payette National Forest to locate the access roads. The trailhead (at 7,200 feet) is about 50 miles north/northwest of Council on US 95. The rugged forest road is not generally free of snow until mid-July. Don't even think about driving this road unless you have a high-clearance 4WD vehicle.

Upper Pittsburg Landing is probably the most easily accessed trail on the Idaho side of the HCNRA. FS Road 493, accessed from US 95 at Whitebird, is a 19-mile, well-maintained steep gravel road suitable for passenger cars. The road is generally open during the winter, but a 4WD vehicle with chains is recommended. Winter storms can be fierce over 4,200-foot Pittsburg Saddle. This is where you'll find the trailhead for the **Snake River National Recreation Trail** and connector trails leading from the river up into the Seven Devils.

The following are the main trails on the Idaho side of the HCNRA

Be sure to obtain an area map before setting out. This wild and windy landscape is short on trees, long on wildflowers, wildlife and distant vistas. Fire danger is high in summer and early fall.

You'll need four to five days to complete the 27-mile **Seven Devils Loop Trail**, beginning at the Windy Saddle trailhead. You can either follow Trail #101 around the east side of the Seven Devils to its junction with Trail #124, or take #124 around the west side of the Seven Devils to where it joins #101.

Travel to or from the high country and the river is highly challenging because of the extreme gradient and changeable trail conditions. Camping spots are limited because of the steep grades.

**These trails generally follow the
main drainages coming out of the Seven Devils.**

The 11½-mile **Sheep Creek Trail #53** offers the most diversity in scenery and conditions. The **Devils Farm #114** and **Bernard Creek #58** trails are primitive and difficult to find in places.

The **Snake River National Recreation Trail** is 35 miles long and parallels the river, sometimes dipping to river level, sometimes skirting above it over rock outcroppings. The trail does not go through to Hells Canyon Dam/Hells Canyon Boat Launch. There are no loop options. If you don't wish to retrace your route, you can contract with a jetboat or float operator to take you either upriver from Pittsburg Landing to trail's end, from where you can hike back down, or to pick you up at trail's end after your upriver hike. Float and jetboat operators are listed in the *On Water* section of this chapter, below.

The Snake River National Recreation Trail traverses some of North America's most ecologically varied terrain. The deep gorge below Hells Canyon is a geologist's, botanist's and bird lover's dream. The canyon's oldest rocks are remnants of volcanoes formed in the Pacific some 270 million years ago. Several plants, including the Snake River biscuitroot, have been identified only here. Peregrine falcons are often seen hang gliding the air currents in search of prey. Eight-foot sturgeon laze in deep river holes (if you catch one, you must release it). The canyon is rich in human history, too. Almost everyone skedaddled out of here in summer because of the scorching heat, but the Nez Perce wintered in the canyon. Homesteaders and ranchers wintered themselves and their stock here, too. Some over-wintering of sheep and cattle continues. You may want to set aside several days to enjoy this unique place. Try to avoid Hells Canyon in the summer months, unless you are a seasoned desert rat.

Snake River of Hells Canyon is an indispensable companion to any Hells Canyon trip, whether on foot, horseback, raft or jetboat. This book, written by Johnny Carrey, Cort Conley and Ace Barton, relates the often explosive story of the people whose lives were changed by this deep rift in the Earth and the river that runs through it. Available in Idaho bookstores and other outlets, or from Backeddy Books, PO Box 301, Cambridge, ID 83610 (☎ 208-257-3810).

Hiking Outfitter

- **Northwest Voyageurs** offers multi-day hikes into the Seven Devils Wilderness that can include hikes to He Devil and She Devil Peaks, both over 9,000 feet high. PO Box 370, Lucile, ID 83542. ☎ 800-727-9977. Fax 208-628-3780.

Travel With Llamas or Horses

 Many of the trails described in *On Foot* double as horse trails. If you travel with horses, contact the applicable National Forest ranger station for detailed information on accessing the back-country with your animal. Assuming that few, if any, readers will be traveling with their own Old Dobbin in tow, this book elects to focus on outfitters offering such trips.

Several outfitters offer horseback and/or horse- or llama-supported trips in the Payette National Forest and the Hells Canyon National Recreation Area. Those listed in this book are licensed by the State of Idaho and are IOGA members. Be sure to ask plenty of questions. Determining the price and length of the trip should be only for starters.

Horseback Outfitters

- **Bigfoot Outfitters, Inc.** offers customized multi-day trail rides and pack trips into the Seven Devils Mountains, plus fishing excursions in Seven Devils lakes. They also do combination vacation packages in cooperation with river-rafting outfitters. Box 498, Riggins, ID 83549. ☎ 208-628-3068.

- **Cascade Recreation** offers four-day river-rafting and horseback-riding trips. See *Payette Rivers Outfitters* below.

- **Deadwood Outfitters, L.L.C.** has a base camp with cabins and a bunkhouse on the Deadwood River east of Cascade Reservoir. Tom and Dawn Carter offer day horseback rides, multi-day pack/fishing trips, customized family vacation trips, fishing on alpine lakes and Cascade Reservoir, and snowmobiling. Box 412, Garden Valley, ID 83622. ☎ 800-684-3675.

- **High Llama Wilderness Tours, Inc.** has three-day and five-day customized llama-supported treks in the Salmon River Mountains of the Payette National Forest east of McCall. Cutler Umbach, Box AN, McCall, ID 83638. ☎ 800-775-5262 or 208-634-5818.

- **Idaho Afloat** offers six-day combination Lower Salmon River and horsepacking trips. PO Box 542, Grangeville, ID 83530. ☎ 800-700-2414.

- **Northwest Voyageurs** runs fast-paced four-day Gallop, Trot and Paddle trips in the Seven Devils Wilderness and down to Hells Canyon and the Snake. PO Box 370, Lucile, ID 83542. ☎ 800-727-9977.

- **ROW (River Odysseys West)** offers combination horse-back/float trips in Lower Salmon River country. PO Box 579-G, Coeur d'Alene, ID 83816. ☎ 800-451-6034.

On Wheels

Jeeping

 Forest Service and other backcountry roads described under *Touring, above,* are suitable for jeeps and other 4WD vehicles. Trails are not.

Bicycling

Bicycling may be tame in comparison to mountain biking, but as a pleasant family activity it's hard to beat. The Boise Greenbelt has some 23 miles of bicycle paths.

- **Wheels R Fun,** downriver from Julia Davis Park at the end of 13th Street, rents bicycles and skates. ☎ 208-343-8228.

Ponderosa State Park on Payette Lake outside McCall has paved bicycle paths, as does **Hells Gate State Park** on the Snake River, four miles south of Lewiston. Bicycling on the **Lewiston Levee** gets you up close and personal with ships coming and going in this inland deep-water port.

Mountain Biking

The **Ridge to Rivers Trail System** in the foothills north of Boise includes several multi-use non-motorized trails. The **Table Rock trails** just east of the Old Penitentiary loop around 3,658-foot Table Rock. **Scott's Trail,** accessed via the 8th Street Extension, leads to the **Shingle Ridge Trail,** topping out at 5,348 feet and offering a great view of 6,525-foot Boise Peak. From here, you can return to Boise via the primitive **Boise Ridge** and **Rocky Canyon Roads.** You'll need a full day for this one.

You can bike most of the **Payette National Forest trails** described in this chapter's *On Foot* section. The primitive loop road linking McCall, Warren, Big Creek, Yellow Pine and crossing over Lick Creek Summit before heading back to McCall includes a challenging mix of terrains.

Brundage Mountain, near McCall, is a favorite with mountain bikers. Trails for beginners and experts wind down the mountain across mead-

*Wheels-R-Fun in Boise's Julia Davis Park rents bicycles
and rafts for floating the Boise River.*

ows and through forests. Chairlifts will carry both you and your bike to the top. You can rent mountain bikes and helmets. Trail maps are available at the ticket counter.

Trails in the HCNRA are designed for foot and horseback travel. Bicycles and motorized vehicles are not permitted in the Hells Canyon Wilderness.

Outfitted Mountain Biking Trips

- **High Llama Wilderness Tours** offers guided mountain bike touring in the Payette National Forest. Cutler Umbach, Box AN, McCall, ID 83638. ☎ 800-775-5262 or 208-634-5818.

- **Cascade Recreation** runs four-day combination peddle and paddle trips. Bike above the Payette River in the Boise National Forest. A sag wagon follows for laggers. Trade pedals for paddles as you raft two Class IV sections of the South Fork of the Payette. Cascade Recreation, Rt. 1, Box 117A, Horseshoe Bend, ID 83629. ☎ 800-292-RAFT.

- **Nichols Expeditions** has five-day Hot Springs mountain biking trips in the Payette National Forest over single track and forest roads. 497 N. Main, Moab, UT 84532. ☎ 800-648-8488.

- **Northwest Voyageurs** offers two days of mountain biking to Burgdorf Hot Springs and on to the Lower Salmon, plus two days of floating the Lower Salmon. PO Box 370, Lucile, ID 83542. ☎ 800-727-9977.

On Water

Whitewater Rafting

 Idaho's world famous whitewater rafting is one of the reasons, if not the primary reason, why outlanders come to sample Idaho, then return year after year. Idaho's licensed river outfitters are another reason. Pioneers in guided river trips, they continue to set the industry standard. They add new meaning to camping out under the stars, pampering guests with gourmet meals accompanied by the seductive music of the river.

The whitewater rafting season runs from April through September, but varies according to specific rivers and spring runoff conditions. Outfitters schedule trips for particular dates, set in stone according to permit parameters.

Prior to the end of World War II, whitewater river travel was primarily accomplished via sweepboats, cumbersome wooden rafts steered with a long handle (sweep) attached to a rudder. River travel was pretty much limited to transporting supplies to isolated homesteads and mining camps. After the war, some farsighted individuals tried riding the rapids in surplus military rubber rafts. It worked, sweepboats went the way of the Spanish galleon, and the recreational whitewater rafting industry got off to a roaring start. Today, most Idaho whitewater outfitters' crafts of choice are inflatable rubber rafts capable of accommodating a ton of gear or a dozen happily screaming passengers.

Idaho has more whitewater river miles than any state in the Lower 48. For me, the exhilaration of whitewater rafting tops any other high. You concentrate every sinew on paddling through a snarling rapid, while being hit with a drenching wall of cold water, then relax and enjoy the scenery before a guttural roar heralds the next rapid. This western slice of Idaho offers whitewater rafting on some of the West's most exciting rivers: the South Fork of the Payette, the Lower Salmon and the Snake through Hells Canyon.

- The **South Fork of the Payette**'s Class IV and V stairstep rapids guarantee non-stop excitement. There's even a portage around a 25-foot waterfall! One- or two-day trips on this boiling stretch of river between the put-in below Lowman to take-out at Garden Valley are not kid stuff. Participants don wet-suits and helmets and expect to paddle. You don't have to be a super-jock, but you must be in good shape. You'll be so busy paddling that you'll have little time to enjoy the scenery in this deep, narrow rocky cleft in the Earth. It's a fantastic taste of whitewater only an hour and a half from Boise.

- The **Salmon River** flows entirely within Idaho and has no dams, making this Wild and Scenic River the longest free-flowing river in the Lower 48 states. The US Forest Service/Bureau of Land Management awards permits to licensed outfitters and individuals to run the Salmon's three sections; the Lower Salmon, the Main Salmon and the Middle Fork of the Salmon. Put-in dates are assigned by the Forest Service/BLM. More about the latter two rivers in the chapter on *Region 3, Central Idaho.*

Not every stretch of river offers a non-stop whitewater zing. The Lower Salmon alternately lazes and splashes through the splendid Lower Salmon River Gorge between Riggins and the confluence with the Snake below the Hells Canyon National Recreation Area. On its way, it passes through Green, Cougar, Snowhole and Blue Canyons. Several Riggins outfitters offer half-day and full-day floats. Multi-day floats usually put in farther downriver and take out at Heller Bar on the Snake. Rapids seldom exceed Class III. Camping is on white sand beaches. The warm water is ideal for swimming and water games. Moderate, widely spaced rapids mean you can jump out of the raft and swim on a whim. The Lower Salmon is ideal for kids, yet offers enough excitement for grown-ups river rafting for the first time.

You can paddle or not as you please. Many outfitters bring along inflatable kayaks. These are hits with kids and adults wanting to get a feel for kayaking or to just play in the water. The swimming and fishing for trout and smallmouth bass are great, too. This high desert environment is very dry. Summer daytime temperatures often exceed 95°, but nights cool down considerably. Wildlife sightings may include raptors, deer, elk and river otter. The rock formations are awe-inspiring, especially in deep, silent Blue Canyon.

The Lower Salmon and Snake River Canyons are rich in history, having been used by Native Americans as winter camps for thousands of years before white men discovered gold here. Chinese miners soon followed.

The Lower Salmon's Blue Canyon is a place of still water and deep blue hues.

West-Central Idaho

Homesteaders didn't exactly stream into this remote area, but a few hardy settlers came and usually left in discouragment. Most floats include short hikes to sites recalling tribal cultures and the homesteading era.

The Lower Salmon is a good river to self-float, if you are so inclined and have the necessary gear. A permit is required. Contact the **Bureau of Land Management's Cottonwood Resource Area**, Route 5, Box 181, Cottonwood, ID 83522. ☎ 208-962-3245.

The Lower Salmon is ideal for the history and family floats offered by some outfitters. A few operators use dories. These high-sided boats ride over the rapids instead of plunging through them. You feel the thrill, but tend not to get as wet as on a raft.

The Wild and Scenic **Snake River through Hells Canyon**, dropping from 1,688 feet at Hells Canyon Dam to 860 feet at the Oregon-Idaho border 71 miles downriver, offers one of North America's premier multi-day river adventures, with enough whitewater to satisfy the most intrepid whitewater rafter. Some outfitters offer combination rafting and horseback riding trips in the HCNRA.

Best time to go: May and June, when wildflowers are at their peak and the relentless heat has yet to set in.

Outfitters

Except for the Payette Rivers, where your choices are limited, the number of outfitters can be bewildering. Some are big companies offering trips on many rivers, both in and out of Idaho, and employing numerous guides. Others are small family-owned Idaho-based companies that will often tailor trips to your preferences. Many of the guides you'll meet on the river pursue seasonal occupations, allowing them to spend the summer months doing what they love: whitewater rafting. Their "real" jobs may vary from university-level teaching to insurance adjusters, ski instructors, or college students. A lucky few raft Idaho rivers in summer and South American rivers in winter.

Think about what you want in a river trip. Decide how long you wish to be out and whether you prefer rafts, dories or inflatable kayaks. Call around. If you're bringing the kids, find out if the outfitter has special kids' activities, and if river conditions are suitable for kids the age of yours.

Payette Rivers Outfitters

- **Cascade Recreation,** headquartered at Horseshoe Bend on the Payette, runs half-day and full-day trips on the quieter Main Payette and North Fork of the Payette. These are generally suitable for young children. Cascade also has half-day, full-day and two- or three-day trips on the challenging South Fork of the Payette. A four-day combination horseback riding-rafting trip is on offer, also a four-day mountain bike-raft combo trip (see *On Wheels* above). Longtime river runner Steve Jones is the owner/manager. Rt. 1 Box 117A RIO, Horseshoe Bend, ID 83629. ☎ 800-292-RAFT.

- **Headwaters River Company** offers half-day, full-day and two- and three-day trips on the Payette River. Box 1, Banks, ID 83602. ☎ 800-800-RAFT.

- **Idaho Whitewater Unlimited** has half-day, full-day and two-day trips on the Payette. 1042 East Ustick, Meridian, ID 83642. ☎ 208-888-3008.

- **Sawtooth Wilderness Outfitters** includes a two-day South Fork of the Payette float in their Sawtooth Wilderness pack trips. PO Box 81, Garden Valley, ID 83622. ☎ 208-462-3416 (winter), 208-259-3408 (summer). Fax 208-462-3813.

Lower Salmon Outfitters

- **Aggipah River Trips'** owner/operator Bill Berndt runs a less structured river rafting company than many larger outfits. He offers Lower Salmon River floats and can arrange trips covering the entire Salmon River system: the Main and Lower Salmon Rivers and the Middle Fork of the Salmon. Box 425 E5, Salmon, ID 83467. ☎ 208-756-4167.

Betsy Bowen, co-owner of River Odysseys West, shows off the fare enjoyed on Lower Salmon River floats.

- **Discovery River Expeditions, Inc.** runs one-day floats on the Lower Salmon from Riggins. They also offer two- to four-day trips. Box 465, Riggins, ID 83549. ☎ 800-755-8894.

- **Epley's Whitewater Adventures** offers half-day to five-day floats on the Lower Salmon River. Ted and Karen Epley put into the river at Patterson Memorial Park in Riggins. Box 987, McCall, ID 83638. ☎ 800-233-1813.

- **Exodus** offers half-day to multi-day Lower Salmon River floats. PO Box 1231, Riggins, ID 83549. ☎ 800-992-3484.

- **Holiday River Expeditions** has four-day floats through the Lower Salmon River Gorge. A 12-day float on the combined Main and Lower Salmon River is also on offer. PO Box 86, Grangeville, ID 83530. ☎ 800-628-1695.

- **Idaho Afloat** runs multi-day trips through the Lower Salmon River Gorge and six-day combination river and horsepacking trips. PO Box 542, Grangeville, ID 83530. ☎ 800-700-2414.

- **Northwest Voyageurs** offers weekly five-day Lower Salmon floats from May through September. They also do a combination four-day mountain biking-Lower Salmon float trip. PO Box 370, Lucile, ID 83542. ☎ 800-727-9977.

West-Central Idaho

■ **O.A.R.S. (Outdoor Adventure River Specialists)** also features four- and five-day floats on the Lower Salmon using oar and paddle rafts, dories, inflatable kayaks and the Revolution, a two-person kayak-outrigger cross that's great for funning around. They also run dory trips on the full Salmon River System (Main and Lower Salmon and Middle Fork of the Salmon), and have a whitewater dory school. PO Box 67, Angels Camp, CA 95222. ☎ 800-346-6277.

■ **Orange Torpedo Trips** runs three- to five-day Lower Salmon trips using orange inflatable kayaks. Paddle and oared rafts are available on request. PO Box 1111, Grants Pass, OR 97526. ☎ 800-635-2925.

■ **R&C Whitewater Floats** has personalized one- to four-day floats through the Lower Salmon's incomparable canyons. Ray and Chad Christopherson are the owner-operators. Ray also operates **Ridgerunner Outfitters**, offering pack and fishing trips, with his wife, Mary Dawn. PO Box 1193, Kamiah, ID 83536. ☎ 208-935-0757.

■ **R&R Outdoors, Inc.** Rob and Nancy Black have multi-day trips on the Lower Salmon. Ask about pre-trip accommodations at their Adventure Lodge, on the Little Salmon River between New Meadows and Riggins. HC 2, Box 500, Pollock, ID 83547. ☎ 800-574-1224.

■ **ROW (River Odysseys West)** has a variety of multi-day Lower Salmon trips that include horseback/float and raft-supported walking trips, Family Focus trips for families with kids ages 5-12, and ParenTeen Fun floats for families with teenagers. Daring Duckies, a.k.a. inflatable kayaks, offer guests a fun alternative to riding a raft all the way down river. PO Box 579-G, Coeur d'Alene, ID 83816. ☎ 800-451-6034.

■ **Salmon River Experience** runs one-and two-day trips on the Lower Salmon below Riggins, and three- to five-day Salmon River Gorge trips. Chuck and Linda Boyd also offer two-day bike-raft combination tours and a four-day mid-summer eco-study Chinese history tour of the Lower Salmon. This is done in cooperation with the BLM and the Asian American Comparative Collection in the University of Idaho's Laboratory of Anthropology. They also offer three-day Music on the River trips featuring an eclectic mix of professional musicians. 812 Truman, Moscow, ID 83843. ☎ 800-892-9223.

- **Wapiti River Guides** offers multi-day floats on the Lower Salmon. Owner/operator Gary Lane, a professional wildlife biologist turned river guide, runs back-to-earth adventures designed to enhance guests' knowledge of the natural world through which the Salmon flows. Box 1125, Riggins, ID 83549. ☎ 800-488-9872.

Hells Canyon Outfitters

- **Hells Canyon Adventures, Inc.** has one-day rafting on the Snake below Hells Canyon Dam. PO Box 159, Oxbow, OR 97840. ☎ 800-422-3568.

- **Holiday River Expeditions** offers three-day floats through lower Hells Canyon and five-day floats down all 80 miles of this Wild and Scenic River. PO Box 86, Grangeville, ID 83530. ☎ 800-628-2565.

- **Idaho Afloat** runs multi-day trips through Hells Canyon. Bruce and Jeanne Howard also offer six-day combination river and horsepacking excursions in the Hells Canyon National Recreation Area. PO Box 542, Grangeville, ID 83530. ☎ 800-700-2414.

- **Northwest Voyageurs** has three-day and six-day Hells Canyon adventures. They also combine floating Hells Canyon with Seven Devils Wilderness hiking trips. Their four-day Gallop, Trot and Paddle trips include riding in the Seven Devils Wilderness and paddling the Snake. PO Box 370, Lucile, ID 83542. ☎ 800-727-9977.

- **O.A.R.S. (Outdoor Adventure River Specialists)** offers three- and five-day raft and dory trips through Hells Canyon. The company also operates a whitewater dory school with instruction on operating dories in intermediate whitewater. PO Box 67, Angels Camp, CA 95222. ☎ 800-346-6277.

- **R&R Outdoors, Inc.**'s Rob and Nancy Black offer multi-day trips through Hells Canyon. HC 2, Box 500, Pollock, ID 83547. ☎ 800-574-1224.

- **ROW (River Odysseys West)** runs three- and four-day trips in lower Hells Canyon and five- and six-day trips down the Snake from just below Hells Canyon Dam. Horseback/float and raft-supported walking trips are also available. PO Box 579-G, Coeur d'Alene, ID 83816. ☎ 800-451-6034.

West-Central Idaho

Jetboat Trips

Most operators advertise their jetboat trips into Hells Canyon as a way for everyone to get a taste of whitewater exhilaration from the safety of a seat bolted onto a stable craft. "Everyone" includes young children, persons of advanced age and the physically challenged. So it would seem that folks who answer to none of the above might find these jetboat trips on the tame side, even boring. Not so! I get into running serious rapids, but I enjoy the change of pace offered by jetboating from Hells Gate State Park above Lewiston to a turn-around point just above Kirkwood Historic Ranch (see *Touring* for a description of the ranch).

Jetboats' twin engines scoop water in, then jet it out, thus accelerating the craft's powerful forward thrust. These boats plow through rapids, bouncing over larger ones with satisfying smacks, sometimes sending spray sheeting over the stern. Jetboats can seat 60 passengers or more, though most are much smaller. Most are equipped with canopies to shield passengers from the scorching sun.

Heading upriver into Hells Canyon, Idaho is on your left and Washington and Oregon are on your right. The Snake River slides over one of the country's most dramatic state lines. In its depths swim 250-pound sturgeon and quick-silver steelhead trout. Since time before counting, Native Americans have found shelter, food, and water in this canyon called Hells. Petroglyphs adorning rock faces attest to their occupancy over hundreds, maybe thousands, of years. The miners and ranchers who succeeded them also left signs a'plenty, albeit less lasting and less artistic.

Incredible as it may seem to us today, in the late 1800s sizeable steamboats carrying passengers and supplies into Hells Canyon were actually winched over the rapids. The iron eye that secured a winch cable can still be seen imbedded in a rock at Eureka Bar, where the steamboat *Imnaha* broke in two when a cable snapped.

At China Gardens, imagination peoples the place where some 30 Chinese were massacred by outlaws in search of hidden gold (the purported stash didn't exist).

At Nez Perce Crossing, jetboats pass over the spot where Chief Joseph and his people crossed at high flood in the spring of 1877, thus eluding a US Cavalry company led by one General Howard. The outwitted general had expected Chief Joseph to cross at Robinson's Gulch upriver. They had reached White Bird by the time Howard realized he'd been outwitted.

For years, Myrna and Walt Beamer have carried mail, supplies and passengers upriver every Wednesday, year-round, to isolated Hells

*Beamer's Hells Canyon mailboat makes weekly
mail runs to isolated Hell's Canyon ranches.*

Canyon ranches and other outposts of uncivilization. Guests bunk
overnight at the Beamers' Copper Creek Lodge, chowing down on
home-cooked Western-style grub.

Several other outfitters operate up-canyon jetboat trips of varying
lengths. Many schedule stops at historic Kirkwood Ranch.

Hells Canyon Jetboats

Reservations are necessary for Hells Canyon jetboat trips. Most depart
from Hells Gate State Park four miles south of Lewiston, but some leave
from other locations in Lewiston and Clarkston, Washington. Be sure
to check on the launch site when booking your reservation.

Jetboat Outfitters

- **Beamers Hells Canyon Tours** runs day trips up the Snake
  in addition to their Wednesday two-day mail run. They
  also do dinner cruises. PO Box 1243, Lewiston, ID 83501.
  ☎ 800-522-6966.

- **Hells Canyon Adventures, Inc.** runs one-day jetboat tours
  below Hells Canyon Dam. PO Box 159, Oxbow, OR 97840.
  ☎ 800-422-3568.

- **Intermountain Excursions** has one-and two-day jetboat trips from Heller Bar up the Snake and Lower Salmon Rivers. Two-day trippers overnight at a guest lodge on the Lower Salmon. 1120 Bryden Ave., Lewiston, ID 83501. ☎ 208-746-0249. Fax 208-746-4620.

- **Red Woods Outfitter** runs day-long jetboat trips on the Snake River below Hells Canyon. Nolan "Red" Woods also offers jetboat tours of the Lower Salmon River Gorge. HC2 Box 580, Pollock, ID 83547. ☎ 208-628-3673 or 208-628-3744.

- **River Adventures, Ltd.** has one-day jetboat tours on the Snake River in Hells Canyon. Box 518, Riggins, ID 83549. ☎ 800-524-9710.

- **River Quest Excursions**, across the road from Hells Gate State Park, has one-day Hells Canyon jetboat tours. 3665A Snake River Ave., Lewiston, ID 83501. ☎ 800-569-1129.

- **Snake Dancer Excursions** has one-day 182-mile Jet Boat Adventures into Hells Canyon. 614 Lapwai Road, Lewiston, ID 83501. ☎ 800-234-1941.

Canoeing

All the lakes and reservoirs in this region are great for canoeing, especially along shorelines where numerous birds and other wildlife are often sighted. The gemlike alpine lakes in the Payette National Forest and the 30 lakes in Seven Devils Wilderness are especially suited for leisurely canoeing. The rivers in this west-central region are mostly too swift for canoeing, but some stretches of the Main Payette and the Lower Salmon are quiet enough. The Little Salmon River in the New Meadows area also offers some pleasant canoeing.

River Kayaking

While kayakers can go out and play on virtually any accessible stretch of river, the rumptious Little Salmon River near Riggins and the world-class South Fork of the Payette offer extra measures of challenge. Kayakers test their skills in whitewater rodeos on the Little Salmon. The South Fork of the Payette hosts world-class whitewater kayaking competitions. **Cascade Recreation**, on the Payette at Horseshoe Bend, has a complete kayak shop. Nationally acclaimed kayaking teacher Tom Long uses Cascade Recreation's facilities to run kayak schools for all ages. ☎ 800-292-RAFT.

Floating The Boise

Floating the Boise is a summer tradition. A well-developed sense of humor comes in mighty handy. It doesn't matter what you choose to float in, or on. An inner tube, a raft, or anything else that floats and can tow a cooler will do just fine. The idea is to get wet, cool off, splash a lot, swim a little, laugh a lot.

The Boise River chuckles merrily through town for a dozen or so miles. It's sometimes shallow enough to run a tube aground, sometimes swift enough to capsize a raft. **Wheels R Fun**, downriver from Julia Davis Park at the end of 13th Street, rents float tubes and rafts and will transport you and your raft to the put-in spot at Barber Park. ☎ 208-343-8228.

Power Boating & Other Water Fun

Payette Lake, surrounded by summer homes, is the quintessential summertime playpool. This deep high-mountain, fir-fringed lake could have been designed specifically for power boating, waterskiing, personal watercraft, sailing, wind surfing and other water frolics. **McCall** has numerous boaters' support services. Boat-launching is available at Ponderosa State Park and in McCall. The following McCall sports shops sell and rent boats and equipment.

Payette Lake mirrors the north country beauty of Idaho's many natural lakes.

Boating Outfitters

- **Cheap Thrills** rents personal watercraft and everything else you might need to have fun on the water. 622 N. Third Street. ☎ 208-634-7472.

- **Gravity Sports** sells, services and rents rafting and kayaking equipment, plus bicycles and climbing equipment. 503 Pine Street. ☎ 208-634-8530.

- **Rocky Mountain Ski & Sport** rents jet skis, boats and other water toys. 615 N. Third Street. ☎ 208-634-4646.

West-Central Idaho

Fishing

No wonder Idaho fishing is legendary. Fish from these clear waters have sustained Idaho Indians since time out of mind. Salmon, steelhead and other game fish continue to figure in this people's culture. The settlers who came later continued this tradition, albeit without the religious overtones. Today, avid anglers fly into Idaho from throughout the world to cast a fly or hook a steelhead.

The state's 42 species of game fish offer plenty of adventure for casual and dedicated fishers alike. Lakes, rivers, streams, reservoirs – it's your choice. Then choose your method: fly-fishing, spin cast, walk-and-wade, drift or oar boat. That trophy fish is bound to be swimming just out of sight. Trout, Idaho's most popular game fish, can be hooked almost everywhere. In most Idaho waters, you may add a bonus of 10 brook trout to your trout limit.

Idaho Fish

All is not rosy for Idaho fish. Damming the Columbia and Snake Rivers has resulted in drastically reduced runs of chinook salmon and steelhead trout. These ocean-feeding fish must return to their birth streams to spawn. If you have ever watched salmon leap up a waterfall, you have taken part, however vicariously, in one of nature's miracles – a miracle that occurs all too seldom in this technological age. If their spawning run is blocked, the fish cannot reproduce. Hells Canyon dams do not have fish ladders; most Columbia River dams do. Fish ladders are poor replacements for naturally free-flowing rivers, but are better than no ladders at all. Chinook salmon and steelhead trout numbers have been steadily declining as a result of this century's emphasis on irrigation and hydro-electric power. Last-ditch measures are underway to turn this sad situation around, but they may be too late.

Some fish living in this region of Western Idaho fall under the Threatened and Endangered Species umbrella. Bull (Dolly Varden) trout are catch and release. Steelhead fishing is subject to a mess of rules and may not be permitted in the future. Don't even think about fishing for steelhead unless you become conversant with steelhead regulations for the area you wish to fish. Wild Snake River chinook salmon are listed as "threatened" under the Federal Endangered Species Act. Catch and release applies.

Some Idaho rivers and streams have Catch and Release rules. Be sure to consult the current *Idaho Fishing Rule Book* for the rules that apply to the waters where you are headed. Voluntary Catch and Release is encouraged.

Anglers 14 years and older must have a license issued by the Idaho Department of Fish & Game. Non-resident children under 14 may fish without a license if accompanied by a license-holding adult. The adult must include the child's fish in his or her bag limit. You can purchase a license at local license vendors or any Idaho Fish & Game office. ☎ 800-554-8685 for a credit card purchase. A small service fee will be charged.

Be sure to pick up copies of the Idaho Department of Fish & Game's *Official Guide to Fishing in Idaho* and a current *General Fishing Seasons and Rules*, available at local sports shops. Or request copies from the Idaho Department of Fish & Game (600 S. Walnut, Boise, ID 83707. ☎ 208-334-3700. Fax 208-334-2114. E-mail: idfginfo@state.id.us). Idaho fishing information is available at ☎ 1-800-ASK-FISH.

Cold water species, swimming in high mountain lakes and reservoirs and in swift-flowing rivers and streams, include hatchery-raised rainbow and cutthroat trout and coho and kokanee salmon. These waters also contain wild brook and rainbow trout, whitefish and steelhead. Warm water species, living almost exclusively in reservoirs, include wild largemouth and smallmouth bass, bluegill, bullhead and channel catfish, crappie and perch. Consult the above-mentioned fishery guide to determine the best waters for particular species. Consult the rule book for current limits and other important information.

Most visitors like to fish on their own, while some prefer to hire guides, especially for steelhead and other game fish seasons. The following guides are licensed in Idaho and are IOGA members. Some offer multi-day fishing trips. Always ask plenty of questions before choosing an outfitter.

FishingOutfitters

- **Aggipah River Trips'** Bill and Peggy Bernt will arrange customized steelhead and sturgeon fishing trips on the Lower Salmon. Box 425, Salmon, ID 83467. ☎ 208-756-4167.

- **Bigfoot Outfitters, Inc.**'s Harvey Whitten, Ray Ralls and Tom Fliss offer fishing trips to the Seven Devils lakes. Box 498, Riggins, ID 83549. ☎ 208-628-3068, 208-347-2567 or 208-839-2282.

- **Deadwood Outfitters** (see *Travel with Llamas or Horses*, above) focusses on alpine fishing in the Boise National Forest east of Cascade Reservoir. Rt. 1, Box 38, Baker City, OR 97814. ☎ 800-684-3675.

West-Central Idaho

- **Epley's Whitewater Adventures** has one-day steelhead fishing trips on the Salmon River out of Riggins. Box 987, McCall, ID 83638. ☎ 800-233-1813.

- **Idaho Afloat** runs one- to four-day October and November steelhead fishing trips on the Snake and Salmon Rivers. Bruce and Jeanne Howard use a custom 22-foot raft or a driftboat. PO Box 542, Grangeville, ID 83530. ☎ 800-700-2414.

- **Intermountain Excursions** offers fall steelhead fishing on the Snake and Lower Salmon Rivers. 1120 Bryden Ave., Lewiston, ID 83501. ☎ 208-746-0249. Fax 208-746-4620.

- **Northwest Voyageurs** offers fall steelhead and spring and summer rainbow, smallmouth bass, channel cat and white sturgeon fishing in Lower Salmon and Snake River canyons. PO Box 370, Lucile, ID 83542. ☎ 800-727-9977.

- **Red Woods Outfitter**, on the Little Salmon River, offers in-season steelhead, bass, catfish and sturgeon fishing on the Lower Salmon and Snake Rivers. HC2, Box 580, Pollock, ID 83547. ☎ 208-628-3673 or 208-628-3744.

- **R&R Outdoors, Inc.** maintains an Adventure Lodge on the Little Salmon River in Pollock, between New Meadows and Riggins. Rob and Nancy Black offer steelhead and bass trips on the Lower Salmon. HC2, Box 500, Pollock, ID 83547. ☎ 800-574-1224.

- **River Adventures** has in-season sturgeon, steelhead and bass fishing on the Snake in Hells Canyon on Wednesdays. Box 518, Riggins, ID 83549. ☎ 800-524-9710.

- **Salmon River Experience**'s Chuck and Linda Boyd offer two- to five-day drift boat steelhead trips on the Salmon River's Lower Gorge in the fall. 812 Truman, Moscow, ID 83843. ☎ 800-892-9223.

On Snow

 The slice of Idaho anchored by Boise, Lewiston and McCall celebrates winter with downhill ski resorts, the McCall Winter Carnival, and great cross-country skiing and snowmobiling. Getting there poses no more of a problem than most other snow country locations. Main highways are plowed and salted, though big snowstorms can temporarily sock them in. Efforts are made to maintain secondary roads. With some exceptions, Forest Service and other unimproved roads remain unplowed – a boon for Nordic skiers and snow-mobilers. Numerous sports shops and other outlets cater to winter sports needs. Contact the chambers of commerce of the towns near where you wish to ski or snowmobile for a current list of equipment sales and/or rental outlets.

Before starting out, ☎ 208-336-6600 for a current winter road report. If renting a car, consider a 4WD vehicle. Pack emergency supplies in case you become stranded. A cellular phone could be useful, but these phones can be useless in canyon country. Pack a tire-width board, a folding shovel and a bag of kitty litter or other gritty material for traction in case you become stuck. A spirit stove and flares make good sense. Ditto, emergency rations and blankets. Remember: if you find yourself stuck in a snowbank and wish to run your car's engine for warmth (the jury is out on how smart a practice that is), be sure to clear the snow from around your tailpipe so exhaust can escape into the air, not into your car.

Use common sense if you are tempted to travel on unimproved roads. Some areas are not conducive to winter travel or winter sports. The Seven Devils Wilderness is a case in point due to extreme avalanche danger and rugged topography. Hells Canyon can be accessed in winter via Forest Road #493 between Whitebird and Upper Pittsburg Landing. A 4WD vehicle with chains is recommended.

Idaho is north country, snow country. That means button up. Don't underestimate the weather. Pack a parka, wool gloves and scarf, a hat with ear flaps, wool socks and waterproof boots. Wear layers: silk or thermal long johns, turtle neck shirt, wool sweater, parka or wind-breaker. You can get surprisingly warm while cross-country skiing, even in 20° temperatures. Layers allow you to remove or add clothing accordingly. Wear wool, pile or polypropylene clothing, not cotton. Don't forget a pair of gaiters and a hat. Snowmobilers should wear one-piece windproof/waterproof suits and helmets.

Downhill Skiing

This region's downhill ski resorts are small potatoes when compared to the high profile resorts at Sun Valley and other Western locations. Bogus Basin and Brundage Mountain are expanding runs and facilities. Bald Mountain, Cottonwood Butte and Snowhaven, all on or near the Camas

West-Central Idaho

Funky Burgdorf Hot Springs has been a favorite McCall area R&R site for well over 100 years.

Prairie, retain a small town flavor while offering a fair amount of beginners' fun. Short or non-existent lift lines and uncrowded slopes are givens at all five resorts. **Bogus Basin Ski Resort**, in the Boise National Forest just north of Boise, has three chairlifts on both the front and back sides of 7,500-foot Shafer Butte. Its 2,600 acres of skiing terrain include black-diamond runs, long cruisers, powder glades, bump runs and winding bowls, on a total of 58 trails with over 1,800 vertical feet. There's night skiing on 17 runs with over 1,500 vertical feet. Snowboards are permitted. Day lodge and two restaurants. Stay in Boise, or at the slopeside **Pioneer Inn Condominiums**. Bogus Basin, 2405 Bogus Basin Road, Boise, ID 83702. ☎ 208-332-5151. Fax 208-332-5102.

Brundage Mountain, eight miles from McCall, has 1,300 lift-served acres with 38 runs on 1,800 vertical feet accessed by two triple lifts, two double chairs, a platter tow and a handle tow. Salmon River and Seven Devils Mountain views from here are spectacular. Brundage offers guided snowcat skiing over backcountry bowls of untracked powder. Snowboarding is permitted. Day lodge restaurant. No overnight lodging, but McCall has lodgings a'plenty. ☎ 800-888-SKII.

Bald Mountain near Orofino has 15 runs with a vertical drop of 975 feet, accessible via one T-bar and one rope lift. Bald Mountain, PO Box 1126, Orofino, ID 83544. ☎ 208-464-2311.

Cottonwood Butte has seven runs with a vertical drop of 845 feet, accessible via one T-bar and one rope lift. Cottonwood Butte, PO Box 162, Cottonwood, ID 83522. ☎ 208-962-3624. Fax 208-962-5132.

Snowhaven, south of Grangeville, has three runs with a vertical drop of 400 feet, accessible via one T-bar and one rope lift. Snowhaven, 225 W. North, Grangeville, ID 83530. ☎ 208-983-2851. Fax 208-983-2336.

Cross-Country Skiing

This west-central region of Idaho enjoys a heavy snowpack. Add both level and sloping terrain and you have hundreds of miles of cross-country skiing fun.

US Forest Service and BLM trails and backcountry areas offer challenging Nordic skiing for everyone from beginners to advanced telemarkers. Be sure to check in with local Forest Service and/or BLM offices for trail maps and conditions. Then heed rangers' advice. Winter storms often come up fast. Becoming lost and disoriented in whiteout conditions is no joke. If you plan on skiing the backcountry, let someone know where you are going and when you plan to return. Never ski alone. Plan your trip according to the capabilities of the weakest skier in your party.

Bring along emergency supplies: map, compass, water, waterproof matches, high energy food, whistle, knife, flashlight, first aid kit, plastic tarp, sunglasses and sunscreen.

The Idaho Department of Parks & Recreation maintains Park 'N Ski areas in cooperation with ski clubs and local and federal agencies. These groomed trails are accessible by car.

Crawford Park 'N Ski Area is four miles east of Cascade on the Warm Lake Road. The seven miles of marked trails are good for intermediate skiers, but abrupt turns on the downhill section can be challenging.

In the McCall area, **Ponderosa State Park**'s eight miles

of Nordic ski trails are part of the Park 'N Ski program. The Warren Wagon Road is kept open in winter, allowing access to the snow country surrounding **Burgdorf Hot Springs**. The level terrain in Long Valley and the New Meadows area near **Zim's Hot Springs** offers great Nordic skiing.

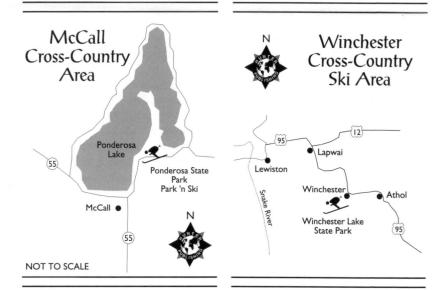

Fish Creek Meadows, nine miles south of Grangeville on Forest Road #221, was one of Idaho's first Park 'N Ski Areas. Five groomed, double-tracked loop trails totaling 12 miles are ideal for both beginning and intermediate skiers. Good play areas appeal to advanced skiers. The ungroomed Fish Creek-Snowhaven Trail connects with Snowhaven Ski Area.

Winchester Lake State Park has a 2½-mile trail through flat and rolling terrain affording views of the woodsy park and gem-like lake.

Snowmobiling

West-central Idaho's hundreds of miles of unplowed Forest Service and BLM roads offer great snowmobiling. Contact the Idaho Department of Parks and Recreation (see Getting Around) to obtain a map showing groomed and ungroomed snowmobiling areas, plus valuable snowmobiling information. You can also check in with local Forest Service and/or BLM offices for snowmobile trail maps and information about roads open to snowmobilers. Be sure to pick up a copy of Idaho Snowmobile Registration Laws & Riding Information. Heed rangers' advice. Winter storms come up fast and hit the backcountry hard. I know. I've been there.

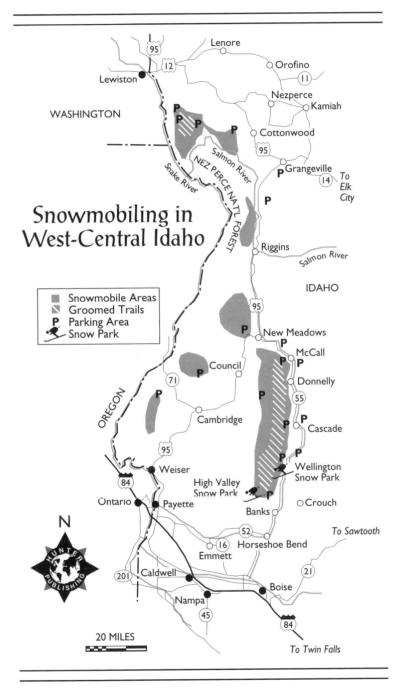

Snowmobiling in
West-Central Idaho

Snowmobile Areas
Groomed Trails
P   Parking Area
Snow Park

WASHINGTON

OREGON

IDAHO

NEZ PERCE NAT'L FOREST

Snake River

Salmon River

Salmon River

Lenore

Orofino

Lewiston

Nezperce

Kamiah

Cottonwood

Grangeville
To Elk City

Riggins

New Meadows

McCall

Donnelly

Council

Cambridge

Cascade

Wellington Snow Park

High Valley Snow Park

Banks

Crouch

To Sawtooth

Weiser

Ontario

Payette

Horseshoe Bend

Emmett

Caldwell

Boise

Nampa

To Twin Falls

N

20 MILES

HUNTER PUBLISHING

Boise, wouldn't you know it, is the only city in the West that can boast a major snowmobile trail right on its back doorstep. The **Highway to Heaven Trail** takes off from 8th Street and heads for the old silver mining town of Idaho City. The three-hour marked and groomed trail continues back toward Lowman and the Sawtooths.

You can pick up the **Winter Wonderland Trail** to McCall from Smith's Ferry, on Hwy 55 north of Boise. The three-hour ride bypasses Cascade and Donnelly before striking out across the mountains into clear country with gentle slopes and bowls. Vistas from 7,900 feet include sweeping views of Cascade Reservoir and Payette Lake. Soak in a thermal hot spring near the Whitelicks area. Trailheads join the main trail at Donnelly and near the West Mountain Lodge at Cascade. The **Railroad Pass Trail** looks in on Warm Lake and connects with trails to Yellow Pine and Deadwood. Much of this expansive area is groomed for snowmobiles.

There are less expansive groomed snowmobile trails and off-trail areas on and around the **Camas Prairie**. The **Gospel Hump Wilderness area** between Grangeville and Elk City is an exciting playground of mountains and valleys.

Cross-Country Skiing & Snowmobiling Trips & Rentals

Most outfitters and guides offering seasonal adventure trips – changing from summer pack trips to fall fishing trips, to winter cross-country skiing and/or snowmobiling – operate in North and Central Idaho.

Outfitters on Snow

- **Blue Moon Outfitters** offers a unique yurt ski-in dining adventure. Cross-country ski or snowshoe a mile to a big, cozy yurt in Ponderosa Park where you will enjoy an ethnic gourmet dinner. PO Box 4281, McCall, ID 83638. ☎ 208-634-3111.

- **Deadwood Outfitters** offers snowmobiling in the Boise National Forest east of Cascade Reservoir. Rt. 1, Box 38, Baker City, OR 97814. ☎ 800-684-3675.

- **Cheap Thrills**, at 622 N. Third Street in McCall, rents snowmobiles, tubes and skis. ☎ 208-634-7472.

- **Rocky Mountain Ski & Sport**, at 615 N. Third Street in McCall, also rents snowmobiles, cross-country skis and other on-snow equipment. ☎ 208-634-4646.

In the Air

Flightseeing

You have to view Idaho from the air to get a handle on the scope and sweep of this splendid country. Seen from a few thousand feet up, the velvety-green fir-clad mountains seem to extend into foreverland. Lakes pinhole the green, so clear that you can see fish swimming in their depths. These sapphire gems may appear to be close enough to touch, yet they often require days of hiking to reach.

Hells Canyon from the air beggars description. The deep gash in the earth seems even deeper when seen in proportion to the canyon walls and the towering Seven Devils Mountains.

Outfitters in the Air

- **McCall Air Taxi**, specializing in access to the Frank Church-River of No Return Wilderness, offers flightseeing trips and city-to-city charters. ☎ 800-992-6559.

- **Pioneer Air Service** has flightseeing trips and air charters from McCall. ☎ 208-634-7127.

- **Grangeville Air Service** ferries passengers to backcountry air strips and offers flightseeing over Hells Canyon. ☎ 208-983-0490.

Kid Stuff

For the most part, what's fun for grownups in this region of Idaho is fun for eight-to-teens as well. Exceptions may include whitewater exceeding Class III and rugged hiking, backpacking, cross-country skiing and snowmobiling trips. Know your child's limitations and try not to exceed them. Err on the conservative side if you're not familiar with the country you'll be going into. Stick with short forays if your child hasn't hiked before. Ditto: Nordic skiing and snowmobiling. Most kids do well on horseback riding trips, providing they have ridden before and/or receive adequate instruction before setting out. Outfitter instruction can vary from casual to extremely good. Be sure to inquire about the level of riding instruction provided when considering a guest ranch or horseback trip.

West-Central Idaho

There's plenty of fun for tagalongs younger than eight. Abilities vary widely among kids in this age group. Plan accordingly so that your adventure is enjoyable for the entire family.

A float trip through the Lower Salmon River Gorge is ideal for kids, offering moderate rapids, plenty of warm calm water for swimming and splashing, big white sand beaches, and interesting Native American, miners' and settlers' sites to explore. Any Lower Salmon float is suitable for kids, especially in late summer when the water is lower.

River Odysseys West (ROW) offers Lower Salmon trips especially designed for families with kids, even including an awesome kids' menu. Their Family Focus trip is for families with kids aged 5-12. ParenTeen Fun adventures are for families with teens age 13-18. All trips include those delightful Daring Duckies (open inflatable kayaks) for hours of fun. ☎ 800-451-6034.

On **Idaho Afloat's** multi-day trips through the Lower Salmon River Gorge, owner/operators Bruce and Jeanne Howard make sure that kids both play and learn. The couple takes kids on short hikes to view Indian petroglyphs and archaeological sites. ☎ 800-700-2414.

Parents are often amazed to discover undreamed-of capabilities in their kids. I was, when my 10-year-old daughter Amy successfully ran Class II rapids after two days of kayaking instruction on the Main Payette River. Tom Long's Cascade Kayak School uses a specially designed kid-friendly approach to teaching the basics of river kayaking while building confidence and self-esteem. Single day private or semi-private lessons are available for both children and adults. Two-week kayak camps are offered for those aged 9-12 and 14-17. **Cascade Raft Company,** ☎ 800-292-RAFT.

R&R Outdoors Inc. has a four-week Youth Recreation Adventure program tailored for teenagers. It includes hiking, fishing, horseback riding, exploring and other fun stuff. ☎ 800-574-1224.

It's a given that downhill ski areas offer kids' programs and ski instruction. When contacting ski resorts, be sure to ask about these programs. Bogus Basin offers free ski lessons to pre-schoolers. Brundage Mountain has lessons for kids aged four and up. Every downhill ski area has at least one beginners' slope or ski area.

Boise's **Julia Davis Park** zoo and children's amusement park are ideal for those times when your little ones have to let off steam. They'll love the bright red Boise Tour Train. The **World Center for Birds of Prey** and the **Morrison-Knutsen Nature Center** are also kid-pleasers. And what child could fail to be fascinated by the Old Idaho Penitentiary's cavernous cell blocks?

For hours of hands-on fun, take the troops to the **Discovery Center of Idaho**. They'll love the amazing incredibubble machine and other participatory science exhibits. 131 Myrtle Street, between Broadway and Capitol Blvd. ☎ 208-343-9895. Open Tues-Sat, 10-5, Sun, 12-5; June-Aug, Tues-Fri, 9-5, Sat, 10-5, Sun, 12-5. Admission fee.

Eco-Travel & Cultural Excursions

 Chuck and Linda Boyd of **Salmon River Experience** offer a four-day mid-summer eco-study Chinese history tour of the Lower Salmon in cooperation with the Bureau of Land Management and the Asian American Comparative Collection in the Laboratory of Anthropology at the University of Idaho. They also run three-day Music on the River trips, featuring an eclectic mix of professional musicians. ☎ 800-892-9223.

Wildlife Watching

Idaho wildlife watchers needn't look far. You might even see peregrine falcons hang-gliding over downtown Boise. You'll almost surely see a group of curious mountain goats topping a ledge in the Seven Devils Wilderness. There's hardly any end to the wildlife you can see in the Seven Devils if you exercise patience. Columbian ground squirrels seem to be scampering everywhere. Black bear and coyote are much shyer. It's a sure bet that you'll see some species of wildlife wherever your hikes, river floats or pack trips, even auto tours, take you. But you won't spot every species native to a given area in every season. Mountain goats are best sighted from July to September, while those hang-gliding peregrines might be evident only in spring.

The following are special wildlife viewing locations in the areas covered in this chapter. Serious wildlife watchers should buy a copy of Leslie Benjamin Carpenter's *Idaho Wildlife Viewing Guide*, available in local bookstores or by sending a check for $6.26, payable to the Nongame Wildlife Program, to the Idaho Department of Fish & Game (600 S. Walnut, Boise, ID 83707. ☎ 208-334-3700. Fax 208-334-2114. E-mail: idfginfo@state.id.us).

Barber Park, on the Boise River east of downtown Boise, is a good place to see wintering bald eagles perched in big cottonwood trees from mid-November to mid-March. Frequently seen resident wildlife include great blue herons, mallards, California quail and numerous other avian species. Mink, muskrats and beavers live along the river.

West-Central Idaho

Montour Wildlife Management and Recreation Area, in the Payette River Canyon off Idaho 55 between Horseshoe Bend and Emmett, is excellent habitat for water birds. In spring and summer, you'll see Canada geese, osprey, golden eagles and numerous species of smaller birds and flycatchers. Great horned owls and red-tailed hawks often nest in large trees on the WMRA's eastern side. Mule deer frequent the area in winter. To see the most waterfowl, take an easy canoe trip from Horseshoe Bend to the Montour Bridge.

Cascade Reservoir frequently resounds to the eerie calls of the common loon. Water birds abound here. In summer, when the reservoir is full, you must observe from the road. You can walk the shoreline in spring, fall and winter. Western and Clark's grebes, bald eagles and osprey nest at the reservoir. Numerous species of uncommon birds can sometimes be sighted. In August, you can watch spawning chinook salmon from a boardwalk at the Stolle Meadows viewing site. There are interpretive signs. At Donnelly, turn off Idaho 55 onto a paved road accessing FS Road 422. The gravel road follows the shoreline for 16 miles, coming out on Idaho 55 at Cascade.

Ponderosa State Park has high concentrations of wildlife. In spring and summer, look for fun critters like Pacific tree frogs, western toads, long-toed salamanders and garter snakes. You might also see a black bear, great horned or barred owls, Swainson's thrush and other song-birds. Red fox, badger and bobcat tracks are sometimes in evidence. Wildflowers abound in spring and summer. So do berries, which are yours for the picking in late summer. The park offers self-guided nature trails, guided walks with park rangers and evening campfire programs.

A Forest Service trail upstream, along the Wild and Scenic Rapid River from the **Rapid River Fish Hatchery**, is a good place to see kinglets, golden eagles, chukar, northern goshawks and other birds. Rattle-snakes, too. The hatchery, offering a close look at chinook salmon and their life cycle, is open daily year-round. To get there, head west on FS Road 2114, 4.4 miles south of Riggins.

The terrain around **Brownlee, Oxbow** and **Hells Canyon Reservoirs** is an important wintering range for mule deer, elk and bald eagles. Bighorn sheep are often spotted near **Hells Canyon Dam**. River otter and chukar are less frequently seen.

Virtually every species of wildlife that inhabits this west-central slice of Idaho at some time or another may be spotted along the **Snake River** in Hells Canyon National Recreation Area, even rare species such as Townsend's big-eared bat. Mild winters make this a favorite wintering area for bighorn sheep, elk, mule deer, mountain goats and bald eagles.

You may see Canada geese, golden eagles and black bear in spring. Rattlesnakes like this arid area, too.

The **Lower Salmon River Canyon** is best accessed by float trip. Watch for numerous raptors as well as mule and white-tailed deer and elk as you float. Hoofed animals are best seen in winter and spring. The catch: the river is not floatable in winter.

Nez Perce National Historical Park, Heart of the Monster Unit is in a low area adjacent to the Clearwater River. Follow a foot trail along the river to see nesting songbirds in spring and summer. This is also a good place to see Canada geese, osprey, beaver, river otter, mink and muskrat. Go at dawn or dusk to see white-tailed deer.

Heavily wooded **Winchester Lake State Park** is home to ruffled grouse, nuthatches, and Stellar's jay. The call of the common loon is often heard over the lake. If you are lucky, you might see a northern flying squirrel or a long-tailed weasel. Coyote will likely make their presence known at night via their characteristic yip-yipping. Nature trails surround the lake.

Craig Mountain Wildlife Management Area, at the lower end of Hells Canyon, is best accessed from Lewiston by road or river. Land access is complicated: obtain a map from the Idaho Fish & Game office at 1540 Warner Ave., in Lewiston. The management area includes species habitats from river level at 800 feet to a mile high. Within that broad spectrum live numerous species of big game and upland birds.

Hells Gate State Park is a great birding area. A two-mile trail from the campground follows the river, offering good opportunities to view many of the 121 bird species recorded in the park. Mammals include cottontail rabbits, white-tailed jackrabbits and yellowbelly marmots.

Festivals & Special Events

 Idaho's diverse peoples throw super-great parties celebrating everything from cowboy culture to music, from whitewater kayaking to crafts. Small town festivals are great for chowing down on good hearty food and kicking up your heels.

Listed below are festivals and special events that occur on an annual basis. All dates are subject to change. Call before solidifying your plans. Chambers of commerce can tell you if their areas plan impromptu events or festivals on the dates of your visit.

West-Central Idaho

February

McCall Winter Carnival, held the first two weeks in February, includes parades, ice sculpture contests, snowmobile and dogsled races, wine tasting, beard and hairy leg contests and the Snowflake Ball. McCall Chamber of Commerce. ☎ 208-634-7631.

First Security Winter Games include just about everything you can do on snow and are held at various Idaho ski areas and winter destinations. For information, contact First Security Bank, Box 15214, Boise, ID 83715. ☎ 208-393-2255. Fax 208-393-2187.

April

Salmon River Jetboat Races, held in Riggins in mid-April, constitute the first leg of the US Championship jetboat race, drawing competitors from as far away as Canada, Mexico and New Zealand. Salmon River Chamber of Commerce. ☎ 208-628-3440.

Lewiston Dogwood Festival, held in mid-April, features an art show, arts and crafts fair, wine and beer tasting, garden tours, concerts and plays. Lewis & Clark Center for Arts & History, 415 Main St., Lewiston, ID 83501. ☎ 208-799-2243. E-mail: dogwood@lcsc.edu.

May

Riggins Rodeo, held in early May, features a parade and rodeo that you watch in a natural canyon "stadium." Salmon River Chamber of Commerce. ☎ 208-628-3440.

Apple Blossom Festival in the Magic Valley town of Payette celebrates apple blossom time and small town life in mid-May. Enjoy old-fashioned delights: an apple bobbing race, hot air balloon rally, talent show, ice cream social, rodeo, pretty baby and pie eating contests, arts and crafts and other activities. Payette Chamber of Commerce, 700 Center Ave., Payette, ID 83661. ☎ 208-642-2362.

Mat'alyma Powwow and Root Feast is celebrated in Kamiah over the third weekend in May. Tribal dancing, give-aways, name-giving and a feast of traditional freshly harvested roots. Non-Indians are welcome to attend as guests of the Nez Perce. Nez Perce Historical Park, Box 93, Spalding, ID 83551. ☎ 208-843-2261. Fax 208-843-2001.

June

Summerfest, Boise is celebrated the first three weekends in June. The Boise Chamber Orchestra, Boise Big Band and other artists perform pop, jazz and classical music in the Boise State University Centennial Amphitheater. Boise State University Music Department, 1910 University Ave., Boise, ID 83725. ☎ 208-385-1596.

Idaho Shakespeare Festival presents a June-September summer season in an outdoor amphitheatre on the Boise River. Idaho Shakespeare Festival, PO Box 9365, Boise, ID 83707. ☎ 208-336-9221. Fax 208-336-6731. E-mail: idshakes@micron.net.

Hells Canyon Days & Bull-A-Rama is celebrated in Cambridge the first weekend in June with a rodeo, miniature toy show, antique power show, custom car show and cruise, square dancing and a horse and tack sale. Boise Convention & Visitors Bureau. ☎ 208-344-7777. Fax 208-344-6236. Web site: http://www.boisecvb.org.

Emmett Cherry Festival celebrates cherry time with a cherry pit spitting contest, pie eating contest, a Civil War encampment, quilt show, fun run, square dancing, horseshoe pitching contest and a carnival. Gem County Chamber, 231 S. Washington, Emmett, ID 83617. ☎ 208-356-3485.

Meridian Dairy Days is held the fourth weekend in June. Once a dairying center, Meridian is now a Boise bedroom community producing more kids than milk. Pancake feed, fun run/walk, community auction, FFA and 4H dairy show, carnival, Dairyland parade. Meridian Chamber of Commerce. ☎ 208-888-2817. Fax 208-888-2682.

Weiser's National Oldtime Fiddlers Contest and Festival, the country's most prestigious fiddlers' event, features country fiddlers sawing away throughout town, plus impromptu jam sessions. The third weekend in June. ☎ 800-437-1280.

Hewlett-Packard International Women's Challenge cycling race is held statewide in late June over a 400-mile range. Women's Challenge, Inc., Box 299, Boise, ID 83701. ☎ 208-345-7223. Fax 208-345-5325.

Boise River Festival, held the last weekend in June, derives its name from an everything-that-floats parade down the Boise. Now it's reduced to a prosaic street parade. Also, a hot air balloon rally, six stages with continuous entertainment, food and more. Boise River Festival Office, 7032 S. Eisenman Rd., Boise, ID 83705. ☎ 208-338-8887. Fax 208-338-3833. Web site: http://www.micron.net/-brf.

Grangeville Border Days Rodeo, held the weekend before July 4, features three days of street fairs, parades and rodeo. Grangeville Chamber of Commerce. ☎ 208-983-0460.

July

Clearwater Riverfest, held in Kamiah over the first weekend in July, features arts and crafts and bluegrass music in the park. Kamiah Chamber of Commerce. ☎ 208-935-2290.

Payette Whitewater Rodeo, on the South Fork of the Payette, is held in mid-July. Championship kayakers' race, surf and perform tricks. ☎ 800-292-RAFT.

Annual International Montour Powwow, held in Montour in mid-July. Native American dancers of all ages perform traditional dances. Arts & crafts and food booths. No drugs or alcohol. Bring lawn chairs. Western Idaho Powwow Association. ☎ 208-343-1528.

Snake River Stampede, held in Nampa in mid-July, is one of the top 25 rodeos in the nation, featuring the world's top-ranking cowboys and cowgirls in action. Snake River Stampede Office, Box 231, Nampa, ID 83653. ☎ 208-466-8497.

First Security Twilight Criterium, one of the most unusual bicycle races in the country, is held at night in downtown Boise in late July. Two cycling races and an in-line skating race. First Security Bank, Box 7069, Boise, ID 83730. ☎ 208-393-2255. Fax 208-393-2187.

Payette Lakes Midsummer Craft & Antique Fair, held in McCall in late July, offers a weekend of homespun crafts and antiques. ☎ 208-634-4151.

August

Yellow Pine Harmonica Festival is held the first full weekend in August. One of Idaho's more offbeat festivals, this foot-stompin' tribute to the harmonica's place in the Old West is centered in one of Idaho's many time-warp gold mining towns. Yellow Pine Enhancement Society, Box 23, Yellow Pine, ID 83677.

Summerfest in McCall, one of the many music festivals popping up throughout the West, is a pop, classic and jazz fest held at the Brundage Mountain amphitheater the first weekend in August. Also, a children's concert and after-hours jazz jam. McCall Music Society, Box 1719, McCall, ID 83638. ☎ 208-634-7762. Fax 208-634-4974.

Hot August Nights, held in Lewiston in mid-August, is a self-styled "blast from the past" featuring music, dancing and a classic car show. Lewiston Chamber of Commerce. ☎ 208-743-6564.

Chief Lookinglass Days, held the third weekend in August, is a traditonal pow wow put on by descendants of Chief Lookinglass of the Nez Perce tribe. Native American dancing and cultural ceremonies. Nez

Perce National Historical Park, Box 93, Spalding, ID 83551. ☎ 208-843-2261. Fax 208-843-2001.

Caldwell Night Rodeo is one of the nation's top PRCA rodeos. The five-night extravaganza is held in late August. Caldwell Chamber of Commerce, Box 98, Caldwell, ID 83606. ☎ 208-459-2060. Fax 208-454-1284.

Council Mountain Festival, held in mid-August, features hot air balloons, dancing, an art show and downhome food. Council Community Visitor Center. ☎ 208-253-0161.

Western Idaho State Fair, held in Boise in mid-August, is Idaho's biggest fair, featuring all the heel-kicking frolics that put state fairs on the West's map of favorite events. Western Idaho Fair, 5610 Glenwood, Boise, ID 83714. ☎ 208-376-3247. Fax 208-375-9972.

September

Lewiston Roundup, held in early September, features three days of top rodeo action. Lewiston Chamber of Commerce, ☎ 800-473-3543.

Art in the Park, held in Julia Davis Park in early September, brings well over 100 artists and crafters together from throughout the country. Food booths, entertainment and over 100 arts and crafts vendors. Boise Art Museum, 670 S. Julia David Dr., Boise, ID 83702. ☎ 208-345-8330. Fax 208-345-2247.

Idaho Historical Society Brown Bag Lunch Speaker Series, held September through May, features noon-hour presentations on subjects pertaining to Idaho history. Idaho Historical Museum, 610 N. Julia Davis Dr., Boise, ID 83702. ☎ 208-334-2120. Fax 208-334-4059.

Clearwater County Fair and Lumberjack Days takes place on the third weekend in September. It celebrates an important facet of Idaho's history and culture with he-man logging competitions pitting loggers from all over the world in axe throwing, two-person hand saw races and other logging skills contests. Orofino Chamber of Commerce, Box 2221, Orofino, ID 83544. ☎ 208-476-4335. Fax 208-476-3634.

Museum Comes to Life, held in late September, celebrates Idaho's living history with hands-on events and demonstrations of 19th-century living. Idaho Historical Museum, 610 N. Julia Davis Dr., Boise, ID 83702. ☎ 208-334-2120. Fax 208-334-4059.

November

Boise Museum After Hours and **Arts for Christmas Sale** are two Boise Art Museum events. After Hours features music, art and refreshments every Wednesday between 5:30 and 7:30 pm in spring and fall. The Arts for Christmas sale, featuring handcrafted items, is held in mid-November. Boise Art Museum, 610 N. Julia Davis Dr., Boise, ID 83702. ☎ 208-345-8330. Fax 208-345-2247.

Festival of Trees, held in Boise in late November, is an extravaganza of lavishly decorated trees and wreaths. St. Alphonsus Special Events Committee. ☎ 208-378-2797.

Where to Stay & Eat

Spur-of-the-moment lodgings and good, hearty small town chow are seldom more than a few miles away. Boise, McCall and Lewiston surprise the palate with a smattering of better-than-average restaurants. Every small town has at least one motel, but keeping an eye open for a bed and breakfast inn can be rewarding. New B&Bs continue to open as home owners and retirees realize the advantages of catering to an increasing influx of visitors to Idaho.

The purpose of this book is to acquaint you with Idaho's wealth of adventures, not to offer town-by-town, motel-by-motel critiques. The lodgings listed below include bed & breakfasts, hotels, resorts and an occasional chain motel to round out the choices. Local chambers of commerce have complete accommodations listings. Reservations are necessary in Boise and in busy, high-profile resort towns, such as Riggins and McCall.

Lodgings

Boise

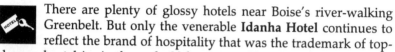

There are plenty of glossy hotels near Boise's river-walking Greenbelt. But only the venerable **Idanha Hotel** continues to reflect the brand of hospitality that was the trademark of top-drawer hostelries in the early 20th century. The Idanha looked pretty grand to Boiseans when it opened in 1901. Proudly situated in the heart of town, it was embellished with corner turrets a full six stories high. For years, the Idanha was *the* place for visiting dignitaries to stay. Eventually, the old lady fell on such hard times that it seemed that she must die. But an expensive renovation is restoring her integrity. The turret suites offer tasteful comfort and a peregrine-eye view of Main Street's comings and goings. Hotel Idanha, 928 Main Street, Boise, ID 83702. ☎ 208-342-3611. Fax 208-342-9690.

Other notable downtown hotels include:

Owyhee Plaza Hotel, a landmark whose renovation has given little attention to its history. 1109 Main St., Boise, ID 83702. ☎ 800-233-4611. Fax 208-381-0695.

Red Lion Riverside is a sprawling complex whose riverside name is misleading, located as it is away from the Greenbelt. Nevertheless, it's a comfortable pad set on a nicely landscaped plot. 2900 Chinden Blvd., Boise, ID 83714. ☎ 800-547-8010. Fax 208-344-1079.

Shilo Inn - Boise Riverside enjoys a prime location adjacent to the Greenbelt, the 8th Street Marketplace and other downtown attractions. 3031 Main St., Boise, ID 83702. ☎ 800-222-2244. Fax 208-384-1217.

The Statehouse Inn is also convenient to downtown attractions. 981 Grove St., Boise, ID 83702. ☎ 800-243-4622. Fax 208-344-5751.

Ustick Inn describes itself as a "residence hotel." The old farmhouse west of town has hostel-style bunks. 8050 Ustick Rd., Boise 83704. ☎ 208-322-6277.

Boise B&Bs

Boise has long since joined Idaho's bed & breakfast boom. Most of those listed below are owner-operated, assuring guests of personal attention.

Bed & Breakfast at Victoria's White House has two guest rooms. 10325 W. Victory Rd., Boise, ID 83709. ☎ 208-362-0507.

Idaho Heritage Inn, in the Warm Springs District, is charming and beautifully appointed. The historic house was the home of the late Senator Frank Church, in whose honor the Frank Church Wilderness Area was named. The six guest rooms are attractive. Idaho Heritage Inn, 109 West Idaho, Boise, ID 83702. ☎ 208-342-8066.

Robin's Nest Bed & Breakfast, in the west end of the city, has four guest rooms. 2389 W. Boise Ave., Boise, ID 83706. ☎ 208-336-9551.

Sunrise Inn Bed & Breakfast is in the hills above Boise. 2730 Sunrise Rim Rd., Boise, ID 83705. ☎ 208-344-0805.

Caldwell & Nampa

Caldwell and nearby Nampa each has a small B&B.

Manning House Bed & Breakfast Inn, 1803 S. 10th Ave., Caldwell, ID 83606. ☎ 208-459-7899.

The Pink Tudor Bed and Breakfast, 1315 12th Ave., Nampa, ID 83651. ☎ 208-465-3615.

West-Central Idaho

Cambridge

This crossroads town has a B&B and two motels convenient to Hwy 71, the well-traveled route to Hells Canyon Dam.

Cambridge House Bed & Breakfast has but one guest room. PO Box 313, Cambridge, ID 83610. ☎ 208-257-3325.

Frontier Motel and RV Park, PO Box 178, Cambridge, ID 83610. ☎ 208-257-3851.

Hunters Inn offers a choice of B&B or motel-style rooms. PO Box 313, Cambridge, ID 83610. ☎ 208-257-3325.

Cascade

Cascade has a whole bunch of motels, plus a B&B and a lodge with guest cabins 26 miles east of town in the Warm Lake area.

North Shore Lodge has eight cabins for rent. 175 N. Shoreline Dr., Cascade, ID 83611. ☎ 800-933-3193.

Warm Lake Lodge & Resort is operated as a B&B. Box 450, Cascade, ID 83611. ☎ 208-257-2221 (summer), 208-382-4274 (winter).

Garden Valley

Warm Springs Creek Bed & Breakfast is the best lodging bet in this hamlet convenient to Payette Rivers kayaking and rafting. HC 76 Box 2540, Garden Valley, ID 83622. ☎ 208-462-3516.

Grangeville, Kamiah, Kooskia, and Orofino have numerous motels.

Lewiston

The general mediocrity of Lewiston's lodgings continues to amaze me. The predictable **Ramada Inn** at 621 21st. St. (☎ 800-232-6730) may be okay if you are in the motel mood. Better is the pleasant **Best Western River Tree Inn**, 1267 Bridge St., Clarkston, WA 99403, ☎ 800-597-3621. This is just across the river. Many guest rooms have river views. Walking and bicycling paths along the nearby levee afford a close-up look at river traffic.

Lewiston B&Bs

The Carriage House B&B, in a pleasant blufftop neighborhood, offers country decor and bounteous breakfasts. 611 5th St., Lewiston, ID 83501. ☎ 208-746-4506.

Shiloh Rose Bed & Breakfast has a three-room guest suite. 3414 Selway Dr., Lewiston, ID 83501. ☎ 208-743-2482.

McCall

McCall is a thriving resort town that's growing apace. Translation: lodging reservations are a must at the height of the summer and winter seasons.

Accommodations Services arranges rentals of privately owned condo units, homes and cabins. PO Box 1522, McCall, ID 83638. ☎ 208-634-7766. Fax 208-634-5150.

1920 House Bed and Breakfast has three guest rooms. PO Box 1716, McCall, ID 83638. ☎ 208-634-4661.

Brundage Bungalows has seven cabins for rent. 308 W. Lake, McCall, ID 83638. ☎ 208-634-8573. Fax 208-634-7359.

The Chateau Bed & Breakfast is on the historic Warren Wagon Road. PO Box 1957, McCall, ID 83638. ☎ and fax 208-634-4196.

Hotel McCall suffered numerous uses and indignities during the hiatus between its salad days and 1989, when Peggy Wheatland rescued it and restored it to a pleasantly appointed B&B. Its situation opposite McCall's busiest corner means that weekend noise could be annoying. Mitigating factors are a lake view and a sense of being where the action is. PO Box 1778, McCall, ID 83638. ☎ 208-634-8105.

Northwest Passage Bed & Breakfast has six guest rooms and an apartment. Box 4208, 201 Rio Vista Blvd., McCall, ID 83638. ☎ 800-597-6658. Fax 208-634-4977.

Shore Lodge, enjoying an idyllic lakeside location west of downtown, is the traditional choice of vacationing Boiseans. Pleasant guest rooms and a restaurant overlook the lake. A private beach and boat dock make it a good family choice. PO Box 1006, McCall, ID 83638. ☎ 800-657-6464.

University of Idaho McCall Field Campus offers moderately priced lodging when the facilities are not in use. Contact the College of Forestry, Wildlife and Range Sciences, University of Idaho, Moscow, ID 83844. ☎ 855-7302. Fax 208-855-5534.

New Meadows

Bear Creek Lodge offers luxury accommodations with fireplaces, jetted tubs and views of mountains and meadows. There is also Nordic skiing, snowmobiling, and a gourmet restaurant. Bear Creek Lodge, PO Box 8, New Meadows, ID 84654. ☎ 208-634-3551.

West-Central Idaho

Hartland Inn & Motel is a B&B in a handsome old house at the crossroads that put New Meadows on the map. A motel is operated in conjunction with the B&B. PO Box 215, New Meadows, ID 83654. ☎ 208-347-2114.

Nezperce

This Nez Perce Indian Reservation town is locally famous for the **Nez Perce Hotel and Dining Room**, with 10 moderately priced guest rooms. PO Box 36, Nezperce, ID 83543. ☎ 208-937-2655.

Riggins

If you're beginning a Salmon River float from here, you may choose to overnight here as well. Riggins has motels, B&Bs and lodges for every taste, from lets-all-eight-of-us-flop-in-one-room to some fairly tony digs. Most are within finger-dipping distance of the Little Salmon River. The majority, with the exception of the **Riverview Motel** (Box 453, Riggins, ID 83549; ☎ 208-628-3041), offer double rooms at under $50 per night. The following have river access or another unique feature. You might want to contact the Riggins Chamber of Commerce for a complete motel list (☎ 208-628-3778).

Half Way Inn is on the Little Salmon River between New Meadows and Riggins. HC 75, Box 3760, New Meadows, ID 83654. ☎ 208-628-3259.

Riggins Motel has a two-bedroom house for rent by the day, plus 19 motel units. Box 1157, Riggins, ID 83549. ☎ 208-628-3041.

Pinehurst Resort Motel, 13 miles south of Riggins, has cabins with kitchen facilities. 5604 Hwy 95, New Meadows, ID 83654. ☎ 208-628-3323.

The Lodge at Riggins Hot Springs is on the Salmon River. PO Box 1247, Riggins, ID 83549. ☎ and fax 208-628-3785.

The Lodge Bed & Breakfast is on the Little Salmon River. PO Box 498, Riggins, ID 83549. ☎ 208-628-3863.

Guest Ranches

Guest ranches are scarce in this part of Idaho.

Mountain Man Lodge & Marina is a scenic 38,000-acre guest ranch offering horseback riding, wagon rides and other ranch-style activities. They also have houseboat rentals, waterskiing and dinner on the Snake River. 2855 Rock Creek Road, Weiser, ID 83672. ☎ 208-355-2626.

Wapiti Meadow Ranch, on the Johnson Creek Road south of Yellow Pine, offers horseback riding, hiking, fishing in high mountain lakes and streams, panning for gold, 4x4 sightseeing, mountain biking, gold mine tours and other traditional and non-traditional guest ranch activities. There is cross-country skiing and snowmobiling over groomed and backcountry trails in winter. Owner Diana Swift offers personalized activities, country cabins and gourmet meals in a rustic mountain meadow setting. If you own an airplane, you can fly in to the Johnson Creek airstrip, five miles from the ranch. Contact Idaho Division of Aeronautics (☎ 208-334-8775) for local flying information. Wapiti Meadow Ranch, H.C. 72, Cascade, ID 83611. ☎ 208-633-3217 or 208-382-3217 (radio phone: 208-382-4336).

Where to Eat

 While some Boise and resort area restaurants keep abreast of current culinary trends, most small town eateries reflect Westerners' traditional preference for steak, burgers and fries. Crossroads café helpings of meat-and-potatoes fare are designed to satisfy loggers and truckers. Stop in at any café to be fed amply and well. You could be out of luck if your tastes tend toward more specialized cuisine.

Boise

Downtown Boise has numerous trendy eateries, some very good, many of the chain genre. The Eighth Street Marketplace has several, as does, believe it or not, Main Street's fancied-up parking garage. Ethnic cuisine is big here, and micro-breweries are catching on fast. At this writing, Boise boasts two: **Harrison Hollow Brew House** at 2455 Bogus Basin Road (☎ 208-343-6820) and **Tablerock Brewpub & Grill** at the corner of Capitol Blvd. and Fulton (☎ 208-342-0944).

Aladdin Egyptian Restaurant, 111 Broadway Ave., serves up Mideastern cuisine and belly dancing. ☎ 208-368-0880.

Bangkok Restaurant, 624 W. Idaho St., is where Boiseans go for Thai food. ☎ 208-336-0018.

The Blue Note, 1805 West State Street, is a fun place to enjoy casual California-style food. Reservations not usually required. ☎ 208-345-9831.

Chapala, Sixth and Main, features authentic Mexican dishes. ☎ 208-331-7866.

West-Central Idaho

Dong Khanh, 111 Broadway Ave., serves Vietnamese food. ☎ 208-345-0980.

Earth Food Café, 2907 W. State St., caters to lovers of natural foods and vegetarians. ☎ 208-342-7169.

The Gamekeeper Restaurant, in the Owyhee Plaza Hotel at 1109 Main Street, offers traditional continental dishes expertly prepared. Dinner only. Reservations suggested. ☎ 208-343-4611.

Onati, 3544 Chinden Blvd., features hearty Basque food prepared the way the Basques like it. ☎ 208-343-6464.

Peter Schott's Restaurant, off the Idanha Hotel lobby at 928 W. Main St., has long been famous for creative continental cuisine featuring Idaho salmon and trout. Generally considered to be Boise's finest restaurant. Reservations suggested. ☎ 208-336-9100.

Renaissance Ristorante Italiano, offering a romantic ambience in the basement of a historic building at 110 S. Fifth St., specializes in Northern Italian cuisine. ☎ 208-344-67765.

Shige Japanese Cuisine, on the second floor of Capitol Terrace at 150 N. Eighth St., has a sushi bar. Other Japanese specialties are also on offer. ☎ 208-338-8423.

Lewiston

Lewiston isn't exactly known for its wide choice of gustatory delights. Lewistonians seeking better-than-average dining in an attractive atmosphere head for **Jonathan's,** at 301 D Street. Located off the town's renovated Main Street, Jonathan's serves continental and Cajun dishes. Reservations are a good idea on weekends. ☎ 208-746-3438.

McCall

Si Bueno Mexican Restaurant & Cantina, across Hwy 55 from the McCall Airport, serves up Mexican food with lots of character, plus kids' specials and the more plebeian steaks and seafood. ☎ 208-634-2128.

McCall Brewing Company. It should come as no surprise to find that this popular resort town has a brew pub offering a casual, rustic ambience with brews and food to match. You'll find it next to Maverik at 807 North 3rd. (Hwy 55). ☎ 208-634-2333.

The Mill Steaks & Spirits, on Hwy 55, is one of those rustic eateries and watering holes beloved by both locals and outlanders. ☎ 208-634-7683.

Nampa

El Charro Café, 1701 First St. N., is worth a drive if you dig really authentic Mexican food. ☎ 208-467-5804.

Camping

This region's camping choices range from an exceptionally well-run **KOA** off I-84 on the eastern edge of Boise (7300 Federal Way, Boise, ID 83706; ☎ 208-345-7673), to three state parks offering facilities for everything from tents to fancy self-contained buses, to US Forest Service and wilderness campgrounds.

State Parks

Ponderosa State Park is a good centralized choice if you wish to explore the trails and other attractions in the McCall-New Meadows area. The campground is open from spring through early fall. The 170 campsites include tent sites and RV sites with water and electrical hookups. Most campsites are fairly privately situated under a canopy of tall ponderosa pines. A few overlook Payette Lake. PO Box A, McCall, ID 83638. ☎ 208-634-2164.

Winchester Lake State Park is a pleasant Camas Prairie camping choice. Open year-round, the park has 75 wooded campsites, many in sight of the lake, some with water and electrical hookups. PO Box 186, Winchester, ID 83555. ☎ 208-924-7563.

Hells Gate State Park, two miles upriver from Lewiston, is an ideal base camp if you're jetboating the Snake and/or wildlife watching in the Craig Mountain Wildlife Area. Riverside campsites enjoy a lawnlike setting. Most campsites have water and electrical hookups. 3620A Snake River Ave., Lewiston, ID 83501. ☎ 208-799-5015.

Riggins (all have RV hookups)

Riverfront Gardens RV Park at Lucile, on the Salmon River 15 miles north of Riggins, is picturesque. HCO 1, Box 15, Lucile, ID 83542. ☎ 208-628-3777.

Riverside RV Park is in South Riggins on the Little Salmon River. Box 1270, Riggins, ID 83549. ☎ 208-628-3390.

River Village RV Park, 1434 N. Hwy 95, Riggins, ID 83549. ☎ 208-628-3746.

West-Central Idaho

Sleepy Hollow RV Park is also on the Little Salmon River. Box 1159, Riggins, ID 83549. ☎ 208-628-3402.

Forest & Wilderness Camping

The **Payette National Forest** maintains numerous campgrounds for self-contained RVs and campers. Some are adjacent to natural hot springs or beside mountain lakes or streams. Check with the district office in McCall for campgrounds in specific areas (☎ 208-634-0700). Not all have drinking water.

The **Seven Devils Wilderness Area** maintains several campgrounds for backpackers and horse-supported trekkers. Snake River/Hells Canyon campgrounds are at Upper and Lower Pittsburg Landing. Check with the HCRA office in Riggins for details (☎ 208-628-3916). Few backcountry campgrounds have potable water. Be sure to inquire about water availability before setting out.

The Panhandle - Moscow to the Canadian Border

Suddenly on US 95 north of Riggins a sign appears: "Entering the Pacific Time Zone." But wait a minute! Isn't this the Rockies, as in Rocky Mountain Time? Not really. Welcome to the Pacific Northwest.

I-90 swaggers across the Idaho Panhandle, entering Idaho just east of Spokane, Washington and exiting near Montana's Lookout Pass. Because of the Panhandle's historic kinship with Washington State, cynics refer to Spokane as Idaho's other capital. In many respects, the Panhandle is a separate entity. Residents harbor a strong sense of identity, preferring the designation "North Idaho" to "Panhandle." Separation from the rest of Idaho or annexation by Washington is bandied about from time to time, though everyone knows that nothing will ever come of it. This sense of separation can largely be attributed to the region's limited north-south access, US 95 being the Panhandle's sole link with the lower half of the state.

Exactly where the Panhandle leaves off and the rest of Idaho begins is up for grabs. Some put the southerly line at the I-90 Corridor, some at the Pacific Time Zone sign on US 95. This Adventure Guide draws an arbitrary line along US 12, the Wild and Scenic Lochsa River Corridor that begins at Lolo Pass, on the Montana-Idaho border. The route parallels the Lolo Indian Trail followed by Lewis & Clark on their 1805 trek to discover the mouth of the Columbia River.

This part of the Panhandle includes a fabulous hunk of wilderness overseen by the Clearwater and St. Joe National Forests. The Lochsa River falls partially within this area. The wild Moyie River cuts a swath in the Panhandle's northeast corner. In between are winding rivers and streams a'plenty, three handsome natural lakes (Coeur d'Alene, Pend Oreille and Priest), mountains both rugged and gentle, quirky historic mining towns, wooded hiking trails, and gently meandering rivers that invite leisurely canoeing.

The Panhandle is a place of contrasts. You can muck for gem-quality garnets or pan for gold by day and dine in lakeside splendor by night. You can visit a theme park celebrating the early days of aviation and chat with crusty characters in a for-real 19th-century ghost town, all in the same day. Wallow in pampered luxury at a state-of-the-art guest

The Panhandle

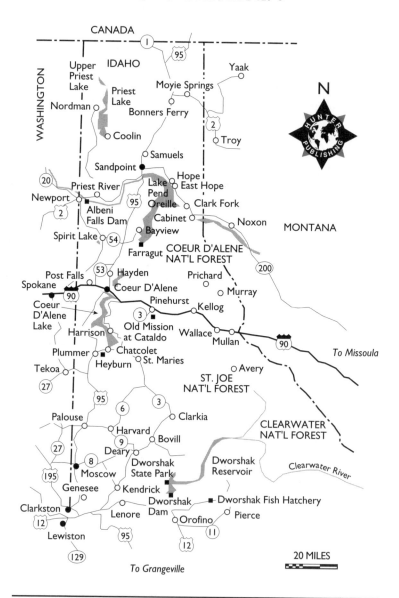

CANADA

WASHINGTON

IDAHO

Upper Priest Lake

Priest Lake

Nordman

Coolin

Yaak

Moyie Springs

Bonners Ferry

Troy

Samuels

Sandpoint

Priest River

Newport

Albeni Falls Dam

Spirit Lake

Hope
East Hope

Lake Pend Oreille

Clark Fork

Cabinet

Noxon

MONTANA

Bayview

Farragut

COEUR D'ALENE NAT'L FOREST

Post Falls

Spokane

Coeur D'Alene Lake

Harrison

Plummer

Tekoa

Hayden

Coeur D'Alene

Pinehurst

Old Mission at Cataldo

Chatcolet

Heyburn

St. Maries

Prichard

Murray

Kellog

Wallace

Mullan

To Missoula

Avery

ST. JOE NAT'L FOREST

CLEARWATER NAT'L FOREST

Palouse

Harvard

Deary

Moscow

Genesee

Clarkston

Lewiston

Clarkia

Bovill

Dworshak State Park

Kendrick

Lenore

Dworshak Dam

Dworshak Reservoir

Clearwater River

Dworshak Fish Hatchery

Pierce

Orofino

To Grangeville

20 MILES

ranch or lakeside resort, or backpack to a wilderness stream and camp beside a waterfall. You can thrill to a whitewater high, or relax on a lake excursion boat. You can vicariously experience historic events as varied as the heroic blazing of the Mullan Road, the Sunshine Silver Mine disaster, an early Catholic mission to the Indians, or a vanished World War II naval base.

Mining and logging have been the Panhandle's traditional meal tickets for well over a century. They still are for some, but tourism is providing ever more bounteous feasts.

This northerly region offers several unique touring opportunities, the one constant being the fabulous photo ops presenting themselves almost any direction you point your camera.

The macho mining and logging heritage that shaped the Panhandle may occasionally be overshadowed by summer playground hype, but reminders continue to haunt the area. Consider setting aside extra time to do the sights if you plan a stay at a guest ranch, a fishing, horseback or backpacking trip or other specific adventure. Many points of interest are convenient to the I-90 Corridor. Wherever you go, whatever you do, be sure to bring your camera.

Tourism is at work in much of the Panhandle, especially in and around the summer resort/lakeside towns of Coeur d'Alene and Sandpoint. Priest Lake folks are rapidly catching on to their own lucrative "gold mine" – outdoor adventures such as fishing, boating and Nordic skiing.

This mini-boom has produced a plethora of uncommonly pleasant bed and breakfasts. The B&B phenomenon has a parallel in the morel mushrooms growing in the humous-rich forests surrounding Priest Lake. Given optimum conditions, mushrooms will sprout. Given an influx of visitors, B&Bs will sprout. Gourmet dining, antique shops and other amenities pop up as well.

The Panhandle is an anything-goes kind of place. Expect to brush up against an eclectic mix of folk: summer vacationers, polo-shirted conventioneers, old folks fishin', backpacking baby boomers, pony-tailed ex-hippies, holidaying families, Coeur d'Alene Indians, savvy wilderness guides, even camouflage-suited survivalists. In decrepit mining and logging towns, you'll come across bearded yarn-spinning characters exuding a crusty individualism evocative of hardened prospectors and loggers, many of them Finns straight from the Old Country.

In recent years, the Panhandle has seen a sizeable influx of Californians and other outlanders, most of whom are proving to be good neighbors. But North Idaho's

remotenesshasalsoattractedquirkywhitesupremacist,
survivalist and other anti-government, anti-you-name-it
types. The Sandpoint and Hayden Lake areas have received
considerable notoriety due to the Randy Weaver standoff,
high profile resident Mike Fuhrman, Aryan Nation and
Christian Identity groups. You may never see any of these
types; and you may not recognize them as such if you do.
A tip: mind your manners if you should happen on closed
gates or "keep out" signs while exploring backroads. These
folks don't just fool around.

Geography & History

The Idaho Panhandle is a four-seasons place: snow-packed in winter, a gentle green in spring, pleasantly cool in summer, radiant with golden aspen and larch in autumn. Because of the heavy stands of fir, spruce, hemlock, larch, cedar, yew and pine, this north country paradise more closely resembles northern Washington than the rest of Idaho.

The Coeur d'Alene, the Selkirk and Montana's Cabinet mountains loom on the skyline. A hefty portion of the Panhandle from Coeur d'Alene north to the Canadian border – taking in Lake Pend Orielle on the east, extending to Priest Lake on the northwest and bumping up against Washington State – enjoys an altitude of some 2,700 feet and lies as level as a frying pan on a campfire trivet. An ancient trench between faults running along its eastern and western edges is responsible for this felicitous geographical quirk. The Panhandle's trio of big natural lakes are remnants of one large lake that covered the area some 30 million years ago.

From the air, the region resembles a child's play cloth dotted with deep blue lakes, crossed by winding rivers, and smudged with thick green forests.

The Panhandle's ore-bearing mountains, less forbidding than the Sawtooths to the south, are cut by deep canyons. The most famous of these is the Silver Valley, through which I-90 slices. These horrendous scars were made when the forests were felled to fuel-belching smelters and for timbers to shore up the labyrinthine silver mines, which in turn produced mountains of slag. The smelters' noxious lead-laden emisions killed any remaining vegetation and poisoned children in the valley's mining communities. Now that the silver boom is history, efforts are afoot to help nature reclaim the valley. The children's impaired mental abilities and stunted lives cannot be reclaimed.

The St. Joe and Clearwater National Forests extend south of I-90 to the Lolo Trail. These big, wild, beautiful lands are bordered by the Bitterroot Mountains on the east and punctuated by peaks rising some 3,000 feet above the floors of canyons. Through those canyons flow the North Fork of the Clearwater and the Lochsa Rivers.

It's easy to visualize the awe with which early 19th-century trappers, men who blazed trails for the loggers, miners and US Forest Service rangers who came later, regarded this land. Beaver, bear, deer, elk, moose, and game birds were abundant. These animals still inspire awe, even by 20th-century standards wherein just a few sightings arouse excitement and pleasure. Animals

Cataldo Mission Church has stood proudly on a rise above the Coeur d'Alene River since the 1840s.

and birds, once trapped and hunted to near-extinction, are on the come-back trail.

American and Canadian trappers followed Lewis & Clark into this wild country, taking enormous quantities of pelts to fuel Europeans' lust for furs. In the 1840s, the legendary Fr. Pierre de Smet established a mission to the Coeur d'Alene Indians. Their descendants are devout Catholics who commemorate the founding of the Cataldo Mission with an annual celebration held on its lovely grounds. It is Idaho's oldest standing structure.

One of the lasting sagas impacting North Idaho is the blazing and construction of the Mullan Road. In 1853 Lt. John Mullan, a US Army topographical engineer, was directed to survey and build a wagon road linking Fort Benton, Montana, at the end of Missouri River steamboat navigation, with Fort Walla Walla, Washington. The road was also expected to establish a right-of-way for the proposed transcontinental railroad. A rough road was completed after nine years – years interrupted by Indian wars and punctuated by incredible hardships. Ironically, only a few immigrant wagons and packers used the road before it was allowed to revert to nature. But the right of way for the Northern Pacific Railway's northern route had been blazed. By 1882, trains were chuffing over Mullan's route – the route followed today by I-90.

The Panhandle

The Bunker Hill Lode

With the railroad came timber barons and loggers fresh from the depleted forests of the East and Midwest. Prospectors came in the 1870s and 1880s. Around 1884, Idaho's silver mining industry received a jump-start that energized the entire Panhandle. Legend has it that a down-and-out prospector named Noah Kellogg was startled to note that his jackass was standing smack dab on an outcropping of rich silver ore. Believe the jackass story or not as you wish, but Kellogg's strike proved to be the fabled Bunker Hill lode. The Sunshine Mine, estimated to be the world's largest silver producer, thrived throughout the first half of the 20th century. Unionization, strikes leading to bloody riots, mine disasters, devastating floods and fires kept Silver Valley folk on edge.

Thanks to the railroad and fancy steamboats, summer trippers were enjoying the irresistible attractions of these north country lakes. From the 1890s through the first two decades of this century, hordes of visitors detrained at Coeur d'Alene to board steamboats promising luxurious lake excursions. Soon sated with such tame diversions, visitors hankered to experience the other adventures offered by this vast and beautiful north country – to hike the trails blazed by the Lewis & Clark Expedition and Lt. John Mullan, to fish the deep forest-fringed lakes. At about the same time, the fledgling US Forest Service began to establish ranger stations in the remote backcountry. While most of these are history, some have been preserved for posterity.

North Idahoans celebrate a legacy handed down by ancestors who came to this enchantingly beautiful place to log, to mine, to seek adventure. Some are still employed in the significantly reduced mining and logging industries. Others work as outfitters, guides and rangers eager to share their backcountry knowledge with visitors like you. Others shape Panhandle tourism in response to the appeal that this place has for casual vacationers. North Idaho's special brand of adventure wears many guises.

Given the national exposure that the Panhandle, especially the Coeur d'Alene area, has enjoyed over the past few years, you might expect to find overcrowding and other less-than-pleasant aspects of tourism overshadowing simple outdoor pleasures. In some places, such as growing Coeur d'Alene and Sandpoint, that may be so. In others, such as the shores of pristine Priest Lake and the wild inner reaches of the Clearwater and Idaho Panhandle National Forests, that is emphatically not so.

Getting Around

Spokane, served by several major airlines and straddling east-west I-90, is most visitors' port of entry to North Idaho. If you wish to explore the Panhandle from south to north, you can fly into Lewiston via Horizon (☎ 800-547-9308) or Skywest Airlines (☎ 800-453-9417), renting a car from Hertz or Budget.

If you are driving, you will doubtless take US 95 north from Boise, I-90 from Spokane, or I-90 or US 12 from Missoula, Montana. If coming in from Canada, you'll enter from Kingsgate, British Columbia. By any route, you're in for a treat.

Driving the Panhandle is generally easy going. Exceptions: some Clearwater National Forest roads through rugged territory south and east of the ancient lake bed. To the east, mountains and deep canyons score the land. Twisting, precipitous roads characterize the terrain along the east side of Lake Coeur d'Alene and on the rolling Palouse. Numerous Idaho Panhandle/Kaniksu National Forest roads meander through the Selkirk Range between US 95 and Priest Lake.

It is strongly recommended that prior to setting out you obtain Idaho Panhandle National Forests travel maps from any Panhandle National Forests district office. Forest Service roads are too numerous to mention individually in this book. Exceptions are fairly high profile roads through areas of particular historical or natural interest.

The Clearwater and Panhandle National Forests maintain a sizeable network of unimproved Forest Service roads leading to a multitude of interesting natural and historical sites. But the roads hide pitfalls for the unwary. Much of this terrain is logging country. You must be prepared to share the roads with logging trucks whose drivers are NOT vacationers seeking a recreational experience. They have deadlines to meet. They're in a hurry. You aren't. They're bigger than you are – much bigger.

Most Forest Service roads are gravel- or dirt-surfaced. Rain can make them slippery and/or cause ruts in the roadway. Some roads are washboarded. Beware of black ice in cold weather. This phenomenon lies in wait for the unwary throughout the Northwest. You can't see it. Just assume it's there if the weather dips to freezing or below. Black ice has upset (literally) many a traveler, not excluding the author of this book.

The Panhandle

Some Forest Service Road Caveats

- Don't let your guard down, ever.

- Drive with your headlights on.

- Slow down. Just because speed limits aren't posted doesn't mean this is the Autobahn. You must be able to stop in half the sight distance; blind corners are as numerous as bunnies in spring.

- Dust ahead indicates traffic ahead.

- Yield the right of way to downhill traffic.

- Pull well off the road if you stop to pick berries or to snap a photo of that mommy and baby deer.

- Don't leave a parked vehicle in front of a closed gate.

- Swerving for animals can be dangerous.

- Use lower gears on downhill slopes; riding the brake can result in no brakes.

- Stay to the right and drive every corner as though you expect to meet another vehicle; chances are you will.

- Pull over in a safe spot to allow faster vehicles (log trucks) to pass.

- Make sure your vehicle is in good working order. Know how it handles in tight situations.

- Carry extra fuel (they don't build truck stops in the wilderness), a spare tire, jack, chains, tools, a fire extinguisher and flashlight.

- Bring enough food and water to last at least two days longer than you plan on being out. Take warm clothing and blankets or sleeping bags. Bring along a cellular phone, but don't expect it to work in deep mountain draws.

Principle highways are well constructed and maintained. Secondary roads are often narrow, always scenic. I wonder if area residents ever lose their sense of awe toward this splendid panorama of sparkling lakes, frolicking rivers, conifer-framed farmland, pine-clad hills, and imposing mountain gorges.

From the south, heavily traveled US 95 climbs onto the rolling Palouse Prairie, looking in on Moscow and continuing on through the Coeur d'Alene Reservation to Plummer. The US 95 route between here and Coeur d'Alene being unremarkable, I prefer to hang a right at Plummer onto Idaho 5 and head for the old Coeur d'Alene Indian town of St. Maries. From here, Idaho 97, the twisty Lake Coeur d'Alene Scenic Byway, follows the lakeshore to meet I-90 10 miles east of Coeur d'Alene. From Coeur d'Alene, US 95 straight-arrows north to Sandpoint at the head of Lake Pend Orielle. It then passes through pleasing farmland to Bonners Ferry and thence to the Canadian border.

All sorts of delightful side trips branch from the US 95 corridor. Some, like the Wild and Scenic Lochsa River Corridor (US 12), may require a couple of days to explore. Others, like the White Pine Scenic Highway (Idaho 3), may consume a pleasant couple of hours.

You can bound across the Palouse on roller coaster roads, follow unimproved roads in the Clearwater National Forest, discover garnets in the St. Joe National Forest. Set aside plenty of time to explore the historic towns and milestones along I-90, saving at least two days for history-rich **Wallace**.

North of I-90, Idaho 54 side-trips off US 95 to **Farragut State Park**, site of a World War II naval base, and to funky **Bayview**, site of a present-day US Navy submarine facility that makes use of deep (1,225 feet at one spot) Lake Pend Orielle.

Set aside at least four days to side-trip west of Sandpoint along the scenic Priest River (US 2) to the **Albeni Falls Dam**, from where you can head north on Idaho 57 to unspoiled Priest Lake.

Paved, gravel and unimproved Forest Service roads penetrate the **St. Joe and Clearwater National Forests**, occupying a chunk of mountains and valleys between US 12 on the south, the Palouse and timbered forests on the west, I-90 on the north and Montana on the east. Many of these roads, some following time-worn trails, lead to historic ranger stations and riveting reminders of old-time prospectors' insatiable quest for gold. Others access deep **Dworshak Reservoir**, thrusting into the backcountry like a crooked saber. Good gravel roads access the Emerald Creek Garnet Area in the St. Joe National Forest, a don't-miss-it opportunity to muck in gooey, goopy mud and emerge with real garnets.

Roads in various states of improvement coil into the **Coeur d'Alene National Forest** north of I-90, looking in on the storied last-holdout mining towns of **Prichard** and **Murray**.

Most of North Idaho's unimproved roads are suitable for passenger cars, though a 4WD/high-clearance vehicle is best for Forest Service roads. Springtime mud and heavy summer and fall rains can bog down the sturdiest car or van. Check road conditions with the local ranger station before setting out.

The Panhandle

Panhandle roads lead to no end of adventures and serendipitous discoveries, so it's a good idea to set aside more time than you think you'll need. Granted, some touristy stuff begs to be ignored. But the region's historic sites and museums highlight riveting, even epochal, pages out of the saga of the West.

Enjoyable hikes, some to historic ranger cabins, are usually fairly close by. The area's three big natural lakes are accessible via good roads looking in at various lakeside locations. Only Priest Lake is fully encircled by roads. This interesting fact highlights the Panhandle's surprising ability to offer adventure opportunities and traditional tourist activities almost side-by-side.

Some lesser lakes and streams can be accessed by road, some not. The fishing is legendary almost anywhere you choose to cast a line or a fly. Chumming up to the natives may produce insider tips on secret lakes and fishing holes. But don't be surprised if your inquiries are deftly deflected.

Except during spring freshets, most Panhandle rivers offer canoeing and leisurely fishing. All have at least some road access.

Information Sources

Idaho Winter Road Report: ☎ 208-336-6600.

Highway Accident/Emergencies: ☎ 800-632-8000.

Bureau of Land Management, Idaho State Office, 1387 S. Vinnell Way, Boise, ID 83709. ☎ 208-384-3300.

Bureau of Land Management, Coeur d'Alene District, 1808 N. Third St., Coeur d'Alene, ID 83814. ☎ 208-769-5000.

Idaho Dept. of Fish & Game, 600 S. Walnut, Boise, ID 83707. ☎ 208-334-3700. Fax 208-334-2114. E-mail: idfginfo@state.id.us.

Idaho Department of Parks and Recreation, Box 83720, Boise, ID 83720-0065. ☎ 208-334-4199. Fax 208-334-3741.

Idaho Outfitters and Guides Assn., Box 95, Boise, ID 83701. ☎ 208-342-1438. Fax 208-338-7830. E-mail: outfitt@aol.com.

Idaho Guest & Dude Ranch Assn., c/o John Muir, 7600 E. Blue Lake Road, Harrison, ID 83833. ☎ 208-689-3295. Fax 208-689-9115.

≈

Clearwater National Forest, 12730 Highway 12, Orofino, ID 83544. ☎ 208-476-4541. Fax 208-476-8329.

Forest Supervisor, Panhandle National Forests, 1201 Ironwood Drive, Coeur d'Alene, ID 83814. ☎ 208-765-7223.

Panhandle National Forests (Kaniksu, Coeur d'Alene, St. Joe), 3815 Schreiber Way, Coeur d'Alene, ID 83814. ☎ 208-765-7457. Fax 208-765-7307.

Panhandle National Forests, Wallace Ranger District. PO Box 14, Silverton, ID 83867. ☎ 208-752-1221.

Panhandle National Forests, Avery Ranger District, HC Box 1, Avery, ID 83802. ☎ 208-245-4517.

Panhandle National Forests, Fernan Ranger District, 2502 E. Sherman Ave., Coeur d'Alene, ID 83814. ☎ 208-765-7381.

Panhandle National Forests, St. Maries Ranger District, PO Box 407, St. Maries, ID 83861. ☎ 208-245-2531.

Panhandle National Forests, Sandpoint Ranger District, 1500 Highway 2, Sandpoint, ID 83864. ☎ 208-263-5111.

Panhandle National Forests, Bonners Ferry Ranger District, Route 4, Box 4860, Bonners Ferry, ID 83805. ☎ 208-267-5561.

Panhandle National Forests, Priest Lake Ranger District, HCR 5, Box 207, Priest River, ID 83856. ☎ 208-443-2512.

❧

Idaho Travel Council, ☎ Idaho Dept. of Commerce, 700 West State St., Boise, ID 83720-0093. ☎ 800-635-7820 or 208-334-2470. Fax 208-334-2631. Web site: www.visitid.org.

Coeur d'Alene Convention & Visitors Bureau, Box 1088 (202 Sherman Ave.), Coeur d'Alene, ID 83814. ☎ 208-664-3194. Fax 208-667-9338. E-mail: cdacc@coeurdalene.org.

Greater Kellogg Area Chamber, 608 Bunker Ave., Kellogg, ID 83837. ☎ 208-784-0821. Fax 208-783-4343. E-mail: kellogg@rand.nidlink.com.

Kootenai County Convention & Visitors Bureau, Box 908 (510 E. 6th Ave.), Post Falls, ID 83854. ☎ 208-773-4080. Fax 208-773-3843.

North Idaho Travel Assn., c/o Greater Sandpoint Chamber of Commerce, Box 928 (US 95 N.), Sandpoint, ID 83864. ☎ 208-263-2161 or 800-800-2106. Fax 208-265-5289. E-mail: chamber@netw.com.

Wallace Visitor Information Center, Box 1167 (#10 River St., Exit 61), Wallace, ID 83873. ☎ 208-753-7151. Fax 208-753-5072. E-mail: rand.nidlink.com.

❧

Dworshak State Park, PO Box 2028, Orofino, ID 83544. ☎ 208-476-5994.

Heyburn State Park, Rt. 1, Box 139, Plummer, ID 83851. ☎ 208-686-1308.

Farragut State Park, E. 13400 Ranger Road, Athol, ID 883801. ☎ 208-683-2425.

Round Lake State Park, PO Box 170, Slagle, ID 83860. ☎ 208-263-3489.

Priest Lake State Park, Indian Creek Bay #423, Coolin, ID 83821. ☎ 208-443-2200.

Touring

The Wild & Scenic Lochsa River Corridor

The Lochsa River Corridor (US 12) consists of 101 miles of eye-feasting splendor and fascinating history. The Lolo Pass Visitor Center anchors the Corridor on the Montana-Idaho line. The western anchor is Kooskia, where the Middle Fork of the Clearwater branches off from the Main Clearwater. The Corridor is innocent of towns, unless you count **Lowell**, population 30 (more or less). Don't allow size to fool you. Where else but in rural Idaho will you find lodging, a commercial campground, gasoline, groceries and other supplies in a community whose residents number fewer than the average family reunion?

From 5,233-foot Lolo Pass to Lowell, the highway follows the Lochsa through a deep cut flanked by steep canyon walls, impressive rock outcroppings and thick forests. From Lowell to Kooskia, the highway follows the Middle Fork of the Clearwater through a gentle valley dotted with bucolic homesteads. At Lowell, the Selway becomes the Middle Fork of the Clearwater.

You can drive the distance in less than two hours, but you'll need at least a full day to do justice to the landmarks along the way. That's not counting side trips on Forest Service roads branching off US 12. You can easily spend several days exploring this country blazed by the likes of Lewis & Clark, the Nez Perce and other tribes, gold prospectors and Depression-era Civilian Conservation Corps (CCC) workers.

The **Lolo Pass Visitor Center**, describing Lewis & Clark's 1805 trek across the Bitterroots and highlighting the area's natural history, serves as an apt introduction to your exploratory journey. Request a copy of *Lewis & Clark Across the Lolo Trail*, a descriptive brochure highlighting the expedition's campsites and other milestones.

You can drive 1½ miles down a logging road east of the visitor center to a campground used by the explorers before they continued west, keeping more or less to the old Indian Lolo Trail. The trail follows mountainous terrain paralleling US 12 and crosses Idaho 11 on the Weippe Prairie before following the Clearwater into Washington. Nine miles west of Lolo Pass, you'll find a fine Western red cedar grove dedicated to the memory of Pulitzer Prize-winning author and conservationist Bernard DeVoto.

The historic **Powell Ranger Station** and yet another Lewis & Clark campsite are a few miles farther on, just south of Powell Junction. Watch for the Lochsa Historical Ranger Station sign. The log building is a

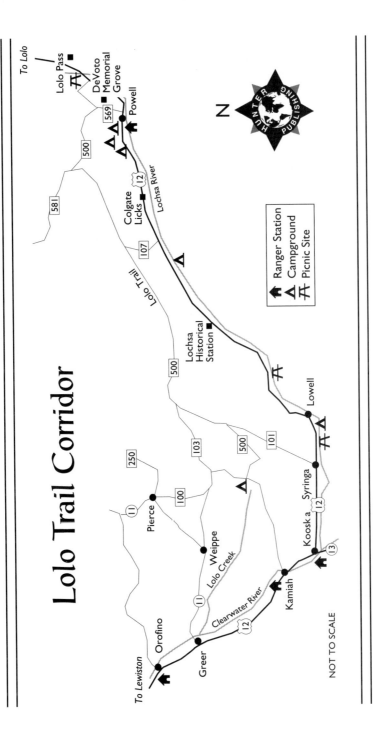

Lolo Trail Corridor

To Lolo

Lolo Pass

DeVoto
Memorial
Grove

569
Powell

500

581

Colgate
Licks

12

Lochsa River

107

Lolo Trail

Lochsa
Historical
Station

500

Lowell

Ranger Station
Campground
Picnic Site

N

HUNTER PUBLISHING

101

500

103

Syringa

Kooska

12

250

Pierce

100

Weippe

Lolo Creek

Clearwater River

13

Kamiah

11

Orofino

Greer

12

To Lewiston

NOT TO SCALE

survivor of many built by the Civilian Conservation Corps in an era when Easterners held Western forests in awe, equating them with heroic legends on the cusp of the civilized world. If you had only a hazy idea of the Forest Service's impact on the West, and of the conservation work undertaken by rangers, the Station's museum will bring it into focus.

At Lowell, Forest Service (FS) Road 223 follows the Wild and Scenic Selway River for 19 miles to the Selway Falls Ranger Station before picking up FS Road 290 to Indian Hill Lookout. The drive along the quiet river (Sel-weh means "smooth water") takes you through fern-edged meadows rich with reminders of a time when Forest Service rangers and CCC workers "roughed it" in a wilderness many miles from civilization. (US 12 wasn't built until 1962).

A few miles west of Lowell, at the one-horse community of Syringa, grandly named for Idaho's official state flower, FS Road 101 heads north and links up with several other roads to make up the **Lolo Trail Corridor**. The Corridor can also be accessed from US 12 via FS Road 569 between DeVoto Memorial Grove and Powell, FS Road 107 halfway between Syringa and Kooskia, FS Road 100 at Kooskia, and Idaho 11 at Kamiah and Orofino. Take at least a day, preferably more, to travel this fabulous place of lofty ridge tops and saddles interspersed with weird rock outcroppings and embellished with huckleberry shrubs. Embellished, too, with history. The tracks of ancient Indians, of the Lewis & Clark expedition, of trappers beyond recall, show themselves sometimes in reality, always in imagination.

The Lolo Trail also comprises the North Idaho portion of the **Nez Perce (Nee-Mee-Poo) National Historic Trail**. Nee-Mee-Poo, meaning the people, is the real name of the Nez Perce. It is thought that the name Nez Perce was bestowed on these people by 18th-century French trappers because some males practiced nose piercing. In 1877, Chief Joseph followed the Lolo Trail when he sought to lead a band of followers to Canada in hopes of avoiding confinement on a small reservation. The trail is part of the National Historic Trails System.

The Lolo Trail Corridor's winding, often steep, dirt roads cover about 100 miles between self-descriptive Parachute Hill on the east to Weippe on the west. High-clearance vehicles are recommended. Don't even think about towing a trailer or driving an RV here. Usually free of snow by early July, the road is accessible into October. Barring an early snowstorm, that is. Be sure to bring water and emergency supplies for both yourself and your vehicle. Check road conditions with

the Clearwater National Forest Headquarters in Orofino before setting out.

This advice holds true if you continue exploring the Clearwater National Forest via the North Fork/Superior Adventure Drive (FS Roads 247/250), beginning on Idaho 11 at the top of a loop looking in on Greer and Orofino.

Chief Joseph

Chief Joseph began the epic trek at Wallowa Lake, Washington, his ancestral homeland. His band crossed the Snake, fought the US Cavalry at White Bird, skirted the Camas Prairie to the Clearwater, and continued across Idaho into Montana. They dipped back into Idaho at 6,985-foot Nez Perce Pass before loosely following the Continental Divide to Camas Meadows west of Yellowstone National Park. Crossing Yellowstone, they struck north into Montana along Clark's Fork, hightailing it for the Canadian border. In the course of their flight, the band of some 250 warriors and 500 women, children and old people fought 2,000 Cavalry men and numerous civilian volunteers in some 20 battles and skirmishes. The exhausted band surrendered after being trapped in the Bear Paw Mountains, just 30 miles short of the Canadian border. Ironically, the Nez Perce were innocent of the depredations that whites associated with Indians. The battle was about land. Chief Joseph and his followers had refused to sign treaties relinquishing their ancestral lands.

The Greer portion of the loop sashays into **Pierce** before joining FS Road 247. Today, Pierce is small pickings. In 1860, Pierce catapulted Idaho to fame and, eventually, territorial status. After a down-and-out Irishman named Elias Pierce struck pay dirt, the town that bears his name waxed wild and raucous. Prospectors are always down and out until they strike gold. The resulting gold rush led to Lewiston's founding and attracted a string of grizzled prospectors and greedy hangers-on longer than a miners' yarn. Inevitably, the strike played out and Pierce followed other North Idaho towns into the timber trade.

Pierce's **J. Howard Bradbury Logging Memorial Museum** at 101 S. Main is situated in a 1928-vintage log cabin. Exhibits include logging and mining memorabilia. Open May 15-Oct 15, Thurs-Sun, 12-4. ☎ 208-435-4670.

The Adventure Drive, culminating at I-90 at Superior, Montana, was completed in 1935 by CCC workers over a route blazed by Native Americans centuries before. Except for Idaho 11 and a 14-mile paved stretch of FS Road 250, the 100-mile route is gravel-surfaced. You can drive your RV or tow your trailer with some confidence, but be sure to avoid the Black Canyon section (low water crossings and occasional rock slides) by detouring onto the FS Road 255 loop at Kelly Forks Work Center.

The Adventure Drive serves to remind you that this was, still is, logging country. Be alert. Speeding logging trucks can paralyze you with fright should you come snout to snout with one on a hairpin turn.

Off FS Road 247, 8.6 miles north of an old Potlatch company town that is aptly, if not imaginatively, named Headquarters, a dirt road leads to 5,520-foot **Bertha Hill**. On this spot, the nation's first forest fire lookout tower was constructed in 1902. The goal: to get a jump on fires threatening the huge fortune in marketable timber stretching for miles in every direction. A sensible precaution, though the Great Fire of 1910 would prove that, once a fire took off in resinous dry timber, there was no stopping it with the primitive fire fighting resources of that period. Even smoke-jumpers and other modern fire fighting technology have been overwhelmed by the fires that have blackened Western forests in recent years.

Watch for wooden flumes along Beaver Creek, remnants of storied log drives down the North Fork of the Clearwater. Farther on, FS Road 250 serves as the gateway to the Mallard Lakes Pioneer Area's granite crags and peaks, home to one of Idaho's largest populations of mountain goats. Look up. Chances are, one or more goats will be looking down at you in a wildlife watching parody.

Both the Lolo Trail Corridor and the North Fork Adventure Road offer seemingly endless opportunities to hike and explore, to fish in gem-like mountain lakes and streams. You'll find primitive campsites along both roads. Maps and brochures can be obtained at the Clearwater National Forest Headquarters in Orofino.

At Kooskia, US 12 heads north and west along the Clearwater River. (See *Touring* in *Region 1* for a description of this lap into Lewiston.)

Dworshak Reservoir

In 1971, the North Fork of the Clearwater's storied log drives faded into history. Construction had begun on the massive Dworshak Dam, and the resulting 53-mile-long Dworshak Reservoir. Today, log booms are towed the length of the reservoir to log-handling sites, where they are loaded onto trucks for transport to Lewiston.

Refer to *Touring* in *Region 1* for descriptions of the dam's visitor center and the Dworshak Fish Hatchery (see page 53).

Idaho 7 makes a steep climb onto the Palouse from the visitor center, affording breath-catching views of Orofino and the Clearwater far below. After 11 miles, a gravel side road makes an abrupt right to Dworshak State Park. Watch for signs. This and other roads accessing the reservoir have incredibly steep inclines down to the shoreline. Some are paved on the lower slopes.

The sprawling reservoir is also accessed by the unimproved Wells Bench Road from Orofino. This road crosses the reservoir before heading for the old sawmill town of Elk River, where it meets Idaho 8. **Elk River Falls**, a mile west of town, is a splendid sight. From Headquarters, the Silver Creek and Musselman Roads loop along the shoreline via Idaho 11, accessing Grandad Bridge and another road to Elk River.

Beyond Grandad Bridge, another road takes an easterly course, meandering over hilly terrain to Clarkia after skirting the reservoir and crossing the deliciously named Breakfast Creek Bridge.

All these confusing directions serve to illustrate the fact that you can reach Dworshak Reservoir by road, but it's no Sunday drive. Pick up a map at the visitor center. On the bright side, these dirt and gravel roads traverse gorgeous mountain and valley terrain through thick fir forests. This backcountry "behind" Moscow and the Palouse Hills offers days of adventuring well off the beaten track.

Moscow & the Palouse

US 95 makes a steep climb just north of the point where the Clearwater River flows west to Lewiston, coming out on the Palouse Hills, commonly but inaccurately referred to as the Palouse Prairie.

National Geographic magazine, and others who like to make such judgements, rate the Palouse among the world's most photogenic places. That may be so, especially when the luminescence that often precedes dusk splashes these undulating hills with striking contrasts in light and shade.

These asymmetrical roller coaster hills, varying from 20 to 80 feet in height, are actually loess dunes shaped by wind, rain and snow. Sunshine and the shadows cast by billowy clouds riding high in a hard blue sky wash these hills with constantly changing movement. The

The Panhandle

springtime green and summertime gold of wheat and legume fields skim over the hills in a dance more graceful than any ballet.

I find it amazing that Palouse farmers manage to till, plant and harvest these hillside fields while keeping their tractors and harvesters from tumbling sideways or backwards end over end down the hills. These skillful farmers produce some of the world's top quality winter wheat and the nation's highest yield of dried peas and lentils.

A network of secondary roads meanders over the Palouse, connecting scattered farmsteads and giving drivers roller coaster thrills. I defy you to drive these roads without losing all sense of direction.

A righthand turn eight miles north of the junction of US 12 and US 95 will get you a look at **Genesee**, a once bustling commercial and rail center named for Upper New York State's Genesee Valley. Though shrunk to half its salad-day size, Genesee remains a charming agricultural town boasting picturesque Victorian homes and elaborate galvanized iron facades fit to turn big city historic districts green with envy.

Stop in at the Genesee City Hall to pick up a brochure describing the town's **historic buildings**, most dating from Genesee's prosperous turn-of-the-century era. An antiques shop at 134 West Walnut St., intriguingly named **Maiden America**, offers treasures reflective of small town Idaho. Genesee is a good place to enjoy a hefty Idaho-style burger before setting out over the Palouse or continuing on to sample Moscow's cultural pleasures.

At first glance, **Moscow** may appear as just another largish trackside town whose attractive downtown boasts the usual complement of modest shops. Looks can be deceiving. This city of something under 20,000 residents, reportedly named for a city in Pennsylvania, not Russia, has thrived since the first settlers arrived in 1869. A superb collection of fine old homes reflects the grandeur dear to the hearts of late 19th-century merchants. Moscow owes its continuing prosperity to agriculture, trade and the University of Idaho, a land grant institution enrolling over 10,000 students. The city's tree-lined streets counterbalance the clean-swept Palouse. You must wander off the main drags to pick up on Moscow's college town ambience.

A rich stew of ethnic students, and the city's smorgasbord of musical, theatrical and other cultural offerings, place Moscow in sharp contrast to the macho cowboy culture of surrounding towns. Here, dim sum supercedes burgers and music festivals supercede rodeos.

You can easily spend a couple of rewarding days exploring Moscow's museums, galleries and antiques shops.

Appaloosa Museum and Heritage Center, at the Idaho/Washington line on Idaho 8, traces the history of Idaho's state horse back to Asian and European stock. It explores the Nez Perce and Palouse tribes' connection with these horses bearing spots on their rumps. The museum also has Native American artifacts. Live Appaloosas are on display during summer months. Open year-round, Mon-Fri, 8-5. Summer hours are extended to include Saturdays from 9-3. Donations welcome. ☎ 208-882-5578.

McConnell Mansion, at 110 South Adams St., houses the Latah County Historical Society and changing exhibits. The circa 1886 showplace mansion, once the home of a prominent Moscow merchant, has been restored and is open for tours. Furnishings reflect the 1890-1930 period. Open year-round except holidays, Tues-Sat, 1-4. No admission fee. ☎ 208-882-1004.

University of Idaho **Geology Displays** are in the second and third floor hallways of the Department of Mining Engineering and Metallurgy, on campus. Displays include an intriguing collection of old mining tools and Idaho gemstones. Open Mon-Fri, 8-5 when school is in session, 7:30-4:30 when school is out. Free admission.

University of Idaho **Campus Galleries**, at Ridenbaugh Hall and on the main floor of the Student Union Building, schedules changing exhibitions. ☎ 208-885-6043.

The Prichard Gallery, 414 South Main, is a part of the university's art facilities. Changing exhibits include the works of nationally known artists. Open Mon-Fri, 10-8, Sat, 10-6. ☎ 208-885-3586.

Moscow's art community stages numerous theatrical, dance and musical presentations throughout the year. Contact the Moscow Chamber of Commerce for current schedules.

From Moscow, you can drive a scenic loop to St. Maries and the southern end of Lake Coeur d'Alene. US 95 runs parallel to the Washington/Idaho line, looking in on the small agricultural town of Palouse before entering the Coeur d'Alene Indian Reservation and linking up with Idaho 5 at Plummer. From here, a pleasant wooded drive passes Heyburn State Park and Chacolet Lake en route to St. Maries.

The eastern lap of this loop is more interesting by far, and is recommended if you have a couple of days to spare and are intrigued at the thought of mucking for gem-quality garnets. Take Idaho 8 east from Moscow, passing the charmingly named hamlets of Deary, Helmer and Bovill. Continue north to Clarkia on Idaho 3 at Bovill, a once-rollicking lumber town founded in 1907 by Hugh and Charlotte Bovill, high-born Brits in search of adventure. The couple ranched and ran a hotel here before decamping for Oregon and greener pastures.

The Panhandle

Mucking for Garnets

Mucking for garnets is messy work.

Clarkia, also a former lumber boom town, sits plunk in the center of Miocene Lake Clarkia, a shallow lake formed from volcanic flows some 20 million years ago.

A significant fossil bed was discovered here in the early 1970s. Specimens include leaves that had retained their autumnal colors, metallic-hued beetles, over 100 woody plant varieties, several aquatic species and over 10,000 plant megafossils representing the life cycle of a Miocene lake.

Clarkia is better known to rock hounds as the closest town to the Emerald Creek Garnet District, the only place in the world where the public may dig for star garnets. You wouldn't expect to find such gems concealed in a yucky creek bed, oozing downhill in otherwise nondescript looking terrain. But it's the only place in the world where star garnets of the six-ray variety have been found. Star garnets of the four-ray variety are found both here and in India.

You are almost guaranteed to take away a handful of garnets, some perhaps of gemstone quality. You're less likely to find a valuable star garnet. But who knows? It's possible.

Garnets are minerals formed in metamorphic rocks that, following their original formation, have been altered in texture and/or composition by heat, pressure, and/or chemically active fluids. The result is a roundish pebble with a grainy blackish crust. The distinctive garnet hue is revealed only when the pebble is cut. The star effect is actually a defect in the garnet.

To reach the garnet digs, hang a left on a dirt road 5½ miles north of Clarkia. Watch for signs to the dig. The Emerald Creek Garnet District is supervised by the St. Maries Ranger District of the Panhandle National Forests.

Permits (at this writing, $10 for adults, $5 for kids age 14 and under) are available from the A-frame building at the end of the road. Each permit allows you to take up to five pounds of garnets in a day. A ranger will direct you to the dig du jour.

Fashionable garnet digging apparel includes shorts or rolled-up pants, rubber boots or disposable sneakers, and a washable T-shirt. I say washable, but the yellowish mud may stain. A change of clothing isn't a bad idea. Bring along a shovel, a coffee can-size container to hold your garnets, a pail for the gunk you muck out, and a screen for washing said gunk to separate garnets from dross.

A young mucker displays her prize, a marble-size garnet.

The digs are in mucky creek beds, so the going is yucky from start to finish. But it's great fun. Kids love getting muddy with parental permission. Rock hound adults take garnet digging seriously, coming day-in and day-out to test their luck. And perseverance.

The Garnet Queen

Self-styled Garnet Queen Louise Darby, a licensed gemologist, cuts and sets gem quality garnets. She also leads garnet digging excursions between Memorial Day and Labor Day. Paying someone to show you how to dig in the muck might seem to be money ill spent when a ranger is on hand to direct your shovel. But Louise has an uncanny ability to judge the location of the best and largest stones from the way the land lies under a tree trunk, or in a crook in the creek. And she's a treasure trove of garnet lore. **Louise Darby**, PO Box 9082, Moscow, ID 83843; ☎ 208-882-9496.

St. Maries & the St. Joe National Forest

Idaho 3 continues through Fernwood and Santa, hamlets whose combined populations would hardly make up a cheering section for a Little

The Panhandle

White Pine Scenic Byway

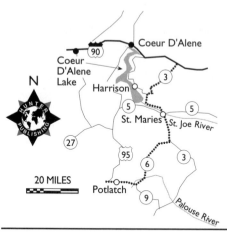

Little League softball game. Here, you pick up the **White Pine Scenic Byway**, which has meandered up Idaho 6 from Palouse through a handful of equally notable hamlets. In the fall of the year, keep an eye open for scattered trees whose yellow needles lend them the appearance of dead conifers. These are deciduous conifers – Western larches, also known as tamaracks.

St. Maries, hugging the St. Joe and St. Maries Rivers, evokes a rustic north country version of Venice. The rivers merge here, draining into Lake Chatcolet, one of a chain of lakes connected to the south end of Lake Coeur d'Alene. A variety of wild rice similar to that found in northern Minnesota is grown commercially in the extensive marshlands dampening the town's toes. The area is a bird watcher's paradise, with osprey nests topping old pilings. Additional nesting boxes have been constructed for the raptors' convenience.

St. Maries' lumbering heyday spanned a half-century. Logs were floated down the rivers and winched into booms which were then floated up the lakes to the Coeur d'Alene railroad terminus. These annual spring log drives must have been some sight. So must have been the accompanying jollity in wide-open saloons and houses of ill repute as loggers celebrated the end of a long winter in the woods.

St. Maries was also a popular steamboat stop. Excursion boats from Coeur d'Alene still cruise up the St. Joe, but turn around before reaching the town.

Paved FS Road 50, the **St. Joe Discovery Road**, heads east along the St. Joe River from St. Maries, looking in on numerous points of natural and historic interest before reaching Avery. Gravel Forest Service roads fork at Avery. The northern route extends to I-90 at Wallace. The other stretch continues along the Wild and Scenic St. Joe to a point where the road takes an easterly course, entering Montana at 7,690-foot **St. Joe Peak** and continuing on to I-90 at St. Regis.

As is the case with all backcountry drives, you must allow plenty of time to enjoy this Discovery Road adventure. You'll no doubt itch to hike some of the numerous trails branching off this road.

This big, beautiful chunk of the **St. Joe National Forest** took the brunt of the fires that devastated North Idaho forests in the summer of 1910. A tinder-dry spring and summer offered ideal burning conditions. By July, 3,000 fires were burning, but were temporarily contained by fire fighters headquartered at the Avery Ranger District. On August 20, strong winds whipped the embers into a voracious fire storm. By the time the conflagrations subsided, 90 people were dead, numerous towns had burned to ashes, and three million acres of forest had been destroyed.

The lessons learned in that disaster prompted the Forest Service to begin an intensive fire fighting program that included the construction of thousands of lookout towers throughout the Northwest.

The **Marble Creek Interpretive Site**, midway up the St. Joe Valley, contains reminders of the area's early 1900s homesteading and logging pursuits. Relics are scattered throughout the drainage – homestead cabins, steam donkeys, logging camps and equipment. These silent sentinels from the past, and the logging operations that continue today, often stand in poignant juxtaposition to one another.

From here, FS Road 321 leads to Clarkia, looking in on **Hobo Cedar Grove**, a protected grove of huge cedar trees that somehow avoided the felling axe. Hike the **Hobo Historical Trail** to see the remains of a loggers' splash dam. The trailhead is two miles north of Hobo Cedar Grove.

Avery, some 10 miles east of Marble Creek, drowses among its memories. The once-thriving railroad town survived the fire of 1910, thanks to back fires set by townsmen after the women and children had been evacuated. The chief attraction is the **Avery Ranger Station**, stoutly constructed of notched logs a year prior to the fire. Touring the station offers an inside view of the Forest Service's historic part in managing the extensive forests of Idaho and the Northwest.

Back in St. Maries, you must choose between two Scenic Byways, both leading to I-90 and Coeur d'Alene.

Stands of tall, straight white pine trees crowd both sides of the aptly named **White Pine Scenic Byway**. The 22-mile corridor comes out at I-90 near the historic Cataldo Mission. More about the mission later.

The Panhandle

Coeur d'Alene: The Lake & the City

The **Coeur d'Alene Scenic Byway** (Idaho 97) leaps uphill from St. Maries, zigging and zagging above the lake in dramatic swoops. You could almost miss **Harrison**, at the bottom of a steep slope 10 miles north of St. Maries. Harrison's situation at the mouth of the Coeur d'Alene River made it an ideal lumber mill site. The town also served as a landing site for steamboats transporting supplies to backcountry mining and timber operations. Today, Harrison, population 225 (more or less), boasts an excursion boat, a lakeside park, a public boat dock and RV park. Often less crowded than bustling Coeur d'Alene, these lakeside amenities offer pleasant camping and boating.

The Crane House, one of Harrison's historic houses, is a museum showcasing local artifacts and photos dating back to the 1890s. Open weekends in summer.

Post Falls, on I-90 seven miles west of Coeur d'Alene city, isn't exactly on the lake, but its situation on the Spokane River, which drains Lake Coeur d'Alene, puts it under the lake's capacious tent. In addition to pleasant riverside parks, Post Falls is notable for the impressive falls for which it was named. An outlet mall draws shoppers.

Over the past decade, Coeur d'Alene has evolved from a friendly small town to a city of over 30,000 and growing. The city's situation is salubrious – at the head of Lake Coeur d'Alene, 30 miles east of Spokane straddling north-south US 95 and east-west I-90. An influx of retirees and other refugees from urban sprawl has attracted numerous businesses catering to their needs. These, and the inevitable tourist-related services, can detract from Coeur d'Alene's considerable charm if you allow them to do so. You will doubtless find much to enjoy if you avoid the commercial-strip tackiness fringing the city, keeping to the original town and fort sites fanning back from the lake.

The downtown area is flanked by a pleasant old-time residential neighborhood. The flossy **Coeur d'Alene Resort** commands a slice of the adjacent lakeshore, spilling to the foot of Tubbs Hill, cherished as the site of city father Tony Tubbs' homestead. Nearby **City Park** and **Independence Point** boast a sand beach, a shady picnic grove and concessions offering everything from waterski rentals to scenic airplane rides. A nearby residential area, Coeur d'Alene's finest, and North Idaho College occupy the parade grounds where Fort Sherman soldiers once snapped to attention.

Coeur d'Alene first gained prominence as the site of a military fort, chosen in 1877 by Gen. William Tecumseh Sherman of Civil War fame (or infamy, if you hail from the South). The city boomed as Eastern lumbermen arrived to capitalize on the area's abundant timber. The new railway and steamship terminals swarmed with prospectors headed for the rich gold and silver veins, some 40 miles to the west, that later became the famed Silver Valley. The tourism flurry of the early 20th century, when trainloads of day-trippers came from Spokane to cruise the lake on paddle-wheel steamboats, merely hinted at the fame and fortune enjoyed by Coeur d'Alene today.

Much of this latter-day popularity can be attributed to the handsome high-rise resort hotel built just over a decade ago by local developer Duane Hagedone. The proposed resort met with heated opposition. The principle objection: a multi-story structure would destroy the shoreline's pristine quality. (Nevermind, that for decades the lake had served as a depository for mining wastes fed into the lake by way of the South Fork of the Coeur d'Alene River). Furthermore, the "eye-sore" would block views of the lake. They needn't have fretted. The resort spurred tourism throughout North Idaho and gave a big boost to an economy on the skids due to a steep decline in mining and logging.

Coeur d'Alene is a fun place to visit. One festival or another always seems to be in progress. The prosperity wave led to a proliferation of bed and breakfasts, each projecting a subtly different ambience. Restaurant fare is satisfyingly varied. The antiques field is fertile with several shops, including downtown's four-story **Wiggett Mall & Marketplace**. Water sports opportunities abound. So do area hiking and biking trails. The **Coeur d'Alene Resort** boasts a miles-long geranium-embellished boardwalk, plus a floating green on its world-acclaimed golf course. This may be the only course in the world where duffers must take care to avoid sending a slice into an osprey nest.

Coeur d'Alene is a good base for exploring the area's numerous museums and historic points of interest. Here, history has a way of reaching out and grabbing you.

Museum of North Idaho, on Northwest Blvd. at Coeur d'Alene City Park, has an old-time blacksmith shop and kitchen, mineral samples and logging equipment. Most interesting is an extensive photo collection covering area Indian culture, early logging and steamship and mining pursuits. Open April-Oct, Tues-Sat, 11-5. Also open Sun in July and Aug. ☎ 208-664-3448.

Fort Sherman Museum, on the North Idaho College campus, has displays relating to Fort Sherman, plus outdoor exhibits of logging and lumbering equipment. Open May 1-Sept 30, Tues-Sat, 1-4:45. ☎ 208-664-3448.

The Panhandle

Old Mission State Park

Each of the numerous landmarks along the 68-mile stretch of I-90 between Coeur d'Alene and the Idaho-Montana line celebrates an event or events that shaped the land and the people of North Idaho. These landmarks are a microcosm of the effect that the nation's westerly push had on the handful of people who were either here in the first place, were just passing through, or stayed to stake a claim.

The stately **Cataldo Mission** crowns a knoll south of I-90 on Mission Flats, at Mile 39 east of 4th of July Summit, a landmark on the old Mullan Road. Chronologically, Old Mission State Park is the logical place to begin a Silver Valley tour. It also points up the fact that, while the valley's silver mines take center stage, many other dramas were played out in this mountain-girt slice of North Idaho.

In 1842, the famous Catholic missionary priest, Fr. Pierre deSmet, established a mission to the Coeur d'Alenes near here at the request of tribal elders. The graceful cornsilk-hued mission, Idaho's oldest standing structure, was constructed circa 1853 by the incredibly talented Fr. Anthony Ravalli. His helpers: two Catholic brothers and an enthusiastic band of Coeur d'Alene tribal members. Remarkable for the time and place, the wattle-and-daub church is hauntingly beautiful both in its design and in the charmingly simple artwork created by Fr. Ravalli from the materials at hand on that remote frontier. A true Rennaisance man, Fr. Ravalli was well-versed in the sciences of the day, including art and mechanics.

The church was virtually abandoned in 1877, when the US Government shifted the Coeur d'Alene lands to approximately their present boundaries south and west of Lake Coeur d'Alene.

Today, the restored mission church and the nearby priests' house are administered by the Idaho Department of Parks and Recreation. The church is no longer used for services, other than an occasional wedding. Once a year, on August 15th, the Coeur d'Alene return to celebrate mass on the Old Mission grounds, to re-enact the Coming of the Black Robes, and to honor their heritage with feasting and dancing.

The Old Mission State Park Visitor Center offers displays and a video show relevant to the Mission and to Coeur d'Alene history and culture. The Visitor Center and buildings are open daily, 8-6, March-Sept; 9-5 pm the rest of the year. The grounds remain open in daylight hours. $2 vehicle fee.

The Silver Valley

The Coeur d'Alene Mining District, a.k.a. Silver Valley, stetches from Pinehurst almost to the Montana state line. The western part of the valley is characterized by denuded hills, slag heaps, tailing ponds, abandoned smelters and other mining structures – detritus of an age when heedless greed stampeded across this once-pristine place, raping the land, polluting the rivers and the air that mine and mill workers and their families breathed.

Today's sharply reduced mining operations – as well as enforced adherence to air pollution and refuse disposal standards – have made big improvements over the heedless methods of former times. The Bunker Hill Superfund Site impacts the entire valley and its tributaries.

Clearly, the pollution problem has not gone the way of the mining moguls. For over a century, Lake Coeur d'Alene has been a repository for arsenic, mercury and other pollutants leaching into tributaries of the Coeur d'Alene River from the mines and mills honeycombing these hills. Massive Superfund cleanups have cleansed many streams. However, 10 inactive mill sites in the Wallace Ranger District of the Panhandle National Forests continue to leach lead and other heavy metals into streams. Seasonal floodwaters carry thousands of tons of metals-laced sediment downstream into Lake Coeur d'Alene – sediments so lethal that migratory waterfowl sometimes succumb after as little as a two-week stay in riverside wetlands. Swan deaths have caused particular concern. Cleanups, costing millions of dollars, are continuing on a priority basis.

Not that you should allow these sad facts to spoil your visit. Pollutants probably have little or no effect on river and lake quality from a recreational standpoint.

On the east, the deep Silver Valley is embraced by darkling mountains covered with thick stands of fir and pine. A few forlorn mining towns huddle among slag heaps at the base of the mountains – legacies of the silver age.

While the valley's rich lodes of silver have long held center stage, large quantities of zinc and lead have also been taken from these mountains,

The Panhandle

Scrap metal sculptor David Dose's caricature of Noah Kellog and his mule graces a Kellog street corner.

to be smelted in the valley. Gold has, and still can be, found hereabouts in relatively insignificant quantities.

Silver Mountain Resort, boasting the world's longest gondola ride (3.1 miles, rising 3,400 vertical feet) in summer and great skiing in winter, rolls over the hills south of Kellogg. The gondola tops one hill before dipping and swooping up another to the Mountain Haus at the top. You can hike down, or return via gondola.

Some years ago, in response to a slump occasioned by the silver bust, Kellogg's movers and shakers angled for the tourist trade by transforming storefronts into a pseudo-Bavarian village. Of more interest is a scattered collection of whimsical sculptures, fashioned by a school teacher from discarded wheels, tractor parts and other metallic flotsam. One depicts a bemused Noah Kellogg watching his prescient jackass unearth a glob of shining silver (see page 106).

Perhaps the succession of mining incidents that rent the valley, from strikes to mine disasters and all the miseries in-between, is best encapsulated by an impressive granite monument to the 91 miners who died of smoke and carbon monoxide poisoning in the 1972 Sunshine Mine disaster. It stands on the north side of I-90 at Mile 54. Take the Big Creek exit.

Drive three miles up the Big Creek Road to see the famous **Sunshine Mine**, one of the world's largest single lode silver producers.

Seldom does a town's past shake hands so charmingly with its present as in **Wallace**, whose entire downtown is on the National Register of Historic Places. This connectedness is as natural as the morning sun slanting over the sheltering hills each day. Wallace eschews tacky tourist traps, projecting instead a serendipitous juxtapositon of modern life and history.

Wallace reached its zenith in the early 1900s when the population soared to 5,000, ranking it as Idaho's third largest town. Straddling the silver-rich Osborn Fault, the town became the financial and logistical center for the state's booming silver industry. Though sharply curtailed, the Coeur d'Alene mining district still produces much of the nation's silver, most from the century-old Sunshine Mine. Wallace's past is strewn with setbacks overcome. The entire business district was destroyed in an 1890 fire. The Great Idaho Fire of 1910 burned a third of the rebuilt town. By 1915, a second rebuilding had been completed. The Northern Pacific Railway Line brought the outside world to this town resting in a fir-clad bowl. Then the Great Depression hit. Silver prices plummeted, and Wallace's population dwindled to its present level of just over 1,000. In many respects, Wallace remains frozen in the Jazz Age.

A serious threat to the town's time-capsule ambience came in the 1970s. I-90 was slated to run smack through downtown, requiring many of Wallace's handsome old buildings to be razed. Thoroughly riled up, the community mounted a campaign that attracted national attention. Led by Harry Magnuson, a grandson of immigrant miners, the town sued the federal government, delaying construction for 17 years. The result: the rerouted I-90 hugs a hill north of downtown.

The splendid cupola-topped Northern Pacific depot, made obsolete when transcontinentel passenger trains gave Wallace the cold shoulder, stood smack in rerouted I-90's path. Moved to a grassy site nearby, the depot was transformed into **The Northern Pacific Depot Railroad Museum**. If you don't set foot in another Idaho museum, you must visit this showcase of one community's triumphs and disasters. Here, the stories of the heroic rescues during the fire of 1910, daily life in a silver boom town, the Northern Pacific's tremendous impact on this and other isolated communities, are told in photographs whose clarity bridges the decades.

To immerse yourself in the spirit of the silver boom era, book a room at the restored **Jameson Hotel**, within spitting distance of the Depot. The former railroad hotel and miners' watering hole survived the Fire of 1910, but failed to surmount the passing of time. A coffee house occupied the ground floor for some years, but the upstairs guest rooms lay dormant for decades. When Harry Magnuson acquired the structure in 1978, he found the upper two floors locked in a time warp. It was as if the proprietor had turned the key and walked away after the last guest hopped a train out of town.

Magnuson restored the guest rooms, introducing an ambience evocative of a typical 1915-era railroad hotel, right down to the bathrooms at the end of the hall. The ground-floor restaurant follows suit, boasting a magnificent mahogany bar and accoutrements to match.

To deepen the time capsule illusion, you might step across the street of an evening to a former bordello. Here, you can take in a Sixth Street

Melodrama performance, presenting turn-of-the-century hiss-and-boo capers based on snippets of local lore. **Sixth Street Melodrama**, 212 Sixth Street, Wallace, ID 83873-1243. ☎ 208-752-8871.

The **Oasis Bordello Museum** is a time capsule of another stripe. The upstairs rooms remain exactly as the girls left them on the 1950s night when the law swooped in. The scene is complete with intimate garments strewn about during the hasty flight of the last of Wallace's notorious ladies of the night. The place was shut up tight, not to be opened for four decades. If you like your history in all its guises, warts and all, this one's for you. Open daily during business hours. 605 Cedar Street, Wallace, ID 83873. ☎ 208-753-0801.

Wallace is a comfortable town for walking, the bowl-like terrain having forced folk to cluster all buildings within a few blocks like figures in a terrarium. Residential streets are lined with front-porch houses harking back to silver boom times. Shops display local crafts, antiques, gourmet foods, minerals and jewelry fashioned from locally mined silver. Yes, tacky souvenirs are on offer, but not to the extent that they intrude on the spirit of this old mining town. Its historical integrity remains firmly in place. A walking tour guide can be obtained at the Depot Museum, the Wallace Chamber of Commerce and points of interest.

Don a hard hat, board a trolley, and take off on a **Sierra Silver Mine Underground Tour**. The mine, a brief trolley ride from downtown Wallace, was formerly used to teach mining techniques to local students. This is not just another hokey tour. As you walk through the mine's main drift or corridor, an experienced miner demonstrates the use of hard rock silver mining tools and techniques. Tours depart the ticket office at 420 Fifth Street daily every 30 minutes, from 9-4, in May, June and September. The last tour leaves at 6 pm in July and August. No children under four. Admission charge. Sierra Silver Mine Tour, Inc., 420 Sixth Street, Wallace, ID 83873. ☎ 208-752-5151.

The **Wallace District Mining Museum**, 509 Bank Street, is a fascinating repository for a rich lode of mining history and lore. A 20-minute video presentation traces the area's mining heritage. The nominal admission fee is discounted for persons taking the mine tour. Open daily in June, July and August, 8-8; to 6 pm in late spring and early autumn. Open the rest of the year on weekdays, 9-4, Sat, 10-4. PO Box 469, Wallace, ID 83873; ☎ 208-556-1592.

Granted, Wallace lacks the down-and-dirty, rough-edged grittiness of early-day prospecting. You'll find that if you head north out of Wallace into the Coeur d'Alene National Forest via FS Road 456. The paved road dips, dives and connives as it makes its crooked way over Dobson Pass and into history.

Welcome to the 1880s, an era when every bewhiskered prospector might strike it rich (or might not); a time when towns seemed to materialize overnight (and as quickly disappear); an age when Saturday nights were for drinking and brawling and "soiled doves," or ladies of the night, ruled the roost.

Turn right onto FS Road 605 at the townsite of Delta, a boom town that failed to outlast nearby Beaver Creek's placer gold. Welcome to the historic **Murray Gold Fields** and the **Murray Adventure Road**. Request a brochure describing the road's points of interest from the Coeur d'Alene BLM office (☎ 208-769-5000) or the Wallace Ranger District office (☎ 208-752-1221).

The gravel road climbs over Kings Pass, and drops into the year 1884. The Lower 48's last big gold rush occurred here, along Beaver and Prichard Creeks to Thompson Pass on the Montana state line. Mining relics strewn along the route tell a silent story.

More than 400,000 ounces of gold ($164 million worth in today's currency) were brought out of the area, swelling the town of **Murray** to some 5,000 souls. Murray dug in and held on while other boom towns went bust. Many original buildings remain, including Idaho's oldest standing Masonic Temple, the former Shoshone County courthouse, the Post Office, the school house, the Sprag Pole watering hole, early log cabins and several false-front structures.

Murray's 20 residents (more or less) refuse to let those heady times go. The town's grizzled old men could be holdovers incarnate from the days when Wyatt Earp came a'visitin' and the incomparable Molly B'Damn allowed miners to assist at her bath in return for the gold dust they sprinkled over the water.

Molly rests in the Murray Cemetery now, but her spirit lives on in the town's annual knee-slappin' **Molly B'Damn days**, when women vie for the honor of being chosen Molly B'Damn for a day. The winner gets to be paraded down the town's single street in a bathtub pulled by miners.

Molly B'Damn

The quintessential shady lady with a heart of gold, Molly grubstaked miners down on their luck and nursed sick ones to health. When smallpox invaded Murray, Molly and her girls took the sick into their house and nursed them. She was so well liked that respectable townswomen returned the favor when she herself fell ill. She died of "quick consumption" at the age of 34.

An effigy of Molly B'Damn, Murray's favorite lady of the night, peers from an upper window of the Sprag Pole Inn.

"Molly," or at least a representation of her, still gazes from an upper window of the **Sprag Pole**. You can belly up to the bar and order a libation and a burger or barbecue in the venerable saloon before stepping into **The Sprag Pole Museum** in another room. And another era – one filled with the memorabilia of over 100 years of placer mining, plus lots of other neat stuff. Open daily during business hours.

Many of the characters frequenting the Sprag Pole still make a living of sorts from gold mining. It's a sure bet that someone will offer to sell you a gold nugget – real gold. Or you can try your luck panning Prichard Creek or one of many tributaries scoring the hills.

For 60 years, "want to" and "don't want to" factions have lobbed verbal bullets over a dirt track running from Murray to Thompson Pass. The road on to Thompson Falls, Montana, has long since been paved. Now, it looks like the Idaho stretch will be paved over by the time this book hits the stores. Some Murray residents salivate at the thought of the increased business the road will bring; others want Murray to remain as it is.

You can try out the new road. Or you can pick up paved FS Road 9 and follow Prichard Creek west to the townsite of Eagle, where Wyatt Earp and his brother are rumored to have owned the White Elephant Saloon and a mining claim.

Prichard Creek empties into the Coeur d'Alene River at **Prichard**, named for A.J. Prichard whose discovery set off the rush of 1884. Not much is left of the town that served as an entryway to the gold fields for prospectors who came upriver on flat-bottomed bateaus. The river also offered a quick exit to those who found it politic to skedaddle.

At Prichard, a right turn onto paved FS Road 208 will take you deeper into the Coeur d'Alene National Forest and to several scenically situated primitive campgrounds. From the pavement's end, a network of forest roads meanders through the wedge of forest bordered by I-90 on the

*The century-old Enaville Resort dishes up Rocky Mountain oysters
and plenty of logging country atmosphere.*

south, the Montana line on the east, US 95 on the west, and the southern tip of Lake Pend Oreille on the north.

The **Magee Ranger Station** sits off FS Road 208, deep inside this gorgeous wedge of backcountry. The station occupies the site of pioneer Charley Magee's early 1900s homestead claim. Most of the buildings were constructed between 1922 and 1935, at the height of the West's ranger station construction boom. The six-room square-hewn log ranger's house could serve as a model for today's popular log homes. The adjacent airstrip was intended as an emergency landing field for World War II fighter aircraft, but never was used as such. The station was decommissioned in 1973, when shifting boundaries put the area in the Fernan Ranger District. It remains as a memorial to a lost way of life.

Or, instead of turning right into the National Forest, turn left at Prichard to follow the gentle Coeur d'Alene River for 20 miles to I-90 at Kingston. After 18 miles, begin watching for a big log and slab building set back from the road on your left (it sports enough racks to caparison a whole herd of elk and stags). This is the historic **Enaville Resort**, alias The Snake Pit, famous (infamous?) local watering hole. Rocky Mountain oysters and other macho foods are served up in an atmosphere that may best be described as rustic rococo with overtones of barbarism and kitsch. Drop in even if you're not thirsty or hungry. It's an experience you won't soon forget.

After retracing your treads to Coeur d'Alene via I-90, you can head for Priest River and the Priest Lake country via Idaho 41, off I-90 two miles east of Post Falls.

Coeur d'Alene to Sandpoint

US 95 scoots, straight as a tepee pole, across the 43 miles linking Coeur d'Alene and Sandpoint. The flatness of this ancient trench is in startling contrast to the ups and downs of the Coeur d'Alene Mining Area.

You'll see the turnoff to **Hayden Lake** a few miles out of Coeur d'Alene, just past the fast-food row straggle. The small town anchoring this lovely lake has received much bad press over the years as the home of a mixed bag of survivalists and doomsday religious sects. Not to worry; it remains a pleasant off-the-beaten-track lake.

You might well rub your eyes in disbelief as a giant roller coaster and attendant amusement park fol-de-rol heave into view just as you thought you were heading into the sparsely populated North Country. But **Silverwood Theme Park** is no Six Flags Over Texas.

Unlike other slicker parks, Silverwood evolved from one man's fascination with vintage aircraft. Gary Norton's 1981 purchase of a run-down airport, and the subsequent purchase of antique airplanes, led in steps to the creation of a Victorian theme village evoking the memories of Charles Lindbergh and early barnstormers. The amusement park rides reflect that heritage. This park offers a fun time for every age and most interests. A museum displays Norton's vintage aircraft collection. A circa 1928 steam locomotive pulls vintage cars through nearby woods. Pilots put such craft as a World War II Super Stearman and a Fokker Tri-plane of Red Baron fame through thrilling maneuvers during the nightly air shows.

Silverwood is open weekends in May and September, daily in the summer months. Admission fees are well under those of higher-profile theme parks. 26225 N. Hwy 95, Athol, ID 83801. ☎ 208-664-3194. Call or write to ask about current hours and admission prices.

Athol never quite made it as a town, but it makes a great junction. US 95 continues on its northward way. Westward bound Idaho 54 heads for Spirit Lake. The westward lap connects Athol with Farragut State Park and Bayview, a funky cross between summer haven and submarine base. Both are on Lake Pend Oreille.

Pretty **Spirit Lake** is one of a bunch of tiny, often hidden Panhandle lakes where the fishing is great and the splashing is, too.

Farragut State Park was developed on the remains of a World War II naval station. Yup. That's right. A naval station in land-locked Idaho. A top-secret naval station was a priority following Japan's attack on Pearl Harbor. Idaho's secluded, land-locked Panhandle was chosen over a vulnerable coastal location. Quick as a sub can dive, the world's second largest naval training facility was built on deep, cold Lake Pend Oreille. Farragut Naval Station had 776 buildings sectioned into six camps housing over 30,000 recruits and support personnel at a time. In all, 293,381 raw recruits were abruptly jerked into manhood here. German POWs performed menial jobs around the station.

Today, all traces of the once-bustling base have vanished. Except inside the park's visitor center. Over the past 15 years, Park Manager Al Leiser has been patiently piecing together bits of memorabilia and snippets of information concerning the facility. The collection gradually grew to become a museum. Former recruits contributed many pieces of the puzzle. Now, it's a full-blown museum mirroring a colorful era – a remarkable resource for remembrance. On display are hundreds of memorabilia: letters, company photographs, snapshots of snowball fights and USO shows and dances; wryly grinning sailors elbow-deep in laundry.

The 4,000-acre park, sited on a peninsula jutting into the Panhandle's largest lake, is a year-round playground boasting dazzling views of the Coeur d'Alene and Bitterroot Mountain Ranges. Black bear, elk, bobcats, whitetail deer and coyote roam forests of ponderosa and white pine, larch and Douglas fir. Mountain goats gambol over rocky ledges. The lake is filled with cold-water fish, the sky bright with mountain bluebirds, Idaho's state bird.

Nearby **Bayview** is worth a look-see. The hamlet's year-round population of some 200 is inflated in summer by "snowbirds" escaping the heat elsewhere. Barbed wire-topped fences and US Navy "Keep Out!" signs interject a discordant note in this northwoodsy setting. Rumor has long had it that bucolic Bayview harbors mysterious top secret goings-on. Now the truth is out: the US Navy's Acoustic Research Detachment tests submarines in this deep, deep lake.

You can catch an excursion boat here, and possibly overhear old-timers spinning yarns about Prohibition days when rum-runners concealed booze, smuggled over the Canadian border, in milk cans.

From Athol, US 95 beelines to Sandpoint, parallel to, but well away from, the lake.

The Panhandle

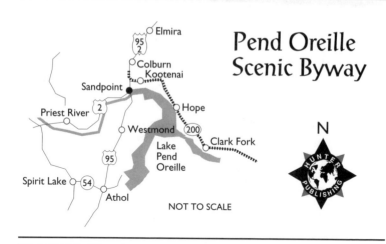

Elmira
95
2
Colburn
Kootenai
Sandpoint
Priest River 2
Hope
Westmond 200
Clark Fork
Lake
Pend
Oreille
95
Spirit Lake 54
Athol

Pend Oreille
Scenic Byway

N

NOT TO SCALE

Curved like a gracefully leaping fish, 43-mile-long **Lake Pend Oreille** is anchored by Farragut State Park on the south and the resort town of Sandpoint on the north. Between is a shoreline dotted with summer homes and backed by mountainous creek-scored terrain. Numerous Forest Service roads traverse this area, linking a growing number of homes and cabins and leading to hiking and biking trails. Idaho 200, the Pend Oreille Scenic Byway, follows the lake's northeast shoreline for some 33 miles.

Sandpoint, posing picturesquely across the Pend Oreille River from the US 95 bridge approach (watch for osprey here), is a summer resort town with aspirations. It has not always been so. Not surprisingly, Sandpoint's heritage includes lumber milling, steamboating and colorful characters whose legacy has been passed on to today's eclectic mix of people: a Buddhist mayor, California transplants, and not a few persons suspected of plotting against the US government.

Be that as it may, this city of 5,200 and counting has gone upscale, seemingly striving to become another Coeur d'Alene. Summer residents, vacationers and wealthy retirees are offered a dizzying array of music and other festivals. The Sandpoint area also has a dazzling wealth of recreational opportunities. Hiking, biking, fishing, water sports, horseback riding, snowmobiling, skiing – you name it.

Bonner County Historical Museum, at 609 S. Ella Avenue in Sandpoint, is a treasure trove of artifacts pertaining to the local Kootenai Indians and Bonner County's logging, mining, railroading and steamboating heritage. Open April-Oct, Tues-Sat, 10-4; Nov-Mar, Thursdays, 10-4. ☎ 208-263-2344.

Sandpoint Fish Hatchery, four miles south of town on Lakeshore Drive, raises rainbow and cutthroat trout, plus sturgeon for reintroduction into the Kootenai River. Visitor information exhibit. Open daily, 8-4. ☎ 208-265-7228.

The North Idaho Panhandle

The **Pend Oreille Scenic Byway** (Idaho 200) follows the northeast shores of the lake, brushing against Kootenai, Hope and Clark Fork.

In 1809, Welsh explorer David Thompson, a Hudson's Bay Company employee, established a settlement on the Hope Peninsula – the first white settlement in the place that would become Idaho. Idaho 200 meets Montana east of the Cabinet Gorge Dam. Behind the dam, in Montana, the Clark Fork River forms a long, slender reservoir. The river empties into Lake Pend Oreille below the dam.

Viewing this dam, yet another monolithic structure taming the West's grand rivers so that lights might glow and washing machines rub-a-dub, makes me wish I could have seen this splendid z-shaped gorge, the river plunging 350 feet below, as the Lewis & Clark expedition did.

Cabinet Gorge Fish Hatchery, just east of Clarks Fork, hatches several million kokanee salmon eggs per year for release into Lake Pend Oreille. Open daily, 7:30-4:30. ☎ 208-266-1431.

Clark Fork Hatchery, on Spring Creek Road, produces rainbow and cutthroat trout. Open daily, 8-5. ☎ 208-266-1141.

Schweitzer Mountain Resort, 11 miles north of Sandpoint, topping a curly-cue road heading west off US 95, is much more than a downhill ski resort. Driving up to this top-of-the-world retreat is well worth your time, even if you have no intention of participating in the resort's numerous activities. The air is bracing, the views of the valley below and the surrounding fir-clothed mountains are endless, and numerous paths and trails invite exploration.

On Schweitzer Mountain and elsewhere in North Idaho, particularly where fires and other depredations have disturbed the vegetation, growths of shocking-pink fireweed color the slopes. Some reach spectacular heights and flower sizes. Other wildflowers also bloom in season, especially if heavy snows cloaked the land during the preceding winter.

US 95 linking Sandpoint and Bonners Ferry follows the Purcell Trench, dredged 32,000 to 80,000 years ago by huge ice lobes plunging south from the Canadian ice fields. Montana's Cabinet Mountains loom on the eastern skyline. The Selkirk Range tumbles on the west, creating a barrier between this corridor and pristine Priest Lake.

In 1992, tragedy struck in a shooting by FBI agents at the Weaver family's cabin on Ruby Ridge, off one of the maze of Forest Service roads winding through the Selkirks. Once more, North Idaho rocketed onto the national stage. The Weavers had joined a lengthy procession of folk who, choosing to dance to a different drummer, looked to Idaho's backcountry for seclusion.

Bonners Ferry's history parallels that of other North Idaho timber towns, with a singular exception: camel trains. Some prospectors imported camels from San Francisco to pack in their gear. Thought to have more endurance than mules, camels proved to be a passing fad. Following the 1863 discovery of gold on nearby Wild Horse Creek, British Columbia, prospectors swarmed over the old Indian trail spanning the Kootenai River. Edwin Bonner made a tidy sum ferrying gold fever sufferers across the river here.

Bonners Ferry's Boundary County Historical Society and Museum, 105 Main Street, displays artifacts and photographs relating to the history of Boundary County. Kootenai (Kutenai) Indian artifacts are also on display. The Kutenai belong to a remote, linguistically separate Algonquin group unrelated to other Western tribes. Their forebears are thought to have migrated westward from the Eastern forests – exactly when, no one knows. A small Kutenai population remains in Idaho; most live in British Columbia.

The **Kootenai Wildlife Refuge** sprawls across 2,700 acres, five miles west of Bonners Ferry, on the Riverside Road. It is habitat for numerous species of waterfowl. (See *Wildlife Watching*.)

At Bonners Ferry you are faced with a choice. You can loop through the Purcell Mountain Area, visiting five mountain lakes via several Forest Service roads. The loop begins at FS Road 1005, four miles north of town. You will come out on US 95 near Eastport.

The other option is to follow US 2 to the Montana line, passing through the small town of **Moyie Springs**. A paved road detours to overlooks affording views of Upper and Lower Moyie Falls. Look for it just to the west of a steel truss bridge soaring 450 feet above Moyie Canyon. The falls are especially spectacular in spring, when the river is at its most feisty.

From Moyie Springs, FS Road 211 follows the Moyie River to US 95 and Eastport on the Canadian border. The Moyie challenges river runners when spring runoff exposes its devilish side. In summer and fall, it becomes a scenic stream running through an idyllic landscape of orchards and hayfields.

Boys leap off Priest Lake's rocky ledges.

The Panhandle

Watch for FS Road 2517, a mile west of Eastport. A couple of miles down the road a sign marks a short trail leading to **Copper Creek Falls**, a 70-foot ribbon of deep forest enchantment. From here, you can follow the 40-mile Purcell Mountain Area loop, coming out on US 95 north of Bonners Ferry. This loop includes several Forest Service roads, some gravelled, some dirt. Obtain a travel map at the Bonners Ferry Ranger District office (1500 Highway 2, Sandpoint, ID 83864. ☎ 208-263-5111) before setting out.

From Eastport, US 95 returns to Bonners Ferry through rolling hills crested with ripening grainfields tended by Mennonite farmers.

Idaho has so many truly scenic drives that designating Scenic Byways must have involved much head scratching. US 2, following the Pend Oreille River west of Sandpoint to the junction with Idaho 57 at Priest River, is one of Idaho's loveliest drives.

Priest River, a sizeable town for these northerly parts, is a good place to stock up on supplies if you're camping on or near Priest Lake. **Albeni Falls Dam**, a few miles to the west, backs up the river clear to Sandpoint. You can tour the dam.

Idaho 57 parallels the chuckling Priest River for a few miles, then veers away from it before reaching the Priest Lake outlet. Numerous Forest Service roads meander through the backcountry on both sides of the highway, coming out at the lakeside hamlet of Coolin. Before setting out, obtain a map at the Priest Lake Ranger District office in PriestRiver.

Priest Lake, Idaho's least developed major natural lake, lies at an altitude of 2,438 feet. The lake occupies a gentle declivity between the Selkirks on the east, some of whose peaks rise to 7,000 feet, and thick forests evocative of the Pacific Northwest on the west. The valley shows evidence of glaciers having retreated as recently as 7,000 years ago.

The peripatetic Fr. Pierre DeSmet happened on the lake, naming it for his Superior General in Rome in what was doubtless a canny political move. Indians renamed the lake Kaniksu, meaning "Black Robe." Great Northern Railway promoters anglicized it to Priest. But Kaniksu stuck. The Kaniksu National Forest sprawls across 1½ million acres of northern Idaho and Washington.

Tucked in a remote corner of Northwest Idaho, Priest Lake has been mostly overlooked by all save loggers and a relatively few summer folk. If you hanker after a true north country experience *sans* the frills of civilization, this lake's for you.

You can drive clear around the lake, the roads breaking only where the Upper Priest River runs through Upper Priest Lake. Summer cabins and a handful of resorts are accessed via gravel roads branching off Idaho 57, which parallels the west side of the lake. "Resort" is a relative term in this backwater. Most consist of simple lodgings, a bar-and-eatery, and a boat rental. Idaho 57 ends at **Nordman,** population 50. A combination store, eatery and post office earns Nordman a dot on the map.

At Nordman, FS Road 302 takes a northwesterly course through dense forest to **Granite Falls** and the **Roosevelt Grove of Ancient Cedars Scenic Area.** These sylvan delights are just over the line in Washington, but Priest Lake folk have long since claimed them.

Ranging from four to 12 feet in diameter and reaching heights of 150 feet, the Roosevelt Grove's stately cedars typify the Northwest's old-growth forests. Sadly, such stands are dwindling, largely because of forest fires, logging inroads and insect infestations. A 1926 fire claimed most of the grove, splitting it into two-acre and 20-acre groves, accessible via a short hike up an old logging trail.

Stagger Inn, the name of the small picnic area at the trailhead serving the Grove and the Falls, recalls the weary firefighters who literally staggered into a fire camp here at the time of the 1926 conflagration.

Two flourishing falls tumble down the North Fork of Granite Creek. If the Roosevelt cedars typify the Northwest's old-growth forests, **Upper and Lower Granite Falls** epitomize the Northwest's multiplicity of streams sashaying down mountains and gorges.

At the Outlet Dam, off Idaho 57, the picturesquely named Dickensheet Road crosses the river and heads for Coolin. It continues north along the lake to curve around the Upper Priest Lake Scenic Area, eventually coming out at FS Road 302. Just past Coolin, the pavement gives way to a good gravelled road.

Drop in at the **Priest Lake Museum/Visitor Center** at Coolin to visit a log cabin built by the CCC in 1935, and to get a fix on local history. The cabin is so warm and cozy, right down to the fish and elk trophies on the walls, that you'll want to move right in. Open daily, Memorial Day-Labor Day, 10-4. ☎ 208-443-2676.

Another cabin, up the lake from Coolin on Eight Mile Island, stands as a tribute to the fortitude of the Vinther and Nelson families. In the early years of this century, the families traveled by train, buckboard and boat to reach the island. The cabin they enjoyed through several generations is on the National Register of Historic Places. The restored cabin houses a museum displaying early photographs, a pelt formerly inhabited by a bear that a family member shot, and other memorabilia. The Priest Lake Ranger District administers the property. Accessible only by boat. Open in the summer months, Wed-Sun, 10-3.

Priest Lake State Park at Indian Creek Bay, a few miles up the lake from Eight Mile Island, occupies a pretty wooded site boasting a fine sand beach. Silent screen star Nell Shipman built a lakefront lodge near here in the 1920s. Shipman, and a 30-member production crew, lived here for three years, making five movies. Supplies were brought up the lake by steam barge in summer, by dog sled in winter. The lodge at Shipman Point has gone the way of silent films.

The Panhandle

Adventures

On Foot

The Idaho Panhandle is laced with superb hiking trails. The varied terrain includes trails for every hiking level, from casual walkers to backpackers itching to experience the backcountry in all its rugged grandeur. Few areas of this size include such a wide range of terrain: level paths through deep forests, rugged trails leading to peaks topping 7,000 feet, trails encircling sparkling lakes and following rushing rivers and chuckling creeks, trails overlooking frothing waterfalls, treks into storied gold mining and logging country, trails culminating in fabulous top-of-the-world vistas.

No matter if your trail is a short one to a scenic waterfall or a lengthy wilderness hike, it behooves you to be alert for bears. Most Panhandle bears are the relatively non-aggressive black bears, but a few grouchy grizzlies are known to roam the territory designated as Grizzly Bear Recovery Habitats. Bears, like most animals, will usually avoid contact with humans. But there is always a chance that you may come upon a sow with a cub or two, or that you may surprise a bear feasting on the wild huckleberries growing in profusion hereabouts. Talking and making noises as you go will usually alert bears to your presence, giving them a chance to skedaddle. Beat a leisurely retreat if you see a bear.

Don't expect black bears to be black in every case. They range through all shades of brown to black. They are smaller than grizzlies and lack grizzlies' distinguishing hump and "dished" facial profile.

If you do encounter a grizzly, try to back out of the situation. Keep calm, avoid eye contact, back up slowly and speak in a soft monotone. Never turn your back on a bear, never kneel and never run. Don't climb a tree unless you have time to climb at least 10 feet before the bear can reach you. Bears and locomotives have much in common: they travel very fast. If you don't have time to reach a tree before the bear does, drop a non-food item such as a camera to distract the bear while you climb.

As a last resort, play dead. Roll into a ball with your hands protecting your face and head. Your backpack will provide some protection. If the bear swats you, roll with it while remaining in a curled position. Don't look up until you are sure the bear has gone. Report all grizzly encounters to the nearest ranger station.

When camping, hang all food and toiletries at least 10 feet off the ground and four feet from any vertical support at night and in the daytime when unattended. Or store them inside a hard-sided vehicle. That does not include coolers, pop-up campers, tents and backpacks.

Hiking alone is never smart, especially in bear country.

Some North Idaho backcountry is prime big game hunting territory. If you plan on hiking in the fall months, be aware of hunting seasons and take sensible precautions, such as wearing bright red or yellow clothing. Before setting out, check with the local ranger district office to inquire about hunting seasons, about trail restrictions and conditions, and to obtain trail maps.

Hiking in the Panhandle calls for the same safety measures as other off-the-beaten-track forays. Here, as elsewhere, careful planning and common sense can make the difference between an adventure whose memory you will long treasure and one you'd prefer to forget.

The Panhandle National Forests ranger districts make several exceptionally clear and useable hiking guides available to the public. Contact either the Panhandlle National Forests supervisor's office in Coeur d'Alene, or the district ranger office for your area of interest.

The Lochsa Corridor

Lewis & Clark hiked the **Lolo Trail** and you can, too. The best way to walk in their footsteps is to begin at the Lolo Visitor Center at the Montana State line. A US Forest Service brochure locates and describes Lewis & Clark landmarks along the trail. You'll find copies at the Clearwater National Forest office in Orofino, and at other regional Idaho and Montana Forest Service offices.

The **Idaho State Centennial Trail** crosses the Lolo Trail, hugging the Montana line as it passes through rugged mountainous country and navigates Thompson Pass. The trail veers west at Clark Fork, traversing the Selkirk Range parallel to Priest Lake before entering British Columbia.

The complete Centennial Trail extends about 1,200 miles from Nevada to Canada, passing through 11 national forests. It crosses the Owyhee Mountains and threads Central Idaho's Frank Church-River of No Return Wilderness before reaching Lolo Pass. The portion of the trail marking Idaho's centennial year uses previously existing trails and a few backcountry roads. Uses, dependent on the terrain, include hiking, horseback riding, cross-country skiing, snowmobiling, mountain biking and motorized trailbiking. Most of the trail is marked with Idaho Centennial Trail signs depicting a map of Idaho.

Two National Recreation Trails meander through Selway River country. The **East Boyd-Glover-Roundup Trail** begins at the end of FS Road 317 (off FS Road 223) at the base of Roundup Mountain. It climbs steeply before descending into the Selway River Canyon. The **Meadow Creek Trail**, beginning at Slim's Camp on FS Road 443 on the west side of the river, follows the creek bottom through lush cedar and fir forest, passing several idyllic waterfalls. A 15-mile hike on this trail ends at the Meadow Creek Station.

Dworshak Reservoir Area

Four trails follow the Dworshak Reservoir shoreline. Each offers great views of the water, plus shore fishing access.

The **Big Eddy Trail** is a good choice if you are camping at Dworshak State Park. The 10-mile trail crosses a small peninsula before following the shoreline to the Big Eddy Recreation Area just north of Dworshak Dam.

The .8-mile **Merrys Bay Trail** hugs the shoreline south of the dam.

The half-mile **Canyon Creek Trail** begins in the vicinity of the Canyon Creek Campground on the reservoir's south shore.

The 2½-mile **Cold Springs Trail**, accessed via the Wells Bench Road, follows the shoreline to the Cold Springs Group Camp.

Palouse Ranger District, Clearwater National Forest

Several Forest Service trails meander off Idaho 6, the White Pine Scenic Route, between Harvard and St. Maries and south of the Palouse Divide Road.

Take FS Road 1960 to connect with the **Gold Hill Mining Area**'s network of trails, looking in on tailing piles and other gold rush leavings. Gold is still being taken from small mines in the area's lower elevations. Be careful not to intrude on private property and/or mining claims. You can survey the area from trails climbing Prospect Peak and Gold Hill.

FS Road 447 leads to the **Laird Park Campground**, a popular Palouse River swimming area, before continuing on through miles of forested multiple use trails. A trailhead serving several other pleasant forested trails is a couple of miles farther up Idaho 6.

St. Maries & St. Joe Ranger Districts, Panhandle National Forests

Some 60 miles of exciting trails wind through the **Marble Creek drainage**, a storied mining and logging area in the St. Maries Ranger District northeast of Clarkia. Most of these trails are open to both hikers and horseback riders. Take FS Road 50 east out of St. Maries. Turn right on FS Road 321, at the Marble Creek Interpretive Site. A map, available at the St. Maries Ranger District office in St. Maries, will guide you to these trails and to the Marble Creek area's numerous landmarks. Old splash dams, steam donkeys and logging campsites will serve to connect you with that era.

FS Road 321 also leads to the **Hobo Cedar Grove Botanical Area**. A half-mile loop trail threads through the 240-acre grove, a dense canopy of western red cedars shading a gentle carpet of lady fern.

The **Big Creek Trail System** lies north of FS Road 50 and south of the Coeur d'Alene Divide. These trails, originally intended for fire control following the devastating fire of 1910, are currently maintained for recreational use. They look in on numerous reminders of the logging and mining pursuits that once rent the silence with a cacophony of sound. Much of this country is rugged, with numerous navigational difficulties, but a few trails are level and have good tread surfaces. Hardy vegetation shows how quickly growth often occurs after a forest fire. Trail lengths vary from the moderately difficult two-mile **Cabin Ridge Trail** to the 15-mile **Big Creek Trail**.

Fernan Ranger District, Panhandle National Forests

If your base camp is one of Coeur d'Alene's luxury digs, you can complete two pleasant nearby hikes between brunch and dinner. **Tubbs Hill** is a cherished landmark nudging downtown. Threatened changes over the years, the most recent involving the logging of trees downed in a 1996 ice storm, have generated vociferous outcries. The view of the lake from the top is reward enough for encountering a zillion other vacationers. The two-mile loop begins at the south end of the parking lot between McEuen Park and the Coeur d'Alene Resort.

The 4.6-mile **Caribou Ridge Trail** linking Beauty Creek, off Idaho 97 (Lake Coeur d'Alene Scenic Byway), with Mt. Coeur d'Alene, also offers splendid views of the lake and surrounding mountains. The moderately difficult trail climbs from 2,200 feet to 4,000 feet and includes four switchbacks. Incidentally, the caribou herds that once roamed the entire Panhandle have long since retreated farther north. However, a re-introduction experiment may be in the works.

The 34-mile **Independence Creek Trail System**, sprawling east of Hayden Lake in the Fernan Ranger District, partially follows the course of a wagon road constructed in the early years of this century to link Lake Pend Oreille and the Lakeview mines with the Independence and Tepee Creek Valleys. To reach the trail system, head north off I-90 at Kingston onto FS Road 209. The paved road meanders along the North Fork of the Coeur d'Alene River, eventually coming out at Bayview on Lake Pend Oreille. The trail then follows the lake shore on a northerly course. Watch for FS Road 258, just before the Honeysuckle Campground. Follow it a short distance to FS Road 904. The road switches back abruptly before arriving at the Independence Creek trailhead. Six side trails branch off the main one. All are open to both hikers and horses; the Independence Creek, Ermine Ridge and East Declaration trails are recommended for trail bikes.

Though hit hard in the 1910 fire, the Independence Creek drainage quickly recovered. Today, this backcountry appears about as pristine as any you will find.

Among the delights of these moderate to moderately difficult trails are numerous waterfalls serving as "fronts" for the nests of drab little birds aptly called water ousels. You may spot them bobbing along the banks or walking underwater in search of insects. Numerous other animals and birds also inhabit this backcountry.

The **Bigfoot Ridge trailhead** is adjacent to the Magee Ranger Station (see *Touring*). Turn off FS Road 422, 2½ miles south of Honeysuckle Campground. The interpretive trail offers insight into the area's numerous conifers.

Wallace Ranger District, Panhandle National Forests

The Wallace Ranger District has many trails in the drainage systems of the North and South Forks of the Coeur d'Alene River. They range from moderate to extremely difficult, are from one to 29 miles in length, and have elevation gains of 100 to 3,850 feet. Most are true backcountry trails, offering adventures for experienced hikers and backpackers. The 18-mile **Stateline Trail** follows a portion of the Centennial Trail across high country ridges. The trailhead is at Mullan off I-90.

Before setting out, contact the Wallace Ranger District office (☎ 208-752-1221) to obtain detailed maps and to learn of any restrictions due to weather and/or fire conditions. Take sensible precautions, and you should experience the adventure of your life.

Sandpoint Ranger District, Panhandle National Forests

The Sandpoint Ranger District has more than 75 trails covering over 275 miles, ranging from the Pend Oreille lakeside environment at 2,062 feet to subalpine environments reaching 7,352 feet in the Selkirk Range. Terrains include dense forests, valley bottoms, barren ridges and meadows. Some border rivers, lakes and streams. Most are accessible by passenger car via Forest Service roads. Before setting out, stop at the Sandpoint Ranger District office to obtain a district map and to check on conditions (1500 Highway 2, Sandpoint, ID 83864. ☎ 208-263-5111).

A handy booklet detailing the most popular trails is also available. The **Gold Hill, Evan's Landing** and **Maiden Creek trails** climb upslope from Lake Pend Oreille. The **Green Monarch Divide, Schafer Peak,**

Delyle Ridge and **Packsaddle Mountain trails** afford splendid views of Lake Pend Oreille and the surrounding mountains. The short **Mineral Point Interpretive Trail** on Lake Pend Oreille's western shore showcases native trees. The **Caribou Lake Trail** is within yodeling distance of Schweitzer Mountain Resort. The **Lake Darling** and **Moose Lake trails** are in designated Grizzly Bear Recovery Habitat.

Bonners Ferry Ranger District, Panhandle National Forests

The Bonners Ferry Ranger District is bordered by the Sandpoint Ranger District on the south, the Priest Lake Ranger District on the west, Canada on the north and Montana on the east. It has some of the Panhandle's deepest forests, handsomest mountains under 7,600 feet, prettiest small lakes, and splashiest waterfalls. Much of this district comprises backcountry fit to please the most intrepid backpacker. There are also several short hikes and interpretive trails, especially in the popular Copper Falls and Robinson Lake areas flanking the Moyie River in the far northeast corner of the state.

The **Selkirk Crest Trail System** follows the rugged mountain crest between the Purcell Trench and Priest Lake. Over two dozen lakes shimmer invitingly in the cirque basins. The headiest elevations skip from 5,000 to 7,600 feet. The **Idaho Centennial Trail's** northerly leg merges with this trail system. To reach the Selkirk Crest Trail System, take Hwy 2 north from Naples to FS Road 402 at Snow Creek Falls. Several trailheads on FS Road 402 access trails south to Ruby Ridge and north to the Myrtle Creek Game Reserve.

A bewildering network of Forest Service and logging roads, penetrating virtually every corner of this district, affords good trail access.

Summer cabins and private homes are accessed via these unimproved roads. It is strongly recommended that you stick to mapped roads and trails and treat private property with respect. Be on the alert for bears, particularly grizzlies, and for hunters in season. I may sound like an over-protective parent, but being aware of possible pitfalls is essential when hiking in unfamiliar territory.

Take time to confer with the Bonners Ferry Ranger District office (Route 4, Box 4860, Bonners Ferry, ID 83805. ☎ 208-267-5561) to determine which trails may best suit your inclinations and levels of expertise.

Priest Lake Ranger District, Panhandle National Forests

If I may be permitted to play favorites, the Priest Lake area has my vote. Perhaps it's due to the contrast between dense conifer forests and that

The Panhandle

unbelievably pristine lake. While other lakes have been abused by pollution, by over use and commercial exploitation, Priest Lake's relative remoteness has ensured that its deep cool waters remain as close to their original glacier-formed state as is possible in this age of heedless progress.

This Brigadoon-like situation even extends to snakes and plants. You'll find poisonous species of neither in the Priest Lake area. Wild huckleberries abound. But every basket of berries conceals a thorn. If you wish to search for the area's famous morel mushrooms, be sure you know how to distinguish them from poisonous fungiforms.

It would be hard to find a hiking trail that does not lead to sunlit wild huckleberry patches or morel mushrooms secreted on the humus-rich forest floor. Searching out morels in spring, summer and fall and picking abundant wild huckleberries from mid-July through August are but two of the delights of this idyllic place. But remember: bears like huckleberries, too.

Like the other Panhandle National Forests ranger districts, the Priest Lake District has more hiking trails than space permits describing. You can locate the backpacking trail of your dreams by perusing a district travel map and conferring with a knowledgeable ranger. The Forest Service makes available a booklet describing the area's most popular trails. The following are some samples.

The **Salmo-Priest area** in the district's northwest corner laps over into Washington, a portion of which is designated as wilderness. Wildlife includes the remnants of Idaho's once-numerous caribou and grizzly bears. The trails system varies from lush old-growth cedar and hemlock forests along the Upper Priest River tributaries to near alpine conditions on 7,572-foot Snowy Top Mountain. The **Little Snowy Top Trail**, with 72 switchbacks, is the most difficult in the district. To access the trails system, take FS Road 1013 off FS Road 302 at Granite Pass.

Granite Falls Trail #301, in the Roosevelt Grove of Ancient Cedars Area (see *Touring*), is at the other extreme of the Priest Lake area's hiking trail ratings.

If rivers and waterfalls thrill you, strike out along the **Upper Priest River/Upper Priest Falls Trail #308**. This seven-mile trail through Idaho's largest cedar forest keeps the river in sight. The often wet trail (wear waterproof boots) dips into numerous springs, creeks and bogs. Boardwalks span the wettest spots. You'll be rewarded by splendid falls just south of the Canadian border (the river flows into Idaho from Canada). This trail is also accessed via FS Road 1013.

The **Beach Trail** and the **Lakeshore National Recreation Trail** meander along the western shore of the lake. The former extends for nine miles from Outlet Bay at the south end of the lake to Kalispell Bay. The latter begins at Beaver Creek and continues south along the lake for 7.6 miles. Both trails are rated "easy." Access to the Lakeshore Trail is via FS Road 1339 from Nordman.

The **Navigation Trail** extends for 10 miles from Beaver Creek, also accessed via FS Road 1339, to FS Road 1013. Ambitious backpackers can spend weeks hiking the entire system of trails west and north of Priest Lake. Some trails interconnect.

If you prefer to do your backpacking without the hassle of locating the best trails and purchasing specialized equipment, you can hire someone else to do it all for you. The following licensed outfitters, members of the Idaho Outfitters and Guides Association (IOGA), offer guided backpacking trips.

Backpacking Outfitters

- **Priest Lake Guide Service** offers customized backpacking trips ranging from one-day hikes to a seven-day Backcountry Adventure. Gary and Pepi Brookshire provide gourmet backcountry meals and all the equipment you'll need. They also offer mountain biking, snowmobiling, and fishing trips. They can arrange horse pack trips and other adventures in conjunction with other outfitters. HCR 5 Box 175 F, Priest Lake, ID 83856-9611. ☎ 800-453-7547. Fax 208-443-0118. E-mail: prstlake@micron.net.

- **Rugg's Outfitting** offers customized hiking trips in the Panhandle National Forests from late spring into early autumn. Head Guide R. Keith Rugg, a Western artist and illustrator, knows where to find the most colorful wildflowers and the most exciting animal sightings. 50 Dry Creek Road, Superior, MT 59872. ☎/Fax 406-822-4240 or 3064. E-mail: spr4240@montana.com or spr3064@montana.com.

Travel with Pack Animals or Horses

North Idaho folk have been getting there with the aid of horses and pack animals of various descriptions since well before gold was discovered in these parts. Most of the Panhandle's backcountry trails are recommended for both horse and foot travel. Some are open to pack animals, but not to horseback riders. Ranger district travel maps indicate restricted trails. Check with the local ranger district office before your plans jell if you will be bringing your own steed and wish to ride or pack into the backcountry.

If you won't be traveling with the family horses in tow you have three options for getting some riding in and/or experiencing pack trips into the backcountry.

1) Though hardly epic adventures, day-long trail rides are always fun. 2) Several licensed outfitters offer multi-day horseback riding and pack-supported trips into the backcountry.

3) Guest ranches offer plenty of riding, plus other fun activities. These are listed under *Where to Stay and Eat*.

Most outfitters offering horseback and/or pack-supported treks double as hunting and/or fishing guides. Some offer specific photography trips. However, every trip is a photographer's windfall, given the Panhandle's endless photo opportunities.

Be sure to ask plenty of questions when choosing an outfitter. What kind of terrain is covered on the trip? Are tents provided, or will you be expected to sleep in the open? What clothing should you bring? What will the weather be like? Are riders matched to horses on the basis of ability and prior riding experience? Is the trip in question suitable for kids?

If you are considering a horseback trip and don't own a pair of Western riding boots, consider purchasing a pair; at least, bring leather-soled footwear with distinct heels. Hiking boots or running shoes can become stuck in the stirrups, causing you to be dragged should you lose your seat. Better to fall off the horse. Be realistic about your riding experience. Passing yourself off as an experienced rider when you've been on a horse three times in your life can have serious consequences. Conscientious outfitters match horses' temperaments to riders' experience for a reason. The right match can make the difference between an enjoyable adventure and emergency evacuation to the nearest hospital.

All that said, the right combination of guide or outfitter, common sense and backcountry terrain should result in a terrific trip. The following Panhandle outfitters offer horseback trips. All are IOGA members. Reservations are advisable.

Day Ride Outfitters

- **Coeur d'Alene River Big Game Outfitters** offers day-long rides on Independence and Coeur d'Alene River trails. Gary and Jan Sylte, E. 11400 Nunn Road, Athol, ID 83801. ☎ 208-683-2154.

- **Rider Ranch**, east of Lake Coeur d'Alene, has day rides, evening dinner rides, hayrides and sleigh rides in winter. ☎ 208-667-3373.

- **Schweitzer Mountain Resort** runs day rides using sturdy Icelandic horses. ☎ 208-263-9555.

- **Western Pleasure**, in the Sandpoint area, offers horseback rides. ☎ 208-263-9066.

Overnight Outfitters

- **Coeur d'Alene River Big Game Outfitters** offers customized weekend horseback trips into the Coeur d'Alene River backcountry. Gary and Jan Sylte, E. 11400 Nunn Road, Athol, ID 83801. ☎ 208-683-2154.

- **Lost Lakes Outfitters** runs horseback trips through Lewis & Clark and Nez Perce Trail country to a camp in the vicinity of three "lost lakes." Trips include fishing for cutthroat trout and sighting moose, otter and feathered wildlife. HC66, Box 226, Kooskia, ID 83539. ☎ 208-926-4988.

- **Moyie River Outfitters** has half-day to seven-day pack-supported horseback trips in the Selkirk Crest, Long Canyon Wilderness and Purcell Range country. Guests fish the Kootenai River and look in on old mines, trappers' cabins, the Kootenai Indian Reservation and other points of interest. In late summer, Stanley and Dolores Sweet offer a weekend "city slickers camp" in the mountains. Guests ride along while the Sweets move cattle to a different range. HCR 85 Box 54, Bonners Ferry, ID 83805. ☎ 208-267-2108.

- **Priest Lake Guide Service** will arrange trail rides and overnight horse pack trips in the Priest Lake Ranger District. Gary and Pepi Brookshire, HCR 5 Box 175 F, Priest Lake, ID 83856-9611. ☎ 800-453-7547. Fax 208-443-0118. E-mail: prstlake@micron.net.

- **Ridgerunner Outfitters** offers summer horseback pack trips from their base camp on Big Creek in the Clearwater

The Panhandle

National Forest. Trips emphasize fishing high mountain lakes and streams, but fishing is only one of the backcountry adventures on offer. Ray and Mary Dawn Christopherson, PO Box 1193, Kamiah, ID 83536-1193. ☎ 208-935-0757. Fax 208-935-0398.

- **Rugg's Outfitting** runs custom pack-supported trips in the Panhandle National Forests from late spring through early autumn. Trips to high country lakes include fishing for rainbow and cutthroat trout. Some trips traverse the Idaho/Montana Stateline Trail, where snowfields linger into August. R. Keith Rugg, 50 Dry Creek Road, Superior, MT 59872. ☎/Fax 406-822-4240 or 3064. E-mail: spr4240@montana.com or spr3064@montana.com.

- **Triple "O" Outfitters** offers seven-day van-supported horseback trips over the Lewis & Clark Trail. Harlan and Barbara Opdahl, Box 217, Pierce, ID 83546. ☎ 208-464-2349 or 2761.

- **World Class Outfitting Adventures** has mule-supported pack trips in the Selway Bitterroot Wilderness area, ranging from two to six days in length. Some excursions include fishing on the Selway River. Jason and Carolyn Clinkenbeard, PO Box 351, Arlee, MT 59821. ☎ 800-203-3246. Fax 406-726-3466.

On Wheels

Cycling & Mountain Biking

North Idaho has a zillion trails open to mountain bikes. The majority are in Panhandle National Forests ranger districts, but some are accessed at ski resorts. Most trails are open to both mountain bikers and hikers, meaning that courtesy toward hikers is a must. Make your approach known well in advance with a friendly greeting, or ring your bell. Use caution when approaching a blind corner. Slow to a walk when passing walkers. Watch for horses on multi-use trails. Coming up behind horses and pack animals without warning can spook the animals, causing serious accidents. Give animals a wide berth when passing and follow horseback riders' directions for safe passing. Some horses are less tolerant of bikes than others.

Refer to *On Foot* for trail descriptions. Some trails fall into the family fun category, but many challenge advanced bikers. Obtain a travel map of the ranger district of interest to you. These maps indicate trail restrictions, multi-use trails, and those limited to two or three uses, such as hiking and biking. A few trails are for hikers only. Ask for a copy of the Forest Service's *Northern Panhandle Mountain Bike Guide*.

Moscow, Coeur d'Alene, Sandpoint, Bonners Ferry, Wallace and most recreation areas have shops where you can rent bikes. Contact the applicable chamber of commerce for a current list.

Some Sample Bike Trails

Mountain biking is big on the **Palouse.** You can even bike in Hog Heaven. No kidding. That's the moniker for a wide-open network of smooth dirt roads and single track where the eastern Palouse meets the northern Rockies. Moderate to more difficult trails vary from one mile to an 18-mile loop. Trails are mostly up at the beginning, with downgrades on the return laps. **Hog Heaven** is accessed at the Giant White Pine area campground on Idaho 6, 18 miles east of the US 95 junction. You may find a trail guide at the campground, or pick up a copy of the *Mountain Bike Guide to Hog Heaven* at Moscow bookstores or bike shops.

Centennial Trail, a paved path not to be confused with the Idaho State Centennial Trail described in *On Foot*, offers a pleasant way for cyclists to take in some beauty spots in the Post Falls/Coeur d'Alene area. The trail begins at City Park in downtown Coeur d'Alene, hugs the lake shore, looks in on Higgins Point, then follows the Spokane River to the Washington line.

The Forest Service's **Canfield Mountain Trail System**, south of Hayden Lake, is designed for use by both mountain bikes and motorized bikes. These 32 miles of trails within the Fernan Ranger District have elevation changes of from 220 to 1,420 feet and are suitable for intermediate to advanced skill levels. Some trails are steep, with ruts, rocks, roots, steep dropoffs and other obstacles. A trail system map is available at the Fernan Ranger District office in Coeur d'Alene. The trail system is accessible from the Shooting Range parking lot. Take Exit 15 off I-90 and head east 5½ miles on County Road 108. This road becomes FS Road 268 at the National Forest boundary. The parking lot is at the junction of FS Roads 268 and 1562.

Silver Mountain Resort, off I-90 at Kellogg, offers great biking. Ride the gondola to the top and bike down or branch out over six trails. Terrain includes a plush drainage through elk habitat, an abandoned railroad bed, a gnarly rock slide, steep ski slopes and views that don't quit. Pick up a copy of the *Silver Mountain Bike Guide* from the information booth at the base of the mountain. ☎ 208 783-1111.

Schweitzer Mountain Resort, 11 miles north of Sandpoint, also does double duty as a ski resort in winter and a bikers' heaven from late June through early September. You can take a chair lift to the summit for expert trails, but other trails can be accessed from the resort complex. This large trail system has offerings from 1½ miles to 5.7 miles in length. Difficulty is rated moderate to expert. Terrain includes alpine meadows strewn with wildflowers and top-of-the-world views. Mountain bikes are available for rent at the resort's Alpine Shop. ☎ 208 263-9555 or 800-831-8810 .

Farragut State Park's nine miles of level trails loop through meadows and forests on old naval roads – ideal for family biking. There are off-road trails as well. Pick up a trail map at the park entrance. A self-guiding tour guide is available for purchase.

A 29-mile loop along the **Lake Pend Oreille shoreline**, skirting the Pend Oreille River and looking in on the Morton Slough Game Preserve affords pleasant biking for skill levels ranging from beginner to intermediate. A portion of this route is on well-traveled roads. Begin at the bike path behind the courthouse in Sandpoint.

In the Priest Lake area, the **Lakeshore** and **Navigation trails** are especially popular with mountain bikers. Both trails begin at the Beaver Creek Campground, the Lakeshore Trail headiug south along Priest Lake, the Navigation Trail striking north along Upper Priest Lake.

Guided Biking Trips

You may prefer to let someone else handle the logistics of your multi-day bike trip. Ask questions. Will the terrain match your biking ability? What is included in the price? Is the trip van-supported? What kinds of bikes are used? What extra equipment is offered? What do you need to bring?

Biking Outfitters

- **Lewis & Clark Trail Adventures** offers mountain bike trips over the Lolo, Lewis & Clark, and Nez Perce Trails. PO Box 9051, Missoula, MT 59807. ☎ 406-728-7609.

- **Priest Lake Guide Service** has one-day to seven-day mountain biking adventures for beginners up to seasoned trail riders. Multi-day trips include camping in some of the area's most scenic backcountry caribou and grizzly bear habitat. Gary and Pepi Brookshire, HCR 5 Box 175 F, Priest

Lake, ID 83856-9611. ☎ 800-453-7547. Fax 208-443-0118. E-mail: prstlake@micron.net.

ATVs, Dirt Bikes, 4-Wheelers

ATVs and other noise-makers may be anathema to hikers and mountain bikers, but for others they are where the action is. Most ranger district trails have restrictions prohibiting motorized bikes and 4-wheelers. Some permit ATVs and dirt bikes. Before setting out, contact the ranger district in the area that strikes your fancy to obtain a backcountry travel map, and to determine which trails are open to which toys.

Wallace

ATVs and their ilk may be shunned in some places, but not in **Wallace**. The old mining town nestled in a bowl just west of the Montana line welcomes ATVs with boundless enthusiasm. An open-streets ordinance passed by canny city fathers means that ATV riders and snowmobilers can access the 1,000-mile network of backcountry trails surrounding Wallace (some are in nearby Montana) literally from their doorsteps. It would be hard to dispute the claim that **Wallace Silver Country Trails** is the world's largest trail system for ATVs, dirt bikes and snowmobiles.

Picture it: Step outside after breakfasting in a cozy B&B, rev up and buzz off for a morning's ride without first loading your ATV on and off a trailer. When the hungries strike, you simply zip back into town for lunch. Afterward, you're off to explore more trails. At sundown, it's back to town for dinner. Park your ATV at, say, the Jameson Restaurant, where the Old West is in full swing. ATV and Old West: some cool adventure combination.

Call ☎ 800-N-IDA-FUN for a guide to Wallace Silver Country Trails and Silver Country's central reservation service. Access information via the Internet at www.silver-country.com.

On Water

If your brand of adventure involves playing in water, on water or under water, then North Idaho, with upwards of 140 lakes and 2,000 miles of rivers and streams, is your kind of place. Few areas of this size offer such a variety of aquatic choices. You can vacation almost without setting foot on dry land. Three big natural lakes, a giant reservoir, numerous small lakes, rivers ranging from placid to fractious, plus silvery mountain streams offer lake excursions and superb whitewater rafting, kayaking, canoeing, scuba diving, fly and drift boat fishing, swimming and more. Heaping helpings of splendid scenery are featured on every activity menu.

Whitewater Rafting

The Panhandle's brace of ructious rivers, the **Lochsa** and **Moyie**, keep a lower profile than the mighty Salmon Rivers and the Snake through Hells Canyon. But don't discount their appeal. They're at their feistiest in late spring and early summer when melting mountain snows swell the rapids. As summer ripens, they quiet down like chastened puppies. The Lochsa and Moyie appeal to serious whitewater enthusiasts who want Class IV and V rapids. Unlike many Idaho rivers, which run through arid and semi-arid country, this brace of rivers slices through lush green mountain valleys of unparalleled beauty.

Unless you are an experienced whitewater rafter and have access to the necessary equipment, don't attempt to raft the Lochsa and Moyie on your own.

Floaters, strong swimmers not excepted, should always wear life jackets when on the water. A wetsuit is a good idea on the friskier rivers and for early season warmth.

The **Selway River** between Selway Falls and Lowell is a laid-back stretch of river that's perfect for day floats. Don't confuse it with the Upper Selway winding through the Selway-Bitterroot Wilderness Area. See page 247 for information on that wild river adventure.

If you wish to float your own boat, consider the **Lower Selway** or the **Priest River** between Outlet Campground and the town of Priest River. Rapids on this stretch seldom exceed Class III. Rafts may drag the bottom due to low water after mid-July, but water volume picks up in the fall. The **Upper Coeur d'Alene River** also lends itself to self-floating. Like all mountain rivers, water levels are highest in spring and early summer. The upper segments of the 120-mile-long Wild and Scenic **St. Joe River** can be challenging, but the lower segments afford great family floating. Contact the Priest Lake, Wallace and/or St. Joe Ranger Districts to obtain detailed information on floating these scenic rivers.

The following outfitters offer trips on the Lochsa, Selway and Moyie. These rivers' relatively short courses translate to shorter trips, worth considering if cost is a factor.

As always, ask questions when contacting a river outfitter. Are wetsuits, helmets and booties provided for Lochsa and Moyie trips? If it's a multi-day trip, will you sleep in tents or on the ground? What about the weather? Cold nights often linger through June in these northern reaches.

Whitewater Outfitters

- **Holiday River & Bike Expeditions, Inc.** runs two-day descents of the Lochsa River. 544 East 3900 South, Salt Lake City, UT 84107. ☎ 800-624-6323. Fax 801-266-1448.

- **Moyie River Outfitters** offers one-day whitewater rafting on the Moyie, and Kootenai River day floats. HCR 85 Box 54, Bonners Ferry, ID 83805. ☎ 208-267-2108.

- **ROW, Inc.** (River Odysseys West and Remote Odysseys Worldwide) has one-day June trips on the Moyie and one-day June and July Lower Selway River floats. Owners and experienced river guides Betsy Bowen and Peter Grubb also offer one- to three-day Lochsa River trips beginning in early May and extending into July. Ask about one-day May floats on the Wild and Scenic St. Joe River. ROW, Inc., PO Box 579, Coeur d'Alene, ID 83816. ☎ 800-451-6034. Fax 208-667-6506.

- **Three Rivers Rafting,** based at Three Rivers Resort on US 12 in Lowell, runs one-day floats on the Lochsa and Lower Selway. Extended trips are also available. HC 75 Box 61, Kooskia at Lowell, ID 83539. ☎ 208-926-4430.

Kayaking & Canoeing

In North Idaho, your kayak or canoe is sure to spend more time in the water than on the roof of your car.

The early season **Moyie** and **Lochsa** challenge the most skilled kayakers. Kayak the quieter **Lower Selway** in spring and early summer for a taste of whitewater, later in the season for laid-back playing.

The **Priest River** between Outlet Campground at the southern end of Priest Lake and the town of Priest River has several kayak and canoe put-ins. The **Upper Coeur d'Alene** and **St. Joe Rivers** also excel as kayaking and canoeing rivers. Fact is, there's hardly a waterway winding through the Panhandle's backcountry and settled terrain that doesn't beg you to launch a kayak or a canoe.

Don't discount North Idaho's Big Three lakes and Dworshak Reservoir for plenty of kayaking and canoeing fun. You can spend days exploring the shorelines, an especially enjoyable pastime on less-developed Priest Lake and along the rugged eastern shore of **Lake Pend Oreille. Lake Coeur d'Alene**'s secluded arms and bays also beg to be explored, but do stick to the shoreline. This slender sprawling lake may appear to be one big playpool, but it's also a commercial waterway threaded by day-cruise boats and tugs hauling huge brailles of logs.

The Panhandle's Hidden Lakes

You may prefer to canoe one or more of the Panhandle's smaller lakes. From the air, they resemble glittering sapphires strewn over the landscape by some generous deity. Some, such as **Spirit** and **Twin Lakes**, are easily accessed by paved roads. Others, like **Chase Lake** in the Priest Lake Ranger District, are tucked into the landscape off Forest Service roads. Contact the ranger district in the area where you wish to frolic to obtain a map showing the locations of these "hidden" lakes.

Canoeing the Coeur d'Alene River is one of life's simpler pleasures.

Among the great pleasures of canoeing North Idaho's lakes and rivers is the opportunity to view feeding waterfowl and deer, moose and other animals drinking at dusk. Osprey nests balance atop pilings in some areas. They are especially evident where Lake Coeur d'Alene disperses into Lakes Chatcolet and Benewah and at the mouth of the St. Joe River.

I recall an idyllic summer day canoeing the lazy Coeur d'Alene River. We paddled past a changing procession of wildlife in wetlands and along higher shorelines. It was like a film, only we, not the birds and animals, were moving. And they were watching us.

Boating & Other Fun Things to Do

If you trailer a boat, this part of the state is for you. Boating and waterskiing enjoy most-favored recreation status on Dworshak Reservoir, Lake Coeur d'Alene, Lake Pend Orielle and, to a somewhat lesser extent, on Priest Lake. These lakes also offer ideal sailing and wind surfing conditions. There are few limits to the scope offered by these big pools of water. Smaller lakes, such as Spirit and Hayden, also offer fun boating.

Most caveats are covered by universal rules of boating courtesy, but each lake has guidelines pertinent to local conditions. Obtain a lake chart before launching your craft. Marinas have charts for sale and are usually glad to offer local boating tips. Some marinas rent power boats, sailboats, personal watercraft, waterskis and/or other equipment. Those that do are listed below under specific lake headings.

Public boat ramps and docks are conveniently on every lake. They are quite numerous on the larger lakes. Public boat access points are designated with bright yellow pilings and docks easily seen from the water.

Dworshak Reservoir is 53 miles long and has 184 miles of shoreline, much of it secluded. Grandad Creek, Dent Acres, Freeman Creek and Canyon Creek boat ramps are open in summer. Bruces Eddy boat ramp is available summer weekends and holidays only. The Big Eddy launch ramp, two miles north of the dam, is open year-round and has marina facilities. Mini-camps scattered along the shoreline include 125 camping sites for boat access only. Stop at the Dam Visitor Center or Big Eddy Marina to obtain a recreation brochure; or request a copy from Dworshak Project, PO Box 48, Ahsahka, ID 83620. ☎ 208-476-3294.

Lake Coeur d'Alene covers 25,100 acres, is about 25 miles long and has 135 miles of shoreline. The average depth is 120 feet. For over a hundred years, this lake has doubled as a popular recreational lake and a busy commercial waterway. The waters at the head of the lake, near the city of Coeur d'Alene, are often crowded, especially on summer weekends.

 Be on the lookout for commercial craft when boating, and particularly when waterskiing. Never ski too close to, or cut across in front of these craft. Quick braking and agile maneuvering is not in tugs' job descriptions. Be mindful of log booms along the shoreline and "dead head" logs lurking just below the surface. These pose a navigational hazard, especially at night.

If you can do it on water, you're pretty sure to be able to do it on this versatile lake. Windsurfing, sailing, waterskiing, jet skiing... you name it.

The Panhandle

Marinas, docks and boat ramps are at several points around the lake. Pick up a chart and a map at any marina. Considering the popularity of this lake, it's surprising that few marinas have boats for rent. Those that do:

- **Best Western Templin's Resort**, on the Spokane River in Post Falls, has pontoon boats, paddle boats and canoes for rent. ☎ 208-773-1611.

- **Boardwalk Marina**, operated in conjunction with the Coeur d'Alene Resort. ☎ 208-765-4000 or call the Resort at 800-688-5253.

- **Gateway Resort & Marina** in Harrison has boats for rent. ☎ 800-FUN-IDAHO.

- **Squaw Bay Resort**, at the northeast end of the lake. ☎ 208-664-6782.

Lake Pend Oreille is Idaho's largest lake, with over 90,000 surface acres. It is 43.2 miles long and 6.25 miles wide, has depths up to 1,150 feet, and includes 111.3 miles of shoreline, much of it thickly wooded. The eastern shore has steep slopes. Launch ramps are available around most of the lake, except for the rugged eastern shore. The most popular launch locations are at the southern tip of the lake at Bayview and Farragut State Park, at Hope on Idaho 200 at the northeastern end, and in the Sandpoint area. Marinas are at Sandpoint, Bayview and Hope. Ask about the best scuba diving locations while picking up your map and chart.

The following marinas make boats and other water toys available for rent:

- **Bottle Bay Resort**, on the west shore opposite Sandpoint. ☎ 208-263-5916.

- **East Hope Marina** rents boats and all sorts of aquatic toys. ☎ 208-263-3083.

- **Holiday Shores Marina**, also at Hope. ☎ 208-264-5514.

- **Hope Marine Services, Inc.** ☎ 208-264-5105.

- **MacDonald's Hudson Bay Resort**, at the south end of the lake next to Farragut State Park. ☎ 208-683-2211.

- **Sandpoint Marina**, owned by the same company as East Hope Marina. ☎ 208-263-3083.

- **Windbag**, on City Beach in Sandpoint. ☎ 208-263-7811.

Priest Lake is really two lakes connected by a slow-moving 2½-mile river dubbed "The Thoroughfare." The lower lake is by far the larger part of this 25-mile-long lake system. The lake's 26,000 acres are of such exceptional purity and clarity as to easily qualify this as Idaho's most pristine lake. Boating and waterskiing are permitted, and it's much less crowded than more readily accessible lakes. Most boaters are thoroughly caught up in Priest Lake's north country aura. Throttle down and watch a gaggle of boys diving from a granite outcropping à la Huck Finn, or a mama duck leading a covey of downy ducklets in stately procession.

Numerous boat ramps and docks ring the lake. Lakeside lodges and resorts have docking facilities for guests trailering boats. Most have boats available for rent.

■ **Priest Lake Marina** also rents boats. ☎ 208-443-2405.

Much smaller **Hayden, Spirit, Hauser** and **Twin Lakes** offer fun boating but have fewer boat ramps and docks.

■ **Tobler Marina** at E. 3400 S. Hayden Lake Road (☎ 208-772-3255) has boat and jet ski rentals.

■ **Lake Haven Resort** on Spirit Lake has boat rentals. ☎ 800-610-3800 or 208-623-2791.

Houseboating

Houseboating is a laid-back option for enjoying these big, beautiful lakes. Several companies rent houseboats for periods of a few days to a week or more.

These houses on pontoons are pretty much standardized, having one or more bedrooms, a bath with shower and a galley.

Before You Rent a Houseboat

■ What is included in the price?

■ Do they charge extra for linens, kitchen utensils and dishes?

■ What should you bring in addition to groceries and libations?

■ Is the houseboat equipped with a depth finder? What about a barbeque grill?

■ Does it have a full bath or just a shower?

■ Is it equipped with a radio or other means of communication?

■ Is a lake chart posted on board?

The Panhandle

- Expect a thorough orientation tour, including a test run, before taking the boat out. This should include familiarity with the controls, a feel for how the boat handles, an understanding of how every aspect of the craft works, and measures to be taken in the event of engine failure or other emergencies.

The following companies rent houseboats. Make reservations well in advance, especially for popular summer weekends.

- **Dock Holidays Houseboat Vacations** rents houseboats on Lake Coeur d'Alene. PO Box 665, Coeur d'Alene, ID 83816. ☎ 208-772-5415.

- **Gateway Resort and Marina** in Harrison, at the southern end of Lake Coeur d'Alene. ☎ 800-FUN-IDAHO.

- Houseboating on pristine Priest Lake can be a delightfully laid-back experience. Contact **Excursions Northwest** to rent a houseboat on this quintessential north country lake. 6525 N. Walnut Road, Spokane, WA. 99207. ☎ 509-926-9196.

Day Cruises

Day cruises are hardly wild adventures, but are enjoyable. Most cruises are narrated. Some companies offer lunch, brunch or dinner cruises.

- **Anchors Aweigh** operates luxury motor yacht day cruises from the 11th Street Marina on Lake Coeur d'Alene. They also feature cocktail and dinner cruises and custom charters. 3525 Fruitland Lane, #18, Coeur d'Alene, ID 83814. ☎ 208-765-0273.

- **Lake Coeur d'Alene Cruises Fun Fleet** is operated in conjunction with Coeur d'Alene Resort. Five large paddle-wheelers depart frequently from Independence Point, just west of the Resort, cruising the northern bays or the length of the lake into the mouth of the St. Joe River. Theme cruises include Sunday brunch and sunset dinner cruises. ☎ 800-365-8338, ext. 7123 to request a brochure.

- *Spokane River Queen* departs Templin's Hotel Marina in Post Falls on cruises of the Spokane River and Lake Coeur d'Alene. Daily cruises and dinner and starlight cruises are offered. ☎ 208-773-1611.

- **Lake Pend Oreille Cruises** departs Sandpoint's City Beach daily in summer for scenic afternoon tours of the northern end of the lake. ☎ 208-263-4598.

Fishing

North Idaho anglers come up with a whopping third of the record fish caught in Idaho. There's something about these deep, expansive cold water lakes that grows 'em big. Lake Pend Oreille's kamloops and bull trout sometimes weigh in at a hefty 30 pounds. Lake Coeur d'Alene's huge chinook salmon and cutthroat trout are legendary. Chinook feed on Kokanee salmon, which are so common that they're considered North Idaho's "bread and butter" fish. Many of the smaller lakes, such as Hauser, Fernan and Twin Lakes, are leaping with bass.

Panhandle rivers and streams, cold-water waterways, almost without exception, support big populations of native brook, bull, brown, cutthroat and rainbow trout and whitefish. Cutthroats are most numerous. Hatchery-raised rainbow trout are released into selected streams.

Preparing for a Fishing Trip

Obtain copies of the Idaho Department of Fish & Game's *Official Guide to Fishing in Idaho* and *General Fishing Seasons and Rules* before even thinking about fishing Panhandle waters. Available at bait and sports shops where fishing licenses are sold. Or request copies from Idaho Department of Fish & Game (600 S. Walnut, Boise, ID 83707. ☎ 208-334-3700. Fax 208-334-2114. E-mail: idfginfo@state.id.us). Idaho fishing information is available at ☎ 1-800-ASK-FISH. For Panhandle Region fishing information, ☎ 208-769-1414. For Clearwater Region fishing information, ☎ 208-799-5010. The Lochsa and Selway Rivers and a big chunk of country north of US 12 is included in the Clearwater Region.

Catch and release rules apply in some waters. Consult the rule book for the regulations that apply to the waters you wish to fish. Voluntary catch and release is encouraged.

You are allowed to add a bonus of 10 brook trout taken from most Idaho streams to your trout limit. Consult the rule book for current limits and other information.

Anglers 14 years of age and older must have a **valid fishing license** issued by the Idaho Department of Fish & Game. Non-resident children under 14 may fish without a license if accompanied by a licensed adult. The adult must include the child's catch in his or her bag limit. Licenses are available at local license vendors or at any Idaho Fish & Game office. ☎ 1-800-554-8685 for credit card purchaes. A small service fee will be charged.

Sometimes obtaining the services of a guide who knows where the big ones are results in a more satisfactory fishing trip than does winging it on your own. As you should when booking any outfitted trip, ask lots of questions before committing. Be sure you understand which items of gear are supplied and which you need to bring along. Ask about clothing; cold, wet weather is no stranger to North Idaho. Wet feet and insufficient warm clothing does nothing to enhance your fishing expedition.

The following outfitters offering fishing trips in North Idaho are members of Idaho Outfitters and Guides Association (IOGA), a strictly regulated professional association whose members adhere to rigid rules of ethics and responsibility. Pack trips, listed under *Travel with Pack Animals or Horses*, often include fishing in high mountain lakes and streams. So do some guest ranches, listed under *Where to Stay and Eat.*

Fishing Outfitters

■ **Priest Lake Guide Service** offers single-party day-charter fishing trips on Priest and Upper Priest Lakes for mackinaw lake trout and other cold water game fish. Veteran guide Gary Brookshire uses a custom-rigged 21½-foot boat that offers protection from the elements. Brookshire also guides chinook salmon and northern pike fishing trips on Lake Coeur d'Alene. HCR 5 Box 175 F, Priest Lake, ID 83856. ☎ 800-453-7547 or 208-443-2956.

■ **Renshaw Outfitting, Inc.** offers five-day fly or spin fishing trips from a deluxe tent camp on Weitas Creek in the Clearwater National Forest. The last five miles into camp are on horseback. Floored tents have wood heat. Jim Renshaw also offers pack mule and horse-supported seven-day fishing trips into high mountain country where lakes and streams are filled with native trout. PO Box 1165, Kamiah, ID 83536-1165. ☎ 800-452-2567 or 208-935-0726 or 926-4520.

- **Moyie River Outfitters** runs day fishing trips on the Kootenai River. HCR 5 Box 54, Bonners Ferry, ID 83805. ☎ 208-267-2108.

- **Ridgerunner Outfitters** emphasizes high mountain lake and stream fishing on their summer pack trips in the Clearwater National Forest. See *Travel with Pack Animals or Horses* (page 151).

- **World Class Outfitting Adventures** combines trout fishing and horseback riding in a two-day Selway River expedition. Jason and Carolyn Clinkenbeard also offer three or more days of cutthroat, bull trout and rainbow fishing from their Paradise base camp. The Selway is a catch and release river. PO Box 351, Arlee, MT 59821. ☎ 800-203-3246 or 406-726-3829. Fax 406-726-3466.

On Snow

Snow comes early to North Idaho and lingers well into spring. If you're into downhill and/or cross-country skiing or snowmobiling and hanker after a comparatively uncrowded playground, you would do well to consider the Panhandle.

Promoters of Schweitzer and Silver Mountain ski resorts may have entertained dreams of becoming a major ski destination similar to Sun Valley, but it hasn't happened. Why? Who knows? The Panhandle is easy enough to reach by flying into Spokane. The Coeur d'Alene Resort provides the most comfortable ski digs imaginable and is only a 45-minute drive from both downhill ski mountains. Not that Schweitzer and Silver Mountain are on the skids. Far from it. It's just that they attract more North Idaho and Eastern Washington skiers than they do jet-setters. This works to your advantage with minimal or no-wait lift lines and wide-open runs, especially in mid-week.

The Panhandle's large expanses of level and gently rolling terrain could have been deliberately placed to gladden the hearts of cross-country skiers. Farragut State Park, five Park n' Ski areas and US Forest Service trails offer hundreds of miles of prime cross-country ski terrain.

It would be no exaggeration to label Wallace the "Little Town that Could... and Did." A decade or so ago, when nearby Silver Mountain Ski Resort was a'building, Wallace folks expected to reap rich rewards by providing food and lodging for skiers. When reality set in, Wallace took a hard look at its back yard; a gorgeous wilderness laced by hundreds of miles of fabulous snowmobile trails. And Silver Country was born. Wallace's

The Panhandle

concept of door-to-trail snowmobiling quickly garnered national recognition as a world-class snowmobiling destination.

Wallace's amenities are unique, but it's far from being North Idaho's only snowmobile playground. Priest Lake and numerous other areas also offer great snowmobiling in a quintessential north country setting.

Preparing for a Ski Trip

Ease of access to these wintery playgrounds is weather-dependent. Main highways are generally plowed and salted, but can offer tough going, or even be closed, should a winter storm hit. The Panhandle's main arteries, I-90 and US Hwy 95, kept clear in all but the worst snowstorms, offer access to Wallace and downhill ski areas. Secondary roads are also plowed, while unimproved roads are sometimes cleared, depending on how much use they have.

Driving on snow is sometimes preferable to driving on roads that appear to be clear and dry. That's when you need to watch out for black ice. You can't see it, but you sure can feel it when your vehicle begins to behave like a drunk on roller blades.

Before starting out, ☎ 208-336-6600 for a current winter road report. Request a 4WD vehicle if renting a car. Pack emergency supplies if you intend to stray off the main highways. A tire-width board, a folding shovel and a bag of kitty litter or other gritty material are helpful if your car mires down. Pack a spirit stove, flares and emergency rations and blankets. Be sure to clear the snow from around your vehicle's tailpipe if you find yourself stuck in a snowbank and wish to run your engine for warmth.

Pack for extreme cold temperatures; never underestimate the fury of north country weather. Wear layers: silk or thermal long johns, turtle neck shirt, wool sweater, parka or windbreaker. Wool socks, waterproof boots, gaiters, a hat with ear flaps, wool gloves and a soft wool scarf are necessities. Layers allow you to remove or add clothing if you become over-warm or chilly. Wool or polypropylene is perferable to cotton. Snowmobilers should wear one-piece wind- and waterproof suits and helmets over hats with ear flaps.

Local sport and ski shops rent and sell winter sports needs. Contact the chambers of commerce or visitor bureaus in the areas you wish to cross-country ski or snowmobile to obtain a current listing of equipment sales and/or rental outlets.

Downhill Skiing

The Panhandle's three ski resorts are serviced by bus from Coeur d'Alene, Sandpoint and Wallace. Due to new management at Schweitzer, however, bus service is iffy at present, though it will probably be resumed. Call Schweitzer at ☎ 800-831-8810 for current busing information. In Wallace, guests of the Wallace Best Western, Wallace Inn, the Jameson Hotel and the Stardust Inn receive complimentary busing to both Silver Mountain Ski Resort and Lookout Pass Ski Area.

Two major ski resorts are in the ascendancy up here where the air is clear and the powder is deep, but a third very low-profile resort offers fun downhill skiing and nary a crowd. **Lookout Pass Ski Area** on the Idaho-Montana line, 13 miles east of Wallace, is especially handy if you are taking in Wallace's snowmobile scene and want to fit in a day of family skiing. The day lodge has a cafeteria, two ski schools, downhill and cross-country ski rentals and a ski shop. Twelve runs over 100 acres are accessed via a double chairlift and a rope tow. Elevation: 4,800 to 5,650 feet. Average annual snowfall: 350 inches. Open daily, late November-early April. Lookout Recreation, Inc., Box 108, Wallace, ID 83873. ☎ 208-744-1392 or 556-7211.

Silver Mountain Ski & Summer Resort, 71 miles east of Spokane at Kellogg, is easily reached via the I-90 corridor. The I-90 location means no winding access roads – a real boon in snow country. There is bus service here from the Coeur d'Alene Resort.

The lodge includes a cafeteria and lounge, a ski shop offering ski and snowboard rentals, and day care facilities. There are 50 named trails on 1,500 acres of developed terrain covering three peaks ranging from 5,700 to 6,300 feet, with a 2,200-foot vertical drop. Lifts include a gondola, a quad, two triples, two doubles and a surface tow. Runs are rated at 15% beginner, 45% intermediate and 40% advanced. Ski instruction is available for children ages five and up, and snowboarding instruction for ages 11 and up. Average annual snowfall: 300 inches. Open daily, late November-early April. Silver Mountain Ski & Summer Resort, 610 Bunker Ave., Kellogg, ID 83837-2200. ☎ 208-783-1111.

Schweitzer Mountain Resort boasts some of the most scenic snow country anywhere. Reached via a seven-mile drive over a well-maintained road off US 95 (the junction is eight miles north of Sandpoint), Schweitzer is both the least accessible and the largest of North Idaho's three ski areas. An overnight lodge and condos, two

The Panhandle

restaurants, night skiing, après ski fun and superb ski conditions make the trip worthwhile. Snowboarders are welcome. The resort also has six miles of cross-country ski trails.

The day lodge has a cafeteria and lounge, a ski shop offering ski and snowboard rentals, and day care. Ski lessons include several options for kids ages 3½ and up.

Trails include 55 named runs on 2,350 skiable acres accessed via one high-speed quad and five double chair lifts. The top elevation is 6,400 feet, the vertical drop 2,400 feet. Runs are rated at 20% beginner, 40% intermediate, 35% advanced and 5% expert. Average snowfall: 300 inches. Open daily, late November-early April.

Schweitzer Mountain Resort, Box 815, Sandpoint, ID 83864. ☎ 800-831-8810.

Cross-Country Skiing

North Idaho offers numerous choices for cross-country skiers. There seems to be no limit to the snow-packed trails snaking through the Panhandle. Most are but a few miles from warm lodgings and hot food – an important consideration in snow country.

Never forget that all the great snow comes from storms, some vicious enough to generate white-out conditions. They often come up with little notice. Check current and expected weather conditions before setting out, pack emergency supplies, and let someone know where you are going and when you expect to return. Never ski alone.

Three Panhandle state parks have Park 'n Ski areas. Call individual parks for detailed information.

- **Farragut State Park**'s former naval station roads become ski trails in winter. There are 7½ miles of groomed trails. The park is four miles east of Athol (25 miles northeast of Coeur d'Alene). ☎ 208-683-2425.

- **Round Lake State Park**'s three miles of trail following the forested shoreline are a beginner's and intermediate's delight. The park also has an ice skating area. ☎ 208-263-3489.

- **Priest Lake State Park**'s **Indian Creek Unit** has 12 miles of groomed trails. The **Soaring Eagle Trail** affords scenic lake views and is rated for intermediate and advanced skiers. Other trails are rated for beginners. The Indian

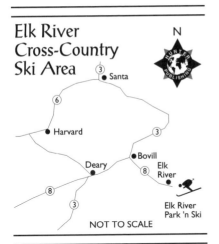

Creek Unit is on the east shore of Priest Lake, 33 miles north of the town of Priest River. ☎ 208-443-2200.

The National Forests include numerous trails for both beginner and expert skiers. Contact the ranger district overseeing your area of interest for current trail conditions and a map. The following trails are just for starters; ask about additional routes.

- The **Panhandle National Forests Fernan Ranger District** maintains three marked loop trails in the **English Point-Hayden Lake area** six miles north of Coeur d'Alene. Grades are generally level to easy. Take Lancaster Road off US 95 to English Point.

- The **4th of July Pass Park 'n Ski area** falls within the Fernan Ranger District. The 12 miles of trails are accessed from a Park 'n Ski trailhead at 4th of July Pass off I-90, 18 miles east of Coeur d'Alene. These trails are suitable for beginners, except for a few short, steep sections requiring advanced expertise.

- The **Mineral Point Trai (Lost Lake Loop) is in the Sandpoint Ranger District**. The 8.9-mile loop trail skirting the west shore of Lake Pend Oreille is suitable for intermediate skiers and some beginners. Deer and numerous species of birds are often sighted here. The trailhead is at the Garfield Bay Campground. Turn off US 95 toward Slagle.

- The **Snow Creek Winter Recreation Area**, a Park 'n Ski area, is in the Bonners Ferry Ranger District. The trailhead is on FS Road 402, off US 95 just south of Bonners Ferry.

The Panhandle

The 13 miles of periodically groomed trails traverse forests and meadows, affording views of the Selkirk Mountain Crest, and are suitable for all difficulty levels.

- Three trails in the **Wallace Ranger District** can be reached via I-90. Take Exit 43 at Kingston, then drive east for 16.8 miles on FS Road 620.

- The **Cedar Creek Trail** begins three miles south of the "Y" in the road at Prichard. This easy sloped trail follows an old road bed and the Coeur d'Alene River, then loops along another road bed to the trailhead.

- The **Cinnabar Trail** begins off FS Road 456, crosses the Cedar Creek Bridge, then follows a snowmobile trail for 1½ miles and continues on through forest and along the river. The last mile is steep, with switchbacks, until it meets FS Road 9.

- The **Kings Point Trail** begins off Trail Creek Road (FS Road 605) and climbs an 8% grade for nearly three miles through a clearcut area. No loop.

- **Hanna Flats at Priest Lake**, in the **Priest Lake Ranger District**, is a good beginners' trail. The marked, groomed loop trail travels through a stand of ancient cedars.

The following North Idaho cross-country trails are designated **Park 'n Ski trails** and are maintained by the Idaho Department of Parks and Recreation.

- The **Elk River ski area**, 20 miles east of Bovill on Idaho 8, adjacent to the community of Elk River, has 24 miles of groomed trails winding through forest and meadows with a look-in at Elk Creek Falls. A good choice for beginner and intermediate skiers.

- The **Palouse Divide Park 'n Ski Area** offers beginner and intermediate skiers 18 miles of trails where the Palouse meets the forested backcountry. Twelve miles of these trails are groomed as weather permits. The trailhead is on Idaho 6, 23 miles east of Potlatch.

Priest Lake Guide Service will be happy to oblige, if you prefer to just concentrate on skiing the Priest Lake area's winter wonderland while someone else leads the way. Pepi and Gary Brookshire teach cross-country skiing techniques and offer ski packages ranging from one-day treks to customized multi-day snow camping treks. They'll even furnish the skis, boots, and poles. Snowmobile in, ski out is also available. HCR 5 Box 175 F, Priest Lake, ID 83856. ☎ 800-453-7547 or 208-443-2956.

Snowmobiling in The Panhandle

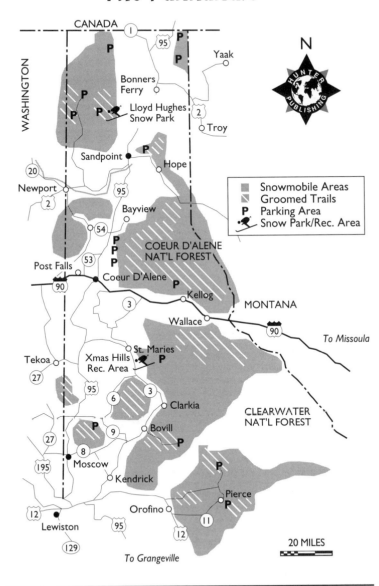

Snowmobiling

Westerners are having a sizzling love affair with snowmobiling and North Idaho is a highly favored rendezvous point.

Numerous backcountry trails attract serious snowmobilers from near and far. A huge chunk of backcountry, stretching from I-90 north to Lake Pend Oreille, bordered on the west by US 95 and on the east by Montana's Cabinet Mountains, is available to snowmobilers. Much of this territory includes groomed trails. Ditto, a big chunk of the Wallace and St. Joe Ranger Districts south of I-90, plus a wide swath northeast of Lake Pend Oreille. The Priest Lake area also offers great snowmobiling, both west of the lake and in the Selkirk Range to the east.

Contact the Idaho Department of Parks and Recreation (Box 83720, Boise, ID 83720-0065. ☎ 208-334-4199. Fax 208-334-3741) to obtain a map of Idaho's snowmobile areas. You can also contact the various ranger districts for information on snowmobile trails under their supervision, plus trail conditions and any restrictions that may be in force. Ask for a copy of *Idaho Snowmobile Laws & Riding Information.*

Snowmobiling can be a great adventure, but can quickly deteriorate into tragedy. Every winter snowmobilers become lost, wandering around the backcountry for days – or worse, dying there. Know your machine and how to repair it. Bring enough gas for an extended ride and pack tools with other emergency gear. Ride in a group and stay on groomed trails. If you should venture off groomed trails, be sure that someone in your party knows the country as well as he does his own house lot.

In **Wallace's Silver Country**, the whole town rolls out the white carpet for snowmobilers. The historic silver mining town is snowmobile-accessible, meaning it's okay to ride in the streets.

Upwards of 1,000 miles of snowmobile trails radiate from Wallace into the forested backcountry. You can rev up your machine on the very doorstep of your lodging. No driving to a trailhead and unloading, then loading up again at day's end. Call ☎ 800-NIDAFUN for more Silver Country information. Or access Silver Country on the Internet at www.silver-country.com.

The following sports shops rent, repair and sell snowmobiles. Contact area chambers of commerce/visitor centers for additional listings.

Snowmobile Sales & Rentals

- **H2O & Snow Sports Rentals**, PO Box 2022, Coeur d'Alene, ID 83816. ☎ 800-H2O-SNOW or 208-665-9933.
- **Orton's Cycle**, 513 Pine St., Wallace, ID 83873. ☎ 208-556-4402.
- **Silver Valley Performance**, PO Box 325, Wallace, ID 83873. ☎ 208-753-4141.

The following outfitters, all members of the Idaho Outfitters and Guides Association, offer guided snowmobile trips:

Guided Snowmobile Trips

- **North Idaho Tours** runs half-day and full-day guided snowmobile tours in the St. Joe country. 201 N. 8th St., St. Maries, ID 83861. ☎ 208-245-1046. Fax 208-245-4299.
- **Priest Lake Guide Service** will arrange customized snowmobile excursions in the forests and mountains surrounding Priest Lake. Gary and Pepi Brookshire, HCR 5 Box 175 F, Priest Lake, ID 83856. ☎ 800-453-7547 or 208-443-2956.
- **Triple "O" Outfitters, Inc.** offers guided and unguided overnight snowmobile trips on ungroomed trails in Lewis & Clark country in the Clearwater National Forest. Lodging is at Mex Mountain Work Center, a US Forest Service facility leased by Triple "O" for the winter months. Bring your own food, sleeping bag and other supplies. Harland and Barbara Opdahl, Box 217, Pierce, ID 83546. ☎ 208-464-2349.

Joining a snowmobile club ride is a great way to make new friends. Contact the following snowmobile clubs/associations for information on club rides.

- **Coeur d'Alene Snowmobile Association.** ☎ 208-772-4369.
- **St. Joe Snowmobile Club.** ☎ 208-245-2983.
- **Silver Valley Snowmobile Association.** ☎ 208-752-8411.

In the Air

The panorama of North Idaho's lakes, forests and mountains comes into magnificent focus when seen from the air. **Brooks Sea Plane Service** has been offering flights over Lake Coeur d'Alene and the Panhandle since 1946. Their excursion and charter flights originate from the City Dock, adjacent to downtown Coeur

The Panhandle

d'Alene. PO Box 1028, Coeur d'Alene, ID 83816. ☎ 208-664-2842 or 208-772-9059.

Some consider parasailing to be the ultimate free-floating adventure. Parasailing 500 feet above Lake Coeur d'Alene captures that experience. Take off and land from a boat. **Coeur d'Alene Parasail**'s motto: "If you can sit, you can fly!" 6115 Dower Rod, Coeur d'Alene, ID 83814. ☎ 208-765-5367 or 208-765-4627.

Silverwood Theme Park owes its existence to founding owner Gary Norton's love of antique aircraft. Nightly summer air shows using vintage planes are popular here. Glider rides and vintage airplane rides are also on offer. Take off from the park's own airstrip to literally soar above the crowds. ☎ 208-683-3400.

Eco-Travel

Wildlife Watching

 North Idaho wildlife is often literally in your face. On hiking trails, on lakes and rivers, even from your car, you're sure to spot osprey, bald eagles, deer, elk and many other animal and bird species. Flashes of color in the trees may herald a mountain bluebird. There's hardly a "best" place to watch for wildlife; it's everywhere. Happening on a deer at a turn in the trail, or spotting a bald eagle high in a cottonwood tree is surely one of life's more sublime experiences.

Accidental wildlife sightings are givens. But if you're a serious wildlife watcher, several prime wildlife viewing areas await your pleasure. Obtain a copy of Leslie Benjamin Carpenter's *Idaho Wildlife Viewing Guide* for descriptions of these habitats and information on the species frequenting them. Copies cost $6.25 and are available from Idaho Fish & Game, 600 S. Walnut, Box 25, Boise, ID 83707-0025.

North Idaho's **Watchable Wildlife** program, coordinated by state and federal agencies, makes it easier to spot and recognize wildlife species in accessible locations. Watch for Watchable Wildlife signs at participating wildlife viewing areas.

The following is a brief rundown of established wildlife viewing areas. Just remember to watch for wildlife wherever you happen to be. And bring along binoculars and/or a camera with a telephoto lens.

If it's moose you want, it's moose you'll get at **Musselshell Meadows** on FS Road 100 (turn off US 12 just before the Clearwater River bridge at Kamiah). This 100-acre area along marshy Musselshell Creek also provides habitat for rare fish and numerous waterfowl. The road surrounding the area permits viewing from your car.

Heyburn State Park on the south shore of Lake Chatcolet, five miles east of Plummer on Idaho 5, affords wildlife viewing virtually from your campsite. Hike the forested trails to glimpse white-tailed deer, chipmunks, badgers, coyotes, black bear and numerous songbirds. Extensive marshes and shallow lakes provide stop-over habitat for waterfowl and nesting habitat for the very impressive great blue heron and osprey. Beavers are also common here; watch for beaver houses resembling untidy piles of sticks. In spring and fall, you'll hear the haunting honk of Canada geese. They break their distinctive V-shaped flight patterns at dusk, gliding to a landing in marshy areas along the lake.

You'll see all manner of wildlife while canoeing the **Coeur d'Alene River Chain of Lakes**. Tundra swans, osprey and great blue heron are but teasers. Deer, elk, muskrat and beaver are often seen in spring and fall, and bald eagles like it here in winter. You can also view wildlife from the shore. The Chain of Lakes is scattered along Idaho 3 for 13 miles between Rose Lake and Thompson Lake. Obtain a brochure, map and wildlife checklist at the Thompson Lake headquarters (Exit I-90 at the Rose Lake Interchange). Exit I-90 at Old Mission State Park to see the visitor center's great blue heron exhibit.

From September to November, you can watch migrating chinook salmon from the frontage road bridge over **Wolf Lodge Creek**, just north of the I-90 bridge crossing. Lake Coeur d'Alene's **Wolf Lodge Bay** attracts up to 60 migratory bald eagles every November. They arrive to feed on kokanee salmon, which come here to spawn and die. Remain in your boat or near your car to avoid disturbing the sensitive raptors. The marshy areas at the mouth of Wolf Lodge and Blue Creeks are fertile birding areas. Wildlife viewing turnouts are located around the bay on Idaho 97.

Farragut State Park is a prime area for sighting wild mountain goats. Bone up on goat lore at the Willow picnic area's outdoor display. Binoculars are available for use in spotting these agile cliff-leapers. Or you may spot them from the water. Most goats are poised to vanish at the mere sign of a human, but these are accustomed to humans and will stare back at you if you sit quietly in your boat.

The **Clark Fork River Delta** is a prime waterfowl-watching area where you may see osprey, bald eagles and shorebirds. From the town of Clark Fork, turn right off Idaho 200 and cross the Clark Fork Bridge. Turn right and drive two miles to the **Johnson Creek Recreation Site**. Avoid the nesting season, if you prefer to explore via canoe.

The Panhandle

Moose also like it here. The Great Spirit seems to have been playing practical joker when He made moose. You'll laugh too, when you see one of these ungainly creatures in the flesh. We keep a couple of moose (not in the flesh) around the house just for laughs.

 A word of caution: moose may present a comical appearance, but they are not to be trifled with, especially in rutting season. If you've ever seen a moose charge, you'll understand why their heads, racks and forequarters are much heftier than their hindquarters.

Moose enjoy a slough in the **Pack River Delta** so much that the highway department has installed signs cautioning motorists to watch out for them. Drive Idaho 200 east of Sandpoint for five miles to a Sportsman Access sign. Follow that road for four miles to Sunnyside. A primitive road invites walking along the west side of the Pack River Delta. Numerous waterfowl can also be spotted here.

Sandpoint City Beach may seem an unlikely place to view wildlife, but migrating birds are attracted to these Lake Pend Orielle sand and mud flats. A short trail leads from here to **Grouse Creek Falls**. In April and May, you can see rainbow trout executing an aerial act up the falls on their way to upstream spawning habitat.

Round Lake State Park affords good wildlife watching around this glacially created "pothole" lake. Water-loving birds and animals are augmented by a few amphibians and reptiles. A foot trail surrounds the lake. The turnoff to the park is 8½ miles north of Sandpoint on US 95.

Look closely at the logs and rocks bordering the **Pend Oreille River**, if you should drive Idaho 2 between Sandpoint and Newport. You may spot painted turtles, Idaho's one and only turtle specie. The area around **Albeni Falls Dam** is a good place to see wintering bald eagles, osprey and other waterfowl.

The **Priest Lake area** abounds with wild creatures. The uncommon harlequin duck nests in the upper Priest Lake drainage. Moose love this largely undisturbed lake and its marshy areas.

The **McArthur Wildlife Management Area**'s 600 acres of marshy lake was Idaho's first land acquisition for the purpose of wildfowl production. Over 150 nesting platforms and 30 artificial islands invite Canada geese and several species of ducks. The best time to visit is late spring through summer when coyotes, moose and white-tailed deer are often seen at dawn and dusk. From Sandpoint, follow US 95 north for 17 miles. Take County Road A4 west to the WMA parking lot.

The **Kootenai National Wildlife Refuge** lies along the bottomlands of the Kootenai River and ranges into the foothills of the forested Selkirk

Mountains. Approximately 218 bird and 45 mammal species frequent the refuge. You can look for them via a 4½-mile auto tour, or from 5½ miles of walking trails. Use of the area is restricted on weekends, and on Tuesdays and Thursdays during the fall waterfowl hunting season. Brochures, maps and a wildlife checklist are available at the Refuge office and at several boxes on the Refuge. From Bonners Ferry, take Riverside Road west for five miles to the Refuge entrance.

The **Purcell Mountains** off US 95, in the vicinity of Robinson Lake, Round Prairie, Copper Falls and the Moyie River, have numerous Forest Service roads leading to secluded lakes. Off these roads are trails where you are likely to spot a wide variety of waterfowl and animals. Moose, too. Contact the Bonners Ferry District Ranger Station for maps and wildlife spotting information (Route 4, Box 4860, Bonners Ferry, ID 83805. ☎ 208-267-5561).

The **Lochsa and Selway River Canyons** offer prime bird, wildfowl and river otter viewing. **Cedar Flats Wetland**, off the Selway River Road, is a white-tail deer fawning ground. You should be able to see moms and fawns in early morning and evening, from early to mid-summer.

Kid Stuff

 Finding something to do in North Idaho that's not kid stuff can be a stretch. Eight-to-teens can have a blast participating in virtually every adventure that their parents enjoy. Exceptions might be rafting the Moyie and Locksa Rivers in high spate (ask river outfitters about a trip's suitability for kids before booking a trip), some snowmobile treks (research trails before setting out), and the more strenuous backcountry hiking and horseback/pack trips.

Many kids in this age bracket are fascinated by the Panhandle's mining and logging heritage. The area's rich trove of natural features, from mosses and berries to beavers and birds, capture their interest.

My 12-year-old daughter, Amy, likes nothing better than tramping through a northern forest, or messing about at the edge of a lake or stream, uncovering interesting flora and fauna (bugs and such) to check against her field guides. She accumulates more knowledge than she'd ever admit to.

North Idaho is also a good choice if you have younger kids in tow. Many **hiking and biking trails** are short and unchallenging enough for the under-eight set. **Horseback rides** by the day or hour are perfect for little ones. **Canoeing** is always fun, and low-water river trips are suitable, depending on your kid's age and venturesomness.

The Panhandle

As with all Idaho guest ranches, Hidden Creek Ranch's corrals are the focus of activity.

Children love water and all the cool things to do on it and in it. Ditto, snow. **Silver Mountain** and **Schweitzer Mountain Resorts** have ski programs for all ages. Schweitzer Mountain's facilities for young children include baby sitting and a day-long ski and play program.

Numerous beaches offer hours of swimming and splashing. Both **Farragut State Park** and **Priest Lake State Park's Indian Creek Unit** have sandy beaches. You can rent personal watercraft at Sandpoint's City Beach and at the public beach adjacent to downtown Coeur d'Alene.

Many adult **rock hounds** are seriously into mucking for garnets at the **Emerald Creek Garnet Area**. But it's kid fun, too. Not only is it a chance to get muddy with nary a no no, but kids emerge from the muck with real gemstones in hand. Adult "regulars" seem to enjoy having children around and sometimes proffer tips on digging. See page 120 for details.

The Panhandle's premier kid pleaser is **Silverwood Theme Park**, on US 95 a few miles north of Coeur d'Alene. Rides ranging from tame simulated antique cars to wild and wet flumes to a really scary roller coaster are great for unleashing high spirits. These, coupled with carnival-type games and numerous shows, even an ice show, keep all ages entertained. Amy and I often overnight at the Silverwood campground across the highway. Come morning, we walk through the pedestrian tunnel to the park and stay all day, retracing our steps to the campground after the evening air show. Unlike more heavily hyped theme parks, this smallish park seems to make a serious effort to remain low-key and folksy. ☎ 208-683-3400 for current hours and prices.

Horses & Kids

Horses and children enjoy a mutual attraction. Most guest ranches welcome kids and many offer activities tailored just for them. Be sure to ask questions about the ranch's horse program when searching out a ranch for your family. How much riding instruction do they offer? Does the ranch rent horses for the season, or are they ranch owned? Are quiet kids' horses available? Are young guests required to attain minimal riding skills before being allowed to go on a trail ride?

Amy and I found that **Hidden Creek Ranch** near Harrison (see Guest Ranches under *Where to Stay & Eat*) has an excellent kids' program crammed with supervised horseback riding, crafts and other fun activities, including overnighting in a tepee. Kids (adults, too) are given instruction in basic horse care and riding skills.

Other fun stuff for children includes **Wallace's Sierra Silver Mine Tour**, riding the **Silver Mountain Gondola**, and **panning for gold** along just about any backcountry creek in the Wallace and Silver Valley mining districts.

The Panhandle

Festivals & Special Events

 If you enjoy the upbeat sense of camaraderie that small town high jinks bring out, North Idaho is your kind of place. Maybe it's the celebratory feeling at the end of a snowy winter, but festivals begin revving up in May and accelerate as the glorious Northern summer progresses. Consider planning your trip around one or more of these festivals.

January

Wallace Sno-Fest, held in mid-January, features a lighted snowmobile parade, guided trail rides and a snowmobile give-away. ☎ 800-N-IDA-FUN or 208-752-8411.

Sandpoint Winter Carnival kicks off the season each year with 10 days of festivities that include snow-sculpture contests, a torchlight parade and lots more wintery fun. Held the last two weeks in January. ☎ 208-263-2161 for further information.

February

Snowflake Arts & Entertainment Festival is a Coeur d'Alene event that's gaining in popularity. Mid-February. ☎ 208-664-3194 for further information.

The **US Dog Sled Races** are held annually on the Priest Lake Air Strip. ☎ 208-443-3191 for dates and other information.

First Security Winter Games are held at Silver Mountain Ski Resort in late February. ☎ 208-784-0821 for further information.

Lionel Hampton Jazz Festival brings some of the world's top jazz musicians to Moscow in late February. Contact the Moscow Chamber of Commerce at ☎ 208-882-1800 for further information.

March

Moscow Mardi Gras & Beaux Arts Ball brings celebrity bands to this college town. Contact the Moscow Chamber of Commerce at ☎ 208-882-1800 for current dates.

May

Moscow's Rennaisance Faire, held the first weekend in May, includes arts, crafts, dragons and wizards. For further information, contact the Moscow Chamber of Commerce at ☎ 208-882-1800.

Wallace's Depot Days features music, food and other events on streets that recently resounded to the roar of snowmobiles. Contact The Northern Pacific Depot Railroad Museum for current dates. ☎ 208-752-0111.

Coeur d'Alene kicks off the summer season with a **Fred Murphy Days** parade in late May. For further information, contact the Coeur d'Alene Chamber of Commerce at ☎ 208-664-3194.

Sandpoint can't seem to allow a month to pass without a festival. The town's annual May **"Lost in the 50s"** weekend features a vintage car parade and other events. ☎ 208-263-2161 for current dates.

The **Post Falls Huck Finn River Fest**, held over Memorial Day weekend, features a carnival, crafts, food booths, a car show and more. ☎ 208-773-5016 for further information.

June

Wallace's Gyro Days got off the ground in 1996, but promises to be a keeper. A carnival, food and other fun abounds as the local Gyro Club chases a Gyro ball down Lead Creek. ☎ 208-753-7151.

A **Strawberry & Chocolate Feast** is held at Sandpoint's Panida Theatre in late June. ☎ 208-263-9191 for particulars.

July

July and August are clearly North Idaho's kick-up-your-heels months, with a boatload of fireworks, festivals and other fun celebrations.

Harrison celebrates July 4th with fireworks. **Spirit Lake's Old Fashioned 4th of July** includes a parade, arts and crafts, games, contests, live music and dancing and a big fireworks display. **Coeur d'Alene's American Heroes 4th of July Parade & Fireworks** starts with a parade and end with a pyrotechnic display.

Bayview Daze celebrates the 4th with a kids' fair, arts and crafts, and a lighted boat parade at dusk. ☎ 208-683-2200 for current information.

Old Mission State Park Historic Skills Fair celebrates pioneer skills in mid-July with some 40 crafts persons demonstrating and selling old-timey items. Watch quilting, spinning, black powder shooting and more. Music by Old-time Fiddlers. Contact Old Mission State Park at ☎ 208-682-3814 for current dates and other information.

Moscow's Rendezvous in the Park festival has received national acclaim for a rich mix of jazz, blues, classical, country and other music performed under the trees at East City Park. Arts and crafts, childrens' activities and silent movies are also featured. Held in mid-July. For further information, contact the Moscow Chamber of Commerce, ☎ 208-882-1800.

St. Maries "SMART" Festival has arts and crafts and a car show over the third weekend in July. ☎ 208-245-3563.

Wallace's Sportsman Days observes hunters' bragging rites with big-game antler racks on display, an elk-bugling contest, black powder shooting and the Idaho Chili Cookoff. Contact the Wallace Chamber of Commerce, ☎ 208-753-7151, for current dates.

Harrison Old Time Picnic features a parade and live entertainment. ☎ 208-664-3194 for further information.

Sandpoint takes the festival sweepstakes with the community's month-long **Festival at Sandpoint**, held from mid-July to mid-August. Under-the-stars ragtime, pop, classical and jazz concerts take place at Memorial

The Panhandle

Field on Lake Pend Oreille. For further information, contact the Sandpoint Chamber of Commerce at ☎ 208-263-2161.

August

Murray's Molly B'Damn Days gets August off to a rousing start. The rip-snorting festival is held in honor of the celebrated Molly B'Damn, Murray's shady lady with a heart of gold. A parade features "Molly" riding in her legendary bathtub. Following the parade, a street fair with beer garden music and food enlivens this old gold mining town. ☎ 208-682-4876 for current dates.

Avery Days' loggers' competition, mountain bike ride through former railroad tunnels and barbecue doesn't quite compare with Molly B'Damn Days, but promises fun if you're down that way. ☎ 208-245-4410 for further information.

Coeur d'Alene's Art on the Green, held the first weekend in August, features arts, crafts and dance festivals. ☎ 208-664-3194.

Sandpoint Arts and Crafts Festival proves Sandpoint's reputation for non-stop festivals. Contact the Sandpoint Chamber of Commerce at ☎ 208-263-2161 for current dates.

The **Coeur d'Alene Indian Pilgrimage** occurs at Cataldo Mission annually on August 15th. The Coming of the Black Robes event celebrates the arrival of Jesuit missionaries to establish a mission among the Coeur d'Alenes. Events include a solemn parade of tribal dignitaries up the hill to the mission church, an outdoor mass, The Coming of the Black Robes pageant in which the historic event is acted out by tribal members, traditional dances, and a round dance in which everyone is invited to participate. The mission church and the adjacent priests' house are open for tours. If you can catch just one event during your trip to North Idaho, it should be this one. ☎ 208-682-3814 for further information.

Wallace's Huckleberry Festival, held in mid-August, celebrates the Panhandle's favorite wild berry with a fine arts exhibition, 5K run, live music and huckleberries galore. ☎ 208-753-7151 for current date.

Post Falls' Festival of the Falls features crafts, food booths and presentations of the play, *The Stories of Q Emlin.* ☎ 208-777-9278 for further information.

The **Old Mission State Park Annual Mountain Man Rendezvous** offers a fix on the West's thriving mountain man sub-culture wherein families relive the early 1800s, when trappers roamed the mountains and met with Indians to trade pelts and yarns. Latter day "mountain men" rendezvous at various locations almost every summer weekend, sleeping in authentic tepees, cooking over campfires, wearing period garb, honing old-time skills. Colorful Peddlers' Row features booths where every conceivable period artifact is sold. Even the food booths sell authentic grub such as Navajo tacos. Call the Old Mission State Park at ☎ 208-682-3814 for current dates.

St. Maries' Paul Bunyan Days is what you'd expect, having logger competitions, a parade, carnival, food booths and more. ☎ 208-245-3134 for futher information.

September

The annual **Farragut Naval Training Station Boot Camp Anniversary Reunion Celebration** is held at Farragut State Park over the weekend following Labor Day. The reunion attracts more Farragut veterans every year. ☎ 208-683-2425 for further information.

St. Joe Outdoor Festival at Avery features muzzle-loading, fly-tying demonstrations, bow shooting, an elk bugling contest, barbecue and more. ☎ 208-245-4410 for further information.

October

Idaho Draft Horse International, held at Sandpoint in early October, has three days of contests and exhibits. For further information, contact the Sandpoint Chamber of Commerce, ☎ 208-263-2161.

Sandpoint Oktoberfest, held in mid-October, has a volksmarch and live entertainment. ☎ 208-263-2161 for current dates.

Where to Stay & Eat

Lodgings

 If you enjoy bed & breakfasts, you'll love the Panhandle. North Idaho proves the axiom that when visitors discover an area, B&Bs can't be far behind. These agreeable establishments range from a couple of guest rooms in the owner's house to sizeable inns run by hired managers. Most fall somewhere in between. They are often marvels of imaginative decor and offer tasty, sometimes sumptuous, breakfasts. Some accept major credit cards, but many smaller B&Bs do not. Ask when you call to reserve.

The Panhandle

Many families, especially those with young children in tow, prefer the privacy and activity choices available at family-friendly resorts. Many motels, especially those of the chain variety, offer some activities ordinarily associated with resorts. Modest motels in remote towns where other accommodations are unavailable are also included below. Again, most accept major credit cards, but ask if in doubt.

US Forest Service Cabins

The US Forest Service makes available lodgings that supercede all others for sheer adventure and an exhilarating sense of roughing it in the backcountry. Amenities vary at these former fire lookout towers and guard station cabins, but most are primitive, with outhouses being the rule. Few have electricity or running water. Some have no water. All have basic furnishings and some type of heat, with wood stoves predominating. Bring your own sleeping bag, utensils and supplies. Most fire lookouts and cabins are accessible by Forest Service roads, but some can be reached only on foot.

Contact the Clearwater, Panhandle, Nez Perce or a participating ranger district to request a *Northern Region Recreational Cabin and Lookout Directory.*

Both the Lochsa and Pierce Ranger Districts of the Clearwater National Forest have two former fire lookout towers for rent. The North Fork Ranger District has a lookout tower and the Cold Springs Cabin for rent. All are in the backcountry adjacent to and north of US 12, the Lochsa Wild & Scenic River Corridor.

The Bonners Ferry Ranger District of the Idaho Panhandle National Forests rents out the Shorty Peak Lookout Cabin and the Snyder Guard Station. The latter is cushy by ranger district standards, having electric heat, hot showers, a kitchen and a horse corral.

The Selway Ranger District of the Nez Perce National Forest rents out the Meadow Creek Cabin and the 60-foot Lookout Butte tower. The former can be reached only on horseback (experienced livestock recommended). Bringing children to the latter is discouraged.

Avery

Scheffy's General Store is an oasis in the wilderness, offering rustic accommodations. RV spaces fishing licenses, supplies and a meat locker. Avery, ID 83802. ☎ 208-245-4410.

Bayview

This town offers surprisingly little in the way of accommodations, considering its lakeside situation. These few are headed by **MacDonald's Hudson Bay Resort, Inc.**, a large facility (for Bayview), with 10 cabins, RV sites and numerous water-related activities. PO Box 38, Bayview, ID 83803. ☎ 208-683-2211.

Scenic Bay Marina has four guest rooms. PO Box 36, Bayview, ID 83803. ☎ 208-683-2243.

Bayview Scenic Motel & RV Park is larger, with eight units. PO Box 70, Bayview, ID 83803. ☎ 208-683-2215.

Bonners Ferry

Bonners Ferry Log Inn, two miles north of town, is a medium size lodging making an attempt at north country atmosphere. HCR 85 Box 6, Bonners Ferry, ID 83805. ☎ 208-267-3986.

B/W Kootenai River Inn at Kootenai River Plaza. ☎ 800-346-5668.

Deep Creek Resort, seven miles south of Bonners Ferry on US 95, promises a pleasant stay. ☎ 800-689-2729.

Mama's Place is a combination bed & breakfast and vegetarian restaurant. Meals are by reservation. 5952 Hwy 95 South (PO Box 5010), Bonners Ferry, ID 83805. ☎ 208-267-7268.

Calder

Calder, 35 miles east of St. Maries on the St. Joe River, is a convenient place to stay if you will be exploring the St. Joe National Forest backcountry.

St. Joe Lodge & Resort has six guest rooms and 20 RV spaces. Rt. 3 Box 350, Calder, ID 83808. ☎ 208-245-3462.

Clark Fork

You might wish to reserve a room at one of Clark Fork's two lodgings if you're wildlife watching and hiking in the area.

River Delta Resort, five miles east of town on Idaho 200, caters mostly to RVers, but has 15 cabins to rent. Box 128, Clarks Fork, ID 83811. ☎ 208-266-1335.

University of Idaho Clark Fork Field Campus makes 15 rooms available to the public when not required for university use. PO Box 87, Clarks Fork, ID 83811. ☎ 208-266-1452.

Coeur d'Alene

Coeur d'Alene has more choices than a huckleberry bush has berries. Listed below are bed and breakfasts and resorts. For motels and house or condo rentals, contact the **Coeur d'Alene CVB,** or **Coeur d'Alene Central Reservations.** PO Box 1933, Coeur d'Alene, ID 83814. ☎ 800-876-8921.

Coeur d'Alene B&Bs

Coeur d'Alene is a B&B lover's paradise, with one to suit every taste. Most accept major credit cards. Some welcome children, but may set age limits; ask before booking a room. Few accept pets.

Amor's Highwood House, conveniently located outside downtown, has two guest rooms. 1206 Highwood Lane, Coeur d'Alene, ID 83814. ☎ 208-667-4735.

Ann & Mel's Log House is private and set away from the busy downtown area. 4850 Long Shadowy Lane, Coeur d'Alene, ID 83814. ☎ 208-667-8015.

Baragar House Bed & Breakfast is in the pleasant Fort Sherman neighborhood at 316 Military Drive, Coeur d'Alene, ID 83814. ☎ 800-615-8422. Fax 765-2427.

Blackwell House, formerly a 19th-century lumber baron's mansion, has eight guest rooms oozing with period decor. 820 Sherman Ave., Coeur d'Alene, ID 83814. ☎ 208-664-0656.

Berry Patch Inn Bed & Breakfast has three comfortable guest rooms. N. 1150 Four Winds Road, Coeur d'Alene, ID 83814. ☎ 800-644-2668.

Coeur d'Alene Bed & Breakfast is handy to downtown. 906 Foster Ave., Coeur d'Alene, ID 83814. ☎/Fax 208-667-7527.

Country Ranch Bed & Breakfast has two pleasant guest suites. 1495 S. Green Ferry Road, Coeur d'Alene, ID 83814. ☎ 208-664-1189.

Cricket-on-the-Hearth is one of Coeur d'Alene's pioneering B&Bs. 1521 Lakeside Ave., Coeur d'Alene, ID 83814. ☎ 208-664-6926.

Greenbriar Inn is a comfortable, rambling B&B in an old neighborhood close to downtown. 315 Wallace St., Coeur d'Alene, ID 83814. ☎ 800-369-0026.

The Warwick Inn is one of several charming Coeur d'Alene B&Bs.

Gregory's McFarland House offers guests a pampered stay in one of five bedrooms, plus breakfast in a light-filled solarium. 601 Foster Ave., Coeur d'Alene, ID 83814. ☎ 208-664-1232.

Highwood House Bed and Breakfast has two cozy guest rooms. 1206 Highwood Lane, Coeur d'Alene, ID 83814. ☎ 208-667-4735.

Katie's Wild Rose Inn, also one of Coeur d'Alene's first B&Bs, is loaded with charm. 5150 Coeur d'Alene Lake Drive, Coeur d'Alene, ID 83814. ☎ 800-371-4345.

Roosevelt Inn Bed and Breakfast has 18 guest rooms. 105 Wallace Ave., Coeur d'Alene, ID 83814. ☎ 800-290-3358. Fax 208-664-4142.

Silver Beach House Bed & Breakfast has two posh guest rooms. 1457 Silver Beach Loop, Coeur d'Alene, ID 83814. ☎ 208-667-5406.

Someday House Bed & Breakfast is in a rural setting. 790 Kidd Island Rd., Coeur d'Alene, ID 83814. ☎ 208-664-6666.

Wolf Lodge Creek Bed & Breakfast is an intimate inn in a pretty area west of town. 715 N. Wolf Lodge Creek Rd., Coeur d'Alene, ID 83814. ☎ 800-919-9653.

The Warwick Inn Bed and Breakfast occupies a classic 1920s bungalow whose three guest rooms are decorated with rare charm. Breakfast on a secluded patio in fine weather. 303 Military Drive, Coeur d'Alene, ID 83814. ☎ 208-765-6565.

The Panhandle

Coeur d'Alene Resorts

Coeur d'Alene has surprisingly few full-service resorts. Make careful inquiries before booking a room or cabin. How close to the lake will you be? What amenities are on offer? Are children welcomed, rather than just tolerated? See nearby Post Falls for other lodgings options.

Anderson's Country Cabin has two guest rooms, a family cabin and horseback riding. East 6495 Sunnyside Rd., Coeur d'Alene, ID 83814. ☎ 208-667-2988.

Arrow Point Resort, on a scenic point jutting into the lake, has chalet-style condo rooms, golf, an indoor swimming pool, beaches and a marina. 715 N. 4th St., Coeur d'Alene, ID 83814. ☎ 208-664-1593. Fax 208-664-2090.

Coeur d'Alene Resort, on the lake, is North Idaho's largest full-service resort. Amenities include several restaurants and a full range of fun things to do. The resort's golf course, complete with a floating green, is said to be world-class. Guest rooms, some graced with splendid lake views and gas fireplaces, are spacious and comfortable. ☎ 800-688-5253.

Elk River

Huckleberry Heaven Lodge covers all the bases with a guest lodge, cabins, condo units, RV spaces, swimming and wild huckleberries. PO Box 165, Elk River, ID 83827. ☎ 208-826-3405. Fax 208-826-3284.

Another option is miniscule **Main Street Cabins**. PO Box B, Elk River, ID 83827. ☎ 208-826-3689.

Harrison

Laid-back Harrison offers an alternative to busy Coeur d'Alene, boasting a B&B, a lodge and a mom-and-pop resort-marina.

Lakeview Lodge is just that, with 21 guest rooms. PO Box 54, Harrison, ID 83833. ☎ 208-689-3318.

Peg's Bed & Breakfast Place has three pleasant guest rooms. 202 Garfield Ave., Harrison, ID 83833. ☎ 208-689-3525.

Squaw Bay Store, Resort & Marina, up the lake from Harrison, has five cabins, a marina and RV spaces. Rt. 2 Box 130, Harrison, ID 83833. ☎ 208-664-6450.

Hayden/Hayden Lake

Hayden Lake is a pretty body of water whose reputation as a haven for survivalists has given it a bad press. The area offers some pleasant lodging choices.

Affordable Inn, 9986 N. Government Way, Hayden Lake, ID 83835. ☎ 208-772-4414.

Clark House on Hayden Lake is a nifty B&B with five guest rooms. E. 4550 South Hayden Lake Rd., Hayden Lake, ID 83835. ☎ 800-765-4593. Fax 208-772-6899.

Hayden Hideaway, on the west side of the lake, has four condo units. 319 Coeur d'Alene Lake Drive, Hayden Lake, ID 83835. ☎ 208-664-2278.

Hope/East Hope

This very resortish area on the east shore of Lake Pend Oreille has more RV parks than places to stay. Nonetheless, several lodging choices are available.

Blue Spruce Lodge Motel, PO Box 306, Hope, ID 83836. ☎ 208-264-5512.

Pend Oreille Shores Resort, 18 miles east of Sandpoint, offers numerous recreational options. 1250 Hwy 200, Hope, ID 83836. ☎ 208-264-5828.

Rainbow Resort, on Idaho 200 in East Hope, has five units. PO Box 217, East Hope, ID 83836. ☎ 208-264-5412.

Red Fir Resort has 12 cabins for rent. 450 Red Fir Rd., Hope, ID 83836. ☎ 208-264-5287.

Kellogg

Kellogg is often overlooked in favor of Coeur d'Alene or Wallace, but the town's eclectic assortment of accommodations range from a hostel to B&Bs to Silver Valley area vacation homes.

Silver Valley Central Reservations makes available rental homes and condos. PO Box 1933, Kellogg, ID 83837. ☎ 800-876-8921.

The **Inn at Silver Mountain** is a sizeable B&B, with nine guest rooms. 305 S. Divison, Kellogg, ID 83837. ☎ 800-SNOW-FUN.

Kellogg Hostel has 80 beds. 834 McKinley Ave., Kellogg, ID 83837. ☎ 208-783-4171.

Kellogg Vacation Homes' 20 homes are available to rent for varying periods of time. PO Box 944, Kellogg, ID 83837. ☎ 208-786-4261.

McKinley Inn, a B&B three blocks from Silver Mountain Ski Resort, has eight rooms. 210 McKinley Ave., Kellogg, ID 83837. ☎ 208-786-7771.

The Panhandle

Patrick's Inn and Steakhouse has 10 guest rooms. 305 S. Division, Kellogg, ID 83837. ☎ 208-786-2311.

Scott's Inn has two cozy B&B rooms. 126 E. Mullan Ave., Kellogg, ID 83837. ☎ 800-767-8581.

Silber Berg Haus celebrates Kellogg's pseudo-Bavarian personality. 625 McKinley Ave., Kellogg, ID 83837. ☎ 208-784-7551.

Silver Ridge Mountain Lodge has nine rental units. 950 W. Cameron Ave., Kellogg, ID 83837. ☎ 800-979-1991. Fax 208-783-1183.

The **Ward's Sunshine House** is a smallish executive retreat. 1 Golf Course Road, Kellogg, ID 83837. ☎ 800-800-6181.

Kooskia

Kooskia is a convenient place to stay if you want to explore the Wild & Scenic Lochsa River Corridor or the Lolo Trail.

Bear Hollow Bed and Breakfast has three guest rooms. HC 75, Box 16, Kooskia, ID 83539. ☎ 800-831-3713.

Ida-Lee Motel is a sizeable mom-and-pop motel for these parts. PO Box 592, Kooskia, ID 83539. ☎ 208-926-0166.

Mount Stuart Inn Motel has 16 units. PO Box 592, Kooskia, ID 83539. ☎ 208-926-0166.

Moscow

A Moscow stay can be very pleasant, with several charming bed & breakfasts and a nice Best Western.

Beau's Butte Bed and Breakfast has two guest rooms. 702 Public Ave., Moscow, ID 83843. ☎ 208-882-4061.

Best Western University Inn is a large high-profile inn at 1516 Pullman Road. ☎ 800-325-8765.

Paradise Ridge Bed and Breakfast is on the Palouse. 3377 Blaine Rd., Moscow, ID 83843. ☎ 208-882-5293.

Peacock Hill Bed and Breakfast is on Moscow Mountain, five miles from town. 1245 Joyce Rd., Moscow, ID 83843. ☎ 208-882-1423.

Naples

If hostels are your thing, you'll be glad to learn that Naples, six miles south of Bonners Ferry, has one.

Naples AYH Hostel has six units. Hwy 2, Naples, ID 83847. ☎ 208-267-2947.

Pierce

Pierce, the backcountry town where North Idaho's gold rush began, is popular with hikers and history hunters. Pierce's lodging choices aren't exactly the Ritz, but they represent rural Idaho at its most... well, rural. Rural prices, too.

Cedar Inn is a country B&B with eight guest rooms. PO Box 494, Pierce, ID 83546. ☎ 208-464-2704.

Pierce Motel, 509 Main St., Pierce, ID 83546. ☎ 208-464-2324.

Post Falls

Post Falls may not be everyone's first lodging choice, but it boasts one of North Idaho's few bona fide resorts, and the Spokane River location is attractive. For further lodging information, call **Post Falls Central Reservation Service** at ☎ 800-876-8921.

Abel & Oliver's Bed & Breakfast offers proximity to Spirit Lake. W. 2225 Hwy 53, Post Falls, ID 83854. ☎ 208-773-6925.

Best Western Templin's Resort Hotel is on the Spokane River, six miles west of Coeur d'Alene. This is a real hotel with 167 guest rooms and numerous resort-type services. 414 E. 1st Ave., Post Falls, ID 83854. ☎ 800-283-6754.

Potlatch

Potlatch, on the northern edge of the Palouse, has a small B&B: **Rolling Hills Bed & Breakfast**, nine miles northwest of Potlatch. Rt. 1 Box 157, Potlatch, ID 83855. ☎ 208-668-1126.

Priest Lake

Priest Lake accommodations run largely to old-fashioned, north-woodsy-style family resorts – the kinds of places where kids are expected to be grubby and grownups need not worry about the "right" clothes. Most have fishing skiffs and canoes for rent. Some welcome the same families back year after year. The family-run Hill's Resort, the granddaddy of Priest Lake resorts, is a summer tradition, welcoming generations of the same families.

Bishop's Marina & Resort is on the southeast shore of the lake at Coolin. Its nine units include an apartment. PO Box 91, Coolin, ID 83821. ☎ 208-443-2191.

Elkins on Priest Lake is on the west side of the lake and has 28 cabins. HCO-1, Box 40, Nordman, ID 83848. ☎ 208-443-2432.

The Panhandle

Grandview Resort, also on the west side of the lake, has been in business for years. HCO 1, Box 48, Nordman, ID 83848. ☎ 208-443-2433. Fax 208-443-2527.

Hill's Resort, Inc. is Priest Lake's version of upscale, with a gourmet dining room serving dishes featuring local wild huckleberries, morels and trout. Some of the resort's 53 units are reserved by the same families from year to year. Hill's is on the west side of the lake at Luby Bay. Reserve way ahead. Open year-round. HCR 5, Box 162A, Nordman, ID 83848. ☎ 208-443-2551. Fax 208-443-2363.

The Inn at Priest Lake proves an exception to Priest Lake's preponderance of resorts. On the southeast side of the lake, the inn has 24 rental units and numerous RV spaces. PO Box 189, Coolin, ID 83821. ☎ 800-443-6240. Fax 208-443-2754.

Kaniksu Resort, near Nordman, is heavier on RV spaces than on accommodations, but does have 10 units. HCO 1, Box 152, Nordman, ID 83848. ☎ 208-443-2609. Fax 208-443-3864.

Old Northern Inn, a B&B near Coolin, has five guest rooms. Box 177 Sherwood Beach, Coolin, ID 83821. ☎ 208-443-2426.

Outlet Bay Resort, on Outlet Bay Road off Idaho 57, is a minuscule place with four units and two guest rooms. HC 5, Box 138, Coolin, ID 83821. ☎/Fax 208-443-2444.

Whispering Waters Bed & Breakfast, also on Outlet Bay Road, has three cozy guest rooms. HRC 5, Box 125B, Coolin, ID 83821. ☎ 208-443-3229.

St. Maries

St. Maries is a good lodging choice if you plan on mucking for garnets in the Emerald Creek Garnet Area (see *Touring*, page 120).

Benewah Resort, five miles west of town on Hwy 5, has five units. Rt. 1, Box 50C, St. Maries, ID 83861. ☎ 208-245-3288.

Knoll Hus Bed & Breakfast has one charming Swedish-inspired unit on a knoll at Mission Point, overlooking Lake Chatcolet's wild rice beds. PO Box 572, St. Maries, ID 83861. ☎ 208-245-4137.

Sandpoint

You have only to count the B&Bs and resortish accommodations to realize that Sandpoint and vicinity is a popular vacation area. Call Sandpoint Central Reservations, ☎ 800-876-8921. Fax 208-263-3705 for alternative lodging information.

TKE Vacation Rentals arranges vacation leases in over 100 homes and other private properties. ☎ 800-765-5539. Fax 208-263-7265.

Angel on the Lake B&B, on Lake Pend Oreille but in town, has four guest rooms. 410 Railroad Ave., Sandpoint, ID 83864. ☎ 800-872-0816.

Bottle Bay Resort & Marina, south of Sandpoint off US 95, has cabins for rent. 1360 Bottle Bay Rd., Sandpoint, ID 83864. ☎/Fax 208-263-5916.

Coit House Bed & Breakfast is conveniently located in town. 502 N. Fourth St., Sandpoint, ID 83864. ☎ 208-265-4035.

Green Gables Lodge is Schweitzer Mountain Resort's answer for those who wish a hotel room or condo close to the action. PO Box 815, Sandpoint, ID 83864. ☎ 800-831-8810.

Lakeside Inn is a large waterside establishment near Sandpoint's City Park. 106 Bridge St., Sandpoint, ID 83864. ☎ 800-543-8126. Fax 208-265-4781.

Mountain View Farm Bed & Breakfast is in a scenic rural area on the Pend Oreille River. PO Box 0150, Laclede, ID 83841. ☎ 208-265-5768.

Page House is an in-town B&B. 506 N. 2nd, Sandpoint, ID 83864. ☎ 208-263-6584.

Pine Woods Bed & Breakfast Home is south of Sandpoint in the Bottle Bay area. 1065 Lignite Rd., Slagle, ID 83860. ☎ 800-366-5851.

River Birch Farm Bed & Breakfast commands a fine location overlooking the Pend Oreille River. PO Box 0280, Laclede, ID 83841. ☎ 800-700-3705.

The Edgewater Resort has 55 units, plus RV spaces. PO Box 128, Sandpoint, ID 83864. ☎ 800-635-2534. Fax 208-263-3194.

Spirit Lake

Two mom-and-pop resorts are on this small, pretty lake.

Lake Haven Resort & Marina has six two-bedroom cabins for rent. HCI Box 17, Spirit Lake, ID 83869. ☎ 208-623-2791.

Silver Beach Resort is primarily an RV resort, but it does have three cabins to rent. 8350 W. Spirit Lake Rd., Spirit Lake, ID 83869. ☎ 208-623-4842.

Wallace

Wallace's accommodations seem to run mostly to motels, disproving my theory that a plethora of visitors inevitably means an upsurge in B&B inns.

Best Western Wallace Inn, just off I-90 on the west side of town, is a convenient modern lodging. 100 Front St., Wallace, ID 83873. ☎ 800-N IDA FUN. Fax 208-208-753-0981.

Jameson Hotel and Saloon is more than a B&B; it's an experience. Book a room at this historic hotel if you wwant to know how it felt to stay in

The Panhandle

a 1915-era railroad hotel. PO Box 869, Wallace, ID 83873. ☎ 800-N-IDA-FUN. Fax 208-753-0981.

Pine Tree Inn is a B&B with two guest rooms. PO Box 1023, Wallace, ID 83873. ☎ 208-752-4391.

The Brooks Hotel, downtown at 500 Cedar Street, has guest rooms and suites, plus RV parking and a resturant and lounge. ☎ 800-752-0469 or 208-556-1571. Fax 208-556-1570.

The Historic Ryan Hotel, 608 Cedar Street, is another historic hotel, but with modern conveniences. ☎ 208-753-6001.

Guest Ranches

Guest ranches have a reputation for week-long experiences heavy on horseback riding and light on comfort. Some take unexpected twists in the trail with downright luxurious amenities. Idaho Outfitters and Guides Association member ranches below have IOGA following their names.

Hidden Creek Ranch (IOGA) is no gritty cow camp. This luxurious guest ranch emphasizes conservation practices. It boasts a log lodge and guest houses oozing Western country decor, gourmet meals, an excellent riding program, numerous other activities, a comprehensive kids' program and the option to participate in observances based on Native American traditions. The ranch

Lazing in a hammock is encouraged at guest ranches like Hidden Creek Ranch.

owns its fine string of horses. Fabulous mountain scenery above Lake Coeur d'Alene. Owners Iris Behr and John Muir offer six-day packages that include meals and activities. 7600 E. Blue Lake Rd., Harrison, ID 83833. ☎ 800-446-3833. Fax 208-689-9115.

Lochsa Lodge Resort (IOGA), near the historic Powell Ranger Station, offers fireside dining, log cabins with woodburning stoves, horseback riding, fishing, hiking, mountain biking, cross-country skiing, snowmobiling and hot springs soaks. Powell Ranger Station, Lolo, MT 59847. ☎ 208-942-3405.

Rider Ranch, near Coeur d'Alene, is a 1,000-acre working cattle ranch with a private timber farm and sawmill that just happens to put up guests. If you're curious about how a real ranch works, this one's for you. You can tag along behind cowhands, go on trail rides and hayrides and dine from a horse-drawn chuck wagon. Owner Linda Rider says "We're not fancy, but we're real." S. 4199 Wolf Lodge Rd., Coeur d'Alene, ID 83814. ☎ 208-667-3373. Fax 208-667-3373.

Shattuck Creek Ranch & Outfitters (IOGA), in the remote Elk River area, is a comfortable lodge serving home-cooked meals. Activities include pack trips, trail rides, fishing, swimming, canoeing, biking, hiking, boating on nearby Dworshak Reservoir, ATV tours. Cross-country skiing and snowmobiling in winter. PO Box 165F, Elk City, ID 83827. ☎ 208-826-3405.

St. Joe Hunting & Fishing Camp, Inc. (IOGA), deep in the St. Joe National forest backcountry, occupies a historic landmark lodge. Guests sleep in rustic but comfortable cabins and enjoy home-cooked meals served family style. Access to this camp on the St. Joe River is by horseback only. Activites include horseback riding, fishing and hiking. All-inclusive packages are from four to seven days. Guided fly-fishing trips cost extra. If you hanker after a real backcountry camp experience, this is it. Owner/operators: Will and Barbara Judge. HCR 1 Box 109A, St. Maries, ID 83861. ☎ 208-245-4002.

Western Pleasure Guest Ranch is a member of Idaho Guest and Dude Ranch Association. Located 16 miles northwest of Sandpoint, the ranch's three cabins are rented by the day. Activities include horseback riding, multi-day rides, wagon rides, sleigh rides and cross-country skiing. 4675 Upper Gold Creek Rd., Sandpoint, ID 83864. ☎ 208-263-9066.

Where to Eat

Every small town has one or more cafés dishing up burgers, fries and such. Beat a trail for resort towns like Sandpoint and Coeur d'Alene if your tastes are more exotic. The following may be the Panhandle's most notable eateries, or may not. They only scratch the surface.

Bonners Ferry

Truckers make tracks for **Three Mile Corner Café**, at the junction of Highways 2 and 95, to load up on chicken-fried steak. My mother, who often chose restaurants that were ringed by big rigs like pigs at a trough, claimed truckers know good food. She was right.

Coeur d'Alene

Coeur d'Alene's gustatory establishments offer continental and ethnic cuisines, plus a real brew pub.

If it's haute cuisine you're after, hie yourself to **Beverly's**. The Coeur d'Alene Resort's signature restaurant serves up fabulous lake views with the chef's impeccably prepared and presented dishes. Reservations suggested. ☎ 208-765-4000.

At **Jimmy D's**, the views are of a downtown street, but the menu is continental. 320 Sherman Avenue. ☎ 208-664-9774.

Papino's offers home-cooked southern Italian food in a modest house at 315 Walnut Street. ☎ 208-765-2348.

Toro Viejo serves up good, inexpensive Mexican fare. Downtown at 117 Second Street. ☎ 208-667-7676.

At **T.W. Fisher's: A Brew Pub** the pretentious name belies the laid-back ambience. Request a brewery tour. Downtown at 204 Second Street. ☎ 208-664-2739.

Moscow

Being a college town, Moscow has its share of hole-in-the-wall eateries serving up coffee, pastries, veggie dishes and such, with reading materials on the side. Exploratory trips often turn up interesting munching. **West Fourth Bar & Grill** also offers serious fare in an adjacent dining room at 313 S. Main St. ☎ 208-882-0743.

Sandpoint

Sandpoint further proves the rule that resort towns attract more varied eateries than do small towns. **Swans Landing**, in the popular Long Bridge area on Lake Pend Oreille, serves up wild game dishes and more in a log cabin ambience. Lakeshore Drive at US 95. ☎ 208-265-2000.

If you favor Northern Italian cooking, try **Ivano's** outdoor dining deck at 124 S. Second Avenue. ☎ 208-263-0211.

Lindy's, Silverwood Theme Park's signature restaurant, is noted for barbecue ribs presented in surroundings paying tribute to pioneer aviator Charles Lindbergh. The downer: you have to pay to get into the park in order to dine here. The upper: you needn't subsist on corn-on-a-stick at this theme park.

Silver Valley

The cuisine here can be terminally bland, but two establishments recall the days when mining and logging produced Paul Bunyan appetites.

Hokey ort's ego is big enough to topple a tree, but the food is really tasty, if your taste runs to thick steaks and fried Rocky Mountain oysters. Don't know what those are? Well... delicately put, they are bulls' nether parts. You'll find the 1880 vintage resort at 1480 Coeur d'Alene Road north of Kingston. ☎ 208-682-3453.

The Historic Jameson invites you to belly up to a big, fancy bar reminiscent of those that once embellished old-time saloons. The dining room serves typically Western fare. In the Jameson Hotel at 304 Sixth Street, Wallace. ☎ 208-556-1554.

Mom's of Mullan will treat you right with Mom's baked chicken and other toothsome delights. At 238 Earle St. in Mullan, a nugget's throw east of Wallace on I-90. ☎ 208-744-1275. It's a toss-up whether **Murray's Sprag Pole Inn Steak & Rib House** is longer on good food or on gold town atmosphere. Whichever, it's a memorable experience. ☎ 208-682-3901.

Camping

Camping, or more accurately RVing, is popular in North Idaho. Flocks of "snowbirds" summer here after wintering in the sunny south. Numerous RV campgrounds and resorts cater primarily to these clients. Assuming that this book's readers prefer real camping, this guide concentrates on state parks and Forest Service campgrounds. Contact local visitor centers if you incline toward RV resorts. Or dial ☎ 800-VISIT-ID to request an *Idaho RV & Campground Directory*. Idaho's extensive state parks system emphasizes the lure of nature, with numerous trails and wildlife viewing areas. Campgrounds are almost invariably placed in scenic lakeside or forested locations. Campsites are usually quite secluded and include separate areas for tents. Facilities include restrooms with hot showers.

Dworshak State Park's **Freeman Creek Campgrounds** are situated in a wooded area at the northern edge of Dworshak Reservoir. The road down to the campgrounds is extremely steep and winding. The steepest stretch is paved. The reservoir is used for irrigation, so expect the water level to fluctuate. Best to visit in spring or early summer if you wish to fish or frolic on the water. In September, the water line may be many mud flats below the boat ramp. The park is 24 miles northwest of Orofino. Follow signs from the Dam visitor center. No reservations. PO Box 2028, Orofino, ID 83544. ☎ 208-476-5994.

Heyburn State Park, on Chatcolet Lake in the Lake Coeur d'Alene Chain of Lakes, is the Panhandle's wildest-looking park and the oldest state park in the Pacific Northwest. Trails lead through thick old-growth fir forests. Marshy areas draw waterfowl. The lake attracts fishers angling for bass, kokanee and trout. The three lakeside campgrounds have a wide range of campsites. No reservations. Rt. 1, Box 139, Plummer, ID 883851. ☎ 208-686-1308.

Farragut State Park, on Lake Pend Orielle at the foot of the Coeur d'Alene Mountains in the Bitterroot Range, is a four-season outdoor lover's paradise. Campgrounds are situated among the trees and near the lake. The centrally located park, halfway between Coeur d'Alene and Sandpoint, is a good choice if you're checking out the fun activities in those communities. Reservations accepted. E. 13400 Ranger Road, Athol, ID 83801. ☎ 208-683-2425.

Round Lake State Park's campsites are shaded by Western red cedar, Douglas fir, Western larch and other large conifers. This small park, situated on cozy Round Lake, 10 miles south of Sandpoint off US 95, is a good choice if you enjoy swimming in water warmer than in most area lakes, and watching a variety of wildlife (see *Wildlife Watching*, above). No reservations. PO Box 170, Sagle, ID 83860. ☎ 208-263-3489.

Priest Lake State Park's three campgrounds offer a variety of choices, all wonderfully scenic, wonderfully pristine. The **Indian Creek Unit** is right on the lake, has a sandy beach, and is the best choice if you have young tagalongs in tow. Open year-round, this is a popular take-off point for cross-country skiers and snowmobilers. The **Lionhead Unit**, 23 miles north of Coolin on the east side of the lake, occupies the site of silent film star Nell Shipman's home and studio. Developed for tent camping, Lionhead's amenities are primitive. This is a good choice if you're exploring the thoroughfare to Upper Priest Lake. Open in the summer and fall months. The **Dickensheet Unit**, beside the Priest River, four miles south of Coolin, offers primitive summer camping. This is a good choice if you're rafting, canoeing or kayaking the river. Reservations are not taken at any of these units. Priest Lake State Park, Coolin, ID 83821. ☎ 208-443-2200.

The US Forest Service maintains numerous primitive campgrounds in the Clearwater and Panhandle National Forests. Some can be reached only on foot or horseback, others by car. I camped once under enormous conifers at the Bumblebee Campground, north of Kingston in the Coeur d'Alene National Forest. It was so remote and quiet, we forgot we had driven in. Contact area ranger districts to obtain maps showing topographical and historical features, as well as campgrounds that are near hiking trails.

Central Idaho

The Frank Church-River of No Return Wilderness

This chapter takes you to the heftiest chunk of Idaho. Plunk in the center is the 2.3-million-acre Frank Church-River of No Return Wilderness. Central Idaho offers the Gem State's most exciting, most literally down-to-earth, splash-and-dash adventures. The two big rivers running through it, the Salmon and the Middle Fork of the Salmon, attract adventurers from the world over. Ketchum/Sun Valley, Idaho's oh-so-trendy resort area, and the North Fork Road, an on-the-edge throwback to times past, point up the contrasts you will find here. This region's western border skirts the eastern edge of hourglass-shaped *Region 1*. The northerly line follows Hwy 12, the Wild & Scenic Lochsa River Corridor, described in *Region 2*.

From here, the eastern edge of *Region 3* follows the rumpled Montana state line south to where Interstate 15 enters Idaho from Montana. The northerly portion of the line hikes across the Bitterroot Mountain Range, skirting the Selway-Bitterroot Wilderness Area and climbing from 5,233-foot Lolo Pass to 10,157-foot Trapper Peak, before dropping to 7,373-foot Lemhi Pass. From here, the state line flirts with the Continental Divide before meeting up with I-15.

A glance at a map reveals a solid green line, an inverted arc, slicing some 400 miles across Southern Idaho from the Montana line to the Oregon line. Comprising parts of I-15 and I-84, plus abbreviated I-86, the line denotes this region's extreme eastern and southern border, stopping short at Boise, described in *Region 1*. From the hamlet of Roberts, 24 miles north of Idaho Falls, to the Oregon line, the merging interstates follow the Snake River Corridor through Idaho's famed potato-growing region. The people living here are largely hardworking farmers, mostly Mormon; the ethos is one of pious earnestness.

Adventure tourism drives scattered towns such as Salmon, Challis and Stanley, situated between the Snake River Corridor and the vast wilderness areas of the Salmon, Challis, Sawtooth, Boise, Payette and Nezperce National Forests. The folks you will meet here differ from Snake River Corridor residents. They are descended from early prospectors and settlers or have come in search of a frontier lifestyle.

Central Idaho

live by guiding visitors on river running, horse packing, fishing, hunting and other backcountry adventures. Life in the open, doing exactly what they want to do where they want to do it, gives these hardy folk a wry sense of humor and a homespun philosophy.

Another brand of tourism drives the Wood River Valley, where Ketchum and the Sun Valley Ski Resort hold sway. Scratch the surface of this area's self consciously Western ethos and you'll find Madison Avenue. This huge chunk of Rocky Mountain splendor is an enormous, tantalizing saddlebag crammed with surprises. Its stunning beauty will emblazon unforgettable images on your memory; its quiet beauty will steal into your soul.

History & Geography

To a large extent, Central Idaho's topographical diversity determined its human history.

This is the ancestral home of the **Lemhi Shoshone, Sheepeater** and **Nez Perce** Indian tribes. These people took sustenance from the land on which they lived and from the rivers running through it, in return treating the land with thankful reverence. Today, the Nez Perce occupy a reservation on the Camas Prairie (see *Region 1*), while the Lemhi Shoshone and remnants of the Sheepeater tribe share the Fort Hall Reservation with the Bannocks of Southeastern Idaho.

Between 15,000 and 2,000 years ago, the area between the northeastern edge of the Snake River Plain and the thrusting Sawtooth Mountain Range experienced a series of violent, earthshaking volcanic eruptions. Lava seeping from fissures flowed south to the Snake River Canyon, creating a weird landscape comprised of layer upon layer of cooling lava. The heart of this volcanic jumble has been preserved as The **Craters of the Moon National Monument**. The deep volcanic ash layering the Snake River Plain is today's fertile soil.

Oregon Trail trekkers, intent on reaching the fabled lands of Oregon and California, failed to recognize the value of the dry terrain over which their wagons passed. It was left to **Mormon** colonizers, whose irrigation methods were producing good crops in the Salt Lake Valley, to realize the potential inherent in the nutrient-rich lava soil. Their descendants still populate the Snake River Plain, cultivating those famous Idaho potatoes and numerous other crops.

Farming, though always a gamble, was a soft life and a sure thing when compared to prospecting for gold.

After the turn of the 19th century, the jumbled mountains and deep narrow river valleys of what would become Central Idaho yielded rich troves of pelts. **Trappers**, commonly dubbed Mountain Men, came to trap and trade with the Indians. Beginning in mid-century, missionaries intent on enlightening the "heathens" began filtering in. Homesteaders followed, but farming was marginal in this harsh country. Few seemed to realize that gold awaited discovery in high mountain fastnesses, although spring freshets washed flecks and nuggets down countless streams into the Salmon River system.

It was only after the California gold rushes played out, and the Civil War decimated the South, that Idaho became the stage for the next **gold rush**. Dejected prospectors and defeated Southerners converged on Idaho. Rip-roaring gold rush towns such as Idaho City appeared seemingly overnight. Other prospectors, preferring to work alone, and

Central Idaho

no doubt to grapple alone with their personal demons, fanned out along the rivers and streams with pans and sluice boxes tied onto pack mules' backs. Chinese miners came, too. They tended to follow Caucasian miners, finding gold in the Salmon River canyons' "played-out" mines.

Adventure travel, Central Idaho's most recent "gold mine," is largely a 20th-century phenomenon. Anglers traveling hundreds of miles to catch fish, only to release them, would doubtless perplex those Native Americans who had for centuries derived sustenance from fishing. But then, Indians didn't build dams to inhibit the salmons' life cycle.

The prospectors who led pack mules over precipitous terrain, who regarded the rivers' turbulent rapids as death traps, would doubtless scratch their heads at the very idea of *choosing* to backpack into the wilderness, of shooting the rapids *for fun*.

It wasn't until after the turn of the 20th century, as Idaho's national forests were established, that an intrepid few started hiking into, camping in, and just enjoying the backcountry. Then, in the 1930s, railroad magnate **Averill Harriman** developed a ski resort on a sheep ranch he had purchased in the **Wood River Valley**.

For most people and for a long time, Idaho and Sun Valley were synonymous. But that gradually changed as adventurers wanting a finer edge to their travel began to discover the endless opportunities that Idaho offers. Conservation followed discovery. In 1968, the late Senator Frank Church's proposed Wild and Scenic Rivers Act was passed by Congress. A decade later, Secretary of the Interior Cecil Andrus, later governor of Idaho, took President Jimmy Carter down the Middle Fork of the Salmon River so that he might have a taste of the proposed wilderness area under consideration by Congress. The **River of No Return Wilderness Area** passed into law the following year. With it came a heightened awareness that America's last frontier is right here in Idaho – a vast, varied frontier awaiting exploration.

In 1984, just weeks before Church's death, Congress changed the name of this wilderness to the Frank Church-River of No Return Wilderness in honor of the man who did more than any other to keep this glorious place free from commercial exploitation and available to adventurers like you.

Getting Around

Most visitors access Central Idaho via the **Boise** or **Sun Valley/Hailey airports**. Boise is served by Delta, Northwest,

United and Southwest Airlines. Horizon (☎ 800-547-9308) and Skywest
(☎ 800-453-9417) serve both Boise and Sun Valley/Hailey.

Central Idaho's lower half is laced with excellent highways: the
Interstate system and US and Idaho Highways 21, 75, 93, 28 and 26. The
northern half is penetrated by a few unimproved Forest Service roads.
Entry to the Frank Church-River of No Return Wilderness Area and the
adjoining Selway Bitterroot and Gospel Hump Wilderness Areas is via
foot or horseback, on water or by bush planes equipped to land at Forest
Service airstrips inside the wilderness areas.

*If you intend to travel into the National Forests
backcountry via unimproved roads, consider using a
4WD vehicle. Some of these roads are accessible in
passenger cars, but 4WD always makes sense, especially
in mountainous areas. Pack as though you expect to be
stranded. It may be high summer, but cold weather, even
snow, is no stranger here in any season.*

*Emergency supplies should include sleeping bags or
blankets, a first aid kit, a spirit stove, flashlights or
lanterns, matches, food for two or three more days than
you expect to be out, a gallon or more of water per person
per day. A two-way radio or cellular phone is a good idea,
though mountainous terrain could interfere with their
effectiveness.*

*Your vehicle's emergency supplies should include one or
two spare tires, a five-gallon can of gasoline, a jack and
other basic tools, jumper cables, kitty litter and a
tire-width board for getting unstuck.*

*Have area maps on board. Always contact a National
Forest headquarters or ranger station before setting out
to obtain maps and current information about any road
closures. A whole range of natural calamities, including
fires in summer and fall and snows, floods and slides in
winter and spring, can lead to road closures.*

*Central Idaho's highways are well maintained
year-round except for certain roads and mountain passes,
such as Hwy 75 over Galena Summit, between Ketchum
and Stanley, that require traction devices in winter.
Some, like the Banner Summit stretch of Hwy 21, may
be closed in winter. You should always expect the worst
and be prepared for it; winter storms can swoop down
suddenly, especially in the higher elevations, bearing
heavy snows and high winds.*

Central Idaho

The principal points of interest outside the wilderness areas can be reached via good paved roads. If you fly into Boise and rent a car there, as most visitors do, you might pick up Hwy 21 (the Ponderosa Pine Scenic Highway) for a swing through the old mining town of Idaho City before climbing to Lowman and thence to the high mountain village of Stanley. Here, you must choose between two routes. Both will take you through some of the most splendid high country you'd ever hope to see through a car window. You can head south on Hwy 75 over Galena Summit into the Wood River Valley, looking in on Ketchum/Sun Valley and the ancillary town of Hailey. Visit the famous Shoshone Ice Caves before picking up Hwy 93, which intersects with I-84 north of Twin Falls. An option is to turn east onto Hwy 20 five miles south of Bellevue for a swing past Craters of the Moon National Monument to Arco, the atomic energy city, and then north on Hwy 93 to Challis. Another choice from Stanley is to head east on Hwy 75 alongside the young, roistering Salmon River, looking in on the Land of the Yankee Fork mining area en route to Challis. From here, the road continues on to Salmon and the North Fork Road, gateway to the Frank Church-River of No Return Wilderness.

These attractions are augmented by numerous hot springs, hidden lakes, historic sites, museums and other landmarks celebrating the area's natural beauty and intriguing history. Many are in out-of-the-way places. Read this chapter's *Touring* section below for more details.

Several sizeable cities (sizeable for Idaho) are strung along the Interstates. Taking their cultural identification with Southern Idaho into consideration, this book will include Idaho Falls in the *Region 4* chapter and Burley, Twin Falls and Mountain Home in *Region 5*. Blackfoot and the Fort Hall Indian Reservation fit nicely into this chapter.

Information Sources

Idaho Winter Road Report: ☎ 208-336-6600.

Highway Accident/Emergencies: ☎ 800-632-8000.

Bureau of Land Management, 1387 S. Vinnell Way, Boise, ID 83709. ☎ 208-373-4015. Fax 208-834-3200.

Bureau of Land Management, Salmon District, Route 2, Box 610, Salmon, ID 83467. ☎ 208-756-5400.

Idaho Department of Fish & Game, 600 S. Walnut, Boise, ID 83707. ☎ 208-334-3700. Fax 208-334-2114 or 334-2148. E-mail: idfginfo@state.id.us.

Idaho Outfitters and Guides Assoc., Box 95, Boise, ID 83701. ☎ 208-342-1438. Fax 208-338-7830. E-mail: outfitt@aol.com.

Idaho Department of Parks and Recreation, Box 83720, Boise, ID 83720-0065. ☎ 208-334-4199. Fax 208-334-3741.

Idaho Guest and Dude Ranch Assoc., c/o John Muir, 7600 Blue Lake Road, Harrison, ID 83833. ☎ 208-689-3295. Fax 208-689-9115.

ᘑ

Boise National Forest, 1750 Front St., Boise, ID 83702. ☎ 208-364-4100. Fax 208-364-4111.

Boise National Forest, Idaho City Ranger District, PO Box 129 (Hwy 21), Idaho City, ID 83631. ☎ 208-392-6681.

Boise National Forest, Lowman Ranger District, HC 77, Box 3020 (Hwy 21), Lowman, ID 83637. ☎ 208-259-3361.

Clearwater National Forest, 12730 Highway 12, Orofino, ID 83544. ☎ 208-476-4541. Fax 208-476-8329.

Nez Perce National Forest, Salmon River Ranger District, Slate Creek Ranger Station, HC 01, Box 70, White Bird, ID 83554. ☎ 208-839-2211.

Payette National Forest, 800 West Lakeside Ave., Box 1026, McCall, ID 83638. ☎ 208-634-0700. Fax 208-634-0744.

Salmon/Challis National Forest, RR Box 600, Challis, ID 83467. ☎ 208-756-2215. Fax 208-756-5151.

Salmon National Forest, Supervisor's Office, Hwy 93 North, PO Box 729, Salmon, ID 83467. ☎ 208-756-2215.

Salmon National Forest, North Fork Ranger District, Hwy 93, PO Box 780, North Fork, ID 83466. ☎ 208-865-2383.

Sawtooth National Recreation Area, Stanley, ID 83278. ☎ 208-726-7672.

Sawtooth National Forest, 2647 Kimberly Road East, Twin Falls, ID 83301. ☎ 208-737-3200. Fax 208-737-3236.

Sawtooth National Forest, Ketchum Ranger District, PO Box 2356, Ketchum ID 83340. ☎ 208-622-5371.

ᘑ

Idaho Travel Council, c/o Idaho Dept. of Commerce, 700 West State St., Boise, ID 83720-0093. ☎ 800-635-7820 or 208-334-2470. Fax 208-334-2631. Web site: www.visitid.org.

Central Idaho Rockies, c/o Sun Valley/Ketchum Chamber of Commerce, Box 2420 (111 Main, Ketchum), Sun Valley, ID 83353. ☎ 800-634-3347 or 208-726-3423. Fax 208-726-4533. E-mail: sunval@micron.net.

South Central Idaho Travel Assoc., c/o Twin Falls Chamber of Commerce, 858 Blue Lakes Blvd., Twin Falls, ID 83301. ☎ 800-255-8946 or 208-733-3974. Fax 208-733-9216. E-mail: tfidcham@cybernethighway.net.

Butte County Chamber of Commerce (Arco), PO Box 837, Arco, ID 83213. ☎ 208-527-8977.

Challis Chamber of Commerce, PO Box 1130, Challis, ID 83226. ☎ 208-879-2771 or 208-879-4267.

Stanley/Sawtooth Chamber of Commerce, Box 8 (Hwy 75), Stanley, ID 83278. ☎ 208-774-3411.

❧

Malad Gorge State Park, 1074 E. 2350 S., Hagerman, ID 83332. ☎ 208-837-4505.

Massacre Rocks State Park, 3592 N. Park Lane, American Falls, ID 83211. ☎ 208-548-2672.

Touring

Boise to Stanley: The Ponderosa Pine Scenic Byway

Touring Central Idaho offers more choices than a conifer has cones. You can be happily pursuing a route to somewhere when you're tempted by a road to somewhere else. Wherever it might lead, you must take it. You've no sooner climbed the Boise Foothills en route to Idaho City on Idaho 21 than a choice like that hits you between the eyes.

Just after Idaho 21 crosses an arm of Lucky Peak Reservoir, you can either continue on as you were, or veer off to the right, skirting this reservoir, as well as Arrow Rock Reservoir and Dam. Following the

The straggling town of Stanley is dominated by the snow-covered Sawtooth Range.

Middle Fork of the Boise River on Forest Road 268 takes you to **Atlanta**, the quintessential historic gold-mining town. Only about 50 hardy types live there now, but in its heyday Atlanta was really something. It was so named after the Georgia city by transplanted Confederates. The mountain-girt valley that would comprise the Atlanta Mining District was discovered in the early 1860s by John Stanley, who lent his name to Stanley Basin. Mining got off to a halting start, but by the 1930s the Atlanta Mining District was Idaho's leading gold producer.

Today, the old town is the center of a network of Forest Service roads and trails reaching deep into the back side of the Boise and Sawtooth National Forests, and the Sawtooth National Recreation Area. This rumpled portion of Central Idaho, between east-west-running Highways 20 and 55, contains the bear's portion of Central Idaho's unimproved Forest Service roads. A *Boise National Forest Travel Map* is essential if you wish to explore the Atlanta Mining District. Pick one up at the Boise National Forest Headquarters in Boise, or at the Idaho City or Lowman Ranger District offices. Inquire about current road and trail conditions at the same time.

While there, you might borrow a copy of the *Ponderosa Pine Scenic Byway Auto Tour* tape, produced by the USDA Forest Service in partnership with Boise State University Radio. This informative tape offers background on the route linking Stanley and Boise.

The Atlanta area is to the serious ghost town explorer what more easily accessed Idaho City is to the casual tourist. Both reflect a time when Idaho was synonymous with gold strikes, but Atlanta better reflects the era's raw flavor.

Atlanta has several Forest Service campgrounds, and you might use one as a base for several days of exploring. Pools fed by thermal hot springs edging the Power Plant Road make the prospect of lingering here all the more inviting.

Back on Idaho 21, you'll soon come to **Idaho City**. This historic mining town isn't exactly a ghost town, considering that upwards of 300 people live here. And it may seem over-hyped after visiting Atlanta. But, four devastating fires between 1864 and 1871 notwithstanding, it does boast a clutch of historic structures recalling a time when the population exceeded that of Portland, Oregon. St. Joseph's Catholic Church rose on a hillside above the town in a mere 30 days following the 1867 fire. This tenacity was typical of Idaho City, Atlanta and other storied "ghost" towns.

Boise Basin Historical Museum, at the corner of Wall and Montgomery Streets, is a good place to bone up on the history of Idaho City and the Boise Basin via a video, interpretive displays and historic landmarks.

Central Idaho

Open daily, Memorial Day through Labor Day, 11-4. Also open by appointment. PO Box 358, Idaho City, ID 83631. ☎ 208-392-4550.

Lowman is 34 scenic miles north of Idaho City. Long a pass-through place, the site of this summer community, spread along a 12-mile stretch of the South Fork of the Payette River, has successively watched Indians, Hudson Bay company trappers and prospectors as they traveled through the valley. In 1989, a forest fire passed through Lowman, destroying several homes and blackening 46,000 acres. Today, the tendency is still to pass through en route to Stanley or to Banks on Idaho 55 via Idaho 17, the infamous Lowman Road (see page 44).

For decades, the 33-mile **Lowman Road** was a hazardous track clinging to steep cliffs above the churning South Fork of the Payette River. It took years for workmen to blast through solid rock in an effort to build a safe roadway. The result afforded breathtaking views of the river far below, with a picturesque descent through verdant Garden Valley before bumping up against Idaho 55. The road was virtually destroyed when a New Year's 1997 storm sent the mountainside slip-sliding onto the road, carrying stretches of roadway into the river canyon below. Road repairs may take a year or more to complete. Inquire at the Lowman Ranger District office, on Idaho 21 north of town, if you are planning to travel Idaho 17. While there, pick up an information packet that includes a guide to camping, trails and numerous hot springs, most accessible from Idaho 21.

A word about Idaho's undeveloped thermal hot springs: unlike the developed variety, the waters of which are often cooled before they reach the pools, many of these are hot enough to cook food. It's not recommended that you do so, but do take care. And keep Fido out. Dogs have been scalded to death in these hot springs.

The 58 miles between Lowman and Stanley could be the longest miles you've ever traveled, if you give in to the temptation to explore the trails leading from the numerous trails and campgrounds between Lowman and 7,056-foot Banner Summit. (The approach to **Banner Summit** is closed in winter.) This is where the scenic byway truly earns its name as it threads a lane of crowding Ponderosa pines.

After Banner Summit, the road skirts the northern edge of the Sawtooth National Recreation Area, leveling off as it passes through lovely high mountain meadows abloom with wildflowers. These flowers are especially colorful in summers following winters of deep snows.

This is the domain of the majestic **Sawtooth Mountains**. The Tetons are famous for the profile presented from Wyoming's Jackson Valley, but their majesty doesn't approach the grandeur of these jagged sawtoothed

The snow-capped Sawtooths lend their reflection to Redfish Lake.

peaks. Keep a southerly eye open for a tantalizing glimpse of this giant's ripping saw about five miles before Stanley Basin heaves into view.

Numerous mountain lakes lie cuddled in mountain declivities. Most are accessible only via foot or horseback. **Stanley Lake** is a fortuitous exception. Turn right at the Stanley Lake sign, drive a short way and here, glistening in a deep dish, reflecting McGown Peak, is the most charming mountain lake you'll find anywhere. The overlook sports a plaque relating some background on the lake. You can camp here and hike a trail to **Bridalveil Falls**.

Stanley Basin, named for the peripatetic John Stanley, was discovered in 1824 by Hudson Bay Company fur trappers. Stanley is divided into Upper and Lower Stanley, the two separated by not much. Apparently, at some time in the past, antipathy seethed between residents of the two.

Occupying a high mountain basin between the Sawtooths and the newly-hatched Salmon River, assailed by heavy snows, Stanley would remain a tiny way station were it not a jumping-off spot for the nearby wilderness area, and for Middle Fork of the Salmon River floats. In summer, the cluster of log structures might be the quintessential mountain village. Come winter, most stand deserted. Tourism drives Stanley. Yet, it avoids the aggressively touristy look to which many such places succumb. Perhaps the splendid setting, between the gurgling Salmon River and the fabulous Sawtooth peaks, helps it to avoid this travesty.

Central Idaho

The mighty Salmon River gathers strength in a field of wildflowers beneath Galena Summit.

Stanley Museum honors the pioneers who settled the Stanley Basin and the Sawtooth Valley. The homey museum is in an Upper Stanley log cabin that formerly housed the Stanley Ranger Station. Exhibits and old-time photos showcase area history. Open May 15 to Sept 15, Mon-Fri, 11-5; Sat and Sun 11-6.

Idaho 21 and 75, fresh from Galena Summit and Sun Valley to the south, meet in Stanley.

Sawtooth Scenic Byway (Hwy 75): Stanley to Galena Summit

It seems best to break the Sawtooth Scenic Byway into two segments, touring from Stanley to Galena Summit now, later picking up Idaho 75 through the Wood River Valley south of Galena Summit.

Idaho 75 slices southward through the lovely Sawtooth Valley. Granite snow-frosted peaks, stretching over 10,000 feet to grab the azure Idaho sky, march in jagged procession on the west. On the east, the less imposing White Cloud Peaks rumble off into the Challis National Forest. The young Salmon River frolics through the Valley, having been spawned beneath 10,225-foot Bromagnin Peak.

One fine summer day, enraptured by the romance of the Salmon, I sought to trace the young river to its source. I pointed my car down a dirt road branching off Hwy 75 below the northern slope of Galena Summit. I drove as far as I could, then walked. I never reached the source, so charmed was I by the sight that presented itself on the wildflower-carpeted meadow. The fingerling river capered willy-nilly through the meadow, like a child chasing a butterfly. I hopped back and forth across it, marveling that such an insignificant stream could grow so rapidly, becoming a tumbling watercourse by the time it reaches Stanley, some 15 miles downstream.

*The **Sawtooth Fish Hatchery**, off Idaho 75 five miles south of Stanley, is open to the public. The Upper Salmon River and its main tributaries have been spawning grounds for ocean-going sockeye and chinook salmon and steelhead trout since time out of mind. The hatchery was established as part of an effort to restore the fish to the headwaters of the Salmon River. Their numbers have dwindled alarmingly due to dam building, habitat despoiling and other factors. Only one sockeye salmon returned to spawn in Redfish Lake in the fall of 1996. Yet, her return was celebrated. The 18-inch fish was captured and transported to the Eagle Fish Hatchery near Boise. Half of her eggs, totaling some 3,000, were placed in Redfish Lake. The fingerlings are free to move downstream. The remaining eggs are being used to increase captive broodstock. Learn about this and other preservation efforts in a tour of the Hatchery. The visitor center is open daily from 8-5 year-round. ☎ 208-774-3684 for tour hours.*

Redfish Lake, snuggled under 10,229-foot Mt Heyburn, 12 miles south of Stanley, is the showpiece of the Sawtooth National Recreation Area. Easily accessible from Idaho 75, this picture-postcard lake boasts a handsome lodge surrounded by log cabins for the renting, a campground, boat rentals and such. The stone visitor center showcases the flora, fauna and geology of the Sawtooth Range. Rangers conduct special tours and campfire programs. Ask to borrow an audio tape describing points of interest along Idaho 75 south of the Stanley Ranger Station, three miles south of Stanley.

Redfish Lake is a recreation center where every level of adventure may be found. You can join guided nature walks or access trails penetrating deep into the Sawtooths, many looking in on hidden mountain lakes.

Central Idaho

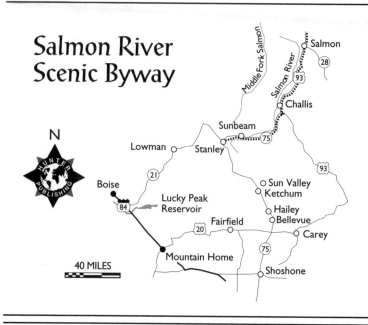

Idaho 75 climbs out of the Sawtooth Valley to Galena Summit, marking the divide between the Salmon and Wood River drainages. The viewpoint atop this splendidly wooded pass affords striking vistas of the Sawtooth Valley and its protecting mountains.

The Salmon River Scenic Byway (Hwy 75): Stanley to Challis

As with many scenic drives, the return trip to Stanley offers a different perspective on this place of extravagant vistas and sparkling close-ups. So it is with some two miles of Hwy 75 east of Stanley. Eastbound, you have a pleasant view of the Salmon, now picking up speed for its run to Challis. Even if you're headed east, turn around at the first riverside campground and retrace your treads to **Stanley**. Otherwise, you'll miss one of the finest vistas anywhere in Idaho.

As you round a curve, the entire Sawtooth Valley opens up. The silver-bright Salmon flows through a grassy meadow spiced with grazing horses and backed by mountains reaching for the sky. The log-built town straddles the river for a ways before meandering upslope.

The State of Idaho has designated Idaho 75 and US 93, covering 161.7 miles from Stanley to the Montana line, as the Salmon River Scenic Byway. "Scenic" it surely is. The two-lane highway is twisty-turny and quite narrow in places, but is well maintained except in the winter months, when driving can be a true adventure. The Byway closely follows the Salmon as far as North Fork, when it travels over steep mountainous terrain to Lost Trail Pass on the Montana border.

Between Stanley and Challis, Idaho 75 tracks the rambunctious Salmon's transformation into a full-blown river. Idyllic Forest Service campgrounds line the river for 13 miles between Stanley and the Sunbeam Dam, inviting you to stay for a time.

My young daughter Amy and I lingered at the Basin Creek Campground – not because it was on the river (it's across the road) but because it's bordered by Basin Creek, one of numerous tributaries gurgling to the Salmon. Amy had acquired gold panning equipment and itched to try it out. She panned for gold while our dog Max and I explored a trail and watched rafters putting into the river. She found gold! These flecks prove that there's still gold in these hills.

The Sunbeam Dam, long since breached, signals the entrance to the historic land of the **Yankee Fork Gold Mining District** and the **Custer Motorway Adventure Road**. If you are at all curious, set aside a day or more to explore this nugget of history lifted whole from that romantic era.

From the 1870s until as recently as 1952, sites along the Custer Motorway were producing gold. By 1910, Bonanza City and Custer had been mostly abandoned, but scattered mines continued to operate.

The Yankee Fork Gold Dredge

In 1940, the Yankee Fork Gold Dredge began chomping up the rocky bed of Yankee Fork Creek, regurgitating stones and separating gold from dross. The dredge closed down in 1952 and sat idle for three decades before a dedicated group of mining history enthusiasts began restoring it. The noisy clatter of this machine, measuring 112 feet by 54 feet by 64 feet high, and resembling an insect from an entomologist's nightmare, has been stilled for good. But tours guided by former dredgemen and their families illustrate the way it worked and offer insight into the working conditions of the men who operated it. The Yankee Fork Gold Dredge is open daily, July 1 through Labor Day, 10-5. Admission fee. ☎ 208-879-5244 for further information.

Central Idaho

Visitors can tour the restored Land of the Yankee Fork Gold Dredge.

The 40-mile Custer Motorway, pushing through rough backcountry from the Sunbeam Dam to Challis's Main Street, was originally a track linking Challis with the mines and settlements scattered along Yankee Fork Creek. In the 1930s, the Civilian Conservation Corps (CCC) improved the roadway, but it remains rough. Passenger cars and RVs have easy going between the Sunbeam Dam turnoff and Custer, but only high-clearance 4WD vehicles should attempt it beyond this point. And then only in summer and early fall.

This road is an evocative place, as I discovered while walking along it one hot summer day when the air was still and all was quiet. I heard the muffled sound of horses' hooves, but not a horse, or another person, was in sight.

If you are into history and things that go bump in the night (or daytime), you'll have a high old time picking through the mining era detritus lying about. Abandoned cabins, stamp mills, cemeteries – it's all there, an extended ghost town fit to entrance even those with only a casual interest in history.

Custer, on the National Register of Historic Places and the District's focal point, is maintained in a state of arrested decay by the US Forest Service and the Idaho Department of Parks and Recreation.

Sammy Holman

Custer was founded in 1870 by one Sammy Holman, a Harvard Law School graduate from Saratoga, New York who gave up a promising practice and headed west to Montana following the death of his fiancée. When his Montana claims played out, he joined the rush to the Boise Basin. He didn't hit pay dirt there either. So he came to the newly discovered Yankee Fork diggings.

For a time it seemed that Sammy was destined for political fame. He gained a reputation for honesty and fairness as Bonanza City's first justice of the peace and sometime judge. But those twin demons, gold fever and strong drink, spiralled him down a different path.

Sammy sold a mining claim off in lots that became Custer City. He stayed around for a time – another mining town character trying unsuccessfully to blot out past misfortunes.

In his 60th year, Sammy left Custer for Clayton, where he and a partner staked a claim that sold for $27,000. Wearing straggly white whiskers, oddments of clothing and patched brogans, his appearance and demeanor belied the brisk young lawyer of three decades before.

Sammy's story, like so many others in that raw land, ended with no burst of success. His life fizzled out in a cabin on the banks of a stream that came to be called Holman Creek.

You can learn more about Sammy Holman, the many other colorful characters who peopled the Land of the Yankee Fork, and how they lived and worked, at the **Yankee Fork Interpretive Center**, at the junction of Idaho 75 and US 93, just south of Challis. The striking glass-and-steel center is chock full of memorabilia, old photos and informative displays relating to Yankee Fork's heyday. The Center is open daily, 9-6. Admission is free.

Idaho 75 tags the Salmon from the Sunbeam Dam until it terminates at US 93. From here, you can drive US 93 south to Arco, or make the run to the busy town of Salmon. More about Arco later.

Challis was founded to supply the mining district. In more recent years, the town has served the needs of area cattle ranchers and recreationists. But this town of 1,300 is probably best known for the Challis Earthquake Fault at the base of nearby Mount Borah, which rumbled to life in 1883.

Central Idaho

A few surviving structures recall the old mining town of Custer.

The quake measured 7.3 on the Richter Scale. Two children were killed by a falling building facade.

For over 100 years, **Challis Hot Springs**, 4½ miles north of Challis on Hot Springs Road, has been popular for riverside camping, picnicking and swimming in a pool fed by thermal hot springs. HC63 Box 1779, Challis, ID 83226. ☎ 208-879-4442.

The Salmon River Scenic Byway (Hwy 93): Challis to Montana

Here, the Salmon flourishes through a corridor widening occasionally to accommodate idyllic homesteads and ranches. A few unimproved roads branch from the highway, heading uphill to look in on some of the hundreds of lakes tucked into the surrounding Salmon National Forest and the Frank Church-River of No Return Wilderness.

A road worth taking is Forest Road 055, the **Morgan and Panther Creeks Road**. This gravel and dirt road slices cross-country, beginning where Morgan Creek meets Idaho 73 on the outskirts of Challis, and ending where Panther Creek flows into the Salmon River beside the North Fork Road. FS Road 055 follows these creeks through flats and under towering ridges. A Forest Service campground is roughly halfway, at McDonald Gulch. Side roads and trails lead to old mines and other signs of past habitation. A high-clearance 4WD vehicle is strongly recommended if you have a mind to explore this rough backcountry.

Stop in at the Salmon National Forest supervisor's office or a local ranger district office to obtain a travel map delineating this and other roads winding through the backcountry and skirting the edge of the Wilderness Area.

The Salmon is a full-flowing river by the time it surges through the town of **Salmon**. The town's situation in a grassy valley surrounded by bare windswept hills reflects its cattle town roots. Salmon's predominating culture harks back to the Mormon ranchers and sheepherders who filtered northward from the Idaho Falls area. A more recent infiltration of river runners and recreationists adds spice.

You can lay down your head for a night, buy a pizza, stock up on supplies, see a movie, catch a Salmon River float trip; or delve into local history at the **Lemhi County Historical Museum** at 210 Main Street. Open April-June and Sept-Oct, from 1-5, Mon-Sat; July-Aug, from 10-5, Mon-Sat. Write PO Box 645, Salmon, ID 83467. ☎ 208-756-3342.

US 93 follows the peaceful Salmon River Valley to North Fork, where the Salmon veers sharply westward. The highway continues on to Lost Trail Pass, where it crosses the Continental Divide and enters Montana. You must continue into Montana on Hwy 93 in order to reach North Idaho via US 12 at Lolo Pass, or I-90 by way of Missoula.

Exploring Down the River Road

Take the left-hand Y off US 93 at North Fork onto FS Road 30, referred to locally as simply the River Road, for a trip into a world overlooked by 20th-century progress. **North Fork** is somewhat of a town, boasting a Salmon National Forest ranger station, a gaggle of motel and cabin-type lodgings and a combination store-café.

The River Road runs finger-dipping close to the swift-flowing, rapids-punctuated Salmon for some 50 miles between North Fork and Corn Creek, the riparian gateway to the Frank Church-River of No Return Wilderness. In 1995, several Canadian gray wolves were introduced in this place characterized by tumbled mountains frowning above the storied river. The wolves continue to thrive, mating and producing offspring.

The River Road is paved as far as Shoup above Panther Creek, at more or less the halfway point, being gravel from there on. **Shoup** is a town on the Official Idaho Road Map. Someone forgot to tell the map makers in Boise that Shoup hasn't been a town in years. The Shoup Store is it –

burger and a few grocery items. Electricity to run the freezer is powered by an ingenious battery pack augmented by a creek tumbling downhill.

John and Patty Houlihan's **Gold Hill Mine** is down the road a piece. An elderly white mule named Daisy serves as the official welcoming committee, standing in the middle of the road until you stop. If your window's open, she'll get acquainted up close and personal. You can tour the more-or-less working mine. The tour schedule is on River Road time: no special hours.

Back before the US Forest Service acquired title to much of the backcountry, this area attracted prospectors and their families. They built cabins along the river and settled in, moving on when prospects dimmed. The Forest Service burned them all. The lilacs that once graced their dooryards bloom still, tenacious reminders of another age. The remaining cabins are on deeded land.

River Road People

The people who choose to live here are a hardy bunch. Some raise gardens and fruit trees on narrow strips of fertile bottomland. Some live in cabins reached via hand-over-hand cable cars sliding high above the river. Some operate mom-and-pop businesses. All are jealous of their way of life. The River Road was one of the country's last bastions of hand-cranked phones, modern service having been introduced but a few years ago. Some folks still bewail that technological toehold. Electricity? No way! Efforts to introduce electrical service have been dealt with swiftly and sternly. River Road folk are self-sufficient souls gladly embracing a vanished way of life.

A few still eke a precarious living from gold. On one of my visits to the Shoup Store I met an extended family with several children, come down from the mountains to purchase supplies. They described their pioneer lifestyle working a mining claim, living off the land, delivering their babies themselves, schooling their children. The youngsters held back until they were given ice cream cones.

The River Road does not lack for "characters." John Booker is a white-bearded former river guide who for years has been more or less building The Outpost, a rustic watering hole set photogenically above the river. On the River Road, you take your entertainment where you find it.

*Cabin dwellers living across the Salmon from the North Fork River
use cable cars to cross the river.*

Hwy 28: Salmon to Interstate 15

Running southeast from Salmon, Idaho 28 travels 106 miles to meet up with I-15, 24 miles north of Idaho Falls. Three minuscule Lemhi River towns, **Baker**, **Tendoy** and **Leadore**, punctuate the loneliness of this route slithering between the Lemhi Range on the west and the Beaverhead Mountains on the east. This is cattle and sheep country. I've often as not been halted by sheep or cattle drives filling the highway with lowing and bleating. Cowboys rounding up strays on horseback color this quintessential Western scene.

Explore the **Lewis & Clark backcountry Byway & Adventure Road**, extending from Tendoy to 7,373-foot-high Lemhi Pass. Here stands a memorial to Sacajawea, the remarkable young Lemhi Shoshone woman who guided Lewis & Clark on their trek to the mouth of the Columbia River. The party reached the crest of Lemhi Pass late in the summer of 1805.

At Leadore, the Lemhi River veers off to the west. The stretch to I-15 is virtually uninhabited, save for Mud Lake, a popular fishing spot 14 miles west of I-15 where Idaho 28 merges with Idaho 33. A gaggle of small lakes fed by Canada Creek, tumbling out of the Targhee Range, lie north of Idaho 28 and 33.

Interstate 15: Hwy 33 to Pocatello

The 45-mile stretch of I-15 between the junction with Idaho 33 and Blackfoot slices through the heart of Idaho's famed potato growing country. At the approach to Blackfoot, a sign offering free potatoes to visitors makes sure you recognize this important fact.

A small museum grandly named **Idaho's World Potato Exposition** offers insight into potato history, planting, harvesting, trivia and anything else you ever wanted to know about spuds. And yes, you will be given a free baked potato, complete with sour cream, at the adjoining lunchroom. Modest admission charge. The Exposition, at 130 NW Main Street (take I-15, Exit 93), is open daily, 10-6, June through September. ☎ 208-785-2517.

The **Bingham County Historical Museum** has a collection of Native American relics displayed in a restored circa 1905 home. Also, dolls and World War II outfits. Open year-round, Wed-Fri, 1-5 and by appointment. 190 N. Shilling Ave., Blackfoot, ID 83221. ☎ 208-785-8065.

The **Fort Hall Indian Reservation** covers a sizeable chunk of land stretching from Blackfoot to well south of Pocatello. I-15 bisects the reservation for some 20 miles between the two towns. A stop at Fort Hall, actually more shopping mall than settlement, could be well worth your time. A sizeable store stocks an eclectic mix of tacky souvenirs and beautiful jewelry, beaded items, objets d'art, dolls, moccasins and traditional-style clothing hand-crafted by residents of the Reservation and other Native Americans.

The 1830s-era post from which Fort Hall derives its name was situated on the Snake River some 15 miles northwest of Pocatello. It has long since crumbled, but you can tour a replica of it in Pocatello's **Ross Park**. Recreated from the original Hudson's Bay Company plans, this conscientiously constructed replica evokes a long-vanished era when mountain men swaggered across the landscape. Take Exit 67 off I-15 to reach the **Fort Hall Replica** and the nearby **Bannock County Historical Museum**. The Fort is open in daylight hours from June to mid-September. ☎ 208-254-6258. The Museum is open daily, Memorial Day to Labor Day, 10-6 and Tues-Sat, 10-2, the rest of the year. ☎ 208-233-0434. Both charge nominal admission fees.

The Idaho State University campus at Pocatello houses the **Idaho Museum of Natural History**. Exhibits reflect the bounteous natural history of Idaho and the Intermountain West. Open year-round, Mon-Sat, 10-6; Sunday 12-5. ☎ 208-236-3168.

Geographically, Pocatello falls within *Region 4*. Because the Fort Hall replica ties in with Fort Hall, described above, and because it is this blandly conservative industrial city's chief point of interest, Pocatello receives mention here. Straggling along the Portneuf River just south of the junction of I-15 and I-86, Pocatello offers comfortable accommodations for those who would tarry.

Oregon Trail Country, Along I-86 & I-84

Traveling westward on I-86, you'll pass **American Falls Reservoir.** This large body of water set amid barren hills backs up behind American Falls Dam, one of a series of dams corralling the Snake and storing the irrigation water that helps all those potatoes to grow.

This is Oregon Trail Country. Contact the **South Central Idaho Travel Association** to request a map and brochure describing the Oregon Trail and other emigrant trails in Idaho. The Main Oregon Trail traveled through Southeastern Idaho (see *Region 4, Touring*) to Fort Hall. From American Falls, I-86 and I-84 closely follow the Main Trail to Heyburn, where I-84 veers away. I-84 picks up the trail at Glenns Ferry (see *Region 5, Touring*), continuing to Meridian, a few miles west of Boise. From there, it again veers away from I-84, following the Boise River until it exits Idaho and heads into Oregon.

Present-day Idaho 26 and 20 more or less trace the route of Goodale's Cutoff between Fort Hall and Fort Boise, where it joined the Main Trail. The cutoff was well traveled after 1862, when gold was discovered in the Idaho batholith. The trek over razor-sharp lavalands through what is now Craters of the Moon National Monument must have been harrowing.

Oregon Trail sites along the I-15 corridor include **Massacre Rocks State Park**, a few miles west of American Falls Dam and the town of American Falls. Here, a skirmish arose between Shoshone Indians and emigrants. Five wagons were attacked and 10 emigrants were killed. Original wagon ruts are visible. Emigrants carved their names on nearby **Register Rock**. Interpretive displays showcase Shoshone and Oregon Trail history. Living history campfire programs take place between mid-May and September.

I-84 skirts a chain of conservative agricultural towns such as Rupert, Twin Falls (see *Region 5. Touring*), Burley and Jerome.The numerous other points of interest along the Snake River as it crosses Idaho west of Burley are south of the river and are described in *Region 5.*

Central Idaho

Atomic & Volcanic Energy

US 26 forms an arc between Blackfoot and Twin Falls, looking in on two places quite at odds with the rest of Idaho. (US 26 parallels stretches of Goodale's Cutoff, taken by Oregon Trail emigrants seeking easier going than the main route along the rugged Snake River Canyon). After 34 sagebrush miles, you'll see a sign announcing **Atomic City**. This, in Idaho, the land of pristine wilderness? Seems there's a worm in every apple.

Atomic City, population 25, is the gateway to the US Department of Energy's Idaho National Engineering Laboratory, sprawling across a huge expanse of off-limits real estate. The facility, a reactor testing station, was established in 1949 by the Atomic Energy Commission. You can tour the inoperative EBR-1 Site. In 1951, **Experimental Breeder Reactor-1**, now a National Historic Landmark, became the first power plant to produce electricity using atomic energy. A roadside sign will indicate if the site is open for tours.

Arco, some 17 miles up US 26, proudly touts the distinction of being the first town in the world to be lit with atomic power. But Arco takes pride in more than that, being situated between the northern edge of the Snake River Plain and the foot of the Lost River Range. The apex of these craggily arid mountains is 12,662-foot **Mount Borah**, Idaho's highest peak and the center of the 1883 earthquake.

Arco sprawls across the junction of US Highways 20/26 and 93. The latter scoots for 78 miles through the Lost River Range to Challis. The US Forest Service has constructed an enclosure on the 20-mile-long fault line. This mini-Earthquake Visitor Center is off US 93, a few miles north of Mackay. Stop in Mackay to check out the **Lost River Museum**'s collection of artifacts casting light on area history. Open Saturday-Sunday, 1-5, or by appointment. ☎ 208-588-2669 or 588-2597.

Nearby **Mackay Reservoir**, a modest body of water backing up the Big Lost River, is a popular fishing spot.

US 93/20/26 heads southwest from Arco through some of the baddest badlands you'll ever see: **Craters of the Moon National Monument**. The Monument square-mile surreal moonscape of lava tubes, cones, caves, craters – remnants of eruptions that began some 15,000 years ago and continued until as recently as 2,000 years ago. Geologists predict that eruptions may reoccur.

Allow at least a day to see Craters of the Moon; several to explore the Monument on foot. It's full of surprises, not the least of which are the many lava tubes and caves awaiting exploration. This may be a desolate moonscape, but numerous species of birds and small mammals find it

Idaho's rocky escarpments are a geologist's dream.

to their liking. Wildflowers color this moonscape in spring. A primitive campground snuggles against huge lava formations. Basic accommodations are available in Arco; classier digs can be found in Hailey and Ketchum.

From Carey, down the road a piece from Craters of the Moon, US 26 follows the Little Wood River to the small town of Shoshone. **Shoshone Ice Caves** are some 15 miles to the north. The icy lava caves are a long-standing Idaho tourist attraction. You can visit them during daylight hours from May to October. Tours are scheduled every half-hour and there's an admission charge. Bring a jacket; the temperature inside the caves is a constant 32°.

From Carey, US 20 continues for some 100 miles through arid foothills to I-84 and Mountain Home. A few miles past Carey, it passes through **Picabo**, home of Olympic skier Picabo Street. Fifteen miles or so farther on, the highway bumps up against Idaho 75, the access route to Ketchum/Sun Valley.

US 20 parallels Goodale's Cutoff for some 125 miles, from Arco to the Anderson Ranch Reservoir turnoff. Sizeable **Anderson Ranch Reservoir**, backing up the Boise River behind the dam of that name, is popular with boaters in summer and snowmobilers in winter. The old mining town of **Rocky Bar** drowses several miles north of the reservoir, at the end of a gravel road. Rocky Bar's relative obscurity proves that some Idaho ghost towns may be highly hyped, but others are where you can find them.

After the Anderson Ranch Reservoir turnoff, US 20 passes through a deep canyon enclosing the ructious South Fork of the Boise River. If you blink you'll miss a sign for **Tollgate**. A historical marker identifies this as the place where tolls were once collected to maintain the rough canyon road, thus enabling prospectors and shady ladies en route to Rocky Bar to avoid the steep Syrup Creek grades on Goodale's Cutoff. One James A. Porter established a fine hotel and dairy here. All that remains are a down-at-heel café closed for repairs, and a nondescript shack.

Central Idaho

Highway 75, Through the Wood River Valley

Nineteen miles north of the US 20 junction, Idaho 75 slides into **Hailey**. This thriving town serves as a commercial adjunct to trendy Ketchum and Sun Valley, 12 miles farther up the Wood River Valley. The **Sawtooth Scenic Byway** begins south of Hailey at Bellevue.

The clean-swept hills surrounding the famed Sun Valley resort area come off second best when compared to the grandeur of the Sawtooth Range a few miles to the north over Galena Summit. This is especially true in summer. Winter snows smooth the contrast. The verdant Wood River Corridor is quite lovely and offers pleasant strolling.

The **Sun Valley** area more than makes up for a lack of dramatic beauty through a festive ambiance and a wide variety of recreational offerings. **Ketchum** exudes happy-go-lucky high spirits. The town of some 2,500 permanent residents swells to many times that number in the winter and summer high seasons. The town center is chock-a-block with trendy shops, restaurants and watering holes exuding a pseudo-Western flavor. You'll not find the real West here, better go to Salmon or Grangeville for that, but it's a fun place nonetheless.

By way of contrast, neighboring Sun Valley's condos and expensive homes present a sedate face. The famous Sun Valley Resort, where it all began, attracts a steady stream of celebrities and well-heeled vacationers.

Adventures

On Foot

The Three Wilderness Areas

If you are an avid hiker or backpacker, this big chunk of Idaho will be to you what a fancy confectioner's window is to a kid. Deciding which part of the wilderness to explore first can be a real challenge. Pity the visitor who has only a few days to sample the delights of the Frank Church-River of No Return, the adjoining Gospel Hump and Selway-Bitterroot Wilderness Areas, and the surrounding National Forest backcountry. Some short, easily accessible trails are available, but trails into the backcountry beckon the time-impaired, causing no end of frustration. Set aside at least a week, preferably a couple of weeks or more, to sample this unspoiled place. You'll itch to return again and again.

After you decide where you want to go and what you want to do, it's time to give thought to personal safety measures and the wilderness's strict conservation mandates.

Contact a Sawtooth National Forest or other forest ranger station before striking out, preferably before leaving home. Request a Travel Map and a set of National Forest and wilderness guidelines and caveats. Read them, then follow them to the letter (see How to Use This Book, On Foot). These big, beautiful chunks of wilderness are here for all to enjoy in perpetuity. It behooves each of us to see that they remain unspoiled for others.

It's important that you take responsibility for your safety and that of your companions. Becoming lost or injured in national forest backcountry is no joke. In a designated wilderness area it can be life-threatening. No mechanized vehicles of any kind, other than light planes permitted to land at designated wilderness air strips, are allowed into these areas. That includes helicopters. Rescue helicopters must obtain special permits that are granted after careful deliberation and only in life-or-death situations.

Confer closely with a ranger regarding the trails you wish to explore. Trails delineated on a map may be impassable due to winter storm damage or for other reasons.

National Forests outside the designated wilderness areas are laced with unimproved roads and are open to mechanized vehicles. You can drive to the trailhead of your choice and commence your hike from there, retracing your steps when your hike is done. This is not the case if you wish to hike into a designated wilderness area. You must either start from a jumping-off point at the edge of the wilderness (check in with the local ranger district first), or charter a plane to take you and your supplies to a wilderness air strip. You can arrange with an air service to have supplies flown in at intervals if you plan on spending some time in the wilderness.

Don't overestimate your backcountry skills. Unless you or your companion is an experienced backcountry hiker with solid orienteering and survival skills, it is strongly recommended that you not attempt to backpack into the wilderness on your own. The Frank Church-River of No

Central Idaho

> *Return Wilderness is especially challenging because of
> trails that ascend and descend thousands of feet in only
> a few miles, and steep dropoffs to creeks or rivers
> thousands of feet below. Hire a guide licensed to lead
> treks into wilderness areas.*

If you do intend to hike in the wilderness on your own, obtain a copy of Margaret Fuller's *Trails of the Frank Church-River of No Return Wilderness* before leaving home. The paperback book costs $14.95 and is available at most Idaho book outlets, or order a copy from Signpost Books, 8912 192nd St., Edmonds, WA 98020.

This exceptionally complete book tells you everything you could possibly want to know about backpacking in this, Idaho's largest wilderness area, plus interesting historical anecdotes. Trails are described in detail, including which topographical map(s) to buy, diffculty rating, length of hike and time required to complete it, elevation gain or loss, highest point reached, and much more. Maps, black and white photos and brief descriptions of some Forest Service trails outside the Wilderness Area are also included.

It would be a disservice to you if this book attempted to cover even a few of the 82 wilderness trails described in Margaret Fuller's book. Better to get the entire picture. Suffice it to state that this pristine area offers backpackers trails with challenges and beauty unparalled anywhere else in the Lower 48.

The **Idaho State Centennial Trail** passes through all three of Central Idaho's wilderness areas. Watch for distinctive signs depicting the Trail.

The 206,000-acre **Gospel Hump Wilderness**, southeast of Grangeville and administered by the Nez Perce National Forest, adjoins its much larger cousin on its northwest flank, across the Wild and Scenic Salmon River. This smaller, more user-friendly wilderness is dominated by 8,345-foot **Gospel Peak** and contains trails looking in on over 200 miles of streams and 35 sub-alpine lakes. Contact the Slate Creek Ranger Station in White Bird for a trail map and detailed trail information before starting out.

You can access trails into the Gospel Hump Wilderness via the Slate Creek Trailhead at the end of FS Road 354, off US 95 near White Bird. Or take FS Road 221 south from Grangeville. It joins FS Road 354 at the trailhead. Idaho 14, paralleling the Clearwater River east of Grangeville offers access to FS Roads 492, 222 and 233. **The Gold Rush Loop Tour** accesses several Gospel Hump Wilderness trails.

The 1.3 million-acre **Selway-Bitterroot Wilderness**, administered by the Bitterroot, Clearwater and Nez Perce National Forests, spills over the Bitterroot Range into Montana. Most of this wilderness lies in Idaho.

Much of it is extremely rugged and mountainous, especially the eastern portion abutting Montana. Copies of the helpful and informative *Selway-Bitterroot Wilderness Primer* are available at the above-mentioned ranger stations. It is recommended that you hire a guide if you or a companion are not skilled orienteers/survivalists.

You can access this wilderness from Salmon by heading north into Montana on US 93 and picking up FS Road 468 at the West Fork Ranger Station, 18½ miles southwest of Darby, Montana. You'll traverse 6,589-foot Nez Perce Pass, the route traveled by Chief Joseph and his people during their 1877 trek to a freedom that was not to be. From here, you can follow portions of the Nez Perce Trail and explore the historic Magruder Corridor, taking side-trips on foot.

A high-clearance 4WD vehicle is a must for the rough single-lane dirt track known locally as the "**Magruder Challenge.**" The Corridor traverses the boundary between the Frank Church-River of No Return and the Selway-Bitterroot Wilderness Areas. There are several primitive campgrounds along the way. Numerous points of interest recalling a time when the hopes of many intrepid prospectors were played out to mostly disappointing conclusions line the 95-mile track.

This Corridor is named for Lloyd Magruder, a 19th-century freighter (wagon driver) whose murder, and his friend Hill Beachy's odyssey to apprehend the murderers, have assumed legendary proportions.

The Corridor ends at the Red River Ranger Station, from where FS Road 222 leads to Elk City. See *Touring, Region 1* for a description of the Elk City Wagon Road and The Gold Rush Loop Tour. Booklets describing these Adventure Roads are available at Nez Perce National Forest ranger stations.

Trails also lead into this wilderness area from Selway Falls. Take FS Road 223 at Lowell. You can also access the wilderness from the Moose Creek and Powell Ranger Stations, both off US 12. It is possible to arrange flights into the heart of the wilderness, utilizing air strips at Moose Creek and Shearer.

The Lowman Ranger District

Many trails in the Lowman Ranger District of the Boise National Forest use Forest Service campgrounds as trailheads. Because of the area's summertime popularity and relative closeness to Boise, these campgrounds and trails may offer a less than solitary experience. Many trails are open to off-road vehicles, further cutting into a sublime backcountry experience. But the pine-forested country is beautiful. And there are hot springs, some adjacent to the South Fork of the Payette River. Access from Idaho 21 and 17 is generally good.

Central Idaho

Stop in at the Lowman Ranger District office on Idaho 21 north of Lowman for a descriptive list of trails.

The Sawtooth National Recreation Area

The foothills of the White Cloud Mountains lie east of Idaho 75 and south of the Salmon River. This country, punctuated by several peaks exceeding 10,000 feet, has rocky trails following creeks draining glacial valleys. This virtual network of backcountry trails is accessed from the south bank of the Salmon River (Idaho 75), and from Forest Service roads branching off Idaho 75 south of Stanley. Some trails are short enough for pleasant day hikes.

The backpacking is world-class in the Sawtooth National Recreation Area, a wedge of rumpled backcountry bisected by the Sawtooth Valley and Idaho 75 linking Stanley and the SNRA Headquarters Visitor Center beneath 8,701-foot-high Galena Summit.

The rugged **Sawtooth Range**, rising to the west of the Sawtooth Valley, includes the 217,000-acre Sawtooth Wilderness, famous for lakes glittering among monolithic peaks. This wilderness has trails enough for a lifetime of challenge and rewards. For many, this alpine country evokes the Swiss Alps. All you need are lederhosen and an alpenstock. Lederhosen are a matter of choice, but an alpenstock makes good sense on trails that seem to be more up than down. This splendid wonderland can be accessed via trailheads at Redfish and Stanley Lakes, and at Hellroaring Creek and Pettit Lake off Idaho 75.

If days' long backpacking treks are not an option, you can make shorter hikes, many ranger-led, from the **Redfish Lake Visitor Center** and numerous other trailheads. Many of these trails are rated easy enough for young children.

The SNRA's "back door" can be accessed via trails branching into the southwestern edge of the SNRA from the storied Atlanta Mining District (see *Touring,* page 207).

The Sawtooth National Recreation Area has several publications describing hiking and other recreational opportunities. Obtain copies at any SNRA visitor center or Sawtooth National Forest ranger station.

The Challis & Salmon National Forests

The Challis Ranger District encompasses 462,312 acres of the Salmon and Challis National Forests. Thirty-five trails await your pleasure. Contact a Challis Ranger District office in Challis or Salmon to obtain the appropriate travel maps, plus the information you need to get started. Be aware that off-road vehicles are permitted on some trails.

The Forest Service roads accessing many of these trails are far too rough for passenger cars, but passable in high-clearance 4WD vehicles. Few trails have campgrounds or access to potable water.

Several trails branch from the **Custer Motorway Adventure Road**, traversing this scarred gold country and looking in on pretty **Bayhorse Lake**. Yet others zigzag into the arid, rumpled country north of the Salmon River and west of the Land of the Yankee Fork. Still more explore the backcountry north of Challis and the Lost River country.

Salmon National Forest trails meander through the high country west of Salmon and North Fork and lead into the Frank Church-River of No Return Wilderness Area. Access is via FS Road 055 along Morgan and Panther Creeks (see *Touring,* page 216). These trails are used by horses and pack trains, which have the right of way. Remember to step off the trail to allow the animals to pass. Be careful not to make any sudden movements or loud noises that might spook the animals.

From the Wood River Valley

Several short trails are accessible on or just off Idaho 75. The West Fork of Prairie Creek Trail, accessed 2.7 miles from Idaho 75 near the end of Prairie Creek Road, downslope from Galena Summit, extends two miles through a lovely glacial basin meadow abloom with seasonal wildflowers.

Hiking a Galena Summit trail will happily prolong your visit to this gorgeously wooded natural barrier between the Sawtooth and Wood River valleys. The **Titus Lake Trail**, accessible across the highway from Galena Lodge, meanders along Titus Creek for three miles. The **Galena Summit Trail** is 1.2 miles long. You can also hike the **Galena Summit Ridge**, but the unmarked trail is rudimentary at best.

Craters of the Moon National Monument

Trails within the Craters of the Moon National Monument and the surrounding wilderness range from the short **Devil's Orchard Nature Trail** to a trail heading south

Camping at Craters of the Moon is apt to be a rocky affair.

through the Great Rift Zone to meet one blazed in 1920, over torturous lava, by Robert Limbert and W.L. Cole. This and other trails explore **Echo Crater**, the **Bridge of Tears** and other lava landmarks.

The Visitor Center offers naturalist-led interpretive walks. A free permit is required for staying overnight in the Craters of the Moon Wilderness. A day-use permit is required for hiking or biking here. Craters of the Moon is a harsh, dry, baking-hot environment. Drink lots of liquids to avoid dehydration. And slather on plenty of sun screen.

Guided Hiking/Backpacking Trips

Several experienced guides spend their lives in these wilderness areas, many leading backpacking, horseback and pack animal-supported treks in summer, hunting and fishing trips in season, snowmobiling trips in winter. Most of the guides listed below are members of the Idaho Outfitters and Guides Association. IOGA members' backcountry knowledge is often encyclopedic. They work hard to see that their appreciation and respect for the wilderness rubs off on their guests, while affording the kind of backcountry experiences that they enjoy with their own families. Campfire yarns and hearty meals cooked in the out-of-doors are integral parts of these trips.

When considering a guided trip, don't be timid about asking questions and more questions. Be open regarding your family's hiking and camping experience, ages, interests, food preferences, health problems and anything else that can make a difference between a great trek and one you'd prefer to forget.

The line is often blurred between backpacking, pack-supported, horseback and fishing trips. Some include all of the above, some just backpacking or just horseback riding. See *Travel with Horses* for trips that are primarily on horseback, *Fishing* for trips emphasizing fishing. Many trips originate at, or are centered around, backcountry lodges or guest ranches. Again, the line can be blurred. See *Guest Ranches* for these. The following outfitters lead treks in Central Idaho's wilderness areas and/or national forests. Pack stock carry your gear on most extended treks.

Hiking Outfitters

- **Bill Mason Sun Valley Outfitters** offers a variety of half- and full-day guided high country hikes. Located on the Sun Valley Mall. ☎ 208-622-9305.

- **Mystic Saddle Ranch** runs five-day packstock-supported hiking treks in the Sawtooth Wilderness, camping near mountain lakes. All you carry is a daypack; guides and horses do the rest. Jeff and Deb Bitton also offer customized trips. Winter address: PO Box 736, Challis, ID 83226. ☎ 208-879-5071. Fax 208-879-5069. Summer address: Stanley, ID 83226. ☎ 208-774-3591. Fax 208-774-3455.

- **Rawhide Outfitters** has one- to three-day hiking trips in the Lemhi Mountain Range south of Salmon. John and Cathy Cranney and Maurice Foland include early morning and evening wildlife "safaris" where you are likely to see elk, deer, antelope and, occasionally, a mountain goat or sheep. 204 Larson St., Salmon, ID 83467. ☎ 208-756-4276.

- **ROW, Inc.,** aka River Odysseys West, offers six-day hikes along the Middle Fork of the Salmon River in the Frank Church-River of No Return Wilderness Area. PO Box 579, Coeur d'Alene, ID 83816. ☎ 800-451-6034. Fax 208-667-6506.

- **Sawtooth Wilderness Outfitters'** Darl and Kari Allred feature customized packstock-supported hiking trips in the Sawtooth Wilderness between their pack station at Grandjean and the old mining town of Atlanta. PO Box 81, Garden Valley, ID 83622. ☎ 208-462-3416 (winter), 208-259-3408 (summer). Fax 208-462-3813.

- **Sun Valley Trekking Company** offers day hiking trips. PO Box 2200, Sun Valley, ID 83353. ☎ 208-788-9585.

- **White Cloud Outfitters** is centrally located in Challis for trips into the White Clouds, the Land of the Yankee Fork and the Frank Church-River of No Return Wilderness. They offer customized packstock-supported hiking trips and three- to five-day Base Camp Hiking Adventure trips. Michael Scott and Louise Stark also offer spot pack services for backpackers who wish to hike on their own and have supplies delivered via horseback to designated dropsites. They also supply horses for backpackers wishing to ride into a campsite. They then return the horses at a prearranged time for the ride out. PO Box 217, Challis, ID 83226. ☎ 208-879-4574. Fax 208-879-5513.

- **World Class Outfitting Adventures** specializes in mule-supported pack trips in the Selway-Bitterroot Wilderness Area. Jason and Carolyn Clinkenbeard also offer spot pack services to the campsite or wilderness destination of your choice. PO Box 351, Arlee, MT 59821. ☎ 800-203-3246 or 406-726-3829. Fax 406-726-3466.

Central Idaho

Climbing & Mountaineering

Possibly the most accessible climb in the Challis National Forest is 12,662-foot **Borah Peak**. Idaho's highest mountain became world famous after the earthquake fault bearing its name cut loose. The peak, 35 miles south of Challis in the Lost River Range, is a fairly easy climb. Access is off US 93 at the "Access to Borah Peak" sign.

Normally, climbing equipment is not necessary if you climb in July or August when the snowpack is light. The vertical elevation from the jump-off point to the top of the mountain is 5,000 feet within a distance of two to three miles. There are no improved trails – just a route blazed by other climbers. The view from the top is incomparable: several mountain ranges, competing for sky space, boast peaks in excess of 11,000 feet.

If you are into serious climbing, the Sawtooth Range, the White Cloud Peaks and the Boulder Mountains are your kinds of places. The **Sawtooths'** sheer walls offer technical climbers lots of challenges. The entire Sawtooth Range is composed of various textures of granite. On a single peak, the rock may vary from hard and sparsely jointed to flaky and ball-bearinged, but proper route selection makes it possible to climb most major peaks on solid granite. Several peaks rise over 10,000 feet, but the bases of many are in the 8,000 to 9,000 foot range, making one-day ascents possible. Many peaks require technical aid on some exposures, but may also be climbed without technical aide via high-angle ridges and talus slopes.

Most peaks in the **White Clouds** and **Boulders** can be climbed without technical aide by off-trail scrambling and boulder hopping. The rock is composed mainly of metamorphosed sediments with some granite and volcanic intrusions. Most of it is highly fractured and loose, precluding high angle technical climbing. Many White Cloud and Boulder peaks and ridges exceed 10,000-11,000 feet.

Do not climb alone. Let someone know your travel route and expected time of return. Sudden fall snowstorms can quickly wipe summer off the map and present life-threatening conditions. Always check your route with a Sawtooth National Recreation Area ranger.

Travel with Horses & Pack Animals

Sure-footed horses and mules are the optimum mode of transportation in Idaho's three wilderness areas, the Sawtooth National Recreation Area and the contiguous national forests.

Backpacking is great for those who are conditioned for steep climbs at high altitudes. But for sheer versatility, horses and mules are hard to beat. Trails and campgrounds are geared to them. Horses and pack strings have the right of way on most backcountry trails. And new vistas open up, when seen from a horse's back.

Chances are, unless you are an experienced backcountry rider trailering your personal horse, you will be signing on for one of the wilderness horse trips for which the West is famous.

 If you are considering using the family nag for backcountry travel, be sure your steed is sure-footed enough to negotiate steep, rocky trails and virtually spook-proof. Outfitters' horses are trained for backcountry travel.

Wilderness horseback trips take you deep into the real West; the unvarnished West experienced by grizzled prospectors leading pack mules into the heart of the land that became the Frank Church-River of No Return Wilderness – the West of Mountain Men, intrepid homesteaders and hard-riding cowboys rounding up strays. This West plays a big part in the lives of folks who live on the perimeter of the wilderness today. They come here to refresh their souls through primitive camping, fishing and hunting, keeping in touch with a lifestyle that shaped their parents' and grandparents' lives. You can do the same.

Many of the outfitters and guides listed below have roots extending deep into this Western ethos. Fine horsemen and women all, they choose their horses and mules with a careful eye for surefootedness and easy-going dispositions. Ideally, horses are matched to riders' experience and abilities.

Central Idaho

Selecting a Horseback Outfitter

When selecting an outfitter, be sure to ask if riding instruction is offered prior to setting out on the trail. This is especially important if you are accompanied by a young tagalong, or are yourself a novice, rusty or inexperienced rider. If you have children, find out if kid-friendly horses are available, if the trip's pace is geared to families, and if any special kids' activities are included. The latter is usually a non-issue. By their very nature, horseback treks offer enough fun stuff to keep the most restive child involved. Most kids eat 'em up.

Other questions might include how long the first day's and subsequent rides will be. First day rides should be of only a few hours' duration so as to ease your muscles into riding condition and keep stiffness and soreness to a minimum. Ask if horses are outfitter-owned or rented for the season. Outfitter-owned is usually preferable. Find out where you will camp and if tents will be provided, what kind of food to expect, what activities are on offer. This is especially important if a child accompanies you, or if you have a special interest such as bird watching, photography or fishing. As always when choosing an outfitter, don't be shy.

The following outfitters are licensed in the State of Idaho and are IOGA members adhering to a strict code of ethics.

Horseback Outfitters

- **Bill Mitchell Outfitters, Inc.** offers three-, four-and six-day pack-supported horseback trips in the Selway-Bitterroot and Frank Church-River of No Return Wilderness Areas, utilizing a high-country camp. Photography opportunities, fishing and side-hikes are integral parts of every trip. 364 McCarthy Loop, Hamilton, MT 59840. ☎ 406-363-4129.

- **Dixie Outfitters**, a mom-and-pop operation owned by Emmett and Zona Smith, offers summer trail rides by reservation from their log lodge in the old mining town of Dixie, sandwiched between the Gospel Hump and Frank Church-River of No Return Wilderness. Dixie's permanent residents number 12. Dixie, ID 83525. ☎ 208-842-2417.

- **Lost Lakes Outfitters** offers horseback trips to a base camp in the vicinity of three "lost lakes" in the Bitterroot Wilderness. HC66, Box 226, Looskia, ID 83539. ☎ 208-926-4988.

- **Mystic Saddle Ranch** has a variety of overnight to five-day pack-supported horseback trips in the Sawtooth Wilderness, looking in on high mountain lakes and traversing historic trails. Jeff and Deb Bitton also offer customized trips. Winter address: PO Box 736, Challis, ID 83226. ☎ 208-879-5071. Fax 208-879-3455. Summer address: Stanley, ID 83278. ☎ 208-774-3591. Fax 208-774-3455.

- **Rawhide Outfitters** runs one- to three-day horse pack trips in the Lemhi Range south of Salmon. Their base camp near Cow Creek has wall tents with cots and solar showers.

Trips emphasize fishing, horseshoe throwing and other activities, along with riding. A good option for families with young children or for those who prefer a more leisurely horseback experience. 204 Larson St., Salmon, ID 83467. ☎ 208-756-4276.

- **Redfish Lake Corrals** at Redfish Lake features Sawtooth National Recreation Area trail rides from 1½ hours to all day. Rides look in on various high country lakes and include overviews of Big and Little Redfish Lakes. Overnight and longer trips are available. Jeff and Deb Bitton, Stanley, ID 83278. Daytime, ☎ 208-774-3311; evening, ☎ 208-774-3591.

- **Renshaw Outfitters** offers summer pack trips emphasizing high mountain lake and stream fishing in the Selway-Bitterroot Wilderness Area. Jim Renshaw, PO Box 1165, Kamiah, ID 83536. ☎ 800-452-2567 or 208-935-0736 or 208-926-4520. Fax 208-935-0788.

- **Rugg's Outfitting** also runs summer pack trips in the Selway-Bitterroot Wilderness Area. Ray Rugg, 50 Dry Creek Rd., Superior, MT 59872. ☎/Fax 406-822-4240.

- **Sawtooth Wilderness Outfitters**, owned and operated by Darl and Kari Allred and family, conduct hourly to full-day trail rides from their Grandjean pack station. Pack trips include a two-day loop through the Sawtooths to Sawtooth Lake, a five-day Float and Ride Vacation beginning with a two-day float on the South Fork of the Payette River, and customized guided pack trips in the Sawtooth Wilderness. PO Box 81, Garden Valley, ID 83622. ☎ 208-462-3416 (winter), 208-259-3408 (summer). Fax 208-462-3813.

- **Shadow Basin Outfitters** offers three- to 10-day horseback trips in the Selway-Bitterroot and Frank Church-River of No Return Wilderness. Ten-day trips include up to 75 miles of horseback travel. Troy and Lori Ginn also operate a professional outfitter and guide school. PO Box 493, Hamilton, MT 59840. ☎ 800-808-4868.

- **Stanley Potts Outfitters** runs seven-day horseback rides in the Frank Church-River of No Return Wilderness Area that include fishing high mountain lakes. This being the area where 35 Rocky Mountain gray wolves have been released in recent years, guests may see wolf tracks and scat or hear their eerie howls. Stanley and Joy Potts also offer special five-day Camping With Wolves interpretive

Central Idaho

trips (see *Cultural Excursions*). Box 61, Shoup, ID 83469. ☎/Fax 208-394-2135.

- **Wally York & Son, Inc.** has pack stock horseback trips of varying durations into the Selway-Bitterroot and Frank Church-River of No Return Wilderness Areas from their base camp about 60 miles east of Elk City. Wally York, whose son, W. Travis York, is the current owner-manager, started the outfitting company in 1932. PO Box 319, Elk City, ID 83525. ☎ 208-842-2367.

- **White Cloud Outfitters** lets you combine a wilderness experience with some creature comforts. Guests hike or ride in to a base camp in the White Cloud Mountains or the Frank Church-River of No Return Wilderness Area, then hike or ride to a different destination each day. Michael Scott and Louise Stark also offer single-day rides in the White Clouds or the Land of the Yankee Fork. Also available is the ultimate wilderness experience: three- to 10-day roving pack trips into the White Clouds or the Frank Church-River of No Return Wilderness. PO Box 217, Challis, ID 83226. ☎ 208-879-4574. Fax 208-879-5513.

- **World Class Outfitting Adventures** runs three- to six-day pack-supported horseback trips in parts of the Selway-Bitterroot Wilderness Area. These include the Elk Creek Meadows area, camping at a traditional Native American campsite, the historic A.P. Cooper homestead, and ridge-running to a USFS lookout tower. Jason and Carolyn Clinkenbeard, PO Box 351, Arlee, MT 59821. ☎ 800-203-3246 or 406-726-3829. Fax 406-726-3466.

Llama Trekking

Llamas are delightful companions on backcountry treks. More biddable, probably more intelligent, than mules, these gentle pack animals actually want to please. They are easily led, even by children. On a "lunch with a llama" trek, my daughter, Amy, happily discovered that llamas love to be petted and fussed over. They add a distinct charm to mountain trekking.

Llama Trekking Outfitters

- **Sun Valley Trekking Company**, PO Box 2200, Sun Valley, ID 83353. ☎ 208-788-9585.

- **Venture Outdoors** conducts Take a Llama to Lunch walks and offers three- to five-day luxury llama treks to alpine lakes. PO Box 2251, Hailey, ID 83333. ☎ 800-528-LAMA or 208-788-5049.

On Wheels

Bicycling & Mountain Biking

 The emphasis on wilderness area backpacking and horseback riding seems to push Central Idaho mountain biking off-track. But the Wood River Valley has over 30 miles of bike paths along the old Union Pacific Railroad right-of-way that invite leisurely family bicycling. Many National Forest trails lend themselves to mountain biking. Check with local ranger districts to determine which are best suited to your skill level.

Guided Biking Outfitters

- **Sun Valley Trekking** leads day-long mountain biking trips. PO Box 2200, Sun Valley, ID 83353. ☎ 208-788-9585.

- **Venture Outdoors** has several day rides over a variety of high mountain trails. They also offer five-day bike trips in the Smoky Mountain Range of the Boise National Forest, a six-day road bike tour that includes a day of rafting the Salmon River and biking in the Yankee Fork Mining Area and Craters of the Moon National Monument. Trips include inn stays and llama-supported rides. PO Box 2251, Hailey, ID 83333. ☎ 800-528-LAMA or 208-788-5049.

- **Wilderness River Outfitters** runs six-day, 95-mile biking trips through the Magruder Corridor and over the Nez Perce Trail in the Selway-Bitterroot Wilderness Area, taking side trips to mountain lakes and streams for fishing. Box 72, Lemhi, ID 83465. ☎ 800-252-6581. Fax 208-756-3959.

Motorbiking & ATVs

Motorbiking is another spin altogether. I'll admit to a measure of perplexity over the contrasting activities thrust on backcountry areas. On the one hand, we have the time-honored backpacking, horseback/pack animal, Nordic skiing tradition. On the other, we have what many consider an excessively noisy intrusion of motorbikes, ATVs and snowmobiles. Be that as it may, if you are into motorbiking or ATVing, Central Idaho has numerous choices.

All kinds of mechanized vehicles, and that includes motorbikes, are prohibited in designated wilderness areas. That leaves plenty of scope on National Forest lands outside the wilderness areas, and in the **Sawtooth National Recreation Area**.

State regulations are available at Forest Service offices and ranger stations. Road and trail restrictions are clearly marked on *National Forest Travel Maps*. Other restrictions may be in force on a temporary basis due to weather or other conditions. Always check with a local ranger district before setting out.

Numerous trails in the SNRA are open to motorbikes and offer plenty of fun and challenge. Pick up a *Travel Plan Map* at any Sawtooth National Forest office. These maps provide information on routes, levels of difficulty, natural features, length of ride and more.

Remember to respect the rights of hikers and horseback riders who may be using the same trail. A Federal regulation prohibits the use of motorbikes and other mechanized vehicles in developed campgrounds.

- **Mulligan's Sun Valley Adventure Center** offers ATV tours. PO Box 2123, Ketchum, ID 83340. ☎ 208-726-9137.

On Water

Whitewater Rafting

The Main Salmon & the Middle Fork of the Salmon

 Over the years, thousands of adventurers have come from throughout the US to float down one of Central Idaho's two high-profile rivers, the mighty Salmon and the rambunctious Middle Fork of the Salmon. There is no more exciting or more fitting introduction to this fabulous state. These true wilderness rivers whoosh through the heart of the Frank Church-River of No Return Wilderness Area, carving the second and third deepest canyons in North America (Hells Canyon is the deepest). Both rivers run their courses within Idaho's borders, as though loathe to leave the place that gave them birth. The 400-mile-long Salmon drains the largest basin within a single state outside Alaska. Both rivers run free and wild, unhindered by dams. The Sunbeam Dam once backed up the Salmon, but the small dam has long since been breached.

Both rivers figure prominently in Idaho history. Indians have lived along their banks for centuries, creating pictographs and petroglyphs that remain for us to ponder. Trappers and prospectors came this way,

The Middle Fork of the Salmon River runs through a land laced with hot springs.

leaving poignant reminders of toilsome lives – a worn boot marking a grave, a mine shaft filled with disappointment. Homesteaders came this way too, leaving, perhaps, a gnarled apple tree or a lilac bush to mark where cabins once stood and lives were once played out.

There was a time when you could explore long-abandoned cabins and other flotsam. No longer. Most of the ones that didn't fall down have been burned or otherwise destroyed in response to Forest Service edicts. A handful of "historically significant" structures, many of them ranger stations, remain. This selective destruction doesn't set well with those who value and respect the struggles of folks who offered their lives to this wild place.

No floater on these two rivers should even think of putting in without taking along the following books relating, mile-by-mile, rapid-by-rapid, the stories of these rivers and the remarkable people who left their marks on them. Copies of *River of No Return* and *The Middle Fork & the Sheepeater War*, by Johnny Carey and Cort Conley, are available at many Idaho bookstores and sports outlets.

Central Idaho

River Running

Legend has it that the Salmon's "River of No Return" appellation came about when members of the Lewis & Clark expedition found the rapids too dangerous to permit canoes to travel upstream. Some say that a National Geographic *magazine* party coined the name in 1935. The romantic-sounding nickname more probably had its genesis with the rivermen who ran scows (sweep-boats) downriver from Salmon or Challis, bringing supplies to isolated homesteads, then abandoned the craft because it was impossible to take them back upstream against the rapids.

In the prospecting and homesteading era prior to the turn of the century until the end of the Second World War, these scows, consisting of boxy raftlike hulls steered by way of long "sweeps" attached to the boats' rudders, were the accepted means of travel on the Salmon. In 1947, one Glen Woolridge ushered in a new age of river travel by successfully taking a plywood boat, propelled by a 22 hp engine, upriver from Riggins to Salmon. Today, jetboats' powerful engines slice through rapids like knives through brie. Restrictions limit their use both in and out of the wilderness area. And there is talk of further limitations.

Today's popular rafting trips down the Salmon and Middle Fork had their genesis in the rubber rafts that appeared in Army Surplus stores after the war. Descendants of these early rafts have been tinkered with and improved, resulting in the commodious self-bailing craft now used to take adventure-seekers down these rivers.

Riggins is generally considered to be the division point between the Lower and Main Salmon. Rafters headed down the Lower Salmon put in at Riggins or near White Bird, while Main Salmon rafters generally meet at Salmon and put in at Corn Creek on the threshold of the wilderness. From Corn Creek, the Wild and Scenic Salmon River runs through the Frank Church-River of No Return and Gospel Hump wilderness areas, emerging at Carey Creek, some 25 miles short of Riggins. Jetboats also ply this last lap.

Choosing between floating the Main or Middle Fork is a tough call. The **Main** is an "easier" and more predictable "pool and drop" river, a series of quiet waters punctuated by rapids ranging from Class II to Class IV. It is more built up, by wilderness standards. Owners of several "grandfathered" guest ranches obtained permits on a renewable basis following the Wilderness Act of 1964. But don't expect the Main to be short on excitement and wilderness ambience.

Most Idaho river trips camp on sand beaches.

The shallower **Middle Fork**, ranked as one of the top 10 whitewater rivers in the world, is much more capricious. The intensity of its rapids is more dependent on water depth, which in turn is dependent on area rainfall or lack thereof. Rapids in the Class III to Class IV range require considerable technical skill, particularly when low water turns the river into a rock garden.

Stanley is the staging area for Middle Fork floats. River trips customarily put in at Boundary Creek, but they fly in to the Indian Creek air strip in low water. The take-out point is at Cache Bar.

Rising in the Sawtooth National Forest north of Lowman, the Middle Fork rollics through the Frank Church-River of No Return Wilderness from south to north, dropping 2,750 feet in 107 miles before emptying into the Main Salmon at Cache Bar, downriver from Shoup. The merging of these two rivers is strikingly apparent as the clear, blue Middle Fork meets the deeper, greener Salmon.

The Middle Fork is pristine in the best sense of the word. Almost entirely within the wilderness area, it laps the skirts of not a single town. Its banks are untouched by civilization, save for a bridge or two carrying horse trails across the river and a couple of "grandfathered" lodges. Hot springs are scattered above the shoreline, some cascading over rocks, thus providing floaters with instant hot showers. Pictographs, reminders of the Native Americans who passed this way, can be seen on towering rock faces.

Central Idaho

Mountain goats, here caught in the Frank Church-River of No Return Wilderness, are curious creatures.

Wildlife, seeming to know no fear, come up close. A mother deer and her spindly spotted fawn nonchalantly trailed through our float party's campsite one morning. The poised mama and baby simply sauntered on their way, taking no notice of us. Another day, I awoke to a rustling in the nearby grasses. I opened my eyes and there, mere feet from my head, a covey of chukkar partridge pecked about on morning patrol, oblivious to my presence.

Floating these rivers is best left to professionals unless you know the river well, have river running expertise and equipment, and wish to deal with the permit process. A finite number of put-in permits is awarded to individuals and outfitters licensed to take parties down designated rivers. Parties must adhere to put-in and take-out dates and locations and camp at assigned campsites, almost always on sand beaches created from spring runoffs.

One- or two-day floats, usually putting in at Riggins or Salmon, are available on the Salmon. Wilderness floats on these rivers are usually of five or six days. Combination floats lof 10-14 days are available. A few outfitters offer epic trips covering the entire Salmon River system.

Running the rapids is the main attraction. But there's much more: hiking the banks to explore old mines and petroglyphs; soaking in thermal pools and swimming; spotting mountain goats, elk or eagles; fishing for trout; reading a book while the river plays background music.

As river trips increased in popularity and outfitters found themselves competing, meals evolved from steak and potatoes to sumptuous repasts transported in huge coolers and prepared in camp kitchens. Dutch oven breads and desserts approach an art form. Outfitters even produce an endless supply of icy cold beer and pop from those seemingly bottomless coolers.

Most outfitters supply tents, but citified habits gradually submit to the river's seductive pull. The first night out, tents sprout like a village of toadstools. The second night, only two or three tents pop up. For the remaining nights, most guests flop their sleeping bags in the open, under stars shining with incredibly intense brilliance. There is no lovelier sleepytime tune than the melody of the river, played out only feet away.

Preparing for a River Trip

As when choosing any kind of outfitter, ask lots of questions. If you have young tagalongs, ask if the proposed trip takes children's needs into consideration. Is your child timid or reluctant to try new experiences, a gung-ho type, reveling in challenges? Running rapids can be frightening for young children; many outfitters set age limits. Twelve is a good first rapids age, though younger kids often take to them like... well, you know.

Ask about the **rafts**. Does the outfitter use oar rafts rowed by a guide while guests ride along? Or do they use paddle rafts offering everyone a chance to paddle? Or a combination of both? Are standard or inflatable kayaks an option? A few outfitters use dories, graceful craft that ride over the rapids rather than through them.

Be sure you understand what kinds of **gear to bring**. Nights can be nippy on the river, but summer days are almost invariably hot in these deep canyons. Be prepared. Bring proper footwear. River sandals are a must; hiking boots a close second. Most outfitters supply lists of gear to bring. You will be cautioned not to bring more stuff than will fit into a duffle-size dry bag. River running is no fashion parade, so a couple of changes of shorts and T-shirts, a pair of jeans and a sweatshirt, should pretty well do it. Some wear swimsuits, but I prefer shorts and a T-shirt in and out of the water. Expect the sun to be searing hot; bring SPF 20 or higher sun screen, sunglasses and a hat.

Know your limitations and those of your companions, especially if you are at the far end of the age spectrum. Running the Middle Fork, in particular, involves a fair amount of rock scrambling if you wish to explore onshore. The time is past when floating these wilderness rivers was only for super-fit adventurers, but they do include experiences that may be beyond some persons' desires or capabilities. Some outfitters offer more "luxurious" river trips than others. Ask about matters of concern to you.

Central Idaho

Most of the guides who will take you downriver lead interesting and enviable lives. Many are moonlighting graduate students, teachers and other professionals who often enrich trips with personal knowledge and experiences. Others are dedicated river rats who run South and Central American rivers in winter. A lucky few change rafts for skis in winter. All have undergone river guide training and are licensed by the State of Idaho.

The outfitters listed below are members of the Idaho Outfitters and Guides Association (IOGA). As such, they are licensed, bonded and adhere to a strict code of ethics. Outfitters are permitted a finite number of guests on each trip. Reserve early!

Salmon & Middle Fork of the Salmon Outfitters

- **Aggipah River Trips** offers six-day excursions on the Main Salmon and the Middle Fork. Customized three- and four-day trips can be arranged. Bill and Peggy Bernt also offer 12-day combined Salmon and Middle Fork trips, plus a whopping 18-day trip on the entire Salmon River system. They will arrange river trips with lodge stays, an attractive option for the physically challenged. They also run combination horseback/float trips. Box 425, Salmon, ID 83467. ☎ 208-756-4167.

- **ARTA (American River Touring Association)** offers five- or six-day Main Salmon floats and six-day Middle Fork trips. They also have a 12-day combination Middle Fork and Main Salmon trip from Boundary or Indian Creek to Carey Creek. 24000 Casa Loma Rd., Groveland, CA 95321. ☎ 800-323-2782.

- **Custom River Tours** runs five-day Middle Fork floats using oar boats and paddle boats. Inflatable kayaks are provided on request. Ken Masoner, PO Box 7071, Boise, ID 83707. ☎ 800-432-4611.

- **ECHO: The Wilderness Company, Inc.** offers Main Salmon floats and a special August kids' float. 6529 Telegraph Way, Oakland, CA 94609. ☎ 800-652-3246. Fax 510-652-3987.

- **Hatch River Expeditions** offers six-day trips on the Middle Fork using oar boats. Paddle boats are an option for floaters in top shape with previous paddling experience and are dependent on enough paddlers signing up for a given trip. Kayaks are provided on request for highly skilled kayakers willing to kayak the full distance. PO Box 1150,

Vernal, UT 84078. ☎ 800-342-8243 or 801-789-4316. Fax 801-789-8513.

- **Holiday River Expeditions** organizes five- and six-day Main Salmon floats using oar boats, plus paddle boats for experienced floaters. Inflatable kayaks are provided on request. A scenic charter flight is included in the fee. PO Box 86, Grangeville, ID 83530. ☎ 800-628-2565 or 208-983-1518. Fax 208-983-1695.

- **Mackay Wilderness Trips** has four- and five-day floats on the Main Salmon and three- and six-day Middle Fork expeditions. They use pontoon boats for camp gear and a combination of oar boats, paddle rafts and inflatable kayaks for guests. They will also extend guests' vacations with mountain or riverside ranch stays. 3190 Airport Way, Boise, ID 83705. ☎ 800-635-5336.

- **Middle Fork River Expeditions** specializes in three-and six-day trips down the Middle Fork of the Salmon River. Jean Ridle and crew have been running the Middle Fork for 17 years. Summer address: PO Box 199, Stanley, ID 83278. Winter address: 1615-21 Avenue East, Seattle, WA 98112. Year-round, ☎ 800-801-5146.

- **Middle Fork Wilderness Outfitters**, owned and operated by Gary and Kitty Shelton and Eric Rector, offers three- to six-day Middle Fork trips via oar and paddle boats and inflatable kayaks. A flight to Ketchum at float's end is included in the fee. PO Box 575, Ketchum, ID 83340. ☎ 800-726-0575 or 208-726-5999.

- **O.A.R.S. (Outdoor River Specialists)** offers five-, six- or seven-day floats on the Main Salmon and six-day Middle Fork trips.
Oar and paddle rafts, dories, inflatable kayaks and unique paddle craft are used on the Main Salmon, oar and paddle rafts and inflatable kayaks on the Middle Fork with dories available in June high water. O.A.R.S. also runs six-day Main Salmon Lodge trips wherein guests spend each night at a different riverside lodge. They also offer 12-day Middle Fork/Main Salmon and 12-day Main/Lower Salmon combo trips, plus an unforgettable 17-day Middle Fork/Main/Lower Salmon trip. PO Box 67, Angels Camp, CA 95222. ☎ 209-736-4677. Fax 209-736-2902. Web site: http://oars.com. E-Mail: reservations@oars.com.

Central Idaho

- **Orange Torpedo Boats,** owned and operated by Eric and Becky Smith, has five- and six-day camping trips on the Main Salmon, as well as early season five-day lodge trips. Guests paddle inflatable "Orange Torpedos" 86 miles downriver from Corn Creek to Carey Creek. Paddle and oar rafts are available on request. PO Box 1111, Grants Pass, OR 97526. ☎ 800-635-2925. Fax 541-471-0995. E-Mail: ott@cdsnet.net. Web site: www.ott@cdsnet.net/business/ott.

- **Outdoor Adventures** has Main Salmon floats complete with "kid coordinators." Box 1149, Point Reyes, CA 94920. ☎ 800-323-4234. Fax 415-663-8617.

- **Rawhide Outfitters,** owned and operated by John and Cathy Cranney and Maurice Foland, offers one- and two-day Main Salmon floats from a put-in near Salmon through the feisty Pine Creek Rapid. This was the rapid that stymied Lewis & Clark in 1805, causing them to characterize the Salmon as "impassable." These are not wilderness trips, but have the advantage of a gold mine tour and wetlands wildlife watching. 204 Larson St., Salmon, ID 83467. ☎ 208-756-4276.

- **R&R Outdoors, Inc.** runs five-day Main Salmon floats. HC 2 Box 500, Pollock, ID 83547. ☎ 800-574-1224.

- **Tour West** offers four-day floats on a 90-mile stretch of the Main Salmon using oar rafts and inflatable kayaks. PO Box 333, Orem, UT 84059. ☎ 800-453-9107 or 801-225-0755. Fax 801-225-7979. E-Mail: twriver@aol.com.

- **ROW, Inc. (River Odysseys West)** has five- and six-day Middle Fork trips. Oar and paddle rafts are supported by a 16-foot sweep boat carrying gear. Guests also have the option of playing around in inflatable kayaks, dubbed Daring Duckies by ROW owners Peter Grubb and Betsy Bowen. PO Box 579, Coeur d'Alene, ID 83816. ☎ 800-451-6034. Fax 208-667-6506.

- **Wapiti River Guides,** owned and operated by Gary Lane, specializes in off-beat trips for the culturally curious. Lane offers a five-day Main Salmon trip entitled "Native Medicine, Magic and Mysteries" designed to enable you to attain harmony and balance in your life. Box 1125, Riggins, ID 83549. ☎ 800-488-9872 or 208-628-3523.

- **Warren River Expeditions, Inc.**, owned and operated by Dave and Thyra Warren, specializes in a variety of six-day Main Salmon trips utilizing paddle boats, self-bailing "incept" rafts and inflatable and hard shell sit-on-top kayaks. Trips include two nights in a lodge. Specialty trips include Grandparents/Grandkids and Seniors Only lodge stay trips. Floats end with either a jetboat ride upriver or an air taxi flight to Salmon. PO Box 1375, Salmon, ID 83467. ☎ 800-765-0421 or 208-756-6387. Fax 208-756-4495.

- **White Cloud Outfitters**, owned and operated by Mike and Louise Stark, gives a different twist on a Salmon River trip: a "Headwaters" day float that ends with a soak at Challis Hot Springs. PO Box 217, Challis, ID 83226. ☎ 208-879-4574. Fax 208-879-5513.

- **Wilderness River Outfitters and Trail Expeditions, Inc.**, owned and operated by Fran and Joe Tonsmeire, offers five- and six-day Salmon River trips, plus nine-day bike/Salmon River combo trips. Also: 10-day combination guest ranch/Salmon River adventures beginning with a four-day stay at Hayden Creek Ranch in the Lemhi Mountains and ending with a float down the Main Salmon. Ask about their spring naturalist-led and September self-improvement trips on the Main Salmon. PO Box 72, Lemhi, ID 83465. ☎ 800-252-6581. E-mail: wro@wilderness-river.com.

- **World Wide River Expeditions**, owned by Richard Jones, leads six-day floats on the Main Salmon and the Middle Fork using oar and paddle rafts and inflatable kayaks. 153 East 7200 South, Midvale, UT 84047. ☎ 800-231-2769 (in Utah: 801-566-2662). Fax 801-566-2722.

The Wild & Scenic Selway River

The Upper Selway, plunging crazily from its source high in the Bitterroot Mountains of Montana through Idaho's Selway-Bitterroot Wilderness Area, is a low-profile river with a high-profile thrill quotient. One launch is permitted daily in order to preserve the river's pristine character. This true wilderness river rivals the Middle Fork of the Salmon for clear, cold water and gorgeous backcountry vegetation. It's a river fit to challenge the hardiest adventurer. Class III and IV rapids are frequent and exciting, with Class V rapids in spring runoff. Private permits are hard to draw.

The following outfitters, both IOGA members, offer upper, or main Selway River trips.

Selway River Outfitters

- **ARTA (American Touring Association)** runs five-day Upper Selway trips from Paradise to Selway Falls, camping on beaches set against meadows and forests. 24000 Casa Loma Rd., Groveland, CA 95321. ☎ 800-323-2782.

- **Whitewater Adventures** is owned and operated by Elwood and Donna Masoner. Guests enter the water at Magruder Ranger Station over Nez Perce Pass from Montana and spend five days threading rapids through the wild Selway-Bitterroot Wilderness before floating the "tamer" Selway to a point above Selway Falls. Trips run from late June to late July, but the Masoners suggest that novice rafters consider one of the later launch dates when the river runs a tad quieter. PO Box 184, Twin Falls, ID 83303. ☎ 208-733-4548.

Kayaking

Expert kayakers can go anywhere whitewater rafters go. See the preceding section on whitewater rafting for river descriptions and outfitters who offer kayaking on Main Salmon and Middle Fork of the Salmon. You must obtain a permit from the relevant National Forest if you wish to kayak the Middle Fork and/or the wilderness portion of the Salmon on your own.

If an extended trip is not your goal, but rather an opportunity to play around for a couple of hours or a day, you can launch your kayak at numerous spots with direct highway access. Providentially, the Salmon follows Idaho 75 and US 93, or vice versa, between Stanley and Challis, between Challis and North Fork, and the River Road between North Fork and Corn Creek.

Probably the most popular play spot is at the confluence of the **Salmon and Yankee Fork**, just east of the old Sunbeam Dam on Idaho 75, 13 miles east of Stanley. The combination of gnarly rapids and steep drops is irresistible. The river is about 200 feet wide here. Depths vary from 12 feet in spring runoff to a mere foot in fall low water.

Another prime play place is farther east, in a 27-mile stretch of the Salmon **between Buckhorn Rest Area and the Torrey's Hold Access Site**. Rapids here are Class I and II, but some are Class III and IV in May and June when runoff is high.

- **Warren River Expeditions, Inc.** offers Kayak Workshops on the Main Salmon. Dave and Thyra Warren also offer Kayak Support Trips in conjunction with Salmon river rafting excursions. See descriptions under *Whitewater Rafting*. PO Box 1375, Salmon, ID 83467. ☎ 800-765-0421 or 208-756-6387. Fax 208-756-4495.

Canoeing

Central Idaho is a land of roistering rivers. Canoeing is a slack-water activity. That pretty much shuts out river canoeing. But an abundance of natural lakes, several having road access, offer ideal canoeing.

Redfish Lake, in the Sawtooth National Recreation Area, offers idyllic waters in the shadows of towering, snow-capped peaks in the Sawtooth Range. Canoes can be rented at the Lodge. Nearby **Stanley Lake** also lends itself well to canoeing.

Many of Central Idaho's mountain lakes can be reached only by foot or on horseback. **Williams Lake**, about 9½ miles up the Perreau Creek Road off US 93 (five miles south of Salmon), is a happy exception. Overnight, get a bite to eat, and rent

Stanley Lake is one of Central Idaho's loveliest.

a canoe or a fishing skiff at Williams Lake Resort, at the head of this small, deep earthquake-created lake.

Quiet reservoirs lend themselves to canoeing, though power boating is often more their style. Ubiquitous in South Central Idaho, they are slack waters behind dams constructed across deep clefts in the foothills of the Sawtooth Mountains and the Snake River Canyon. Vegetation is usually sparser and less spectacular than that fringing natural lakes. Snake River reservoir vegetation runs mostly to sagebrush.

Jetboating

Jetboats are not permitted on the Middle Fork of the Salmon, but are allowed on the Main Salmon if you have a permit. The noisy, gasoline-driven boats' presence on this wilderness river is controversial. Wilderness purists deplore it. Jetboating on the Main Salmon could be curtailed, if not discontinued, at some point in the future. At least for the present, jetboats offer an opportunity to get a fix on this fabled river in one day instead of five. It's a good way for the physically challenged to feel the tug of the Salmon.

The following outfits offer Main Salmon jetboat tours.

Jetboat Outfitters

- **River Adventures, Ltd.** runs Monday jetboat trips from Riggins that include visits to the Polly Bemis Ranch (Polly was a one-time Chinese slave who married a prospector and earned fame in frontier Idaho), and to river hermit Buckskin Bill's home and Museum; also gold panning, hiking, swimming, and trout and bass fishing. And, of course, wildlife watching. Surprisingly, some animals don't seem to mind noisy jetboats. I shot some great mountain goat photos from a jetboat near the Polly Bemis Ranch. Reservations required. Sam Whitten, Box 518, Riggins, ID 83549. ☎ 800-524-9710 or 208-628-3952.

- **White Water West** offers one- and two-day jetboat trips from their River of No Return Lodge 20 miles downriver from Corn Creek. Contact Gail Watt, 1901 W. 200 S., Pingree, ID 83262 (☎ 208-684-4781) or Stan Watt, 202 S. 1400 W., Pingree, ID 83262 (☎ 208-684-3121).

Power Boating

Power boating also seems at odds with the wilderness nature of Central Idaho. But maybe that's what reservoirs are for, in addition to mundane things like flood control and crop irrigation.

Anderson Ranch Reservoir, damming the Boise River 21 miles north of Mountain Home off US 20, is popular with waterskiers.

Several others strung along the Snake River, most notably the sizeable **American Falls Reservoir**, are favored by power boat enthusiasts. **Snake River reservoirs** are so numerous, and the river between reservoirs so wide for such long stretches, that you can hardly tell where one leaves off and another begins.

Numerous marinas and launch sites are along the Snake and in the vicinity of the various reservoirs. Contact local chambers of commerce for information on marinas currently renting boats.

Fishing

Mention steelhead to an angler and the Clearwater and Main Salmon immediately come to mind. The mere mention of fly-fishing conjures up images of illusive trout hiding in Central Idaho's clear mountain streams. Hatchery-raised rainbow trout lurking in the deep, cold waters of countless mountain lakes tempt anglers for whom heaven is a boat, a rod and a lure. Countless adventurers are attracted to the wilderness areas of Central Idaho for the fishing alone.

 If it's steelhead you're after, you'd best look smart and get 'em while you can. There's talk of listing steelhead as endangered. Rick Williams, a Boise biologist heading a group of scientists examining salmon problems in the Pacific Northwest, opines that all anadromous fish could be gone by the middle of the 21st century. Presently, only steelhead with a missing adipose fin, as evidenced by a healed scar, can be taken. All others must be released.

Steelhead Trout

Hazy about just what a steelhead is? In the Snake River drainage below Hells Canyon, and in the Salmon and Clearwater drainages, a steelhead is a rainbow trout over 20 inches long. Like salmon, the young swim to the ocean to mature, returning to their birth waters to spawn. Rules and regulations pertaining to fishing for these handsome fish vary according to river locations. Don't even think about fishing for them, or for any fish, without first obtaining an Idaho fishing license and a copy of the Idaho Department of Fish & Game's General Fishing Seasons and Rules and Official Guide to Fishing in Idaho. These handbooks are available where fishing supplies and licenses are sold or by contacting the Idaho Department of Fish & Game (see *Information Sources*). ☎ 1-800-ASK-FISH for 24-hour Idaho fishing information.

Those in the know rate **Williams Lake** tops for wild rainbows and bull trout. Wild rainbows also inhabit lakes in the **Lemhi Mountains, Stanley Basin, Bighorn Crags** and **Sawtooth Mountains**. Most of these lakes also boast wild brook and cutthroat trout. Lakes in the **White Cloud Mountains** harbor wild cutthroat and hatchery-raised rainbows.

Isolated Williams Lake offers great fishing in peaceful surroundings.

The **Middle Fork of the Salmon** is aleap with wild rainbows, plus Chinook salmon, catch and release steelhead, whitefish and brook and bull trout.

The **Selway River** is also a catch-and-release steelhead stream. Several species of wild trout, including rainbows, are caught here.

The **Silver Creek Nature Conservancy Preserve** in the Wood River Valley, is a world-famous fly-fishing stream. The **Big Wood River, Copper Basin** and the **headwaters of the Salmon River** are also full of trout.

Stop in at a local Ranger District office for information about specific lakes and streams, should you wish to fish on your own.

Signing on with an outfitter for a fishing trip fitting your particular vision of angling heaven may be the best bet. You can expect to get some fishing in on most backpacking, horseback, pack and river running trips (see the sections of this book pertaining to these activities). But if it's fishing and more fishing you're after, the following IOGA-member outfitters will do you proud.

Fishing Outfitters

- **Aggipah River Trips** arranges special Salmon River system fishing trips for trout, steelhead, smallmouth bass or sturgeon. They also offer fly-fishing trips using either small inflatable rafts or McKenzie drift boats. Box 425, Salmon, ID 83467. ☎ 208-756-4167.

- **Mackay Wilderness River Trips** leads Middle Fork of the Salmon driftboat fishing expeditions designed for serious fly fishers. They maintain a ratio of two anglers to one guide. They also offer customized wilderness lake and/or stream fishing excursions. 3190 Airport Way, Boise, ID 83705. ☎ 800-635-5336. Web site: http://www.mackay.org.

- **Middle Fork Wilderness Outfitters** offers five-day fall flyfishing trips on the Middle Fork of the Salmon. PO Box 575, Ketchum, ID 83340. ☎ 800-726-0575 or 208-726-5999. Fax 208-726-7086.

- **Mystic Saddle Ranch** conducts guided multi-day fly-fishing horse pack trips on the Main Salmon and the Middle Fork of the Salmon. Jeff and Deb Bitton also offer spot pack fly-fishing trips with or without food. This option can be more economical because you pay only for your supplies, the use of the horse, and the guide's fee for leading you to the camp site. Winter address: PO Box 736, Challis, ID 83226. ☎ 208-879-5071. Fax 208-879-5069. Summer address: Stanley, ID 83278. ☎ 208-774-3591. Fax 208-774-3455.

- **Rawhide Outfitters** offers half and full-day spring and fall steelhead fishing trips on the Salmon. John and Cathy Cranney, 204 Larson, Salmon, ID 83467. ☎ 208-756-4276.

- **Red Woods** guides spring and fall steelhead trips and in-season fishing for sturgeon, bass and trout on the Salmon. He uses a 26-foot aluminum jetboat to get to where the fish are. Nolan F. Woods (Red), HC2, Box 580, Pollock, ID 83547. ☎ 208-628-3673 or 628-3744.

- **River Adventures, Ltd.** has spring and fall Salmon River steelhead fishing trips. Sam Whitten, Box 518, Riggins, ID 83549. ☎ 800-524-9710 or 208-628-3952.

- **Silver Creek Outfitters** leads a variety of customized and non-customized fishing trips that include spring steelhead fishing on the Salmon and fly-fishing in Silver Creek, Big Wood River and Big Lost River in the Pioneer Mountains east of Ketchum. They also offer winter fishing on the Big Wood River, a free fly casting clinic, and can arrange guided fishing trips on Anderson Reservoir and other waters. 507 N. Main Street, Ketchum, ID 83340. ☎ 208-726-5282.

Central Idaho

- **Stanley Potts Outfitters** runs five- and seven-day pack animal-supported wilderness high mountain lake rainbow and cutthroat fishing trips. Stanley and Joy Potts have been running wilderness pack trips since 1964. HC-64, Box 61, Shoup, ID 83469. ☎/Fax 208-394-2135.

- **Wally York & Sons, Inc.** offers July 1 through September 10 pack-supported horseback fishing trips in the Selway-Bitterroot and Frank Church-River of No Return Wilderness Areas. Excursions begin at the family's base camp about 60 miles east of Elk City. The York family has been leading wilderness fishing trips since 1932. PO Box 319, Elk City, ID 83525. ☎ 208-842-2367.

- **Wapiti River Guides'** Gary Lane offers March through November driftboat trout and steelhead fishing trips on the Main Salmon. Box 1125, Riggins, ID 83549. ☎ 800-488-9872.

- **Warren River Expeditions'** Dave Warren runs six-and seven-day lodge-supported steelhead fishing trips on the Salmon. Box 1375, Salmon, ID 83467. ☎ 800-765-0421 or 208-756-6387.

- **White Cloud Outfitters** offers spring steelhead fishing on the Salmon between Torrey's Boat Launch and Iron Creek. Mike and Louise Stark use driftboats on these day trips. PO Box 217, Challis, ID 83226. ☎ 208-879-4574. Fax 208-879-5513.

On Snow

So venerable is Sun Valley Ski Resort, and so effective its PR efforts, that most people exhibit an almost Pavlovian response when winter in Idaho comes to mind: winter = snow = winter sports = Sun Valley. That's okay, as far as it goes. Sun Valley is undeniably the Mercedes of the Idaho winter sports scene. If you can do it on snow, you can do it at Sun Valley. And do it in luxury.

But Sun Valley is only one facet of the Central Idaho snow scene. The region's sparkling valleys and snow-choked backcountry represent heaven on Earth for Nordic skiers and snowmobile enthusiasts. Getting there can be a tad dicey when winter storms hit, but highways are generally kept free of snow and ice between storms. Side roads and Forest Service roads are less well maintained. If people live along a road, it's plowed. If no one does, it probably isn't. Many Forest Service roads are transformed into Nordic skiing and snowmobile trails in winter.

Use common sense when driving on winter roads. ☎ 208-336-6600 for the Idaho winter road report before setting out. A 4WD vehicle can save you lots of grief. Wear layers and pack emergency gear. Blankets, extra food, a spirit stove, a shovel, a wide board or mat, kitty litter and a spare tire are basics. Visualize yourself stuck in a snowstorm and add whatever other items you would need to stave off frostbite and stay alive until you can dig yourself out or until help arrives.

Expect roads leading to downhill and cross-country ski areas to be maintained as well as is possible, given the possibility of sudden snowstorms.

Downhill Skiing

Idaho is peppered with small ski areas favored by the locals. One such is **Soldier Mountain**, 12 miles north of Fairfield in the Sawtooth National Forest. Turn off US 20 at Fairfield, 57 miles northeast of Mountain Home. This old-fashioned family-style ski area tucked in the foothills of the Sawtooths was recently purchased by entertainers Bruce Willis and Demi Moore. Word has it that an expansion is afoot.

The mountain has a vertical drop of 1,400 feet. Lifts include two doubles, one rope and one handle. There are 42 runs and snowcat skiing is available. **Soldier Mountain Ranch & Resort** has a restaurant and lodgings. Soldier Mountain Ski Area, Inc., PO Box 279, Fairfield, ID 83327. ☎ 208-764-2506.

Sun Valley is a world-renowned mecca for downhill skiers. These slopes can't approach the heart-thumping moguls and black diamond runs of, say, Utah's Alta or B.C.'s Whistler, but Sun Valley does offer a fabulous downhill skiing experience with all the frills you would expect from a first-class ski resort. The "Beautiful People" aura established by the likes of Ernest Hemingway, Olympic Gold Medalist and four-time World Champion figure skater Scott Hamilton, and countless other celebrities, is thrown in free of charge. Who knows whom you might run into on the slopes? Not literally, one hopes.

The Sun Valley area has the advantage of being accessible via Horizon Air (☎ 800-547-9308) and Delta connection, and SkyWest Airlines (☎ 800-453-9417), flying into nearby Hailey from Boise and Salt Lake City.

Sun Valley has a 3,400-foot vertical drop with 78 impeccably groomed runs on 2,054 skiable acres. Thirteen lifts, including seven high-speed

Central Idaho

quads, cut lift lines. The resort's highest point is 9,150-foot Bald Mountain.

Snowboarding has grown so in popularity, and become so readily accepted, that it will be an official Winter Olympics event beginning with the 1998 Games. Snowboarders are welcome on most Sun Valley slopes.

Ski schools and skiing and snowboarding clinics are available for all ages and levels of expertise. These include both private and group instruction.

Sun Valley offers every amenity you might expect, and some you won't. The Resort is a village in itself, with numerous lodgings, restaurants, ice skating arenas, hot tubs, shops and more.

Skiing Sun Valley can be pricey, depending on the lodgings you choose and the frills you take advantage of. More economical options are available in and near Ketchum, close enough to Sun Valley to be its Siamese twin. The byword: reserve early.

Sun Valley, ID 83353. ☎ 800-634-3347 or 208-726-3423. Fax 208-726-4533.

Nordic/Cross-Country Skiing

Numerous cross-country ski trails, both groomed and ungroomed, fall within National Forest boundaries. Groomed trails offer pleasant skiing over predictable terrain.

Backcountry trails are for adventurous, experienced and highly skilled Nordic skiers. Avalanche danger can be high. Check with the local ranger station for trail information before setting out. Check in with SNRA Headquarters in Ketchum or the Stanley Ranger Station if you plan to ski in the Sawtooth National Recreation Area. The SNRA's Avalanche Report number: ☎ 208-622-8027.

Ask the appropriate ranger station or SNRA personnel for a list of suggested emergency supplies and gear. Never ski the backcountry alone. Let someone know where you'll be going and when you plan to return.

The Nordic ski trails mentioned below are for the exclusive use of cross-country skiers. Trails permitting both skiing and snowmobiling are described under *Snowmobiling,* below.

Sun Valley has both downhill and Nordic skiing adventures in one handy locale. A complete Nordic Center offers ski rentals, Nordic skiing instruction for all ages, and 25 miles of groomed trails with a warming

Idaho City Cross-Country Ski Area

To Lowman

Banner Ridge Park 'n Ski

21

3.5 miles

Little Beaver Creek

Gold Fork Park 'n Ski

2 miles

Edna Creek

▲ Pilot Peak

Whoop-Um-Up Park 'n Ski

Idaho City 18 miles

21

N

Mores Creek Pass

cabin placed in just the right spot. Gourmet ski tours and illuminated night skiing are also special treats.

Beginning at Hailey, mile upon mile of groomed cross-country ski trails meander up the **Wood River Valley** to the top of Galena Summit, side-tripping through whisper-quiet, fir-embellished country along the way. A separate ungroomed trail loops off Idaho 75 to **Alturas Lake**. These fee trails are maintained by the Sawtooth National Forest and the Blaine County Recreation District. Passes are available at the Ketchum CVB, SNRA Headquarters, Galena Lodge and area sports shops. ☎ 208-788-2117 for further information.

The **Stanley Ranger Station Trail** is a gentle four-mile loop winding through wooded moraines at the base of the looming Sawtooths. It is groomed following most snowfalls.

The Idaho Department of Parks and Recreation maintains three Park 'n Ski areas **north of Idaho City on Idaho 21**. All have restrooms and plowed parking areas.

- **Whoop-em-Up**, 18 miles north of Idaho City, is a 6.6-mile marked, but not groomed, trail complex. Downhill trail sections are challenging and require advanced skills, but other areas are suitable for beginner to intermediate skiers.

- **Gold Fork**, 20 miles north of Idaho City, has 14.9 miles of weekly groomed trails with some steep downhill runs. Practiced beginners would do well here.

- **Banner Ridge**, 23½ miles north of Idaho City, has 14½ miles of marked trails suitable for beginner to expert skiers. There are gorgeous ridgetop views and open bowls for off-trail skiing.

Craters of the Moon National Monument may seem an unlikely place to ski, but first impressions can be misleading. The Loop Road through these convoluted lava fields affords great cross-country skiing. The visitor center is open year-round.

Nordic Ski Lodges & Guided Ski Touring Services

As these lodges are also Nordic ski centers, I have opted to place them in this section instead of under lodgings.

- **Busterback Ranch** is a full-service ski-touring facility in the Sawtooth Valley, 20 miles south of Stanley. Forty miles of groomed trails wind through rolling, forested terrain dominated by the Sawtooth Mountains. Equipment rentals, ski lessons, lodging and food service are available. Star Route, Ketchum, ID 83340. ☎ 208-774-2217.

- **Buffalo Hump Lodge**, in the vicinity of Elk City, offers ski touring and telemarking in the Gospel Hump Area and the Salmon River portion of the Frank Church-River of No Return Wilderness. Getting there is as much fun as the skiing. Access is via the Snowbus, a snow-groomer equipped with a cab for guests and gear. PO Box 303, Elk City, ID 83525. ☎ 208-842-2220.

Ski Guides

The following guide services offer a variety of ski tour options.

- **Mulligan's Sun Valley Adventure Center** runs guided cross-country ski tours and numerous other activities. PO Box 2123, Ketchum, ID 83340. ☎ 208-726-9137.

- **Sawtooth Mountain Guides'** Kirk Bachman offers one-hut and hut-to-hut skiing in the Sawtooth Mountains. PO Box 18, Stanley, ID 83278. ☎ 208-774-3324.

- **Sun Valley Trekking Company** leads guided backcountry hut-to-hut ski touring, one-day ski tours, backcountry skiing, telemark instruction and multi-day wilderness ski treks. PO Box 2200, Sun Valley, ID 83353. ☎ 208-788-9585.

- **Sun Valley Heli Ski** takes skiers into the high backcountry for trackless skiing. Their Club Vertical packages include cross-country skiing and overnighting in a yurt. PO Box 978, Sun Valley, ID 83353. ☎ 800-872-3108. Fax 208-726-6850. E-Mail svheli@sunvalley.net. Web site: www.destinationnw.com/svheliski.

- **Venture Outdoors** offers a whole sledload of alpine touring, Telemark, hut skiing, track skiing and snowshoeing trips ranging from day trips to their six-day cross-country hut-and-yurt trips. PO Box 2251, Hailey, ID 83333. ☎ 800-528-LAMA or 208-788-5049.

Snowmobiling

Central Idaho's long draws, spacious valleys and fir-crested slopes seem made for far-ranging snowmobiling. Forest Service and other unimproved roads become instant snowmobile trails when winter silences the land and the snows drift in. In winter, snowmobiles replace horses as the preferred, if not the traditional, mode of backcountry tansportation.

This country is cold, often bitterly cold. Insulated suits and boots, heated gloves and socks, gaiters, scarves, ear-covering wool hats under safety helmets are musts in this country. Make sure your machine is in good working order. Pack tools, spare parts, a folding shovel and extra gasoline. A survival pack including food and matches is a wise idea. Every winter, a few snowmobilers become lost, disoriented in sudden white-outs, or experience engine failure and are forced to overnight in makeshift shelters. Most make it out alive; some don't. Never go out on the trail alone. Let someone know where you will be snowmobiling and when you plan to return.

Many snowmobile trails are used by cross-country skiers. Be alert for skiers and snowshoers and give them a wide berth. Do not drive across a ski track that has been set parallel to the machine track.

Contact a ranger station or BLM office in the Salmon area for snowmobile travel plan maps, Idaho snowmobile registration laws and riding information, plus local snowmobile rental shops. A guide to snowmobiling in Idaho that includes a map of designated snowmobile areas and groomed trails can be obtained from the Idaho Department of Parks and Recreation (Box 83720, Boise, ID 83720-0065. ☎ 208-334-4199. Fax 208-334-3741).

Central Idaho's wilderness areas keep their winter silences to themselves, but numerous other locations offer great snowmobiling over both groomed and ungroomed trails. The following areas are maintained jointly by the Idaho Department of Parks and Recreation and local snowmobile clubs. All have parking areas; some have vault toilets.

Maclomson Parking Area is the gateway to over 300 square miles of sagebrush hills and scattered pockets of aspens at 4,000 to 8,000 feet

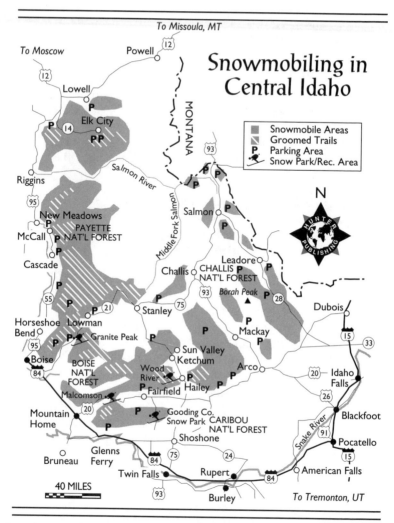

Snowmobiling in Central Idaho

To Missoula, MT

To Moscow

Powell

12

12

Lowell

P

To Moscow

P

Elk City

14

P P

Riggins

95

New Meadows

P

McCall P PAYETTE NAT'L FOREST

Cascade

P

55

P

Horseshoe Bend

95

P

Lowman

P P

Granite Peak

Boise

84

BOISE NAT'L FOREST

Malcomson

Mountain Home

20

Glenns Ferry

Bruneau

Twin Falls

93

Burley

Legend:
- Snowmobile Areas
- Groomed Trails
- P Parking Area
- Snow Park/Rec. Area

MONTANA

Salmon River

Middle Fork Salmon

93

P P

P

Salmon

P

Leadore

P

P

Challis

CHALLIS NAT'L FOREST

93

Borah Peak ▲

75

Stanley

P

28

Dubois

Mackay

P

P

15

33

Sun Valley

Ketchum

Arco

20

Idaho Falls

Wood River

P

Fairfield

P

Hailey

26

Gooding Co. Snow Park

CARIBOU NAT'L FOREST

Shoshone

75

24

Snake River

91

Blackfoot

Pocatello

15

American Falls

To Tremonton, UT

40 MILES

N

HUNTER PUBLISHING

elevation in the vicinity of Anderson Ranch Reservoir and Soldier Mountain, off US 20. This popular snowmobiling area is convenient to Boise and I-84.

Should Sun Valley's downhill skiing pall, you can drive to Hailey and zoom off on the **Wood River Recreation Area**'s 200-plus miles of trails over open sagebrush-covered hills, valleys and mountains.

Granite Creek Snow Park, three miles east of Idaho City, includes 150 miles of snow-packed Forest Service roads. Terrain is rolling to steep, with both timber and clearcuts.

Gooding County Snow Park, 20 miles north of Gooding on State Highway 46, offers over 150 square miles of open terrain featuring rolling sagebrush and grasslands with some high desert rimrock canyons.

Wide-open ungroomed snowmobiling areas in the vicinity of **Challis, Salmon** and the **North Fork Road** beckon experienced riders.

For the ultimate snowmobiling adventure, consider covering the entire distance **between Lowman and Stanley,** climbing and descending numerous summits and passes and exploring both groomed and ungroomed side trails along the way. The aggregate climb is almost 3,000 feet. South of Stanley, you can explore seemingly endless trails, both groomed and ungroomed, through the lovely Sawtooth Valley. These mountain fastnesses, dominated by the spectacular Sawtooths, assume a quite different character from summer's sun-dappled meadows and sparkling lakes. Dense forests of Ponderosa pine, their branches heavy with snow, creak and whisper in the cold mountain air.

Stanley has become a thriving snowmobile village. There was a time when the town hibernated in winter like a summer-fattened bear. Many eateries and lodgings do take long winter snoozes, but as many remain open to serve snowmobilers and Nordic skiers. You can snowmobile clear into and through town, as long as you keep your speed to 10 mph. *Sawtooth Country Trail Maps* are available at local outlets, the Stanley Ranger Station or the Sawtooth National Recreation Area Headquarters.

The following lodgings remain open for the convenience of snowmobilers. Several Stanley businesses rent snowmobiles and prepare trail lunches.

- **Custer Cabins,** on Idaho 21 between Stanley and Stanley Lake, has furnished two-bedroom cabins. PO Box 358, Stanley, ID 83278. ☎ 208-774-3768.

- **Creekside Lodge** has kitchenette accommodations. PO Box 110, Stanley, ID 83278. ☎ 800-523-0733 or 208-774-2213.

- **Danner's Log Cabin Motel** rents rustic log cabins with kitchenettes. Box 196, Stanely, ID 83278. ☎ 208-774-3539.

- **Jerry's Motel** also has kitchenettes. HC 67 Box 300, Stanley, ID 83278. ☎ 800-972-4627 or 208-774-3566.

- **Mountain Village Resort** is a large two-story motel complex with a restaurant, shopping, and a service station. PO Box 150, Stanley, ID 83278. ☎ 800-843-5475 or 208-774-3661.

- **Sawtooth Rentals** has cabins and rooms to rent, plus snowmobile rentals and gear. They also offer guided snowmobile trips. Stanley, ID 83278. ☎ 208-774-3409 or 208-734-4060.

- **Smiley Creek Lodge,** between Stanley and Ketchum on Idaho 75 at the non-town of Sawtooth City, also offers lodging, dining, snowmobile rentals and servicing, and guided snowmobile trips. HC 64, Box 9102, Ketchum, ID 83340. ☎ 208-774-3547.

- **Elk City,** at the end of Idaho 14 east of Grangeville, has also made a name for itself among dedicated snowmobilers. Numerous riding areas with miles of groomed trails and open country include Elk Summit Loop, Red River Hot Springs, Siegel Creek and the historic Nez Perce Trail.

- **Dixie,** winter population 12, is farther down the track, almost in the Gospel Hump Wilderness. Here, Emmett and Zona Smith, owners and operators of Dixie Outfitters, maintain a laid-back bed & breakfast-style snowmobilers' lodge in their spacious log house. Zona also serves up lunch and dinner by prior arrangement. Dixie, ID 83525. ☎ 208-842-2417.

- **Mulligan's Sun Valley Adventure Center** offers snowmobile tours. PO Box 2123, Ketchum, ID 83340. ☎ 208-726-9137.

Dog Sledding & Other Snowy Adventures

Snowshoeing, once *the* way to explore the backcountry in winter, has largely gone the way of wool plus fours. However, some people are bringing it back. If snowshoeing appeals, you can don your snowshoes and go wherever cross-country skiers go. At least one outfitter offers guided snowshoeing treks (Venture Outdoors, see page 258).

Snowshoeing may seem a tad archaic, but dog sledding is increasing in popularity. And why not? Alaska doesn't have a monopoly on winter wonderlands. This is a sport requiring an experienced guide and trained dogs. The family pooch just won't cut it.

- **Sun Valley Sled Dog Adventures** offers 1½-hour, half-day, full-day and overnight dog sled expeditions. Overnight trips include some snowshoeing and cross-country skiing. Overnighters stay and sup in a remote 1870-era cabin. Guests ride in a sled pulled by eight Alaskan huskies. Box 3687, Hailey, ID 83333. ☎ 208-788-3522.

There is something about horse drawn sleigh rides with harness all a'jingle that strikes a nostalgic chord. The Sun Valley area is ideal for this cozy-up winter activity.

- **Mulligan's Sun Valley Adventures** offers romantic horse drawn dinner sleigh rides. PO Box 2123, Ketchum, ID 83340. ☎ 208-726-9137.

- **Sun Valley Resort** has dinner sleigh rides to historic log Trail Creek Cabin. Built in 1937, this was where Ernest Hemingway and other personalities celebrated New Year's Eve. Reserve through Sun Valley Resort or at ☎ 208-622-2135.

Ice Climbing

Mount Borah, Idaho's highest peak, may offer fairly tame summertime climbing, but it's another basket of snowballs altogether in September, when early snows and frigid temperatures cause ice to build on the higher reaches. **Wilderness River Outfitters** offers two gnarly five-day Mt. Borah ice climbs in September, when the range lands below sport only dustings of snow. PO Box 72, Lemhi, ID 83465. ☎ 800-252-6581. E-mail: wro@wildernessriver.com.

Ice Skating

Rounding out Central Idaho's snowy adventures is that perennial favorite: ice skating. **Sun Valley Resort** is famous for shows featuring champion skaters. Indoor and outdoor skating rinks are also at the disposal of amateur skaters.

In the Air

Bush Flights

 Idaho's bush pilots are as legendary as Alaska's. And well they might be. Flying in Central Idaho can be every bit as tricky. Designated wilderness areas being off-limits to motorized vehicles, the transport ball falls squarely in bush pilots' court. Wilderness airfields offer access for backpackers, anglers and campers. Bush pilots will fly in supplies by prior arrangement. They will also fly folks to wilderness and backcountry guest ranches not otherwise accessible except by horseback. Most offer flightseeing trips.

In low-water years, when the Middle Fork of the Salmon above Indian Creek is too shallow to float, outfitters charter planes to fly guests to the Indian Creek Air Strip. Missing out on floating several miles of river is more than compensated for by seeing the wild country you will be floating through from the air.

- **Bob's Air Service**, (☎ 208-879-2364), **McCall Wilderness Air** (☎ 208-756-4713), **McCall Air Taxi** (☎ 800-992-6559), **Pioneer Air Service** (☎ 208-634-7127), **Arnold Aviation** (☎ 208-382-4336), **Grangeville Air Service** (☎ 208-983-0490), **Sun Valley Heli Ski** (☎ 800-872-3108) and **Wild Blue Yonder Aero Taxi** (☎ 800-267-9069) ferry passengers and freight into wilderness areas from airstrips at Stanley, Challis, Salmon, Hailey, Grangeville and McCall.

Ballooning, Soaring, Paragliding & Other Adventures

Sun Valley is the place to find in-air adventures. Perhaps all this activity is centered in the Wood River Valley because of the moneyed people who flock here like exotic hummingbirds to nectar. These adventures aren't cheap. But they're fun. These companies cover the gamut.

- **Mulligan's Sun Valley Adventure Center** offers hot air balloon rides. PO Box 2123, Ketchum, ID 83340. ☎ 208-726-9137.

- **Sun Valley Heli Ski** has flightseeing and cross-country tours in addition to heli skiing. PO Box 978, Sun Valley, ID 83353. ☎ 800-872-3108. Fax 208-726-6850.

- **Sun Valley Paragliding** takes off at Mount Baldy. It also offers paragliding instruction, mountain thermal flying clinics, cross-country flying seminars and adventure travel excursions. 260 First Ave. North, Ketchum, ID 83340. ☎ 208-726-3332. Cell: 208-720-0852. Fax 208-726-1149.

- **Sun Valley Soaring** has both winter and summer glider rides. PO Box 119, Hailey, ID 83333. ☎ 208-788-3054.

Kid Stuff

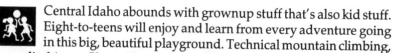 Central Idaho abounds with grownup stuff that's also kid stuff. Eight-to-teens will enjoy and learn from every adventure going in this big, beautiful playground. Technical mountain climbing, ice climbing, Class V river running and rigorous wilderness

backpacking trips are beyond the capabilities of young children and most teens. But there's lots more.

 Know your child, what he or she enjoys and is capable of accomplishing. It may be best to ease into kids' adventure experiences so as not to dampen their enthusiasm or make them feel like failures. Most children love a challenge, but it's no fun when the challenge is beyond their capabilities. This is especially true for younger tagalongs. Many outfitters post minimum ages for their trips.

The older crew will be anxious to try just about anything that offers a challenge and a chance to show off. One of the advantages of an outfitter-led trip is that an authority figure other than Mom or Dad is on hand to see that teenagers don't try anything stupidly dangerous. If you don't know the territory, you may not realize that a given activity is dangerous until too late. There's no counting the number of teens who every year become stranded on shelves and narrow precipices and have to be rescued, sometimes by helicopter.

Wilderness adventures are ideal for teens going through the stage where they wouldn't be caught dead associating with Mom and Dad. All of a sudden, they find that the whole family enjoys doing something in common. When everyone is having fun with no peers watching, teens may even grudgingly admit that their parents are cool dudes.

Most guest ranches make an effort to attract families by offering fun stuff for kids. When considering a guest ranch, be sure to ask what there is for youngsters to do, if the ranch has a supervised kids' program, and if child-friendly horses are available. Supervised kids' programs allow parents to enjoy activities on their own while knowing that the kids are happily occupied.

Following is a grab bag of fun stuff having special appeal for kids.

- Central Idaho creeks, kids and **gold panning** were made for each other. Purchasing a gold panning kit for your young'un and turning him or her loose in a safe, shallow creek assures hours of fun for the kid and goofing-off time for you. Gold panning kits are available in many stores where souvenirs and sporting goods are sold.

- Sun Valley offers a **kids' ski school**, plus free skiing for children 15 and under; only one child per parent qualifies for free skiing. ☎ 208-622-2248.

- Sun Valley operates a **playschool** for children of families staying at a Sun Valley Resort. It includes pony rides, swimming, hayrides, ice skating and other fun stuff. ☎ 208-622-2248.

- Sun Valley also has a Monday-Friday **day camp** for kids ages six through 14. Participants enjoy biking, hiking, ice skating, swimming, trail rides, field sports and more. ☎ 208-622-2133.

- **Bill Mason Sun Valley Outfitters** offers childrens' fly-fishing classes and just-for-kids guided fishing trips. PO Box 127, Sun Valley, ID 83353. ☎ 208-622-9305.

- Many river outfitters include special kids' activities on **Main Salmon trips**. The Main Salmon, as one outfitter pointed out, is "a 78-mile-long sandbox."

- **Outdoor Adventures** employs coordinators to lead age-appropriate activities such as bug collecting, making music with natural objects, gold panning, story telling, stick carving and sand castle building. Box 1149, Point Reyes, CA 94920. ☎ 800-323-4234. Fax 415-663-8617.

- **ROW (River Odysseys West)** has a special children's menu. Box 579-GX, Coeur d'Alene, ID 83814. ☎ 800-451-6034.

- **ECHO: The Wilderness Company** hosts an August kids' trip featuring crawdad hunts, stone-skipping contests and nature hikes. 6529 Telegraph Way, Oakland, CA 94609. ☎ 800-652-3246. Fax 510-652-3987.

Eco-Travel & Cultural Excursions

In a very real sense, every trip into Central Idaho's wilderness areas, whether on foot or horseback, via raft or dory, is an eco-trip. The stringent ecological parameters mandated for wilderness travelers and campers ensure that. But some outfitters, realizing the rich lode of potential learning experiences, offer educational trips designed to help guests appreciate these wilderness areas.

Eco-Travel Outfitters

- **Oregon River Experiences** teams up with Elderhostel to offer educational Main Salmon trips for seniors. Audubon naturalists narrate in a downriver "floating classroom." 2 Jefferson Parkway #D7, Lake Oswego, OR 97035. ☎ 503-697-8133. Fax 503-697-8133.

- **Salmon River Outfitters** takes Darcy Williamson, author of *Rocky Mountain Wild Foods*, along on special six-day Main Salmon River trips. Williamson teaches guests to identify wild foods and medicinal herbs. Guests sample dishes featuring 28 plants common to the Salmon River region. Williamson also shares her knowledge of Indian lore with guests. Box 1751, McCall, ID 83638. ☎ 208-634-4426.

- **Silver Cloud Expeditons** owner Jerry Myers is a curious naturalist who brings the animal world to life for guests on six-day Main Salmon trips. He shows guests over 200 specimens: animal skulls, bones, furs and scat samples. Box 1006, Salmon, ID 83467. ☎ 208-756-6215.

- **Solitude River Trips** offers six-day Orvis-endorsed women-only fly-fishing trips on the Middle Fork of the Salmon. Guests learn to fish for catch-and-release native cutthroat trout, often catching as many as 25 fish a day. Guides and guests are all women. Box 702, Salmon, ID 83467. ☎ 800-396-1776.

- **Stanley Potts Outfitters** has interpretive Camping With Wolves horseback trips to Central Idaho's wolf introduction area. Participants are taught to identify wolf scat, tracks and howling, and may see current wolf activity. If denning activity is located it will be monitored with spotting scopes while participants remain far enough away so that the wolves will not be bothered. HC-64, Box 61, Shoup, ID 83469. ☎/Fax 208-394-2135.

- **The River Company** runs naturalist-led day trips on the upper Salmon River. Guests learn to identify wildlife common to the area. Box 2329, Sun Valley, ID 83353. ☎ 208-726-8890. Fax 208-726-8895.

- **Wapiti River Guides**, owned and operated by Gary Lane, specializes in off-beat trips for the culturally curious. Lane offers a five-day Main Salmon trip entitled "Native Medicine, Magic and Mysteries" designed to enable you to attain harmony and balance in your life. Box 1125, Riggins, ID 83549. ☎ 800-488-9872 or 208-628-3523.

Wildlife Watching

Including a section on where to watch wildlife in a chapter on Central Idaho seems like overkill. Wildlife comes with the territory. You can't avoid seeing animals and birds here. You are likely to enjoy serendipitous wildlife watching experiences while hiking, river rafting, horseback riding and camping. I've found that deer, bears, mountain goats, moose, birds and waterfowl appear when least expected. This is their home and I'm a visitor.

Serious wildlife watchers may prefer designated wildlife areas. Many are well off the driven path. These places often require hiking or horseback riding to reach. These and other Central Idaho wildlife viewing areas are described in detail in Leslie Benjamin Carpenter's Idaho Wildlife Viewing Guide. Copies are available at Idaho bookstores, or by sending a check for $6.25, payable to the Nongame Wildlife Program, to Idaho Fish & Game, 600 S. Walnut, Boise, ID 83707.

The following wildlife viewing areas are relatively easy to find.

Minidoka National Wildlife Refuge, near Minidoka Dam on the Snake River and along Lake Walcott, is a fine place to view migratory waterfowl. The refuge has Idaho's only nesting white pelicans, some 40 pairs of them. Mammals include mule deer, pronghorn, beaver, muskrat and coyote. Turn off I-84 at Rupert and drive six miles northeast on Idaho 24. Proceed through Acequia, then turn east for six miles on County Road 400 N. to the refuge headquarters on the north side of Minidoka Dam. There are three south shore access roads.

An 18-mile stretch of the **Upper Salmon River** between Salmon and North Fork is a cottonwood riparian bottomland and a veritable Eden for a variety of songbirds and waterfowl. The area has a great blue heron rookery and osprey nest platforms. Mammals include river otter and pronghorn, white-tailed and mule deer. You can view wildlife from the road, from the river, or walk in from the Wagonhammer Springs Forest Service campground.

Deadwater Slough and the Salmon River Canyon (FS Road 30) between North Fork and Corn Creek is also a rich wildlife watching area with a variety of birds and waterfowl, bighorn sheep, elk, mountain goats, and very occasionally mountain lion and bobcat.

Redfish Lake is favored by a variety of songbirds. A boardwalk nature trail traverses river otter and beaver habitat, including active dams.

Silver Creek Nature Conservancy Preserve has numerous waterfowl and wading fowl, including sandhill cranes, American bittern and long-billed curlew. Migratory birds often include tundra swans and bald eagles. To reach the Preserve, drive west from Picabo on US 20.

Turn left just past the turnoff to Gannett. Go two miles to the Preserve headquarters.

Craters of the Moon National Monument harbors the predictable racers, rattlesnakes, gopher snakes and short-horned lizards. Unexpected wildlife include great horned owls near the openings to lava caves, mountain bluebirds (Idaho's official state bird), golden-mantled ground squirrels, yellow-bellied marmots, pika and a host of other birds and mammals.

Festivals & Special Events

 From foot-stompin' fiddlers' festivals and rodeos to Sun Valley's trendy events, Central Idaho serves up heaps of fun and frolic. The following schedule may include festivities worth planning your trip around. Call ahead to confirm dates and locations. Last-minute changes can and do occur.

Memorial Day Weekend

Hailey kicks off the summer season with **Springfest,** a celebration with live entertainment and upwards of 100 arts and crafts booths. Hailey Chamber of Commerce. ☎ 208-788-2700.

June

Jerome celebrates **Live History Days** with demonstrations of pioneer skills that include authentic farming practices, cooking, spinning, weaving and other skills reflecting local heritage. Held in early June. ☎ 208-324-2711.

Burley is the scene of the **Idaho Regatta,** a late-June speedboat spectacular on the Snake River featuring upwards of 90 power boats. Mini-Cassia Chamber of Commerce. ☎ 208-436-4793.

Sun Valley Resort presents a mid-June through September **outdoor ice show extravaganza** featuring world-class Olympic and professional skaters. Shows are presented every Saturday at dusk. ☎ 800-635-8261.

July

Hailey celebrates July 4th with **Days of the Old West** featuring a parade, old-fashioned button barbecue, a rodeo, fireworks and dancing. Hailey Chamber of Commerce. ☎ 208-788-2700.

Central Idaho

Rupert puts on a typical small town **4th of July celebration** with a rodeo, fireworks and more. Mini-Cassia Chamber of Commerce. ☎ 208-436-4793.

Salmon has celebrated **Salmon River Days** for five days overlapping the 4th of July weekend since 1958. Lemhi and Salmon River Valley communities join in presenting a Little Britches Rodeo, Shakespeare in the Park, raft and kayak races, a parade, a staged bank robbery and other high jinks. Salmon Valley Chamber of Commerce. ☎ 208-756-4935.

Shoshone throws an **old-time fiddlers' jamboree** in mid-July. Contact City Hall, ☎ 208-886-2030.

Stanley is the scene of the **Sawtooth Mountain Mamas Arts and Crafts Fair**. Upwards of 100 crafts booths, old-time fiddlers, barbecue dinner and pancake breakfast. Stanley/Sawtooth Chamber of Commerce. ☎ 208-774-3411.

Sun Valley Music Festival attracts classical and jazz performers from far and wide. July/August. Sun Valley Center for the Arts and Humanities. ☎ 208-726-9491.

August

Salmon Balloon Fest blooms with numerous colorful balloons in mid-August. ☎ 208-756-4935.

Burley is the scene of the annual six-day **Cassia County Fair and Rodeo**, held the second week in August. This downhome event features a rodeo, farm and ranch and 4H exhibits, carnival rides and food. Burley Chamber of Commerce. ☎ 208-678-7230.

September

Ketchum celebrates **Wagon Days** over Labor Day Weekend with a parade touted as the largest non-motorized parade in the West, band concerts and more. Sun Valley/Ketchum Chamber of Commerce. ☎ 800-634-3347.

October

Sun Valley Resort closes the summer season in mid-October with an annual **Swing 'n' Dixie Jamboree** featuring bands from throughout the US and Canada, dancing to Big Band sounds, plus ragtime, traditional jazz and swing music. ☎ 800-634-3347.

Where to Stay & Eat

Central Idaho serves up pretty nearly any kind of accommodation and cuisine that you might fancy. The catch: you must choose the right place to indulge your preferences.

Just about every small town can satisfy simple tastes running to downhome steak-and-fries and clean-but-basic lodgings. Great, if you're not choosy and are willing to try something different. Adventure Guides are all about trying unaccustomed experiences.

If you like luxury and are darned if you're going to do without it on vacation, the Wood River Valley is for you. With some exceptions, luxury digs and sophisticated cuisine are givens in the Sun Valley-Ketchum area. Luxurious B&Bs and ski condos abound. You'll find B&Bs elsewhere, too, though not as many or as luxe.

Forest Service Cabins

At the rustic end of the scale, the US Forest Service rents out two historic Nez Perce National Forest cabins and a fire lookout tower. The **Jerry Walker Cabin**, on the Crooked River 15 miles southeast of Elk city, has a fireplace, firewood and a cookstove, but no drinking water. Inquire at the Elk City Ranger District (☎ 208-842-2245).

You must traverse a rugged trail to reach **Meadow Creek Cabin**, 36 miles southeast of Lowell. Experience with horses is recommended.

Lookout Butte Tower is 15 miles southwest of Lowell over primitive roads. Children are discouraged because of the dangers inherent in the 60-foot-high tower. Both the Tower and Meadow Creek Cabin are in the Selway Ranger District (☎ 208-926-4258).

Lodgings

Anderson Ranch Reservoir Recreation Area

Deer Creek Lodge, at Anderson Ranch Reservoir, has both accommodations and camping. HC87 Box 615, Pine, ID 83647. ☎ 208-653-2454.

Fall Creek Resort & Marina has 10 guest units, a spa and a restaurant. 6633 Overland Rd., Boise, ID 83709. ☎ 208-653-2242.

Feather River Motel is in the historic town of Featherville. HC87, Box 560, Pine, ID 83647. ☎ 208-653-2310.

Atlanta

Greene Valley Retreat, a mile north of this old mining town, has 18 rooms rented on the American Plan (room and meals, one price). PO Box 39, Atlanta, ID 83601. ☎ 800-864-2168 or 208-864-2168.

Blackfoot

Alder Inn Bed & Breakfast has three guest rooms. 384 Alder St., Blackfoot, ID 83221. ☎ 208-785-6968.

The Riverside Inn is a largish motel on the Snake River. PO Box 490, Blackfoot, ID 83221. ☎/Fax 208-785-5000.

Burley

Burley has little to recommend it except as a stopping place en route to somewhere else. Chain motels are good choices here.

Best Western Burley Inn & Convention Center is Burley's premier option, with 128 units. 800 N. Overland Ave., Burley, ID 83318. ☎ 800-599-1849 or 208-678-3501. Fax 208-678-9532.

The Budget Motel of Burley is a more economical choice. 900 N. Overland Ave., Burley, ID 83318. ☎ 800-635-4952 or 208-678-2200.

Dixie

Dixie, a jump away from the Frank Church-River of No Return Wilderness Area, is a last-frontier town whose lodgings reflect this ambiance.

Dixie Store & Motel has seven units. PO Box 67, Dixie, ID 83525. ☎ 208-842-2358.

Lodgepole Pine Inn calls itself a resort, probably because you can get a meal here. PO Box 71, Dixie, ID 83525. ☎ 208-842-2343.

Elk City

Elk City has an amazing assortment of lodgings for a town whose population barely tops 400. That's because of the backcountry surrounding this old mining settlement.

Canterbury House Inn Bed & Breakfast, outside Elk City, keeps two rooms ready for guests. PO Box 276 (501 Elk Creek Rd.), Elk City, ID 83525. ☎ 208-842-2366.

Elk City Hotel can put up 15-plus guests. PO Box 356, Elk City, ID 83525. ☎/Fax 208-842-2452.

Elk City Motel & Lodge has 20 units. PO Box 143, Elk City, ID 83525. ☎ 208-842-2240.

Junction Lodge is on Hwy 14, six miles before Elk City heaves into view. HC67, Box 98, Grangeville, ID 83530. ☎ 208-842-2459.

Prospector Lodge & Cabins, five miles north of Elk City, has 12 guest cabins and offers horseback riding. PO Box 270, Elk City, ID 3525. ☎ 208-842-2557. Fax 208-842-2593.

Red River Hot Springs is at the Elk City area's historic hot springs. Elk City, ID 83525. ☎ 208-842-2587.

Fairfield

This gateway to Soldier Mountain Ski Resort boasts a historic Union Pacific Depot, now a museum. Not bad for a town of some 350 souls. Fairfield's accommodations reflect this up-and-coming town's size.

Country Inn has 16 units. PO Box 393, Fairfield, ID 83327. ☎ 208-764-2247. Fax 208-764-2483.

Motel 68 has 12 units. PO Box 285, Fairfield, ID 83327. ☎ 208-764-2211.

Soldier Mountain Ranch & Resort is at Soldier Mountain Ski Area, 9½ miles from Fairfield, and has 17 rental cabins. Box 279, Fairfield, ID 83327. ☎ 208-764-2506. Fax 208-764-2927.

Gooding

Gooding Hotel Bed & Breakfast has six guest rooms and eight Hosteling International dorm rooms. 112 Main St., Gooding, ID 83330. ☎ 208-934-4374.

Idaho City

Idaho City Hotel's ambiance reflects that of this historic "ghost town." PO Box 70 (215 Montgomery St.), Idaho City, ID 83631. ☎ 208-392-4290. Fax 208-392-4505.

One Step Away Bed Breakfast & Lodging has four comfortable guest rooms just a step away from Idaho City's historic attractions. PO Box 55 (112 Cottonwood St.), Idaho City, ID 83631. ☎ 208-392-4938.

Central Idaho

Prospector Motel is small but the name says it all. PO Box 70 (517 Main St.), Idaho City, ID 83631. ☎ 208-392-4290. Fax 208-392-4505.

Jerome

Jerome may be an unlikely overnight stop unless you wish to take in Live History Days in early June. Two mid-size motels cater to attendees.

Crest Motel, 2983 South Lincoln, Jerome, ID 83338. ☎ 208-324-2670.

Holiday Motel, 401 W. Main, Jerome, ID 83338. ☎ 208-324-2361.

Lowman

A long-time summer retreat for Boiseans, this town was hit hard by the 1989 forest fire. Then came the heavy snows and mudslides of the winter of 1996-97. Two lodgings are hanging in there.

New Haven Lodge, on Idaho 21 at Milepost 76, has six guest rooms. HC 77 Box 3608, Lowman, ID 83637. ☎ 208-259-3344.

Sourdough Lodge and RV Resort, on Idaho 21 at Milepost 84, has six units, two guest rooms and a restaurant. HC77 Box 3109, Lowman, ID 83637. ☎ 208-259-3326.

Mackay

This is a good overnight choice if you plan to hike the Lost River Range.

Martini's Mountainside B&B has two guest rooms. PO Box 456 (4718 Old Loop Road), Mackay, ID 83251. ☎ 208-588-2940.

Pocatello

Pocatello is not a charming town, or particularly interesting except for the Fort Hall replica, which is worth staying over to see. A brace of B&Bs softens Pocatello's hard edges.

Hales Half Acre Bed & Breakfast, 10 minutes north of town on Hiline, has two cozy guest rooms. Route 2, Box 26, Pocatello, ID 83202. ☎ 208-237-7130.

Liberty Inn Victorian Bed & Breakfast has four in-town guest rooms. 404 S. Garfield, Pocatello, ID 83204. ☎ 208-232-3825.

Salmon

Salmon owes its summertime popularity to its namesake river, running smack through the middle of town, plus convenient proximity to the backcountry. Alternatives to a flurry of forgettable motels include three area B&Bs and two laid-back resorts some distance from town.

Broken Arrow is a rustic self-styled resort at tiny Gibbonsville, 33 miles north of Salmon on US 93. Hwy 93 N., Gibbonsville, ID 83463. ☎ 208-865-2241.

Greyhouse Inn Bed & Breakfast, 12 miles south of Salmon on US 93, has four guest rooms. HC 61, Box 16, Salmon, ID 83467. ☎ 208-756-3968.

Heritage Inn offers five comfortable in-town guest rooms. 510 Lena St., Salmon, ID 83467. ☎ 208-756-3174.

Syringa Lodge is an eight-room bed & breakfast 10 blocks from Salmon city center. PO Box 583 (2000 Syringa Drive), Salmon, ID 83467. ☎ 208-756-4424. Fax 208-756-3373.

Resort, hugging the shore of 15 miles southwest of Salmon off US 93, has motel type accommodations with lake views, a restaurant, recreation hall/lounge and boat rentals. PO Box 1150, Salmon, ID 83467. ☎ 208-756-2007.

Shoshone

Governor's Mansion is a seven-room B&B. PO Box 326 (315 S. Greenwood), Shoshone, ID 83352. ☎ 208-886-2858.

Shoup

Accommodations along the River Road (FS Road 30) come under the heading of basic with lots of atmosphere.

Smith's Guest House is a peaceful pad overlooking the Salmon.

Central Idaho

Ram's Head Lodge, a River Road tradition, has four guest rooms and a bunkhouse. It's 33 miles downriver from North Fork. The Rams Head has a sometime eatery and a most-of-the-time bar. HC 64, Box 44, Shoup, ID 83469. ☎ 208-394-2122.

Shoup Store and Café has three rental cabins. RR 2, Box 1, Shoup, ID 83469. ☎ 208-394-2125.

Smith's Guest House, the last sign of habitation before Corn Creek, rents out a comfortable three-bedroom, two-bath house in a gorgeous riverview location. 49 Salmon River Road, Shoup, ID 83469. ☎ 800-238-5915 or 208-394-2121.

Stanley

Stanley is awash in lodgings – quite an accomplishment for such an isolated town. Just in the past eight years, Stanley has grown from a two-motel-and-scattered-cabins town to a popular destination with enough roofs to cover a whole platoon of adventure seekers. The lodgings listed below include B&Bs and those having some particular features to recommend them.

Creek Side Lodge has 14 units overlooking Valley Creek and the Sawtooths. PO Box 110, Stanley, ID 83278. ☎ 800-523-0733 or 208-774-2213.

Custer Cabins, on Idaho 21 between Stanley and Stanley Lake, has four cabins to rent. PO Box 358, Stanley, ID 83278. ☎ 208-774-3768.

Danner's Log Cabin Motel has nine rental cabins. PO Box 196, Stanley, ID 83278. ☎ 208-774-3539.

Jerry's Country Store & Motel is on the river in Lower Stanley. HC 67 Box 300 Hwy 75, Stanley, ID 83278. ☎ 800-972-4627 or 208-774-3566.

McGowan's Salmon River Cabins rents 15 log cabins and a two-bedroom, two-bath house. PO Box 91, Stanley, ID 83278. ☎ 208-774-2290. Fax 208-774-3307.

Redfish Lake Lodge, Redfish Lake's focal point (after the Sawtooth Mountains) and activity center, has 36 lodgings that include both rooms and cabins. PO Box 9, Stanley, ID 83278. ☎ 208-774-3536.

Sessions Lodge is a B&B on Idaho 75, 12 miles south of Stanley. HC 64, Box 9696, Stanley, ID 83278. ☎ 208-774-3366.

Sunbeam Village, 12 miles down the Salmon from Stanley, has 14 rental cabins. HC 67, Box 310, Stanley, ID 83278. ☎ 208-838-2211.

Torrey's Burnt Creek Inn is a small resort 21 miles east of Stanley on Idaho 75. HC 67, Box 725, Clayton, ID 83227. ☎ 208-838-2313.

Sun Valley/Ketchum

Inexpensive accommodations are hard to find in this celebrity hangout, though mid-price digs do exist. Listed below are B&Bs and other recommendable accommodations. Contact the Sun Valley/Ketchum Chamber of Commerce or Sun Valley Area Reservations (☎ 800-635-1076) for a complete lodgings list that includes motels. Ask about condo rentals too.

The Heidelberg Inn is a pleasant mid-price hostelry especially appealing to families with children. My child and large dog received a gracious welcome. Some units have fireplaces and microwaves. PO Box 5704, Ketchum, ID 83340. ☎ 800-284-4863 or 208-726-5361. Fax 208-726-2084.

The Idaho Country Inn, at 134 Latigo Lane in Ketchum, is a largish B&B. PO Box 2355, Ketchum, ID 83340. ☎ 208-726-1019. Fax 208-726-5718.

The Knob Hill Inn is more inn than B&B, with 24 guest rooms. PO Box 800, Ketchum, ID 83340. ☎ 800-526-8010 or 208-726-8010. Fax 208-726-2712.

The Pinnacle Inn, at the base of Warm Springs' ski lifts, has five guest rooms and four suites. PO Box 2559, Sun Valley, ID 83353. ☎ 800-255-3391 or 208-726-5700. Fax 208-726-2877.

The River Street Inn's eight parlor suites are pricey, but worth the money for a B&B with class. PO Box 182, Sun Valley, ID 83353. ☎ 208-726-3611. Fax 208-726-2439.

Sun Valley Resort takes Central Idaho's high profile sweepstakes with a wide choice of accommodations (546 units), several restaurants and a heaping plateful of adventure opportunities and other fun things to do. Sun Valley Rd., Sun Valley, ID 83353. ☎ 208-622-4111. Fax 208-622-3700.

Guest Ranches

Central Idaho has a guest ranch for every taste. Many are used as base camps for trail rides, camping trips, river floats and other excursions. Meals are, without exception, hearty and delicious. Menus range from traditional Western beef and beans to gourmet cuisine.

To pick a guest ranch, study brochures, looking closely at the photographs. Do the people having fun look like your kind of people? Ask pointed questions designed to narrow the field. Decide on the activities you prefer. Horseback riding is

*usually a given, but not always the entire show.
Riverside ranches offer swimming, fishing and floating.
Many high-mountain ranches combine hiking and
fishing. Get a fix on the ranch's comfort level. Rustic
may mean just that and be more primitive than you
bargained for. Request sample menus if you have food
preferences. If you have kids, find out what activities, if
any, are designed for them. Ask about the horses; are
they kid-friendly, and how much riding instruction is
given before kids (adults, too) are permitted to go on trail
rides. See page 179 for additional tips.*

Most of the following ranches are owned and operated by Idaho
Outfitters and Guides Association members (IOGA) as indicated.

Bill Mitchell Wilderness Vacations (IOGA) offers two- , three- or
five-day summer stays at a rustic base camp deep in the backcountry.
Accessed by horseback. 364 McCarthy Loop, Hamilton, MT 59840-9146.
☎ 406-363-4129.

"Camp Stanley" (IOGA) is the nickname for a tent camp created by
three horsepack outfitters adjacent to Redfish and Alturas Lakes in the
Sawtooth Valley. The idea is to offer families and groups an easily
accessible base camp. You call the shots for everything from meals (you
cook, or they'll cook) to guided horseback trips. The outfitters will do
the rest. The lakes offer swimming, canoeing, fishing or just beach
lounging. Contact the following outfitters: **Mystic Saddle Ranch**, Fisher
Creek Road, Stanley, ID 83278 (☎ 888-722-5432); **Sawtooth Wilderness
Outfitters**, Box 81, Garden Valley, ID 83622 (☎ 208-462-3416) or **Pioneer
Mountain Outfitters**, 3267 East 3225 North, Twin Falls, ID 83301.
(☎ 208-734-3679).

Diamond D Ranch (IOGA) rests in a gentle valley among pine-clad hills
in the Challis National Forest northwest of the Yankee Fork Adventure
Road. You can drive to the ranch, or fly in via charter plane. A handsome
Forest Service-brown lodge is surrounded by comfortable cabins and a
swimming pool. Activities include daily trail rides, hayrides, picnics,
gold panning, stream and lake fishing, Western crafts and campfire
tales. Tom and Linda Demorest claim that they have to hog-tie their kids
every fall to get them to leave the ranch for Boise and school. Winter
address: PO Box 1555, Boise, ID 83701. ☎ 208-336-9772. Summer
address: Box 35, Stanley, ID 83278. ☎ 800-222-1269.

Happy Hollow Vacations (IOGA) is a working ranch whose owners,
the Martin Capps family, just happen to enjoy having guests. Located
in the mountains of the Salmon River country, this ranch offers
comfortable accommodations, trail rides and pack trips, Main Salmon

floats, and spring and fall steelhead fishing. All of this in addition to finding out first hand how a working ranch operates. HC61, Box 14, Dept. O, Salmon, ID 83467. ☎ 208-756-3954 or 208-756-2997.

Indian Creek Guest Ranch (IOGA) is on Indian Creek, in a canyon two miles up from the River Road (FS Road 30) and 11 miles downriver from North Fork. This small, laid-back ranch has four guest cabins, each with a private bath. Propane provides lighting. Wood is used for cooking hearty family-style meals, for heat, and to fire up the hot tub. Activites include trail rides and hiking. Mary Bullard and James Bower, HC64, Box 105A, North Fork, ID 83466. ☎ 208-394-2126.

Guests may try their luck in Idaho Rocky Mountain Ranch's trout stream.

Idaho Rocky Mountain Ranch, a member of the Idaho Guest & Dude Ranch Association, has been a Sawtooth Valley fixture since 1930. The classic log lodge is listed on the National Register of Historic Places. The surrounding cabins are delightfully old-timey, yet include modern conveniences. Many have working fireplaces. Backing against the White Cloud Mountains, the ranch enjoys spectacular sunsets in which the jagged Sawtooths stand silhouetted against a flaming red sky. Ranch-arranged activities include horseback rides to secluded mountain meadows and lakes, hiking, mountain biking, fishing the ranch's stocked pond, and cross-country skiing. Managers: Bill and Jeanna Leavell, HC 64 Box 9934, Stanley, ID 83278. ☎ 208-774-3544.

Mackay Bar Ranch (IOGA), just inside the Frank Church-River of No Return Wilderness Area, sits at the confluence of the Main Salmon and the South Fork of the Salmon River. Access is by air taxi from McCall or by jetboat from Riggins. Guests settle into comfortable cabins. Activities include trail rides, jetboating, hiking, swimming, fishing, or simply walking in the woods. Spring and fall steelhead fishing is also on offer. Mackay Bar Corporation, PO Box 7968, Boise, ID 83707. ☎ 800-854-9904 or 208-344-9904.

Middle Fork Lodge (IOGA), in the Frank Church-River of No Return Wilderness Area, is accessible by air taxi only. The log lodge and cabins include a restored 1898 homestead designated as a National Historic Site. Cabins have private baths and electricity. Activities include trail

Central Idaho

rides, pack trips, hiking, stream and river fishing, swimming in the ranch pool, gold panning, trap shooting and cross-country skiing. PO Box 64, Challis, ID 83226. ☎/Fax 208-362-9621 or 208-879-2203.

Salmon River Lodge (IOGA) is across the Salmon River from Corn Creek Campground, at the edge of the Frank Church-River of No Return Wilderness Area. Getting there is a trip in itself: you drive from North Fork to the end of the River Road (FS Road 30), where the Lodge's jetboat will pick you up for the short ride to the complex. Most guests use the lodge as a base for a whitewater trip down the Salmon. Multi-day floats are an option. Others use it as a base for pack trips into the wilderness, for McKenzie drift boat steelhead fishing, or for wilderness trout fishing treks to nine high-mountain lakes. Wildlife watching is a constant. PO Box 927, Salmon, ID 83467. ☎ 800-635-4717 or 208-756-6622. Fax 208-756-3033.

Shepp Ranch (IOGA), across the Salmon River from the famed Polly Bemis Ranch, is accessible by air taxi or by jetboat from Riggins. The historic ranch is situated on such a fertile shelf of land that meals often include fresh-picked berries and vegetables. Ranch-raised animals and trout fresh from the river round out the "from scratch" cuisine. Accommodatons are in comfortable riverside cabins. Activities include floating the Salmon, jetboating, trail rides, swimming, fishing for trout and steelhead, trap shooting, cookouts, volleyball, and just enjoying the ranch's idyllic setting. Jerry Hopfenbeck, PO Box 5446, Boise, ID 83705. ☎ 208-343-7729.

Sulphur Creek Ranch (IOGA) is deep within the Frank Church-River of No Return Wilderness Area, some three miles east of the Middle Fork of the Salmon River. The ranch enjoys a picturesque setting in a forested high mountain valley. The weathered log lodge and cabins are mirrored in a private trout lake. Access is by bush taxi or private plane to the ranch's 3,300-foot grass airstrip, or via a five-mile horseback ride from the nearest road. Activities emphasize horseback riding, but fishing and just loafing are options, too. Tom Allegrezza, 7153 E. Emerald St., Boise, ID 83704. ☎ 208-377-1188.

Twin Peaks Ranch (IOGA), in a mile-high valley some 18 miles west of the town of Salmon, fronts on the Salmon River Gorge and backs onto seemingly endless miles of mountains tumbling to the sky. Lodgings include both modern cabins and original log cabins dating to 1924, when the ranch was founded. Horseback riding is paramount at this 2,850-acre ranch; an overnight pack trip into the high country is the high point of many guests' visit. Other activities include pond and river fishing, trap shooting, dancing to live Western band music, and swimming in the ranch's heated pool. PO Box 774, Salmon, ID 83467. ☎ 800-659-4899 or 208-894-2290. Fax 208-894-2429.

Wild Horse Creek Ranch (IOGA), in the Pioneer Mountains 20 miles east of Sun Valley, represents the upscale side of the guest ranch spectrum. Modern log and stone buildings afford civilized comfort. An outdoor swimming pool is at guests' disposal. Unlike most guest ranches, activities such as trail rides, pack trips and guided fishing and hunting trips cost extra. By-the-day room rates include breakfast only. PO Box 398, Mackay, ID 83251. ☎ 208-588-2575.

Where to Eat

 There may be no deeper rift between dining styles anywhere in the West than in Central Idaho. On one side are eateries serving up the hearty home-style meals that evolved from the foods of early homesteaders and ranchers. On the other side are the trendy, tasty dishes turned out by Sun Valley/Ketchum chefs. Cafés satisfying burgers and fries tastes land somewhere in the middle.

Included in these extremes are restaurants that quite consistently (no one's perfect) deliver a high degree of culinary perfection, and eminently avoidable hash houses. The following suggestions strive to showcase the former, while giving the latter a wide berth.

Arco

Passing through Arco? Get to **Pickle's Place** around noon for some serious Western grub. 440 S. Front St. ☎ 208-527-9944.

Challis

Not much doing in Challis, gastronomy-wise. Best not to set your standards too high in any Central Idaho town, for that matter. Apple dumplings set Challis's log **Y-Inn Café** apart from run-of-the-corral small town cafés. Check out the weekend prime rib buffet at the adjoining **Challis House**. 1200 N. Main St. ☎ 208-879-4426.

Pocatello

Pocatello dining mostly reflects the blandness of Southern Idaho's Mormon-inspired cooking. The following are Pocatello's alternatives.

Eduardo's, serving traditional Mexican fare, is a happy surprise. 612 Yellowstone Ave. ☎ 208-233-9440.

The Sandpiper, one of a chain of restaurants serving most sizeable Idaho towns, is a good choice when all else fails. Steak and seafood dishes in a pleasant atmosphere. 1400 Bench Road. ☎ 208-233-1000.

Salmon

Salmon's restaurant fare reflects both the town's cowtown roots and the more recent influx of river rafters. Pizza, burgers and typical mom-and-pop cafés abound.

Shady Nook, on US 93 North, is an exception if you enjoy steak or trout and don't mind being stared down by big game trophies. ☎ 208-756-4182.

Stanley

Stanley has no dirth of eateries, mostly of the ho-hum genre. A general rule in towns swelled to bursting with vacationers is that the fare offered by restaurants adjacent to the bigger and showier lodgings is apt to be bus-tour basic. The same is true in Stanley.

An exception is the **Kasino Club**, serving up well-prepared meats and poultry, plus nightly pasta specials. 21 Ace of Diamond Ave. ☎ 208-774-3516.

Galena Lodge, roughly halfway between Stanley and Ketchum, is known for homemade soups and bread, plus burgers and other hearty appetite pleasers. Open for lunch and après-ski. At Galena Summit on Hwy 75. ☎ 208-726-4010.

Sun Valley/Ketchum

You can allow your taste buds to romp in this mining and sheep town turned trendy. But you may suffer from pocketbook shock. A Central Idaho constant: restaurant fare is priced according to how high a profile the area enjoys. You can eat well for much less in, say, Arco, than at Sun Valley. But there is no comparing the cuisine and ambience. You pay for what you get. Sun Valley/Ketchum offers the widest variety of cuisines in Idaho. Here, the challenge is not finding a recommendable eatery, but narrowing the field. If the following list seems to be heavy with fine restaurants, it's because casual moderately priced drop-in eateries are in relatively short supply. Prix fixe menus, offered by some establishments, can lighten the shock to your purse.

Beach Café characterizes itself as "Ketchum's Main Street Hot Spot." We don't understand the relevancy to mountain-girt Idaho. But the typical ski resort fare is tasty, particularly "Low Tide" appetizers.

Lunch, après ski, dinner. Sun Valley Road & Main St., Ketchum. ☎ 208-726-0051.

Chandler's specializes in generous portions of American home-cooked entrées. Nightly prix fixe menu. Dinner only. Reservations appreciated. Trail Creek Village, 200 S. Main St., Ketchum. ☎ 208-726-1776.

China Pepper serves up sizzling-hot Thai, Hunan and Szechuan specialties and features a sushi bar. They also offer take-out. Dinner only. 511 Building, Ketchum. ☎ 208-726-0959.

Desperado's features authentic Mexican cuisine prepared *sans* lard. Lunch and dinner. Corner of 4th and Washington, Ketchum. ☎ 208-726-3068.

Hungarian Radish specializes in European cuisine prepared with Hungarian flair. The skiers'-appetite winter prix fixe menu lightens up in summer. Lunch and dinner. Reservations requested. 200 S. Main St., Ketchum. ☎ 208-726-8468.

Ketchum Grill prepares pizzas, fish and meats on a wood-burning grill. Dinner only. Reservations accepted. 520 East Ave., Ketchum. ☎ 208-726-4660.

Michel's Christiania & Olympic Bar is the place to dine if you have a hankering for traditional French cuisine. Patio dining in summer. Dinner only. Reservations recommended. Sun Valley Road, Ketchum. ☎ 208-726-3388.

Ore House serves traditional ski resort fare. The kids' menu is one of the best I've seen. No hot dogs and grilled cheese sandwiches, with nary a veggie in sight, but rather scaled-down versions of grownups' dishes. They also have a vegetarian menu. Lunch and dinner. Reservations welcome. Sun Valley Village. ☎ 208-622-4363.

Otter's garden dining room features continental cuisine and Pacific Northwest specialties. Dinner only. Reservations preferred. 180 6th St. at Second Ave., Ketchum. ☎ 208-726-6837.

Salvatore's specializes in authentic Italian cuisine. Dinner only. 111 Washington Ave., North Ketchum. ☎ 208-726-3111.

Sun Valley Lodge Dining Room plays elegance to the hilt. No T-shirted wait staff here, but rather tux-clad waiters serving continental cuisine with nary a misstep. The ambience is enhanced by a string quartet romancing diners from a marble staircase. Reservations requested. ☎ 208-622-2150.

Central Idaho

Camping

Central Idaho camping choices cover almost as much territory as its wilderness areas.

Backpackers can throw down sleeping bags almost anywhere within the designated wilderness areas, but must adhere to conservation guidelines. The Forest Service does maintain a few primitive wilderness and Sawtooth National Recreation Area campgrounds. Strictly observing rules of wilderness conduct is obligatory; you pack it in, you pack it out. No exceptions.

> *Wilderness Areas are maintained by the Nez Perce, Boise, Challis, Payette, Salmon and Sawtooth National Forests. Obtain a copy of Camping and Picnicking in the National Forests of Idaho, a US Department of Agriculture Forest Service publication, from any Forest Service or ranger district office. Look up the relevant National Forest, then check in with the local Ranger District for trail and camping information and wilderness conduct guidelines specific to the area in which you wish to camp. Be sure to inquire if potable water is available.*

Central Idaho has dozens of **National Forest campgrounds**. The majority are primitive and most, but not all, have potable water. You can reserve a campsite at some of the more popular campgrounds. Again, check with a local ranger station.

- The US Forest Service maintains pleasant wooded campgrounds at **Stanley** and **Redfish Lakes**. The Stanley Lake campground's small size reflects this lightly used lake's ambience, while the Redfish Lake campground is quite extensive. All campsites have easy lake access; some have lake views. Contact the Sawtooth National Recreation Area (2647 Kimberly Rd., Twin Falls, ID 83301. ☎ 208-737-3200. Fax 208-737-3236).

State parks are usually good camping choices, but in Central Idaho they are conspicuous for their absence. However, two state parks offer pleasant stopovers off I-84 and I-86. Hefty dollops of Oregon Trail history are thrown in at no extra charge.

- **Massacre Rocks State Park** has camping beside the Snake River, where numerous birds and waterfowl are often spotted. No reservations. Take Exit 28 off I-86. 3592 N. Park Lane, American Falls, ID 83211. ☎ 208-548-2672.

- **Three Island Crossing State Park**'s grassy campground (see pages 347, 379) overlooks the Snake and the three islands that caused Oregon Trail emigrants such grief. Take the Glenns Ferry exit off I-84. No reservations. PO Box 609, Glenns Ferry, ID 83623. ☎ 208-366-2394.

A **private campground** can be a welcome sight if you find yourself in an area lacking state park or Forest Service campgrounds. The following have something special to recommend them.

- **Pocatello KOA** may be a good choice if you have kids and need to overnight in the Pocatello area. Kids love KOAs. My Amy is as enthusiastic about the backcountry as any kid, yet her eyes light up at the sight of a KOA sign. Why? The swimming pool, other kids, and games. The Pocatello version has a bewildering 85 spaces. Take Exit 71 off I-15. 9815 W. Pocatello Creek Rd., Pocatello, ID 83201. ☎ 800-562-9175 or 208-233-6851.

- **Challis Hot Springs** has enjoyed local popularity for generations. Only a line of brush separates campsites from the Salmon River. A thermally heated swimming pool is the main attraction. HC 63, Box 1779, Challis, ID 83226. ☎ 208-879-4442. Fax 208-879-5349.

- **Resort**, 15 miles southwest of Salmon off US 93, has 20 RV spaces set on a hill overlooking the lake. Amenities include a restaurant, game room and fishing boat rentals. PO Box 1150, Salmon, ID 83467. ☎ 208-756-2007.

Region 4

Eastern Idaho

The slender slice of Idaho east of Interstate 15 and west of the Tetons projects dual characters shaped by disparate cultures. The legacy of the Mormon farmers and ranchers who filtered north from Utah in the late 19th century is very strong. The legacy of the explorers, trappers and prospectors who bucked the challenge posed by the rugged Wyoming and Montana mountains to the east and north is less palpable – increasingly buried by modern life and twisted by tourism.

For all of that, this area, crossed by successive waves of Oregon Trail emigrants and dominated by the Teton Range, appeals to travelers attracted by its unique mix of human and natural history and traditional Western adventures. You won't find vast wilderness areas here. You will find forested gorges, wetlands and chiseled uplands in the shadow of the Grand Teton Mountain Range. Seemingly in concert with most residents' conservative lifestyle, the terrain is less intimidating than that of macho Central Idaho. Even the austere Tetons reflect this. The frontside over in Wyoming rivals the Sawtooths in majesty, lending illusion, but less substance, to the gentler backside sloping into Idaho.

The Tetons – several lakes and sizeable reservoirs, a tangle of chuckling rivers, notable wildlife watching areas, a saucer-shaped caldera ideal for horseback riding, and a wildly funky hot springs town – offer a wide variety of adventures.

Scattered across southeastern Idaho's rolling terrain are towns seemingly folded in on themselves. Homes cluster around Mormon meeting houses like sheep in a holding pen. Streets wide enough to U-turn six span of oxen pulling a loaded freight wagon mirror those of Salt Lake City, where the concept originated with Mormon leader Brigham Young. The sense of 1920s-era déjà-vu extends to courteous townspeople who are more than happy to offer directions or to chat, especially on the subject of religion – their religion.

Adequate lodgings and eateries are seldom farther than a few miles distant. A town has to be miniscule indeed not to boast at least one café serving predictable fare. Pies and doughnuts are staples. Just don't expect a good cup of coffee or a glass of wine.

Inhibitions tend to be looser in the area north of St. Anthony, along the Tetons and in the US 20 corridor that signals the approach to Yellowstone National Park.

Geography & History

Southeastern Idaho differs geographically from the bulk of the state, which is drained by the Columbia River and its tributaries. From Blackfoot Reservoir south, numerous creeks drain into **Bear Lake** and then into the **Great Salt Lake** – an interesting distinction when you consider the area's close Utah ties. Scored by the **Bear** and **Portneuf Rivers**, the southern third of this region is characterized by low mountains – timid extensions of Utah's Wasatch Range. Thus, the north-south valleys became natural corridors for migrating Mormons.

Today, potato fields green the land between Blackfoot and Rexburg. To the south, cattle graze the arid hills and narrow valleys over which toiled emigrants on the Oregon Trail and the Hudspeth Cutoff. The faint outlines of Oregon Trail wheel ruts are still visible, as are the various landmarks that were recorded in emigrant diaries.

The **Caribou Mountains**, cut by the Snake and Grays Lake Outlet, dominate the mid-section of *Region 4* as far east as the Blackfoot Reservation and north to the Snake. The Targhee National Forest kicks in north of here. Forested lands punctuated by waterfalls fringe the Tetons. North of **Ashton** lies one of the strangest phenomena in a state full of them: the near-level 18-by-23-mile caldera of a large shield volcano from the Pleistocene Age. This caldera, one of the world's largest, is covered with stands of pine interspersed with meadows and lakes.

Idaho's first non-Indian permanent settlements were established by **Mormons** in the state's southeast corner. **Franklin** dates from 1860, when Oregon Trail emigrants were still trekking across Idaho. At Soda Springs, the main trail branched northwest to merge with the Lander Cutoff. The Hudspeth Cutoff headed almost due west from here to meet the California Trail.

Since time unremembered, this country had been home to the **Shoshone**, and later the **Bannock Indians**. An uneasy, but generally peaceful, coexistence between natives and Mormons was destroyed on the morning of January 29, 1863, when the US Cavalry, under the command of Col. Patrick Connor, attacked a Shoshone village. The cavalry killed over 400 villagers, women and children as well as men, burned 70 tipis, appropriated some 175 horses, and left the few survivors to die. More persons died here than at Little Big Horn or Wounded Knee. The debacle entered history books as the Battle of Bear River. Justice was served when, in the late 1980s, the truth escaped the mire of historic prejudice. Today, the site near Preston is officially commemorated as the Bear River Massacre Site.

Meanwhile, the mountain man saga was winding down in the Caribou and Teton Mountains to the north. The heady days when the likes of

Eastern Idaho

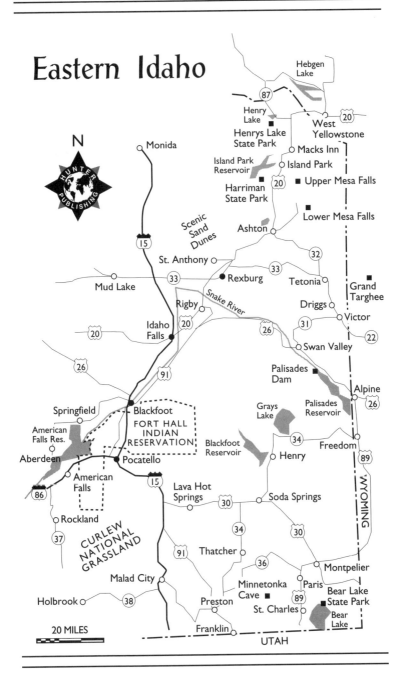

N

Monida

Hebgen Lake

87

Henry Lake
Henrys Lake State Park

West Yellowstone 20

Macks Inn

Island Park Reservoir
Island Park

Upper Mesa Falls

Harriman State Park 20

Lower Mesa Falls

Scenic Sand Dunes

Ashton

15

St. Anthony

32

33

Mud Lake 33

Rexburg

Tetonia

Grand Targhee

Rigby

Snake River

Driggs

31

Victor

Idaho Falls 20

26

22

20

Swan Valley

26

91

Palisades Dam

Alpine 26

Springfield

Blackfoot
FORT HALL INDIAN RESERVATION

Grays Lake

Palisades Reservoir

American Falls Res.

Blackfoot Reservoir

34

Freedom

89

Aberdeen

Pocatello

Henry

WYOMING

American Falls

15

Lava Hot Springs

Soda Springs

86

30

Rockland

37

CURLEW NATIONAL GRASSLAND

34

30

Thatcher

91

36

Montpelier

Malad City

Minnetonka Cave

Paris

Bear Lake State Park

Holbrook

38

Preston

89

St. Charles

Bear Lake

20 MILES

Franklin

UTAH

Eastern Idaho

John Colter, Manuel Lisa and Andrew Henry blazed trails through the history of the West had run their course. Homesteaders arrived, harvesting the caldera's wild hay and bringing cattle to graze the valleys. In 1872, Yellowstone National Park, across the border in Wyoming, was authorized. Over the decades, the trickle of curiosity seekers and adventurers, using Idaho as a convenient route to the park, increased to a torrent of vacationers. Today, US 20 between Ashton and West Yellowstone, Montana, threads a gauntlet of tourist come-ons.

John Colter

John Colter is best known as the man who discovered the thermal geysers and hot pots that later formed the nucleus of Yellowstone Park. But when he regaled folks back in St. Louis with tales of these wonders, few believed him. A member of the Louis & Clark expedition that blazed a trail to the Pacific in 1804-06, the tall Virginian subsequently accepted an offer to guide a beaver trapping expedition on the upper Missouri. He remained in the bush for four years. He didn't set out to establish the US fur trade in the Rocky Mountains. That just kind of evolved from his love of wilderness living.

Colter's most celebrated exploit occurred in 1808, when he and a partner came upon a party of 500 Blackfeet. Had not his partner shot before parlying, the meeting would have been peaceable. After the partner was shot full of arrows, Colter was stripped and tortured. When a chief asked how fast he could run, the wily Colter lied that he was slow as a turtle. Giving him a 30-second lead, the braves made him run for his life. Off he went, running barefoot over rocky scree and prickly pear thorns, headed for the Jefferson Fork six miles away. He soon left all his pursuers in the dust, save one. When that lone warrior drew near, Colter tripped and dispatched him with his own lance. Reaching the river, Colter hid under a raft of driftwood. After nightfall, he swam five miles downriver. The next day, he resumed running and ran 200 miles in seven days to safety at Manuel Lisa's fort on the Bighorn River. Though naked, dehydrated, starved, feet flayed by rocks and thorns, Colter recovered quickly and soon returned to the bush.

In 1810, he decided to leave, paddling 2,000 miles downriver to St. Louis. He bought a farm and tried to settle down. But it rankled him that few believed his tales of the wonders in the Rocky Mountains. Drink and disappointment overtook him and he died a bitter man.

This brand of tourism is an offence you can accept or not. Several area guest ranches offer a taste of the true West. Area lakes afford prime fishing. Wildlife viewing areas abound. And funk sometimes mixes it up with conservatism.

Getting Around

Eastern Idaho's principle access points are **Pocatello** and **Idaho Falls**. Pocatello is served by Skywest (☎ 800-453-9417) and Horizon Airlines (☎ 800-547-9308). Idaho Falls is served by Delta Airlines and regional carriers Skywest and Horizon Airlines. Major car rental agencies do business in both cities.

Interstate 15 provides access from Salt Lake City to the south and from Montana to the north. Feeder highways, including US 91, 30, 26 and 20, branch from I-15, providing direct or indirect access to Bear Lake, Grays Lake, Palisades Reservoir, Lava Hot Springs and other southeastern Idaho points of interest, Grand Targhee Ski Resort, and the Targhee National Forest's numerous natural attractions.

Most secondary roads and highways serve towns, farms and ranches, assuring fairly good maintenance year-round. But heavy snowfalls, particularly in the higher elevations, can hamper road crews. Some highways are snow-packed in winter. But that's the universally preferred alternative to the dreaded black ice.

Forest Service roads are open to mechanized vehicles. Most are suitable for passenger cars, but a 4WD vehicle is recommended for carefree driving, particularly in mountainous terrain. Before setting out, inquire about current road conditions at the local ranger station or BLM district office.

Much of this region may be "tamer" than other sections of Idaho, but don't let down your defenses. Follow the driving and emergency precautions set forth elsewhere in this book. Pack winter survival gear for both yourself and your vehicle. Winters can be severe, with wind-driven snows sweeping across the area and colliding with the Tetons. Summers are generally pleasantly cool.

Eastern Idaho

This is take-your-time country. Don't rush down highways and byways. Meander, so as not to miss side trips offering interesting historical footnotes. Historical markers provide insight into the events that shaped this land and the people who chose to live on it. Many small towns have museums designed to preserve as well as showcase cherished relics of the past. Many are lovingly maintained by The Daughters of Utah Pioneers. Pioneer-constructed homes and public buildings drowse in old Mormon towns such as Preston, Paris, Chesterfield and Franklin.

This is also Oregon Trail country. You will follow portions of the Oregon Trail and the Lander Cut-Off as you meander along the Bear Lake-Caribou Scenic Byway (US 30) and the Pioneer Historic Byway (Idaho 34). Many landmarks noted in emigrant journals remain visible, as do some portions of actual trails.

An illustrated map and brochure, *Oregon Trail in Idaho*, is available at BLM offices and through the Idaho Travel Council and associated offices. A descriptive map of the Lander Cut-Off through Idaho and Wyoming is available at local BLM and Forest Service offices. These publications, offering insight into the trail and its landmarks, are invaluable in tracing the trail through Idaho.

Deviate off the main highways to take in spectacular under-hyped natural attractions such as Upper and Lower Mesa Falls and Minnetonka Cave.

Eastern Idaho's three state parks, Bear Lake, Harriman and Henry's Lake, reflect distinctive slices of Idaho's natural and human history. Boating, scuba diving and ice fishing are big at Bear Lake. Harriman State Park is the legacy of an era when railroad and copper tycoons carved out remote retreats for themselves and their friends. Glacier-created Henry's Lake offers superb trout fishing.

Wherever you choose to explore in Eastern Idaho, you can count on easy and pleasant traveling, good access to amenities, and many days worth of touring and adventure possibilities.

Information Sources

Idaho Winter Road Report. ☎ 208-336-6600.
Highway Accident/Emergenies. ☎ 800-632-8000.

♨

Bureau of Land Management, Idaho State Office, 1387 S. Vinnell Way, Boise, ID 83709. ☎ 208-384-3300.
Bureau of Land Management, Idaho Falls District, 940 Lincoln Road, Idaho Falls, ID 83401. ☎ 208-524-7500.
Bureau of Land Management, Pocatello District, Federal Building, 250 S. 4th Ave., Suite 172, Pocatello, ID 83201. ☎ 208-236-6860.

Idaho Dept. of Fish & Game, 600 S. Walnut, Boise, ID 83707. ☎ 208-334-3700.

Idaho Outfitters and Guides Assoc., Box 95, Boise, ID 83701. ☎ 208-342-1438. Fax 208-338-7830. E-mail: outfitt@aol.com.

Idaho Guest & Dude Ranch Assoc., c/o John Muir, 7600 E. Blue Lake Rd., Harrison, ID 83833. ☎ 208-689-3295. Fax 208-689-9115.

Idaho Department of Parks and Recreation, Box 83720, Boise, ID 83720-0065. ☎ 208-334-4199. Fax 208-334-3741.

ﻉﺎ

Caribou National Forest, 250 South Fourth Ave., #187, Pocatello, ID 83201. ☎ 208-236-7500. Fax 208-236-7503.

Caribou National Forest, Malad Ranger District, 75 S. 140 East (PO Box 142), Malad, ID 83252. ☎ 208-766-4743.

Caribou National Forest, Montpelier Ranger District, 431 Clay, Montpelier, ID 83254. ☎ 208-847-0375.

Caribou National Forest, Soda Springs Ranger Station, 421 West. 2nd South, Soda Springs, ID 83276. ☎ 208-547-4356.

Targhee National Forest, Box 208, St. Anthony, ID 83445. ☎ 208-624-3151. Fax 208-624-7635.

Targhee National Forest, Ashton Ranger District, 30 South Yellowstone Highway, PO Box 858, Ashton, ID 83420. ☎ 208-652-7442.

Targhee National Forest, Dubois Ranger District, PO Box 46, Dubois, ID 83423. ☎ 208-374-5422.

Targhee National Forest, Island Park Ranger District, PO Box 20, Island Park, ID 83429. ☎ 208-558-7301.

Targhee National Forest, Palisades Ranger District, 3659 E. Ririe Hwy, Idaho Falls, ID 83401. ☎ 208-523-1412.

Targhee National Forest, Teton Basin Ranger District, PO Box 777, Driggs, ID 83422. ☎ 208-354-3421.

ﻉﺎ

Idaho Travel Council, c/o Idaho Dept. of Commerce, 700 West State St., Boise, ID 83720-0093. ☎ 800-635-7820 or 208-334-2470. Fax 208-334-2631. Web site: www.visitid.org.

Southeastern Idaho Travel Assn., c/o Lava Hot Springs Foundation, Box 498, Lava Hot Springs, ID 83246. ☎ 800-423-8597 or 208-776-5500. Fax 208-776-5723.

Bear Lake Convention & Visitors Bureau, Box 26 (2661 US Hwy 89), Fish Haven, ID 83287. ☎ 800-448-BEAR or 208-945-2333. Fax 208-945-2072.

Yellowstone-Teton Territory Travel Committee, c/o Eastern Idaho Info. Visitor Center, Box 50498 (505 Lindsay Blvd.), Idaho Falls, ID 83405. ☎ 800-634-3246 or 208-523-1010. Fax 208-523-2255.

ﻉﺎ

Bear Lake State Park, PO Box 297, Paris, ID 83261. ☎ 208-945-2790.

Eastern Idaho

Harriman State Park, HC 66, Box 500, Island Park, ID 83429.
☎ 208-558-7368.

Henry's Lake State Park, HC 66, Box 20, Island Park, ID 83429.
☎ 208-558-7532.

Touring

Bear Lake to Lava Hot Springs

You have only to glance at the rendering of extreme southeast Idaho on the *Official Idaho Highway Map* to understand that driving from here to there in logical sequence is nigh unto impossible. But we'll try.

Three highways, US 91 and 30 and Idaho 36, access this area from I-15. A more direct route to Bear Lake is via US 89 from Logan, Utah. Idaho 36 connects with I-15 at the small agricultural town of Malad, not to be confused with Malad Gorge between Jerome and Glenns Ferry. If you are approaching from the south, you can take this route to Preston. If you're coming from the north, access US 91 from I-15 at the non-town of Virginia. Both routes involve climbing over wind-swept hills and passing through hamlets that appear to have left the world behind.

Preston, originally given the unglamorous name of Worm Creek, dates from 1888. Unlike many old Mormon agricultural towns, Preston's 3,700 residents enjoy a mild prosperity reflected in tidy streets lined with respectable brick homes. Some houses have two front doors; separate entrances for separate wives. Some, but not all, polygamous families lived under one roof. It was more common for each wife to maintain a separate home in which to raise her children. Scraping sustenance from the soil was paramount at first, but as time went on Brigham Young's admonition to make the desert bloom as the rose was taken literally. So it is that these small towns announce their presence from afar, appearing as leafy oases surrounded by sere hills. Most yards are planted with well-watered grass and neat ranks of flowering plants and shrubs, including roses.

Two and a half miles north of Preston on US 91, where the road crosses the Bear River, you'll find a historic marker identifying the site of the **Bear River Massacre**. The actual site is across the highway from the sign, about a half-mile west, above Battle Creek ravine. A gravel road leads to the site, considered sacred by members of the Shoshone tribe and honored by all Native Americans. Now a National Historic Landmark, the site is slated to become a National Monument. See page 288 for the story of this incident.

Franklin, Idaho's oldest settlement and the site of an **Idaho Pioneer Association Museum**, is eight miles south of Preston on US 91. The Main Street museum houses pioneer relics and photos. Open May-September, Mon-Fri, 10-noon and 1-5, or by appointment. ☎ 208-646-2437.

Franklin barely tops 475 souls, but the town has been on a roll ever since Idaho instituted a state lottery. Pious Utah scoffs at the very idea of starting a Utah lottery. But that doesn't keep its residents from making tracks for Franklin. The border town consistently racks up the most lottery sales of any Idaho town.

Idaho 36 takes a northeasterly course from Preston, traveling through widely-flung ranchlands to merge with US 89, the southerly lap of Idaho's **Bear Lake-Caribou Scenic Byway**, at the grandly named hamlet of Ovid. This 26-mile drive to the Utah state line is one of the state's loveliest. No splendid mountains and rivers, but rather a succession of hamlets evoking pioneer times, none exceeding 600 souls.

A few miles south of Ovid, you'll come to **Paris**. This, the first Mormon settlement in the Bear Lake Valley, was founded in 1864 by Charles Rich, husband of six wives and father of 51 children.

The circa 1884 **Paris Tabernacle**, on the National Register of Historic Places, remains one of the finest examples of the Mormon Church's 19th-century tabernacle building fixation. Historic wood and brick homes project an innocent charm quite at odds with the Tabernacle's ambitious architecture.

The **Paris Museum**, containing hand-fashioned antiques and flotsam from the attics of pioneer families, makes available a brochure identifying many of the town's 100 or so historically significant structures. Located on Main Street, the museum is open daily, Memorial Day-Labor Day, 10-4.

Your first glimpse of shimmering-blue Bear Lake comes just before you reach **St. Charles**. Strong stone houses, hugging who knows what secrets to themselves, stand in pretty gardens above the lakeshore. St. Charles is the birthplace of Gutzon Borglum, the sculptor who carved the presidential faces at Mount Rushmore, South Dakota.

Bear Lake, a remnant of prehistoric Lake Bonneville, was a favorite mountain man rendezvous site. Concentrations of soluble carbonates cause Bear Lake to glisten like a brilliant deep-blue sapphire. An altitude of 5,923 feet assures cool summers and shivery winters. Just over half of the 20-mile-long, seven-mile-wide lake is in Utah. Idaho may not have the cougar's share, but it does boast the lake's deepest waters. A

208-foot-deep trench along the faultline below the eastern shore is a magnet for scuba divers.

The lake's upward-sloping western edge offers perfect raspberry-growing conditions. Bear Lake and raspberries are synonymous in many Utahns' and Idahoans' minds. Others equate Bear Lake with Bonneville ciscos, also called Bear Lake sardines. The silvery fish can grow to seven inches and are caught in winter, usually through the ice. The locals claim that the fish is found nowhere else on Earth.

Fish Haven, a hamlet of 100 souls three miles north of the Utah line, was once a Shoshone summer campsite; no doubt because of the superior fishing. A commercial fishery operated here at the turn of the century, but both states outlawed commercial fishing at Bear Lake in the 1920s. The nearby **Bear Lake National Wildlife Refuge** occupies the northern end of the lake. Like Loch Ness, Bear Lake is said to have a monster. Some claim, with tongue held firmly in cheek, to have seen it.

If you plan to play at Bear Lake, you will find lodgings at **Garden City**, Utah, seven miles south of Fish Haven. If camping, you can pitch your tent at Bear Lake State Park on the eastern shore.

Just north of St. Charles, you may have noticed a sign directing drivers down a gravel road to **Minnetonka Cave**. A half-mile path through the limestone cave trails past soda straws, stalactites, helictites, cave coral and flowstone formations. The US Forest Service opens the cave to visitors daily, June 15 through Labor Day.

Retrace your treads to Ovid and continue on US 89 to **Montpelier**. This crossroads town grew up around the Clover Creek Grazing Area, a popular Oregon Trail resting place. A new **National Oregon Trail Center** is on the exact site of this early rest area. Under construction as this book goes to print, the Center is expected to open in the summer of 1998. Interactive films and displays will offer visitors you-are-there insight into the Oregon Trail experience. Forty-one Oregon Trail paintings by noted Idaho artist Gary Stone will form the centerpiece of a hypothetical "journey" through 19th-century Idaho. The Center is at the junction of US 89 and 30. Contact the Bear Lake Convention & Visitors Bureau (☎ 800-448-BEAR) for current information.

Southeast-branching US 30 parallels the Oregon Trail route for a time before the highway gyrates south and the trail heads due east. An Idaho Highway Historical marker identifies **Big Hill** at Milepost 141.7. This descent out of the Bear River Mountains was one of the most feared impediments on the trail. The trail entered Idaho from Wyoming at **Border Summit**. Hang a left on the first road just north of the summit and drive 0.6 miles. From here, looking southwest, you should be able

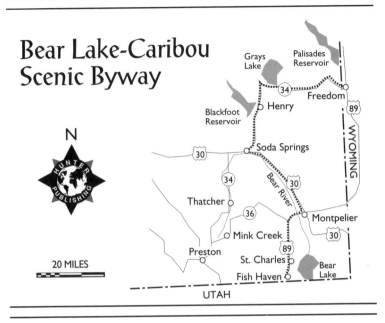

Bear Lake-Caribou Scenic Byway

Grays Lake

Palisades Reservoir

34

Freedom

Blackfoot Reservoir

Henry

89

WYOMING

N

30

Soda Springs

34

30

Bear River

Thatcher

36

Montpelier

Mink Creek

30

Preston

89

St. Charles

20 MILES

Fish Haven

Bear Lake

UTAH

to see faint trail tracks climbing out of the valley in a southwesterly direction.

The **Bear River-Caribou Scenic Byway** (US 30) heads north from Montpelier, checking in at **Soda Springs**, another favorite Oregon Trail rest area. Numerous emigrant diaries mention the spring coursing from beneath the ground here, claiming that the cool water tasted like "sodey-water." And so Soda Springs got its name.

It still tastes like sodey-water; some detect a faint root beer flavor. A park and pavilion surround the famous spring, two miles north of town (watch for signs). A dusty, noisy Monsanto Chemical Co. plant producing elemental phosphorus is directly uphill from the spring. The price of progress.

Not to be outdone by Yellowstone's Old Faithful, Soda Springs boasts a geyser on a timer. In 1937, workmen trying to locate a hot water source for a community swimming pool tapped into a geyser. The pool died aborning, but a timer was installed and every hour on the hour the geyser swooshes spectacularly to a height of some 150 feet.

The Daughters of the Utah Pioneers maintain Soda Springs's **Pioneer Historic Museum**. Located between 1st and 2nd Streets, the museum is open June 1 to October 1, from 1-4. ☎ 208-547-3890.

The 21-mile drive through the Portneuf Valley over US 30 between Soda Springs and Lava Hot Springs is a gateway to some fascinating footnotes in Southeast Idaho history.

Six miles west of Soda Springs, watch for a small sign announcing the **Niter Ice Caves.** Turn south, then watch for another small sign a couple of miles down the road. If you find yourself in tiny Grace, you've gone too far. The lava-formed ice cave is straddled by a scruffy dirt road. No hype here, only a scramble through the remains of one of those strange phenomena that pioneering settlers turned to advantage. These ice caves once served to cool a family's food supply.

Back on the highway, watch for directional signs to Bancroft and Chesterfield. Bancroft is another cookie-cutter farming town, but **Chesterfield** is something else again. This quintessential Mormon pioneer village is often referred to as a ghost town, but ghost town it's not, at least not in the usual sense of the word. No romantic mining flotsam here, but rather a self-righteous farming village teetering on the edge of arrested decay. A few families live here, but the meeting house and most of the sturdy old homes cast empty eyes to the wind-swept hills, imparting an eerie aura to this place of memories astride the Oregon Trail route. The entire village has been placed on the National Register of Historic Places. Daily tours are available from guides working at various projects in the village. A visitor information center is at 3111 Moses Lane.

Water ranges from very, very hot to just hot in Lava Hot Springs pools.

Lava Hot Springs never harbored any illusions of righteousness. As a town, it grew like a wildflower turned to the sun of opportunity. As a spa, it took root long before white men seized the deep declivity in the Portneuf Valley for their own.

Since early times, warring Indian tribes laid down their tomahawks when gathering to bathe in these geothermal springs that kicked out six million gallons of odor-free mineral water per day. Mountain men soothed their weary bones in the 110° waters. Some say that Oregon Trail emigrants also enjoyed the waters, but Lava Hot Springs is not on any known Oregon Trail route. In 1900, the US government ceded the springs to the state of Idaho. Thus began the development of one of Idaho's most popular, albeit funky, playgrounds.

The pool complex, kept open year-round by the state-owned Lava Hot Springs Foundation, is the focal point of this village on the banks of the happy-go-lucky Portneuf River. A close second is an Olympic-size outdoor swimming and diving pool, open only in summer. Modest fees are charged to use these facilities.

In winter, you'll find an unlikely mix of sore-muscled skiers, arthritic seniors and Salt Lake City yuppies soaking in the warmer of these stairstep pools. The waters' heat quotient declines in relation to each pool's distance from the source spring. Overflow water swells the Portneuf and fills the swimming pool.

In summer, the clientele shifts a tad in favor of "snowbirds," vacationing families and roaming hippies. Any season, the village's official roll of 420 souls swells to bursting.

Lava Hot Springs's merchants reflect the laid-back nature of the place, often with amusing culture clashes. This is especially evident in mid-July when a **Mountain Man Rendezvous** comes to town. The entire town is overtaken by buckskin-clad mountain men and women, "Indians" in full regalia, and assorted hangers-on. Tepees sprout along the river, traders' row sets up shop, Dutch ovens bubble beside campfires, calico-clad young'uns dart hither and yon, and a good time is had by all.

The mountain man culture is very much alive in the West. Entire families go to great expense to accumulate authentic costumes and gear. Rendezvous are held at various locations every weekend from spring through fall. Some latter-day mountain men attend every rendezvous, returning in spirit to a time when their role models roamed free. Nevermind that come Monday they must return to today's workaday world.

Lava Hot Springs is remote from most folks' workaday world. Campgrounds of various stripes line the river at both ends of town. Racks of tubes resembling doughnuts on steroids await adventurers bent on tubing the river. Gift and T-shirt shops, eateries, lodgings ranging from 1930s-style motels to toney B&Bs throng the town, wedged tightly between the river and a steep bluff. Across the highway, freight trains pound the tracks, creating a deep resonance throughout the valley.

Behind all the hoopla, you can make out the handsome facades of commercial buildings dating back to the early 20th century. Townspeople take pride in the unfolding history of this unique place. The **South Bannock County Historical Center**, housed in a former bank building, features an exhibit entitled "Trails, Trappers, Trains and Travelers."

Eastern Idaho

Doubling as a research facility, the museum has a good collection of photos, documents and artifacts. Open daily year-round, noon-5. ☎ 208-776-5254.

Lava Hot Springs can also be reached directly from I-15 via the McCammon exit.

Bywaying It: Soda Springs to Ashton

Return to Soda Springs via US 30 to pick up Idaho 34, the northerly stretch of the Bear Lake-Caribou Scenic Byway leading to Grays Lake. Here, the road becomes the **Pioneer Historic Byway**, paralleling a portion of the Lander Cut-Off. The cut-off was the preferred route for emigrants wishing to avoid some 50 miles of alkaline desert between South Pass and the Green River.

In 1965, **Grays Lake** was set aside as a National Wildlife Refuge (see *Wildlife Watching,* below). Watch for a directional sign to the Wildlife Refuge Headquarters. From here, you can access FS Road 117 for a scenic drive along Tin Cup Creek, looping to join Idaho 34 a few miles farther on.

Pick up US 89 at Freedom, a high-country ranching community whose main street traces the Idaho-Wyoming state line. From here, a scenic drive through the Wyoming side of the Snake River Range will bring you to Alpine, from where you can return to Idaho via US 26.

The Snake River enters Idaho here. But just as the Snake begins its epochal journey across the state, the channel disappears into the easternmost of the myriad reservoirs and dams built to tame this once-feisty river. US 26 runs the length of **Palisades Reservoir** between wheat fields and the Caribou Mountains. This reservoir is very popular with boaters and anglers.

At **Swan Valley**, a small crossroads community that has earned some fame as a fly-fishing mecca, you have a choice between continuing on US 26 to Idaho Falls, or swinging north on the Teton Scenic Byway (Idaho 31, 33 and 32).

The former is the main route between Jackson, Wyoming and Idaho Falls, site of a wedding-cake-white Mormon temple and mother hen to a clutch of nearby farming towns. Among these is **Rigby**, the boyhood home of Philo T. Farnsworth, who produced the first all-electronic television image at the tender age of 20. The farm boy-cum-inventor is little known, his pioneering work on television and the cathode ray tube patents having been gobbled up by RCA.

The **Teton Scenic Byway** skirts the Tetons for 70 leisurely, sometimes twisty, miles and affords Idaho's most splendid views of the massive mountain range's back side. In autumn, miles of shimmering aspens turn the landscape to gold. The road is snow-packed in winter. The occasional Forest Service road invites exploration.

The Byway passes through **Grand Valley**, a grassy mountain-girt expanse of land discovered in 1810 by John Colter, the mountain man adventurer credited with stumbling upon the geysers and other natural wonders that became Yellowstone National Park. Today, **Victor** and the more sizeable town of **Driggs** serve the needs of valley hay farmers and passing tourists. Driggs makes hay while the snow flies, it being the jumping-off place for Idaho's answer to Jackson Hole Ski Resort.

At Victor, Idaho 33 veers eastward to Teton Pass, the northernmost cross-mountain route to Jackson.

At Driggs, a partly paved, partly graveled road snakes skyward to **Grand Targhee Ski and Summer Resort**. Grand Targhee's dirty little secret: it's actually in Wyoming, but a situation on the back side of the Tetons gives it such close ties to Idaho that it might as well be in Idaho. The pleasant resort offers a baker's dozen of winter and summer adventures.

The Byway terminates at **Ashton**, a thriving ranching and tourist town straddling US 20.

Potatoes & Piety: Idaho Falls to St. Anthony

Idaho Falls owes its existence to potatoes and piety. The city's low skyline is dominated by the **Mormon temple**, at the falls of the Snake. The **riverside park** in the vicinity of the temple is a pretty oasis in this otherwise uninspiring city of some 43,000.

Bonneville County Historical Society maintains a museum at 200 Eastern. This ambitious museum showcases the Idaho Falls area from pre-history to the atomic era. Open year-round, Monday-Friday 10-5, Saturday 1-5. ☎ 208-522-1400.

US 20 becomes an expressway at Idaho Falls, zipping through potato fields to Rexburg and on to St. Anthony, from where it two-lanes to West Yellowstone, Wyoming.

Rexburg is the home of Mormon Church-owned Ricks College, where the offspring of the faithful embark on four-year adventures in learning and faith building.

Six miles north of Rexburg, Idaho 33 heads west to the **Teton Dam Site**, three miles east of Newdale. Watch for a directional sign to a spot

Eastern Idaho

overlooking a hole in the Earth. For a brief span of time, the breached dam at the head of this former reservoir held back the waters of the Teton River. By June 5, 1976, the 9½ million-cubic-yard earthen dam, under construction since 1972, had been completed and the reservoir was almost full. At 8:30 am, two leaks were reported. A hole appeared at 10 am. Bulldozers attempting to plug the hole nose dived into the rapidly expanding gap. At 11:52 am the dam split like an over-ripe melon, sending 80 billion gallons of water downstream, destoying farms and homes, and killing those who failed to scramble to safety.

The **Teton Flood Museum**, at 51 North Center Street in Rexburg, features exhibits pertinent to the dam failure, plus local history. Open May-September, Mon-Fri, 10-5, plus Saturdays from June-August. The balance of the year, the museum is open Monday-Friday, 10-4. ☎ 208-356-9101.

Some 13 miles up US 20 is **St. Anthony**, whose claim to fame is another of the strange phenomena gracing the Gem State. The **St. Anthony Sand Dunes** were formed by quartz sand deposited by prevailing winds over the course of a million years. Undulating over an area some 35 miles long and five miles wide in places, these are said to be the highest sand dunes in the state, possibly in the country (the latter claim may be a flight of local fancy). Dune-buggying the St. Anthony Sand Dunes is *the* local sport. Located northwest of town, the dunes can be reached by following Fourth Street north to Red Road.

Henry's Country: St. Anthony to Henry's Lake

From the dunes, a Forest Service road heads north into the Centennial Mountains on the Montana border. Kilgore, population 11, is the only settlement hereabouts. Before attempting to drive this remote road, contact the Targhee National Forest office to ascertain any road closures or restrictions (Box 208, St. Anthony, ID 83445. ☎ 208-624-3151. Fax 208-624-7635).

If you're in a hurry to reach Island Park, Harriman State Park, Henry's Lake or Yellowstone Park, you should continue on busy US 20, bee-lining it north from Ashton. The **Mesa Falls Scenic Byway** is the more scenic choice by far. To pick up the Byway, head west from Ashton on Idaho 47.

The narrow road meanders through 28 miles of sun-dappled forest. Lushly green and wildflower-sprinkled in summer, this forest turns a lovely green-gold in fall. Hiking here is a splendid adventure. The road is closed to all but snowmobiles in winter.

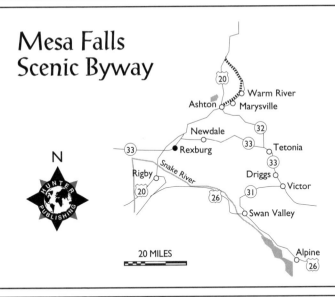

Mesa Falls Scenic Byway

N

20 MILES

The Byways' chief attractions are 114-foot-high **Upper Mesa Falls** and 65-foot-high **Lower Mesa Falls**. Between these falls, the Henry's Fork River shoulders through a deep, narrow gorge, kicking up a foaming fuss as it roisters to join the Snake River near Rexburg. In May, the Upper Falls' waterflow peaks at an incomprehensible 64,632,000 gallons per hour. By late August, the rate has dropped to about half that. You can view these falls from many angles via a series of walkways and platforms and a stone overlook built by the CCC in the 1930s. The sight of the falls is splendid indeed; the steady pounding of the water defies description.

The derelict, yet still handsome, 1907-32 vintage **Big Falls Inn** recalls an era when visiting the wonders of the West defined adventure. The log inn served as a way-stop for travelers en route to Yellowstone National Park. US 20 was constructed in the 1950s, side-lining what had been the main route to Yellowstone.

The Byway ends at US 20, seven miles south of **Island Park**, a sprawling tourist town adjacent to Island Park Reservoir on Henry's Fork. The area's level terrain seems all the flatter to eyes accustomed to seeing mountains. It may not be your idea of what a volcanic landmark should look like, but you are smack in the center of the **Island Park Caldera**. The surrounding stands of pine, interspersed with meadows and lakes, are ideal for hiking, horseback riding and Nordic skiing.

Eastern Idaho

Unfortunately, this lovely place is marred by the clamor of tourist enterprises lining US 20 at Island Park, and straggling for miles along the highway. But nuggets of gold shine through the dross.

Harriman State Park is a nugget of inestimable value. Locals still refer to the sprawling 10,700-acre park as the Railroad Ranch. The spread was incorporated as the Island Park Land and Cattle Company following the 1880s purchase by three controlling shareholders of the Oregon Short Line Railway. By 1911, Union Pacific President E.H. Harriman had become a joint owner. His sons, Roland and Averell, later gained control of the property. Running cattle was secondary to use as a family vacation retreat.

In 1977, the Harrimans deeded the ranch to the State of Idaho with the stipulation that the proposed park's first consideration would be wildlife conservation.

Roland Harriman's rationale for the deed was telling, in view of the commercialism that today drives the Island Park area: "Because we all felt such lasting gratitude for our many years of a full life at the Railroad Ranch, and because we just could not face the prospect of its becoming nothing more than an uncontrolled real estate development with hot dogs and cheap honky-tonks, and because we could foresee the necessity for preserving such property for the enjoyment of future generations."

The park, which includes two lakes and frontage on Henry's Fork, is a delightful place to hike, watch wildlife, ride horseback, cross-country ski, and simply to enjoy the silent beauty that so enthralled the Harrimans and their friends.

A couple of miles north of Island Park, unimproved County Rt. A2 slices cross-country to Dubois, looking in at Kilgore and intersecting the aforementioned Forest Service road connection with the St. Anthony Sand Dunes. This mountainous route skirts the caldera and two US Department of Agriculture Sheep Experiment Stations.

A few miles farther north, FS Road 421 heads off US 20 to **Big Spring**, the headwaters of Henry's Fork and the site of the **John Sack Cabin**. This cabin, listed on the National Register of Historic Places, is open to visitors in the summer months. The area's numerous roads, delineated on the *Island Park Ranger District Travel Map*, resemble the trails of a confused snake. Many roads are closed or restricted. Check in with the Island Park Ranger District before surrendering to the temptation of exploring them.

Another 10 miles north on US 20, watch for a sign announcing **Henry's Lake State Park**. This glacially formed lake, enlarged somewhat by a dam on Henry's Fork, is widely considered to be one of the West's finest trout fishing venues. You can camp right on the water. Families and other travelers have camped on the shores of this lake for centuries. They include Flathead Indians, Chief Joseph's ill-fated band and the pursuing US Cavalrymen, Jim Bridger and other mountain men, and Major Andrew Henry. The lake's namesake was the leader of an exploratory expedition that passed through this area in 1810, "discovering" the lake and river – known for centuries to Native Americans.

The road forks just north of the turnoff to Henry's Lake. Idaho 87 heads north, entering Montana at 6,836-foot **Reynolds Pass**. US 20 continues on to West Yellowstone, entering Montana via 7,072-foot **Targhee Pass**. Named for Tarhgee, a Bannock chief, this pass is on the route Chief Joseph and his band took in their 1877 attempt to reach a supposed freedom in Canada. Long before John Colter discovered the Yellowstone country, the Shoshone used the pass en route to a buffalo hunting area there.

Adventures

On Foot

Much of Southeastern Idaho is privately owned crop and ranchland, and off-limits to hikers. You can hike on BLM grazing lands. The Caribou and Targhee National Forests maintain trail systems in mountainous areas. These mountains shelter the populated valleys west of the Tetons. Most trails are open to horses as well as hikers. Horses have the right of way. You must step 10 feet off the trail and remain there until horses are out of sight, or until they have advanced 50 yards ahead. Do nothing that might spook these animals, many of which are working cow horses.

If you enjoy hiking through fairly level terrain, check out **Harriman State Park** and **Targhee National Forest** lands near Island Park.

Many trails are day hikes and demand no more than normal common sense precautions. Pack a supply of insect repellent, especially around lakes. Other trails, in the Tetons, are as remote and as difficult as any in the Sawtooths or the Central Idaho Wilderness Areas. Never underestimate weather and trail conditions. Never overestimate your hiking ability and that of your companions. See page 9 for detailed backcountry hiking precautions.

Eastern Idaho

Much of the Targhee National Forest is critical grizzly bear habitat. Grizzles don't observe Yellowstone National Park boundaries. They don't observe the rules of common courtesy, either. It is essential that you take all possible precautions. Before heading out, be sure to contact a local ranger district for grizzly bear dos and don'ts and to learn about recent sightings.

The **Caribou National Forest** sandwiches several relatively small trail systems into Southeast Idaho's crop and ranchlands, a boon if you are touring the area or playing water games in Bear Lake and wish to get in some hiking. Much of this is BLM rangeland. Ranchers and their families have trailed their cattle and sheep into this high country for well over 100 years. The cows won't bother you. Just watch out for cow patties. Before setting out, stop in at a Caribou National Forest ranger station (see page 293 for addresses) to obtain a travel map and to acquaint yourself with current trail restrictions.

Cariboo Jack

Don't expect to see caribou. The animals never roamed here. Caribou National Forest owes its name to one Jesse Fairchild, aka Cariboo Jack. A prospector in the Fraser River mining district before moseying southward to try his luck in Idaho, he couldn't seem to put that place out of his mind. So eloquent were his tales of the Canadian caribou country that the mountain where he finally made his big strike just naturally came to be named for him. Well, so goes the story anyway. But there was no doubt as to the richness of the strike. It set off a gold rush that lasted 20 years and produced $50 million worth of placer gold. Mining relics from that era still moulder in the vicinity of Caribou Mountain, west of Grays Lake.

The northerly end of the **Wasatch Range**, just west and north of Bear Lake, is especially attractive to hikers, having several undeveloped springs, both hot and cold, and peaks in excess of 7,000 feet.

The Caribou National Forest's largest backcountry expanse hugs the Idaho-Wyoming line north of Bear Lake to Grays Lake and Palisades Reservoir. Hiking and horseback riding trails, usually one and the same, network through this country, shaking hands with landmarks bearing names like Suicide Pass and Stump Peak. Traces of their colorful sojourn here have gone the way of time, but it's enough to know that your boots may be walking in the moccasin tracks of intrepid mountain men such as Jim Bridger and Jedediah Smith.

Jim Bridger

Born in Richmond, Virginia in 1804, Jim Bridger moved with his parents to the St. Louis area at age eight. Young Jim was apprenticed to a blacksmith. But the lure of the West grabbed him, never to turn him loose. At 18, he threw down his tongs to join a fur-trapping expedition to the headwaters of the Missouri River.

Bridger trapped the Rockies for the next 20 years. He came to embody the swagger and derring-do of fabled men in a fabled time. He claimed to be the first white man to lay eyes on the Great Salt Lake and seems to have been a part of virtually every mountain man/Indian rendezvous from Bear Lake north and west through Idaho, Montana and Wyoming. In 1830, he and his partners consolidated a scattering of trapping and trading interests, forming the Rocky Mountain Fur Company.

In 1843, Jim established Fort Bridger, a trading post on the Oregon Trail in Wyoming. But he couldn't stay put. For years he roamed the West, scouting and guiding for various expeditions. He discovered Bridger's Pass in Wyoming and got himself embroiled in more feats and scrapes than any one life could seemingly ever contain. Bridger didn't cotton to the Mormons or they to him. He got the worst of an 1853 skirmish with members of the new cult and retired to lick his wounds for four years. Then the US Army launched a campaign against the Mormons and Bridger signed on as a guide.

The "Old Man of the Mountains" swashbuckled across the West until 1868, guiding, exploring, yarning. He died at his Missouri farm in 1881.

The mountains and flats within the Targhee National Forest also knew the silent padding of their moccasins. Smoke from their campfires curled into the crisp mountain air. The grizzlies, elk, beaver and other animals you may see here today are likely descended from animals taken by these legendary mountain men.

 TIP *The Teton, Ashton and Palisades Ranger District offices make available a descriptive list of trails. In addition, the Targhee National Forest has a helpful Recreation Guide*

Eastern Idaho

covering hiking, camping and points of interest in the Forest. Travel maps, available for a nominal sum, are useful adjuncts. Be aware that motorized and mechanized vehicles are permitted on some trails, though many are restricted. No map can replace discussing trail conditions and restrictions with ranger district personnel.

The very thought of hiking through shifting sand dunes may make your legs ache, but surrealistic light and shadow playing over the **St. Anthony Sand Dunes** makes for interesting hiking.

The **Sand Creek Wildlife Management Area**, north of the Dunes, offers superb wildlife watching from upland desert trails. (See *Wildlife Watching*, below).

Harriman State Park's 20-mile-plus multi-use trail system winds along Henry's Fork, loops around Silver Lake and sashays along Golden Lake. Trails include both level terrain and ridgetop climbs. The one-mile **Ranch Loop** looks in on the historic Railroad Ranch buildings. The 5½-mile Ridge Loop passes through several forest communities on its 400-foot climb to top the ridge. The ridgetop affords a splendid view of the Tetons.

A half-dozen day-hike trails branch upward from **Grand Targhee Resort** to top Peaked Mountain, Fred's Mountain and the Teton Valley overlook. Most of these trails are fairly short, but are ski-run steep. Grand Targhee offers guided backcountry treks.

Travel on Horseback & with Pack Animals

Most trails in the Caribou and Targhee National Forests are open to both hikers and horses and pack animals. Assuming that you will not be traveling with Old Dobbin in tow, we'll skip National Forest horse etiquette parameters. If you will be trailering the family steed, be sure to contact a local ranger station for current regulations and trail restrictions pertinent to horse travel.

Most outfitters offering one-day trail rides operate out of self-styled resorts. **Harriman State Park** may be your best trail ride bet short of staying at one of these resorts, or visiting a guest ranch. Well-mannered ranch horses traverse many of the same trails used by the Harrimans and their guests. Special rides are offered in the September and October elk mating season. Riders trail up-mountain to where they can hear the resonating bugle of bull elk as they vie for the attentions of lady elk.

Grand Targhee Ski and Summer Resort is a good bet if you fancy riding in the Tetons. The resort's **Bustle Creek Outfitters** runs trail rides lasting from one hour to overnight. They also offer hayride dinners, chuckwagon cookouts and riding lessons. And they will arrange customized high country wilderness pack trips. Reservations required. ☎ 800-827-4433, extension 1355.

Central Idaho's wilderness areas have attained such an intriguing backcountry mystique that the majority of horseback/pack trip outfitters have permits to operate these areas. Conversely, more traditional "dude" ranches operate in the skirts of the Tetons.

See *Guest Ranches* for ranch stays offering horseback riding.

On Wheels

Bicycling & Mountain Biking

 Mountain bikes are permitted on many National Forest trails used by hikers and horses (see *On Foot*). Local ranger district offices have current information on these trails.

Many **Harriman State Park** trails are perfect for leisurely family bicycling. Mountain bikes are also permitted on these trails.

Grand Targhee Ski and Summer Resort permits mountain biking on hiking trails. Expanded mountain biking trails wind through scenic **Rick's Basin**. The resort hosts the **Grand Targhee Cross-Country Mountain Bike Race** over the July 4th holiday.

ATVs

For many, the **St. Anthony Sand Dunes** are synonymous with ATV adventures. A portion of the dunes area is restricted, but most of the sandy 10,000-acre playground is open to ATVs and motorized mountain bikes.

Many roads in the **Caribou** and **Targhee National Forests** are open to ATVs, but as many or more are restricted. Observe road signs. Better yet, visit local ranger district offices to make sure which is which.

On Water

River Floats

The **South Fork of the Snake River** flows northwest from Palisades Dam to the confluence with Henry's Fork near Menan Buttes. The entire length of this flat-water river covers 64 miles, but launch ramps at several locations offer the option of shorter floats. This is not a wilderness river in the sense of the Salmon and the Snake through Hells Canyon. It follows US 26 for some 15 miles, at which point it enters a beautiful cottonwood-fringed canyon several hundred feet deep. The canyon opens to a floodplain and runs through farmland to the Henry's Fork confluence.

Though not considered a whitewater river, the South Fork of the Snake poses some unique hazards. Take care to avoid water diversion structures located at intervals on the river. The water runs very fast near these diversions, creating whirlpools and standing waves that can overturn canoes and small boats. There is a high danger of being swept through diversion canal headgates, with fatal results. Other hazards include swift currents around bridge support piers and rocks. You should not attempt to float this river on your own unless someone in your party knows the river and is an experienced rafter.

The BLM, the US Forest Service and the Idaho Department of Fish & Game make available a helpful Boater's Guide to the South Fork of the Snake River. The guide includes maps and charts. Pick up a copy at any office of the above agencies.

All of that aside, the South Fork of the Snake offers much in the way of scenery and serenity. And the fishing is world-class. So is the wildlife watching. Deer, elk, moose, mountain goats, nesting bald and golden eagles, great blue heron and over 126 species of non-game birds frequent the river banks and the cliffs above the river.

- Until recently, outfitters offering floats on this river were scarce as fleas on a fish. IOGA member Lon Woodard, owner of **Drifters of the South Fork**, now offers two-day drift boat floats through the river's scenic canyons. The trip includes overnighting at a riverside camp with such almost unheard-of amenities as carpeted wall tents with cots, flush toilets, showers and a sweat lodge. Woodard also runs day-long group floats. PO Box 148, Swan Valley, ID 83449. ☎ 800-490-1204 or ☎/Fax 208-483-2722.

The **Portneuf River**, where it trips through Lava Hot Springs, is hardly a world-class whitewater river. But tubing this short, tumbling stretch is splashing great fun, especially on a hot summer day. Tubes can be rented from concessions at the town bridge.

Natural Lakes

Eastern Idaho's three major natural lakes couldn't be more different from one another. **Henry's Lake** is all business: fishing business. **Grays Lake**, actually a large shallow marsh with little open water, is also all business: wildlife refuge business.

Bear Lake's business is recreation in and on the water. Power boating, waterskiing and personal watercrafting are big here. The winds swooping down over the lake off the surrounding hills bring ideal windsurfing conditions. The steep drop just off the eastern shore, at **Bear Lake State Park's East Bench Unit**, is popular with scuba divers. Water-related gear can be rented at Garden City, Utah, a few miles south of the state line on the west side of the lake.

Reservoirs

Eastern Idaho, particularly the lower half, is specked with reservoirs, most under 100 acres in size, that are designed to hold river water and/or snow melt runoff for crop irrigation.

A typical reservoir's "life" cycle goes like this. Spring snow-melts fill it until, by early summer, it is brim-full. As summer progresses, the reservoir is drawn down until, by fall, the water level is several feet lower. In winter, the remaining water freezes over. River reservoirs commonly retain steadier water levels than mountain reservoirs that are dependent almost entirely on snow-melt. Spring is an anxious time, when farmers pray for warm days and cold nights, thus assuring a gradual thaw. Sudden heat spells cause rapid thawing, resulting in flooding, wasted water and low reservoir levels at the start of the growing season. In drought years, water may be drawn down to a point where fish can no longer live.

Most reservoirs are stocked with trout and other species of fish. Small reservoirs, such as **Portneuf Reservoir** near Chesterfield and **Foster Reservoir** near Preston, offer pleasant canoeing, though nearby canoe rentals are nearly non-existent. Most of these reservoirs are surrounded by low sagebrush hills. The larger **Palisades, Blackfoot** and **Island Park Reservoirs** have more varied scenery.

Canoeing

You may find a rental concession, but if you are a serious canoer you might bring your own canoe. Chambers of commerce can usually supply current lists of concessionaires.

At several viewing areas, canoeing is a quiet and natural way to watch wildlife. The following areas, described in this region's section on *Wildlife Viewing*, offer pleasant canoeing: the water trail at **Big Springs**, the **Sand Creek Wildlife Management Area**, **Market Lake Wildlife Management Area**, and selected stretches of the **South Fork of the Snake River**.

Fishing

Long ago, a higher power cloned rowboats fitted with outboard motors and guys casting for trout. So it is that, on any day from ice-melt to freeze-over, boatloads of anglers can be seen trying their luck on every lake and reservoir in Eastern Idaho.

Hatchery trout and bass are released into reservoirs, while rivers and lakes contain both wild and hatchery-raised species.

Henry's Lake is one of the state's best venues for cutthroat trout, cutthroat-rainbow hybrids of up to 10 pounds, and Temiscamie brook trout. Wild cutthroat had best be wary of anglers in **Bear River, Henry's Fork, Teton River**, and the **South Fork of the Snake River**. **Island Park Reservoir** has good coho salmon fishing.

Bear Lake has four endemic fish species: Bear Lake and Benneville whitefish, Bear Lake sculpin and Bonneville cisco. The Mackinaw fishing is also good. Cisco runs occur in January when ice fishing holes appear as suddenly as mining shacks in gold rush days. Cisco is the only sport fish in Idaho that can be legally taken with dip nets.

If you plan on any fishing at all, be sure to obtain copies of two Idaho Fish & Game Department publications: The Official Guide to Fishing in Idaho and General Fishing Seasons and Rules, available wherever Idaho fishing licenses are sold, or from the Idaho Fish & Game office in Boise (PO Box 25, Boise, ID 83707). The publications are gold mines of information on where to find which fish, fishing season dates, identifying species,

record catches, exceptions and restrictions, general fishing rules and other helpful information.

If you still have a question regarding fishing in Idaho, ☎ 1-800-ASK-FISH, an Idaho Fish & Game and Sport Fishing Promotion Council 24-hour angling hotline.

Many anglers consider the South Fork of the Snake River to be one of the premier dry fly-fishing streams in the country, if not the world.

- Spence and Linda Warner's **South Fork Lodge** offers guided flyfishing on the South Fork. Services include lodge stay/fishing packages, RV camping, full-day guided fishing and a fully stocked fly shop. PO Box 22, Swan Valley, ID 83449. ☎ 800-483-2110 or 208-483-2112. Fax 208-483-2121.

- Lon Woodard, owner-operator of **Drifters of the South Fork**, runs customized guided fly-fishing trips on this famous river. Airport pickup and lodging at an area B&B can be arranged. PO Box 148, Swan Valley, ID 83449. ☎ 800-490-1204 or ☎/Fax 208-483-2722.

On Snow

Heavy snows sweep into Eastern Idaho with demonic fury, slamming into the Tetons, drifting in the valleys, lying heavily on croplands and the level Island Park area. This annual blitz fails to thrill ranchers, who must struggle through the snow to get hay to cattle and sheep, and often to hungry deer and elk. But it does thrill downhill and Nordic skiers and snowmobilers. Indeed, there is as much, maybe more, to do here in winter as in summer.

Main roads are kept open, though they could be snowpacked due to heavy or sudden storms. Many side roads, such as the Mesa Falls Scenic Byway, are left to the drifts. You are unlikely to find impassable roads if your destination is a popular recreation area such as Grand Targhee Ski and Summer Resort or on a main route of commerce. Unless, of course, a snowstorm hits. In that event, it may be advisable to hole up.

You may have noticed a preponderance of high-clearance 4WD vehicles in your meanderings across Idaho. People who live in snow country know from experience that these hardy workhorses are the way to go. Request one if you rent a vehicle in winter.

Eastern Idaho

Load up on emergency gear if you plan on driving any distance at all, especially in sparsely settled areas. Prepare to be stuck in the snow and/or stranded for a few hours or even a couple of days. Kitty litter or other gritty material, a shovel and a tire-width board will aid in digging your vehicle out. Sleeping bags and/or blankets, extra-warm clothing, high-energy foods, and possibly a spirit stove and a cellular phone are necessary precautions.

Grand Targhee Ski Resort is *the* big draw for downhill skiers and 'boarders. Other winter adventure-seekers can't wait to strap on cross-country skis or snowshoes, or to jump onto a snowmobile for a roaring good time.

Downhill Skiing & Snowboarding

Grand Targhee Ski and Summer Resort, on the backside of the Tetons, has it all: 42-feet of annual snowfall, two mountains totaling 3,000 eminently skiable acres ranging from 8,000 feet altitude at the base to 10,250 feet atop Powder Mountain, snowcat skiing on Powder Mountain. The full service resort village offers a wide range of comforts and fun activities. The poolside fitness center and a new spa serve up an array of workouts and treatments. The ski school serves both grownups and kids. Advanced ski clinics, including NASTAR and NASTAR race clinics, are offered at intervals throughout the ski season. Other specialty programs include off-trail and snow cat powder workshops.

Grand Targhee jumped on the snowboard craze early on, not just grudgingly permitting 'boarding, as many ski resorts do, but actually encouraging the sport with snowboard clinics.

The lift-served mountain has a 2,200-foot vertical rise and 1,500 skiable acres, 300 of which are groomed. It is accessed via two new quad lifts, three double chairs and one surface lift. The longest groomed run is 2.78 miles. There are 1,200 acres of powder runs. Ten percent of the runs are for beginners, 70% intermediate, and 20% advanced.

Powder Mountain, open to snowcat skiing, has 1,500 skiable acres with a 2,800-foot vertical rise. The longest run boasts 3.2 miles of magnificent powder.

You can reach the Grand Targhee Resort by flying into either Idaho Falls or Jackson, Wyoming. The resort is up-mountain from Driggs – 87 miles by good roads from Idaho Falls. Jackson is half the distance from Grand Targhee as compared to Idaho Falls, but the road over Teton Pass is dicier in winter.

Ski Hill Road, Box SKI, Alta, WY 83422. ☎ 800-TARGHEE or 307-353-2300. Fax 307-353-8148.

Eastern Idaho has two low-profile ski mountains where the lift lines are short and the fun quotient is high.

Kelly Canyon Ski Area, east of Ririe, is a favorite with Ricks College students. The mountain has a vertical drop of 1,000 feet. The 23 runs are accessed by four double lifts. PO Box 367, Ririe, ID 83443. ☎ 208-538-6261. Fax 208-538-7735.

Pebble Creek Ski Area, near Pocatello, has a vertical drop of 2,000 feet. The 24 runs are accessed by two double lifts and one triple. PO Box 370, Inkom, ID 83245. ☎ 208-775-4452.

Cross-Country Skiing/Snowshoeing

Unless you are an experienced backcountry skier with a good fix on the terrain, it's adviseable to stick with marked trails. Several cross-country trails are located in the Caribou and Targhee National Forests. Check with the appropriate district ranger station for current information.

Island Park
Cross-Country
Ski Area

All but one of the Idaho Department of Parks and Recreation's Eastern Idaho Park 'n Ski areas are in the northeastern corner, where the terrain and scenery seem to have been designed for Nordic skiing.

The exception is **Trail Canyon**, located 12 miles northeast of Soda Springs on Trail Canyon Road. A convenient 35-mile drive from Lava Hot Springs makes it possible to top off a day of skiing with a soak in the famous thermal pools.

The 10-mile trail system is groomed periodically, depending on weather conditions. Trails suitable for all levels of ability traverse terrain that

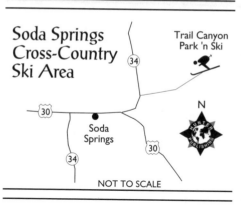

Soda Springs
Cross-Country
Ski Area

NOT TO SCALE

ranges from open meadows to thick conifer and aspen forests. The warming shelter and vault toilet are shared with snowmobilers.

As you might expect, the **Ashton** and **Island Park** areas offer prime cross-country skiing.

Fall River Ridge Park 'n Ski Area is 10 miles east of Ashton on the Cave Falls Road. The seven miles of trail, including several loops, are suitable for beginner and intermediate skiers. Rolling meadows are interspersed with stands of aspen and lodgepole pine. Skiers and snowmobilers share one mile of trail. The trails are groomed periodically, weather permitting.

The Bear Gulch/Mesa Falls Trail, seven miles northeast of Ashton on Mesa Falls Forest Service Road 47, is one of Idaho's most scenic trail systems. The nine-mile trail begins with a steep one-mile climb, then parallels a snowmobile trail to Upper and Lower Mesa Falls, where it branches away from the snowmobile trail, traveling along the canyon rim before returning to the trailhead. Recommended for intermediate and advanced skiers. The trail is groomed periodically, weather permitting.

In winter, **Harriman State Park**'s 21 miles of hiking trails are transformed to a Nordic skier's and snowshoer's delight. Trails include opportunities for all levels of ability. A colony of trumpeter swans winters here, as do a variety of other animals.

The Brimstone Trail is a quarter-mile north of the Island Park Ranger Station on US 20, near Ponds Lake Resort. The nine miles of trails, varying between gentle grades and downhill runs through groves of trees, afford views of Island Park Reservoir, Box Canyon and the Buffalo River. Suitable for all levels of ability.

The Buffalo River Trail, also accessed from the Island Park Ranger Station, trails the Buffalo River through pine forests. Gentle grades make this an ideal trail for beginning skiers. Both trails are goomed periodically.

If your group includes both Nordic and downhill skiers, **Grand Targhee Ski and Summer Resort** might be the answer. The resort's Nordic Center includes nine miles of groomed trails tracked for traditonal and skating techniques and offers lessons from PSIA certified instructors.

Snowmobiling

Given a snow cover that rivals any in the country, it's not surprising that the roar of the snowmobile is heard throughout Eastern Idaho. These machines are both workhorses and passports to winter fun. Ranchers use them for getting hay to their stock. Residents use them for grocery runs over snow-choked roads. Kids ride them as naturally as they ride horses in summer and fall. Folks come from afar to snowmobile some of the best trails west of Yellowstone.

 If you trailer your own machine, be sure to obtain a copy of the Idaho Department of Parks and Recreation's Idaho Snowmobile Registration Laws & Riding Information by contacting Parks & Recreation's Boise headquarters (Box 83720, Boise, ID 83720-0065. ☎ 208-334-4199. Fax 208-334-3741) or stopping at any ranger district or BLM office. You must register your machine. ☎ 208-334-4199 for information on where to purchase a tag. Also request a copy of Ride the Endless Trails of Idaho, which includes a descriptive map of snowmobile areas throughout the state.

A glance at this map reveals a larger concentration of groomed snowmobile areas in Eastern Idaho than in any other section of the state (the Wallace area and the territory anchored by Idaho City, Cascade and Lowman are close seconds).

Remember: this is north country, the land of biting cold winters. Impressive wind chill factors further reduce temperatures that often dip well below zero with no help from the wind. Don't skimp on clothing: insulated coveralls over long johns, gaiters, heated gloves, a hat with ear covers and a helmet. Carry extra gasoline, spare parts, high-energy food and survival gear in case you have to spend the night in a makeshift shelter. Don't go out alone. Let someone know where you and your party are going and when you plan to return. Know your machine and don't take macho chances.

The **Bear Lake** area anchors a network of some 250 miles of groomed trails, plus extensive spreads of marked, ungroomed trails ranging from 6,000 to 9,000 feet in altitude. **The Minetonka Trail** is one of the most popular. Contact a local Caribou National Forest ranger station for current information (see page 293 for addresses).

From a point east of Idaho Falls, you can zoom all the way to Alpine, Wyoming over a network of open, groomed trails skidded between

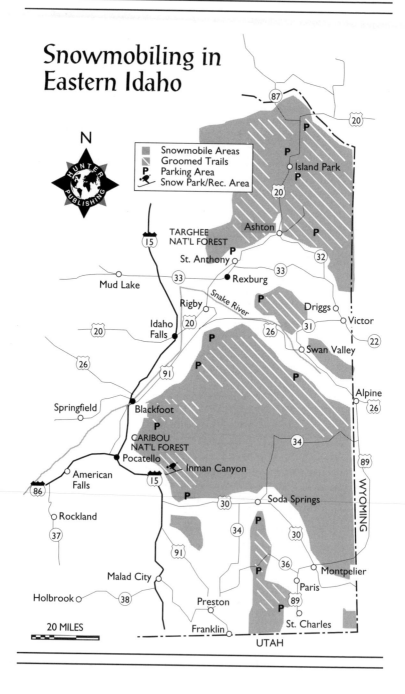

Snowmobiling in Eastern Idaho

N

Snowmobile Areas
Groomed Trails
P Parking Area
Snow Park/Rec. Area

87

20

P

P

Island Park

P

20

TARGHEE
NAT'L FOREST
15
P
St. Anthony

Ashton

P

32

33

33

Mud Lake

Rexburg

Snake River

P

Driggs

Victor

Rigby

Idaho
Falls
20

26

31

22

20

Swan Valley

26

P

91

P

Alpine
26

Springfield

Blackfoot

P

34

89

CARIBOU
NAT'L FOREST

Pocatello

Inman Canyon

89

American
Falls

15

WYOMING

86

P

30

Soda Springs

Rockland

34

P

30

37

91

36

Montpelier

Malad City

P

Paris

Holbrook

38

Preston

89

P

St. Charles

20 MILES

Franklin

UTAH

Grays Lake and **Palisades Reservoir**. The trailhead is at **Bone**, more a store than a town. Contact the Pocatello or Palisades Ranger District for current information.

Eastern Idaho's gnarliest snowmobile country includes the mountain passes between the **Greater Island Park area, West Yellowstone** and **Yellowstone National Park**. This is snowmobiling adventure par excellence. thrilling hill climbs, powder bowls, trails over 8,000-foot-high mountains culminate with a ride through the snowy streets of West Yellowstone, transformed in winter from tacky tourist mecca to alpine village. Contact the Island Park Ranger Station for current information.

Where there's good snowmobiling there are sure to be snowmobile rental and repair shops. The following will get you off to a roaring start. Contact area chambers of commerce for information and a current list of other rental options.

- **Sawtelle Sales, Service & Rentals**, Hwy 20 & Milepost 396, Island Park, ID 83429. ☎ 800-273-1950 or 208-558-7818.
- **South Fork Lodge**, PO Box 22, Swan Valley, ID 83449. ☎ 800-483-2110 or 208-483-2112. Fax 208-483-2121.

Dog Sledding & Sleigh Rides

Any snow country worth its powder must offer opportunities to enjoy dog sledding and horsedrawn sleigh rides. **Grand Targhee Ski Resort** comes through with both (PO Box SKI, Alta, WY 83422. ☎ 800-TAR-GHEE).

You can feel the dogs' excitement as your sledge skims the snow under a frosty winter sky. Hour-long mushes are available every day all day.

Grand Targhee sleigh rides mix cultures with a Western-style Dutch oven dinner in a yurt. Contact the Resort Activities Center to book both.

Mountain River Ranch, near Ririe, offers winter sleigh rides in addition to a range of other seasonal activities. Tran R. King, 98 N. 5050 East, Ririe, ID 83443. ☎ 208-538-7337.

Kid Stuff

 It's not easy to find an Eastern Idaho adventure that isn't good for kids. You may want to fit your tagalongs with blinders when driving US 20 in the Island Park area, lest they clamor to stop the car at every chainsaw sculpture, ice cream and souvenir stand. Tacky come-ons aside, there's no end to this region's fun and educational possibilities. If your kids are like mine, they'll enjoy checking out the flora, fauna and geological points of interest identified by wildlife area interpretive signs.

By all reports, the new **National Oregon Trail Interpretive Center** at Montpelier will be every bit as fascinating for kids as for parents. Your little ones will love it if it's half as interesting as the Oregon Trail centers at Baker and Oregon City, Oregon (my daughter and I spent hours soaking up trail lore at each). But most children can take just so much educational stuff. The time is bound to come when they welcome an opportunity to splash and dash sans parents. You'll welcome it, too.

Lava Hot Springs' Olympic-size pool is just the place. If your kids are old enough and are good swimmers, you can leave them at the pool while you enjoy a peaceful soak in the Foundation Pools' famous hot waters. And do heed your tagalongs' importunings to rent a tube for a wild plunge down the Portneuf River.

The volcanic activity that shaped Idaho's geologic history also produced numerous thermal hot springs. Resorts of various sizes and kinds have sprung up around many of these.

Downata Hot Springs, just a skip over the hills from Lava Hot Springs, has a water slide and a miniature golf course. 25901 Downata Road, Downey, ID 83234. ☎ 208-897-5736.

Riverdale Resort, in a pleasant valley near Preston, also offers water slide fun. 3696 N. 1600 East, Preston, ID 83263. ☎ 208-853-0266.

Grand Targhee Ski and Summer Resort offers a whole bunch of seasonal just-for-kids' activities recalling grand old summer camps. These activities may include horseback riding, hiking, mountain biking, insight into the environment and scaling the resort's climbing wall. A good way for both kids and parents to gain space for themselves.

In winter, Grand Targhee's Kids Club goes the extra slalom beyond the expected downhill ski lessons with fun stuff like sledding, snowplay, a gym class and more. Ask about family ski vacation packages. Young children's day care can be arranged through the resort.

Eco-Travel & Cultural Excursions

Grand Targhee Ski and Summer Resort arranges Winter Wildlife Tours offering insight into animals' and birds' amazing ability to thrive in a place that receives 500 inches of snow annually and where the temperature regularly dips to 20° below zero. These naturalist-led snowshoe excursions seek out tracks and signs of winter wildlife. Through them, guests learn how to decipher their winter survival adaptations. Participants also visit the world of creatures living under the snowpack. Contact the Grand Targhee Ski School, Box SKI, Alta, WY 83422. ☎ 800-TARGHEE, Ext. 1352.

Targhee Institute, at Grand Targhee Resort, schedules a variety of instructional natural and Western history programs for the fall and winter months. Elderhostel programs are scheduled for the summer months. To obtain a current schedule, contact Targhee Institute, PO Box 335, Alta, WY 83422. ☎ 800-TARGHEE or 307-353-2233.

Wildlife Watching

Eastern Idaho abounds with easily accessible wildlife refuges, preserves and management areas. Major wildlife viewing areas are described below. The excellent *Idaho Wildlife Viewing Guide*, by Leslie Benjamin Carpenter, includes detailed information on numerous other areas where you can view both rare and common wildlife. Most Idaho bookstores stock the book, or you can order a copy by sending a check for $6.25, payable to the Nongame Wildlife Program, to Idaho Fish & Game, Box 25, Boise, ID 83707-0025.

Bear Lake National Wildlife Refuge, at the northern end of Bear Lake, has the flooded meadows of sedges, rushes and grasses, and dense stands of bulrushes, that make ideal nesting habitat for migratory birds and small mammals. The refuge includes one of North America's largest nesting colonies of white-faced ibis. In September, over 100 sandhill cranes feed on refuge grain fields. Large animals include mule deer and a few moose. Trails inside the refuge are available to hikers and cross-country skiers. From Montpelier, drive west on US 89 for three miles. Turn left at the refuge's directional sign onto Bear Lake Country Airport Road. The refuge is five miles farther on. You can pick up a brochure and map on-site, or at the refuge headquarters in Montpelier.

Cherry Springs Nature Area has three self-guided interpretive nature trails, two learning centers and an amphitheater. Over 100 documented species of birds have been seen here. Small mammals, plus coyote and red fox, call this place home. Sagebrush and juniper habitats encourage the sagebrush lizard, Western skink and Western rattlesnake. In addition to the nature trails, you can explore several hiking trails via trailheads on roads accessing Mink Creek, East Fork Mink Creek and South Fork Mink Creek. To reach the Nature Area from Pocatello, head southeast on the Bannock Highway for four miles, then turn south onto FS Road 231. This road follows Mink Creek. After another four miles, watch for Nature Center signs.

Big Springs, kicking out 120 million gallons of water per day, supports protected rainbow trout that grow to enormous size. You can view the fish from a half-mile trail. Watch for osprey, bald eagles, black bear, moose, muskrat, elk and white-tailed deer. Located on FS Road 59, six miles from Mack's Inn.

Harriman State Park is famous for its trumpeter swans. Up to 5,000 of them winter here. Several breeding pairs are present year-round. Other birds, waterfowl and animals indigenous to this area can also be seen. Maps and bird checklists are available at park headquarters.

Sand Creek Wildlife Management Area, north of St. Anthony and near the St. Anthony Sand Dunes, is a good place to see high desert wildlife. Moving sand dunes, lava tubes, broken lava reefs and cinder buttes are habitat for numerous songbirds and animals. The **Sand Creek Ponds Area** is habitat for waterfowl and muskrats. Wildlife can be viewed from a roadway or from trails along the dikes. Maps, brochures and directions to the area are available at the Management Area headquarters at 758 N. 2000 East in St. Anthony (☎ 208-624-7065).

Market Lake Wildlife Management Area's northern edge is a good place to view wintering elk and pronghorn sheep. The extensive marshes and a canal, surrounded by farmland and elevated sagebrush and basalt outcroppings, attract large numbers of waterfowl. Exit I-15 at Roberts (Interchange 135). Turn north at the T intersection and follow this road to the end past the Main and Triangle Marshes. Follow signs to Sandy Marsh and the refuge headquarters, where a map and checklist are available.

The **South Fork of the Snake River** provides 45 miles of prime wildlife viewing. The US Fish and Wildlife Service has classified the dense cottonwood forests lining the river for 18 miles between Heise and Henry's Fork as Idaho's most important fish and wildlife habitat site. The canyon below the Swan Valley bridge has the state's largest population of nesting bald eagles. Over 80 species of birds can be seen in the river corridor, as well as beaver, river otter, raccoon, moose and other animals. The **Cress Creek Nature Trail**, two miles downstream from Heise, has a 0.75-mile walk through several habitat types. Points along the river corridor can be accessed via boat ramps placed at frequent intervals along the river. **Grays Lake National Wildlife Refuge**, a large shallow marsh backed by 9,803-foot Caribou Mountain, is a scenic location for viewing one of North America's largest breeding concentrations of greater sandhill cranes. It is also a reintroduction site for endangered whooping cranes, whose eggs are hatched under sandhill crane foster parents. As many as 3,000 cranes may be present from late September to early October. May and June are the best months to see other wildlife. The refuge visitor center has interpretive exhibits, maps and checklists. A high overlook adjacent to the headquarters gives a wide-angle view of the refuge and includes an observation platform with a spotting scope. Drive north from Soda Springs on Idaho 34 for 33 miles. Turn north on the gravel road encircling the marsh.

Festivals & Special Events

January

 Lava Hot Springs Snow Festival features sledding, a cross-country ski race, a chili feed and a snowman contest. ☎ 800-548-5282 for current dates.

February

Bear Lake Winter Carnival honors the famous Bear Lake cisco and features a sledfull of wintery high jinks. ☎ 800-488-BEAR for current dates and other information.

May

St. Anthony's Fishermen's Breakfast, held in late May, marks the beginning of fishing season. Various fun activities follow a free breakfast. South Fremont Chamber of Commerce, ☎ 208-624-4455.

June-September

Pierre's Playhouse at Victor presents the Teton Valley Players in an old-fashioned melodrama, complete with a Dutch oven chicken dinner. Call Pierre's Playhouse, ☎ 208-787-2249, for reservations.

July

Rexburg's Whoopee Days/4th of July Parade features a rodeo, an arts & crafts show, a public picnic and more. ☎ 208-356-5700.

Teton Valley Hot Air Balloon Races are held at Driggs over the 4th of July holiday. The festival brings out 30-40 hot air balloons in a race backdropped by the Grand Teton Mountain Range. Driggs Chamber of Commerce, ☎ 208-354-2500.

Idaho Falls Snake River Settlers' 4th of July festivities kicks off with a parade and goes on to step back in time with a variety of old fashioned activities held in Tautphaus Park. Fireworks conclude the festival. Idaho Falls Chamber of Commerce, ☎ 800-634-3246.

Eastern Idaho

Rockin' the Tetons Music Festival, held at Grand Targhee Resort in mid-July, includes two days of rock, blues and reggae. ☎ 800-TAR-GHEE.

Mountain Man Rendezvous-Pioneer Days Celebration, held at Lava Hot Springs in mid-July, celebrates Idaho history in Lava Hot Springs' own off-beat style. Mountain Man rendezvous, held throughout the West in the summer months, are colorful throwbacks to annual meetings between trappers, traders (mountain men) and Indians. Participants step back into the pages of Western history by dressing in authentic garb, living in tepees, cooking over campfires, conducting a lively Traders' Row. Lava Hot Springs Foundation, ☎ 208-776-5221.

Butch Cassidy Bank Robbery Re-enactment is held in Montpelier the third weekend in July. ☎ 800-488-BEAR.

Oregon Trail Rendezvous Pageant, held in Montpelier in late July, features a Dutch oven supper, a live action pageant showcasing Oregon Trail history in Southeast Idaho, plus dancing on the real Oregon Trail. ☎ 208-945-2333.

Snake River Regatta is celebrated in Ashton in late July. Participants jump into anything that floats for races down Henry's Fork. ☎ 208-652-3987 for current dates.

River Park Festival, featuring arts and crafts, is held in Idaho Falls the last weekend in July. ☎ 800-634-3246.

Idaho International Folk Dance Festival is held in Rexburg the last week in July. Dance troupes from throughout the world perform. Rexburg Chamber of Commerce, ☎ 208-356-5700.

August

Island Park Stampede, held the first weekend in August, features cowboys whooping it up rodeo-style on the shore of Henry's Lake. ☎ 208-558-7755.

The annual **Shoshone-Bannock Indian Festival** is held at Fort Hall in early August. The celebration of Indian culture includes dancers in traditional regalia, games, art and the **All-Indian Old-Timers' Rodeo**. Call the Blackfoot Chamber of Commerce, ☎ 208-785-0510, for current dates.

A **Bluegrass Festival**, hosted by Grand Targhee Ski and Summer Resort, is held in early August. ☎ 800-TARGHEE.

War Bonnet Round-Up, Eastern Idaho's oldest rodeo, is held in Idaho Falls in August. ☎ 208-523-1010 for current dates.

Bear Lake County Fair & Rodeo is held the third week in August. ☎ 800-488-BEAR.

Soda Springs Geyser Days take place in late August. A community potluck, karaoke dancing, bed races and a Dutch oven dinner are just a few of the activities celebrating Soda Springs' famous timed geyser. ☎ 208-547-2600 for current dates.

Famous Preston Night Rodeo features three nights of PRCA rodeo with top rodeo performers, plus a carnival. ☎ 208-852-2703 for current dates.

September

The Eastern Idaho State Fair at Blackfoot kicks off September. The typical Western event features a rodeo, horse and pig races, a demolition derby, top name stars and more. Blackfoot Chamber of Commerce: ☎ 208-785-0510.

Idaho Spud Days are celebrated in Shelley in late September. This annual celebration of Idaho's famous potatoes, held in the heart of potato growing country, features an assortment of events and attractions. ☎ 208-357-7662.

Late November - December

Idaho Falls' Parade of Lights is held the Friday evening immediately following Thanksgiving. Lighted floats parade around the Snake River Greenbelt. ☎ 208-523-1010.

Preston's Festival of Lights, held from late November through December, opens with a Veterans Day parade, a musical, and the lighting of what some consider the best light display in Idaho. ☎ 208-852-1969.

Where to Stay & Eat

Lodgings

Bed & breakfasts are your best lodging bets in Southeastern Idaho. The area is liberally sprinkled with motels of the ho-hum mom-and-pop genre, easily located and usually not requiring reservations unless some big local event, such as July's Oregon Trail Rendezvous pageant in Montpelier, is under way. The picture changes as you travel north into Teton country. Here, choices run largely to resorts that range from beds with activities attached to the high-profile full-service Grand Targhee Resort. Guest ranches are also big here. Ask about the activities on offer when choosing a resort.

National Forest Cabins

These secluded rental cabins are great choices if you don't mind roughing it, and the rents are reasonable. All are in remote locations often requiring a 4WD vehicle, foot power, snowmobile or cross-country skis to reach. Many have no potable water.

The *Caribou National Forest*, **Soda Springs Ranger District**, makes three former guard stations available for year-round use. They sleep six or eight and have propane stoves and fridges. Contact the Soda Springs Ranger Station (421 West 2nd South, Soda Springs, ID 83276. ☎ 208-547-4356) for further information and to reserve your hideaway.

The *Targhee National Forest* has a few rental cabins in the **Dubois, Ashton** and **Palisades Ranger Districts**. Contact the applicable ranger station.

The lodgings listed below reflect this area's regional differences. Motels are not included unless alternatives are unavailable in the area, or unless a given motel offers some particular advantage.

Ashton

Jessen's RV/Bed & Breakfast, two miles south of Ashton on US 20, covers the field with three cabins, three guest rooms and 22 RV spaces. 1146 So. 3400 E., Hwy 20, Ashton, ID 83420. ☎ 800-747-3356 or 208-652-3356.

Bear Lake

Bear Lake Bed and Breakfast at Fish Haven has four cozy guest rooms. 500 Loveland Lane, Fish Haven, ID 83287. ☎ 208-945-2688.

Downey

Downata Hot Springs, a rustic resort developed around a thermal hot spring, has seven B&B-style guest rooms, plus camping. PO Box 185 (25900 S. Downata Rd.), Downey, ID 83234. ☎ 208-897-5736. Fax 208-897-5672.

Driggs

Grand Targhee Ski and Summer Resort is in Wyoming but lists the Driggs zip code. The full-service resort offers a variety of lodging choices in a glorious forested mountain setting deep in the Targhee National Forest. PO Box SKI, Alta, WY 83422. ☎ 800-TARGHEE.

Grand Valley Lodging will arrange vacation home rentals throughout Teton Valley. PO Box 191, Driggs, ID 83422. ☎ 800-746-5518 or 208-354-8890.

Teton Creek Bed & Breakfast has four attractive guest rooms. 41 S. Baseline Rd., Driggs, ID 83422. ☎ 208-354-2584.

Idaho Falls

Idaho Falls is bereft of B&Bs, but does offer a selection of chain motels, some on the River Greenbelt.

Comfort Inn, 195 S. Colorado, Idaho Falls, ID 83402. ☎ 208-528-2804.

Holiday Inn Westbank, 475 River Pkwy, Idaho Falls, ID 83402. ☎ 800-432-1005. Fax 208-529-9610.

Shilo Inn overlooks the Snake River. 780 Lindsay Blvd, Idaho Falls, ID 83402. ☎ 800-222-2244. Fax 208-522-7420.

Stardust Best Western also overlooks the Snake. 700 Lindsay Blvd., Idaho Falls, ID 83402. ☎ 800-527-0274. Fax 208-529-8361.

Irwin

McBride's Bed and Breakfast pays special attention to guests staying in their single guest room. PO Box 56 (half-mile off Hwy 26 on Valley Drive), Irwin, ID 83428. ☎ 208-483-4221.

The Lodge at Palisades Creek, on the South Fork of the Snake, offers resort-style activities. Seven units. PO Box 70, Irwin, ID 83428. ☎ 208-483-2222. Fax 208-483-2227.

Island Park

Island Park is big on resort-style accommodations.

Island Park Village Resort, one mile north of Macks Inn, features 66 units in a resort atmosphere. HC66, Box 12, Island Park, ID 83429. ☎ 208-558-7502. Fax 208-558-7450.

Lucky Dog Retreat, one mile off Big Springs Road, is a five-unit resort run on the American plan. PO Box 128, Island Park, ID 83429. ☎ 208-558-7455. Fax 208-558-9042.

Eastern Idaho

Sawtell Mountain Resort, on US 20 one mile north of the village of Macks Inn, has 36 units. PO Box 250, Macks Inn, ID 83433. ☎ 800-574-0404 or 208-558-9366. Fax 208-558-9235.

Staley Springs Lodge, a resort on the northwest shore of Henry's Lake, has 18 rental cabins. HC66, Box 102, Island Park, ID 83429. ☎ 208-558-7471. Fax 208-558-7300.

Lava Hot Springs

Home Hotel and Motel, smack in the center of town, is no beauty, but a Lava Hot Springs tradition. PO Box 67, Lava Hot Springs, ID 83246. ☎ 208-776-5507.

Hot Springs Village Condominiums are located away from the hoopla area, west of the Olympic pool complex on the Porneauf River. PO Box 156, Lava Hot Sprngs, ID 83246. ☎ 208-776-5445.

Lava Hot Springs Inn's 17 art deco guest rooms, in a one-time hospital, are close enough to the river for its gurgle to lull you to sleep. PO Box 420, Lava Hot Sprngs, ID 83246. ☎ 208-776-5830.

Oregon Trail Lodge is another Lava tradition. Its eight units are on Main Street, where the action is. PO Box 600, Lava Hot Springs, ID 83246. ☎ 208-776-5000.

Riverside Inn & Hot Springs is a historic hotel-cum-B&B whose 16 rooms have been fancied up to a fare-thee-well. Lava Hot Springs luxe. PO Box 127, Lava Hot Springs, ID 83246. ☎ 800-733-5504 or 208-776-5504. Fax 208-776-5504.

Royal Hotel Bed and Breakfast's four guest rooms occupy the upper floor of a historic hotel oozing atmosphere. PO Box 476, Lava Hot Springs, ID 83246. ☎ 208-776-5216.

Montpelier

Best Western Crest Motel is a sizeable hostelry at 243 North 34th St., Montpelier, ID 83254. ☎ 800-528-1234 or 208-847-1782. Fax 208-847-3519.

Blue Sage Inn Bed & Breakfast offers trout fishing, horseback riding and Dutch oven suppers in addition to a soft bed and a hearty breakfast. 89989 US Highway 30, Montpelier, ID 83254. ☎ 208-847-0263.

Budget Motel, 240 North 4th St., Montpelier, ID 83254. ☎ 208-847-1273. Fax 208-847-3519.

Preston

Deer Cliff Inn, eight miles up Cub River, off US 91 south of Preston, has four rental cabins. 2106 N. Deer Cliff, Preston, ID 83263. ☎ 208-852-0643.

Plaza Motel is an in-town alternative at 427 S. Hwy 91. PO Box 24, Preston, ID 83263. ☎ 208-852-2020.

Rexburg

Rexburg accommodations are much in demand year-round because of its college town status. Reservations are advised.

Best Western Cottontree Inn is a 100-unit giant. 450 West 4th South, Rexburg, ID 83440. ☎ 208-356-4646. Fax 208-356-7461.

Days Inn has 43 quite adequate units. 271 South 2nd West, Rexburg, ID 83440. ☎ 208-356-9222. Fax 208-356-9242.

Ririe

Heise Hot Springs puts Ririe on the map. This modern family-oriented resort overlooking the Snake River has hydrojet pools and other water-related features. 5116 Heise Rd., Ririe, ID 83443. ☎ 208-538-7312. Fax 208-538-7466.

St. Anthony

Best Western Weston Inn is medium-size as such chain motels go, but comfortable withall. 115 South Bridge, St. Anthony, ID 83445. ☎/Fax 208-624-3711.

Riverview Bed & Breakfast offers travelers four pleasant guest rooms. 155 E. 3rd South, St. Anthony, ID 83445. ☎ 208-624-4323.

Soda Springs

Soda Springs runs to low-tariff, medium-size motels.

Caribou Lodge & Motel, 110 West 2nd South, Soda Springs, ID 83276. ☎ 800-270-9178 or 208-547-3377. Fax 208-547-2663.

J-R Inn, 179 West 2nd South, Soda Springs, ID 83276. ☎ 208-547-3366.

Trail Motel and Restaurant, 213 East 200 South, Soda Springs, ID 83276. ☎ 208-547-3909.

Eastern Idaho

Swan Valley

South Fork Lodge, four miles west of Swan Valley on US 26, is a resort whose focus is fly-fishing (see *Fishing,* page 313). Eleven rooms are available. PO Box 22, Swan Valley, ID 83449. ☎ 800-483-2110 or 208-483-2305. Fax 208-483-2121.

Swan Valley Bed & Breakfast has five comfortable rooms. PO Box 115, Swan Valley, ID 83449. ☎ 800-241-SWAN or 208-483-4663.

Guest Ranches

Area guest ranches range from lodgings with horses and board, to working cattle ranches, to ranch "resorts," where guests arrive decked out in designer jeans and boots. It's a good idea to sound out prospective ranches in relation to your family's vacation needs before plunking your money down. Guest ranches are seldom one-night stands; they require guests to sign on for a full week of Western-style fun and games. Look closely at each ranch's brochure. Most are full of people having fun, but do they look like your kind of people, wearing your kind of clothing? Do kids figure in these happy vignettes?

Ask questions and more questions. Are the horses ranch-owned or rented nags? Is the ranch kid-friendly with horses and activities to match? Are special kids' activities on offer? What is the food like? What activities, in addition to riding, are on offer? Are the accommodations cabins or lodge rooms? Inquire about the altitude if high altitudes are a problem for you. Is there a refund policy in case you realize after a few days that it's not for you?

Unless otherwise noted, the ranches listed below are members of the Idaho Guest and Dude Ranch Association.

Granite Creek Ranch is operated in conjunction with a 3,000-acre working cattle ranch and farm. The ranch buildings are situated at the base of a densely forested mountain. This family-oriented ranch offers special children's programs. In addition to the standard trail rides and other horse activities, guests are invited to help with chores ranging from feeding baby farm animals to helping mend fences. There's plenty of fishing and hiking, too. Cattle drives, roundups and branding are seasonal activities. Ask when they occur, if you wish to take part. Guests sleep in rustic cabins. Meals include cookouts. The ranch season is June through September. Carl and Nessie Zitlau, PO Box 340, Ririe, ID 83443. ☎ 208-538-7140. Fax 208-538-7876.

Hansen Silver Ranch, on Rainey Creek, assigns each guest a horse matching his or her ability to use for the duration of the stay.

Riding lessons are all in a day's ranching and trail rides range up to full-day rides to the top of Fallcreek Mountain Range. Other activities include guided fly-fishing on the Snake, mountain hikes, floating the Snake, and Dutch oven cookouts. Brett Hansen, PO Box 112, Swan Valley, ID 83449. ☎ 800-277-9041 or 208-483-2305. Fax 208-483-2305.

Jacob's Island Park Ranch is a working cattle ranch offering a hatfull of activities in addition to riding. These include covered wagon treks, boat tours of Island Park Reservoir, professional rodeo events, cattle drives and Western hoedowns. Families are welcome. This ranch is open in winter so that guests might take advantage of the Island Park area's excellent cross-country skiing and snowmobiling. Stays can be as short as overnight. Guests stay in cabins. Mitch Jacobs, 2496 N. 2375 East, Hamer, ID 83425. ☎ 800-230-9530, 208-662-5260 or 208-662-5251.

Medicine Lodge Cowboy Experiences offers cattle drives and hands-on working ranch activities. Sleep in a converted school house. Silver Spur Outfitters, PO Box 406, Dubois, ID 83423. ☎ 208-374-5684.

Moose Creek Ranch, secluded (no TV) in the heart of the Tetons, offers a stagecoach ride, swimming in a heated pool, chuck wagon dinners, a whitewater float trip and live Western show and cookouts. In addition, there is an instructional riding program in which guests become involved in the care of their horses. A smaller number of guests permits program flexibility and personal attention. Roxann and Kelly Van Orden, PO Box 350, Victor, ID 83455. ☎ 800-676-0075 or 208-787-2784. Fax 208-787-2284.

Teton Ridge Ranch, 1,600 acres of sheer beauty, is about as upscale as a ranch gets. This isolated mountain ranch, entertaining 12 guests at a time, tailors activities to guests' desires. Guest suites have wood-burning stoves, Jacuzzis and private porches. You may choose horseback riding, soaring, fishing, river floats, skiing, cycling, and more. Wines are served with dinner. Albert Tilt, 200 Valley View Rd., Tetonia, ID 83452. ☎ 208-456-2650. Fax 208-456-2218.

Tincup Mountain Guest Ranch, a member of the Idaho Outfitters and Guides Association, has been around for a long time – since 1888 when ancestors of owners David and Lorie Haderlie homesteaded the spread on the Idaho-Wyoming border. It is still a working cattle ranch. Surrounded by three national forests, Tincup's emphasis is on riding endless forest trails where wildlife viewing is part of the action. Guests bed down in private log cabins and chow down on hearty Western food.

Eastern Idaho

Stays can be as short or as long as desired. Unlike most ranches, Tincup is not on the American Plan; you pay separately for lodging, meals and horseback rides lasting from an hour to overnight pack trips. PO Box 175, Freedom, WY 83120. ☎ 800-263-2368 or 208-873-2368.

Where to Eat

 If your dining preferences run to steak and potatoes, chuck wagon beans and Dutch oven dishes, you're in luck. If you go for gourmet pastas and fresh fruits and veggies, you're out of luck. But the Western dishes can be tasty indeed. The fare dished up in predominantly Mormon territory is usually less tasty. This slender list of eateries reflects the scarcity of notable dining experiences.

Driggs

Grand Targhee Ski and Summer Resort is one of the few places in Eastern Idaho where discriminating diners can relax and enjoy. Several restaurants are on tap, as listed below. ☎ 800-TARGHEE to reach them all.

Skadi's features contemporary American and continental fare and specialty beers in a relaxed mountain atmosphere. And there's a children's menu. Open for breakfast, lunch and dinner.

Trap Bar features innovative lunches, après ski snacks and dinners in a ski bar atmosphere.

Wild Bill's Grille serves up traditional Western fare with flair.

Idaho Falls

With few exceptions, one place is about as good as another in this town awash in family-style chain eateries. But Idaho Falls boasts the supreme oxymoron, a memorable airport restaurant. **Runway 21** is notable for freshly flown-in seafood and fancy desserts. ☎ 208-522-3202.

Lava Hot Springs

Lava Hot Springs eateries tend to turn over from season to season; no loss considering the dubious quality of the dishes on offer. The one constant is the **Royal Hotel's ground level pizza parlor**. A player piano livens things up, and the pizza is okay. ☎ 208-776-5216.

Montpelier

Here, local color goes a long way toward enhancing the traditional Western steak and potatoes. Try them at **Butch Cassidy's**, at 260 N. Fourth Street. ☎ 208-847-3501.

Rexburg

Don't expect viands prepared with gourmet flair, let alone a wine list, in this and other Mormon towns. **Me 'n Stan's**, a family restaurant at 167 W. Main Street, serves up good, if not imaginative, fare. ☎ 208-356-7330.

Victor

If restaurants touting "home cooking" or "like Mom makes" turn you off, you just might be converted by the **Painted Apple Café** at 55 N. Main Street. Displays of local crafts and acoustic music enliven the home-style fare. ☎ 208-787-2039.

Camping

Eastern Idaho camping can be primitive, resort-like, or may fall somewhere in-between. The Caribou and Targhee National Forests maintain numerous primitive campgrounds, some of which are accessible via cars. Others can be reached only on foot or on horseback. Many, but not all, have potable water and toilets. For current campground information, contact the local ranger district office.

Two state parks offer camping in Eastern Idaho. Both are operated on a first-come, first-served basis.

Henry's Lake State Park appeals primarily to anglers, but proximity to Harriman State Park's hiking, wildlife watching, horseback riding, biking, fishing and Western history lore make it a good family camping option. Sites are right on the lake. HC66, Box 20, Island Park, ID 83429. ☎ 208-558-7532.

Bear Lake State Park's East Bench Campground is popular with scuba divers. The scenery, other than the lake and surrounding clean-swept hills, is unremarkable. No RV hookups, but there's a dump station. PO Box 297, Paris, ID 83261. ☎ 208-945-2790.

Private campgrounds include several built around thermal hot springs. Others listed below are in areas where public camping, particularly for RVs, is unavailable.

Eastern Idaho

Henry

Whitelocks Marina & RV Park, on Blackfoot Reservoir, 18 miles north of Soda Springs off Idaho 34, has 50 RV hookups and lake access. 3429 Hwy 34, Henry, ID 83230. ☎ 208-574-2208.

Idaho Falls

Idaho Falls KOA is a whopper with 167 spaces. Most children love KOAs for the chance to swim in a pool with other kids. KOAs tend to be uniformly well run, but are also uniformly close to major highways. 1440 Lindsay Blvd., Idaho Falls, ID 83402. ☎ 208-523-3362.

Island Park

Pond's Lodge has cabins and 50 campsites. PO Box 258, Island Park, ID 83429. ☎ 208-558-7221.

Red Rock RV & Camping Park, on Henry's Lake, has 44 RV spaces and a tent area. HC66, Box 256, Island Park, ID 83429. ☎ 208-558-7442.

Staley Springs Lodge, also on Henry's Lake, has 44 campsites. HC66, Box 102, Island Park, ID 83429. ☎ 208-558-7471. Fax 208-558-7300.

Wild Rose Ranch, another Henry's Lake property, has 60 RV spaces and offers horseback riding. 340 W. 7th South, Island Park, ID 83429. ☎ 208-558-7201.

Lava Hot Springs

No fancy RV parks here, but rather laid-back mom-and-pop campgrounds where something always seems to be on the fritz. Most campsites overlook the river. Few tent spaces; numerous RV spaces. Best bets:

Cottonwood Family Campground's 111 shaded spaces sit above the river on the eastern edge of town. The owners are anxious to please. PO Box 307, Lava Hot Springs, ID 83246. ☎ 208-776-5295.

Lava Ranch Inn Motel & RV Camping, with 52 spaces, is situated on the river a mile west of town. 9611 Hwy 30, Lava Hot Springs, ID 83246. ☎ 208-776-9917. Fax 208-776-5546.

Montpelier

Montpelier KOA, two miles east of town on Hwy 89, has 50 RV spaces and a tent area. PO Box 87, Montpelier, ID 83254. ☎ 208-847-0863.

Rendezvous Village RV Park has 30 campsites. 577 N. 4th St., Montpelier, ID 83254. ☎ 208-847-1100.

Preston

Deer Cliff Store, Café and RV, eight miles up Cub River Canyon, has only 11 spaces, but the scenery is okay. 1942 N. Deer Cliff Rd., Preston, ID 83263. ☎ 208-852-3320.

Ririe

Heise Hot Springs, overlooking the Snake River, is open year-round except for November. The family-oriented resort centers around the thermal hot springs. PO Box 417, Ririe, ID 83433. ☎ 208-538-7312.

St. Anthony

Informal RV and tent camping is available at **St. Anthony Sand Dunes** on a first-come, first-served basis.

Eagle's Nest RV/Campground is a mile south of town and has 100 spaces. 395 N. 2200 East, St. Anthony, ID 83445. ☎ 208-624-3051.

St. Charles

This small town overlooking Bear Lake has three well-located campgrounds for enjoying the lake's recreational attractions.

Bear Lake Hot Springs' large pools and campground are on the shore of Bear Lake. Open May-September. PO Box 75, St. Charles, ID 83272. ☎ 208-945-2494.

Cedars & Shade Campground has 100 spaces and is on the east shore of Bear Lake. PO Box 219, St. Charles, ID 83272. No telephone listed.

Minnetonka RV & Campground has 20 spaces. PO Box 6, St. Charles, ID 83272. ☎ 208-945-2941.

Swan Valley

South Fork Lodge, on the South Fork of the Snake, has 48 RV spaces in addition to lodging facilities and fly-fishing headquarters. PO Box 22, Swan Valley, ID 83449. ☎ 800-483-2110 or 208-483-2112. Fax 208-483-2121.

Victor

Teton Valley Campground has 30 camp spaces, plus cabins. PO Box 49, (128 Hwy 31) Victor, ID 83455. ☎/Fax 208-787-2647.

Eastern Idaho

Southern Idaho

Southern Idaho's sweep of raw land, of monolithic rocks, sagebrush desert and juniper-strewn mountains, seems more like an extension of Utah, Nevada and Oregon than part of the Gem State. It's a wild place, this land west of Interstate 15 and south of I-84, tumbling northward from Utah and Nevada, sharing the inscrutable Owyhee Mountains with Oregon – a wild place where cattle and mustangs graze. It's a hard, challenging land. Only the waterfall-splashed Magic Valley clinging to the Snake River and the northwestern corner's fertile Treasure Valley wedge have accommodated well to civilization. A scattering of wineries attests to the region's extremes.

The villages hunkered down astride the few roads seem to be looking backward, still ruminating over the legendary characters who chanced to pass through a century or so ago. Yards flaunting lilac and rose bushes give brave testimony to hardships overcome only by dint of perseverance and punishing toil.

This land graphically reflects water's civilizing influence. Settlers came to places where a spring, a river or a stream soaked the soil. Homesteads and villages took root. The more reliable the water supply, the larger the settlement. Thus, Twin Falls and other Snake River towns. Thus, dusty hamlets edging eternities of parched monotony.

As you travel this area, you'll note a marked dichotomy between these villages and the prosperous agricultural towns strung along I-84 like so many Christmas tree lights – a dichotomy spawned by commerce.

This region's ruggedness is reflected in the do-it-yourself nature of the adventures it offers. Rock climbers rank the City of Rocks National Reserve among the country's top rock climbing challenges. The Owyhees are destitute of hiking trails – just a few bad and badder roads scoring 500 square miles of desolation hunkered under a relentless sky. Except for outfitters running the Owyhee/Jarbridge and Bruneau River systems, and a scattering of guided cultural adventures, it's just you and the elements.

Blatantly touristy attractions are notable for their absence. A possible exception is Silver City, that most venerable of ghost towns. Getting there requires a high-clearance 4WD vehicle. So much for main-line tourism.

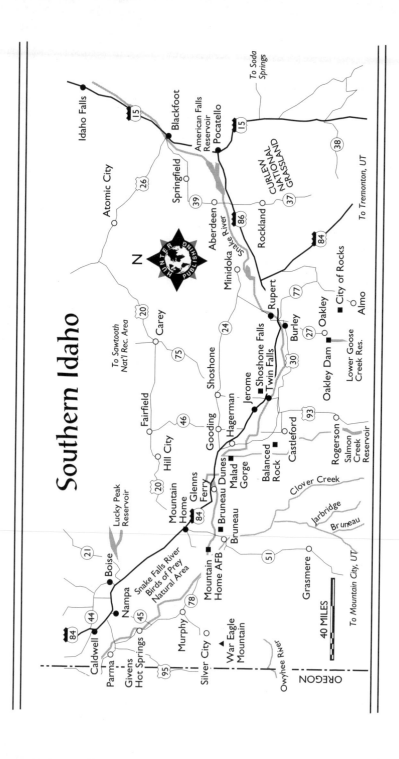

Southern Idaho

History & Geography

The Oregon Trail crossed and re-crossed Southern Idaho. The Main Trail followed the south side of the Snake as far as present-day Glenns Ferry. Here, most trekkers island-hopped across the Snake at treacherous Three Island Crossing. Others chose the South Alternate, a mostly dry track along the bluffs above the Snake. It rejoined the Main Trail just west of Old Fort Boise. The Hudspeth Cutoff angled across Southern Idaho from Soda Springs, meeting the California Trail north of City of Rocks. Following the beginning of the railroad era, the Kelton Stage Road (linking Boise with the railroad at Kelton, Utah) passed through City of Rocks and joined the main Oregon Trail near present-day Murtaugh.

Remnants of these trails remain more visible in this largely undisturbed region than in most other areas traversed by emigrants bound for Oregon, Utah and California. Tracking them down can be an absorbing adventure. The Idaho Travel Council makes available an *Oregon Trail in Idaho* map that includes descriptive text, as well as a National Park Service map delineating the entire Oregon Trail.

The last westward-bound wagons' dust had hardly settled when gold-fevered prospectors hit pay dirt in the Owyhees. In 1863, one Michael Jordan led a group of prospectors south from the Boise Basin in search of the apocryphal Lost Blue Bucket Mine. They didn't find it. Instead, they saw color along the stream that came to be named Jordan Creek. Word got out. By the time this placer gold had been depleted, rich lodes of silver and gold were being discovered on nearby War Eagle Mountain. The rush was on, bringing prospectors, outlaws and other enduring, but seldom endearing, characters who peopled legendary 19th-century gold camps.

While Southwestern Idaho rocked to mining camp ribaldry, the grasslands between I-15 and where I-84 makes a diagonal swing north from Utah were being discovered by Mormons, who saw promise in the valleys nestled in the Blue Spring Hills. Scant promise, as it turned out. Today, isolated ranches, grazing lands and dry-farmed wheat fields sprawl across these windy, farflung spaces.

To the north and west, on the bluffs across the Snake from the future town of Hagerman, herds of equine fossils lay buried under layers of sand and soil.

Southern Idaho

Small Horses

Some five million years ago, at the beginning of the Pliocene epoch, Southern Idaho was covered by a lake enjoying a sub-tropical climate. Camels, saber-toothed tigers, small horse-like animals (*Equus simplicidens*) and other mammals roamed the marshy shore. Ice ages and the subsequent Bonneville Flood spoiled this happy situation.

In 1928, rancher Elmer Cook showed some fossil bones he had unearthed to Dr. H.T. Stearns of the US Geological Survey. Stearns passed them on to Dr. J.W. Gridley at the US National Museum (Smithsonian Institution) who opined that they had belonged to a fossilized horse. The rest, as they say, is history. Today, Hagerman Fossil Beds National Monument is considered the world's richest deposit of terrestrial Upper Pliocene fossils. Some 150 skeletons of these small horses, now believed to be more closely related to the African Grevey's zebra, have been uncovered.

The spring-fed canyons cut by the Snake and a series of reservoirs fashioned by man define the northern edge of this region. The Snake's waters exert little or no influence on the landscape to the south. This parched land, at about 4,500-foot elevation, is furnace-hot in summer, biting cold in winter. The Owyhee Mountains swagger into view on the west. Historically regarded with deep respect, the jumbled mountains, canyons and high desert wedged between the Snake and the Oregon line command no less respect today. Perhaps the story of how the mountains came by the name "Owyhee" defines the awe that even experienced backpackers feel toward these bonafide badlands.

The Owyhees

Captain Cook spelled "Hawaii" as "Owyhee." We seldom see that spelling today, but it stuck in Idaho. Reference Boise's Owyhee Hotel. In the winter of 1818, three Hawaiian trappers set out from the Boise Basin to explore the mountains to the southwest. (The thought of Hawaiians braving a winter in the Idaho wilderness gives one pause). They never returned. The mountains that swallowed them have been called The Owyhees ever since.

It fits that the Owyhees should be home to one of the country's largest herds of wild horses. The Bureau of Land Management (BLM), overseers of the area's federal lands, has raised the hackles of ranchers and recreationists by limiting stock grazing and public access to the Owyhees in an effort to protect the herd. Catching sight of a wild stallion running before his mares, manes and tails spreading on the wind, is an experience to treasure.

Getting Around

Southern Idaho is accessed by air via **Boise** or **Twin Falls**. Boise is served by Delta, Northwest, United and Southwest Airlines. Horizon and Skywest fly into Boise from regional destinations. Twin Falls is served by two regional carriers, Horizon (☎ 800-547-9308) and Skywest (☎ 800-453-9417).

Avis, Budget, Dollar, Hertz and National rental cars are available at the Boise Air Terminal; Avis, Budget, Hertz and National at the Twin Falls Airport.

Southern Idaho points of interest can be accessed by several highways and lesser roads branching southward from I-84 and US 30, which parallels I-84. You can approach from Utah via I-84 or I-15; from Nevada, take US 93 or Idaho 51.

This region includes two designated scenic byways. The **Thousand Springs Scenic Byway** (US 30 along the south side of the Snake) is a good two-lane highway. The **Owyhee Uplands National Backcountry Byway**, known locally as the Mud Flat Road, is paved with gravel, dirt, coyotes and adventure. Snow usually socks it in from October to May.

Patches of Southern Idaho managed by the Sawtooth National Forest include the Albion Mountains, the Black Pine Mountains, and the Sublett Range east of US 93, plus the Cedar Creek and Salmon Creek Reservoir country south of Twin Falls. The **Curlew National Grassland**, wedged between I-84, Idaho 37 and the Utah line, is managed by the Malad Ranger District of the Caribou National Forest.

Many of Southern Idaho's most intriguing points of interest are accessed via unimproved roads. These bear cautionary signs strongly suggesting high-clearance 4WD vehicles. Summer and early fall are the best times to drive these roads. Many are closed in winter. Spring thaws and sudden rainstorms can turn them into mud bogs.

The **Owyhee Badlands**, administered by the BLM, will challenge you from the get-go. Devilish roads, and there are darned few roads of any kind, lead to challenging backpacking adventures that can punish or

Southern Idaho

Cattle drives serve as reminders that Idaho remains a part of the Old West.

reward, depending on your preparations and conditioning. The absence of trails should tell you something: this is no place for the faint-hearted or for inexperienced hikers out for a day's jaunt.

The spectacular canyonlands of the **Owyhee Desert**, also managed by the BLM, speak to desert lovers. Here, and throughout Southern Idaho, private and BLM range lands are often indistinguishable. If you must open a gate, be sure to close it behind you. Watch for stock on the road. Slow down or stop while animals meander off to the side of the road. Don't honk your horn. Resist the temptation to nudge a cow. Take your cue from her. She's in no hurry. You shouldn't be, either. Expect stock to behave unpredictably. If you come upon a cattle drive, stop and await drovers' directions. Cow hands are usually courteous and will clear a path for you in good time.

The people you meet in these remote areas may seem crusty on first acquaintance. But most are shirt-off-their-backs types with a self-reliance prompted by isolation. In this country, lives can depend on helping the other guy out. Life is basic, stripped of non-essentials. If ever there was a place where designer jeans and $500 boots look out of place, this is it.

 Dress in layers (a flannel shirt is indispensable) and be prepared for any kind of weather. This is high desert. Blazing hot days give way to chilling nights, even in mid-summer. Shorts may be cool, but if hiking you'll be

better off with long pants and high-top boots, the better to deflect those pesky cheatgrass thistles. Pack sleeping bags, blankets, extra food and water, matches, a spirit stove, a compass, a good water filter, extra gasoline, a spare tire or two, a can of pressurized flat fixer, a "Handyman" type jack, a shovel, flashlights and fresh batteries. The more remote dirt tracks call for heroic measures: a winch installed on your vehicle or a come-along and chain or cable. Stay off these side roads when they are wet.

Staying in your vehicle is good advice if you become mired down. If you do leave your vehicle, post a note on the dashboard noting the time, date, the direction you plan on taking and when you expect to return. This advice also holds if you park in a remote area while hiking or backpacking.

Be well acquainted with your vehicle. Know how to drive it on muddy roads and in bad weather. Survival gear is vital. Except for the Snake River Corridor, this region is very sparsely settled. If a town's population tops 100, it's not only a metropolis, it's a miracle. And settlements are more far-flung than potatoes in a gleaned field.

This place of extremes whets the appetites of adventurers with widely differing outlooks. Oregon Trail chasers and on-the-edge rock climbers mixing it up at City of Rocks is a good example. Little middle ground exists. Casual day hikers and cyclers are more likely to prefer, say, the Stanley or McCall areas. Hard-muscled rock climbers and backpackers eat up the challenges posed by terrain that didn't come casually by the appellation "badlands."

Information Sources

Idaho Winter Road Report: ☎ 208-336-6600.
Highway Accident/Emergencies: ☎ 800-632-8000.

≥∙

Bureau of Land Management, Idaho State Office: 1387 S. Vinnel Way, Boise, ID 83709. ☎ 208-373-4015.
Bureau of Land Management, Boise District: 3948 Development Ave., Boise, ID 83705. ☎ 208-384-3300.
Bureau of Land Management, Burley District: Rt. 5, Box 1, Burley, ID 83318. ☎ 208-677-6641.

Southern Idaho

Bureau of Land Management, Deep Creek Resource Area: 138 S. Main, Malad City, ID 83252. ☎ 208-320-4766.

Bureau of Land Management, Jarbridge Resource Area: 2620 Kimberly Road, Twin Falls, ID 83301. ☎ 208-736-2350.

≈♣

Caribou National Forest, Malad Ranger District, 75 South 140 East, Malad, ID 83252. ☎ 208-766-4743.

Sawtooth National Forest, 2647 Kimberly Road East, Twin Falls, ID 83301. ☎ 208-737-3200. Fax 208-737-3236.

Sawtooth National Forest, Burley Ranger District, 2621 S. Overland Ave., Burley, ID 83318. ☎ 208-678-0430.

City of Rocks National Reserve, PO Box 169, Almo, ID 83312-0169. ☎ 208-824-5519.

≈♣

Idaho Dept. of Fish & Game, 600 S. Walnut, Boise, ID 83707. ☎ 208-334-3700. Fax 208-334-2114 or 334-2148. E-Mail: idfginfo@state.id.us

Idaho Outfitters and Guides Assoc., Box 95, Boise, ID 83701. ☎ 208-342-1438. Fax 208-338-7830. E-Mail: outfitt@aol.com.

Idaho Department of Parks and Recreation, PO Box 3720, Boise, ID 83720-0065. ☎ 208-334-4199. Fax 208-334-3741.

Idaho Travel Council, c/o Idaho Dept. of Commerce, 700 West State St., Boise, ID 83720-0093. ☎ 800-635-7820 or 208-334-2470. Fax 208-334-2631. Web Site: www.visitid.org.

Southwest Idaho Travel Assn., c/o Boise Convention & Visitors Bureau, Box 2106 (168 N. 9th, Suite 200), Boise, ID 83701. ☎ 800-635-5240 or 208-344-7777. Fax 208-344-6236. E-Mail: admin@boisecvb.org.

South Central Idaho Travel Assn., c/o Twin Falls Chamber of Commerce, 858 Blue Lakes Blvd. North, Twin Falls, ID 83301. ☎ 800-255-8946 or 208-733-3974. Fax 208-733-9216. E-Mail: tfidcham@ cybernethighway.net.

Touring

Emigrants, Raptors & Sand Dunes

Assuming that most Adventure Guide readers will be starting from Boise, this *Region 5* driving tour begins by picking up US 95 at Exit 3 off I-84. It takes in Hagerman and Magic Valley sights, continuing east to I-15 before backtracking to explore roads leading to City of Rocks, Silver City and the Owyhees.

The area of extreme Western Idaho tucked between I-84 and the Snake is the Treasure Valley at its most bucolic. Flourishing potatoes, hops, onions, sugar beets, even grapes, strut through fields transformed from scrubby sagebrush to regimented plenty by Snake River water.

Near Parma, the Snake swallows the Owyhee and Boise Rivers before lazing northward to define the line between Idaho and Oregon. Near the confluence, the Hudson's Bay Company established **Old Fort Boise**, not to be confused with the Fort Boise later constructed in Boise.

The fort was used as a stopping place for Oregon Trail emigrants until 1854, when a massacre near present-day Middleton led to its closing. Flood waters have long since washed away all traces. A big stone bear on the Old Fort Boise Game Reserve marks the fort's probable site. Turn west off US 95 onto the Old Fort Boise Road, three miles north of Parma.

A full-size replica of Old Fort Boise stands in Parma, on Idaho 20/26 east of the US 95 junction. A museum and authentic pioneer cabin are open for tours Friday through Sunday, 1-3, during June, July and August. Call the Parma City Hall to arrange a tour at other times. ☎ 208-722-5138 or 722-5086.

Idaho 20/26 loops to meet I-84, which negotiates Boise's industrial and bedroom community corridor before speeding to Mountain Home and thence to Glenns Ferry over 63 miles of wind-swept desolation. **Mountain Home**, a misnomer if I ever met one, supports Mountain Home Air Force Base. The Snake snuggles up to I-84 just west of Glenns Ferry. From here to a point north of Idaho Falls, the river and the Interstate play catch-up. Better to take US 95 from Parma to Caldwell. Here, you can pick up Idaho 78 for a swing along the Snake that mostly parallels the Oregon Trail's South Alternate. You'll be glad you did.

A slight detour is in order to visit the famous **Ste. Chapelle Winery**, if you're into wineries and wine tasting. Pick up Idaho 55 at Marsing and proceed as though you were returning to I-84. The highway jogs sharply. Watch for Lowell Road. Turn right and voila! You're in French wine country; vineyards, chateau and all. Open Mon-Sat, 10-5, Sunday 12-5. Winery tours are available on the hour. ☎ 208-344-9074.

Marsing invites a pause to check out a stand selling fresh local produce. The false front **Tin Husky Mercantile** lends an Old West atmosphere to this sleepy agricultural town. The shop is crammed to the rafters with antiques and other dusty stuff. You can't miss 'em; they're both on the main drag.

Idaho 78 skirts the Snake for some 20 miles southeast of Marsing, affording tantalizing glimpses of blue water. Here and there, a road or track bearing a Sportsmen's Access sign heads toward the river. Most lead to boat ramps and fishing camps.

Southern Idaho

Twelve miles southeast of Marsing, you'll come across **Givens Hot Springs**, one of only a handful of landmark sites along the Oregon Trail settled by emigrants. Milford and Martha Givens remembered the hot springs where they and other emigrants paused to bathe and wash clothes begrimed by dust and distance. In 1881, the couple returned to establish the pool and baths that still bear their name.

Archaeological evidence indicates that the site has been more or less continually settled for 5,000 years. Today, Givens Hot Springs offers visitors a warm indoor mineral pool and a spacious picnic and camping area shaded by mature trees. The pool is open afternoons. ☎ 800-874-6046.

Eight miles past Givens Hot Springs, Idaho 78 veers away from the river. North of the highway and out of sight, the Snake runs between high, steep canyon walls pocked with ledges and crevices affording nesting habitat for bald eagles, peregrine falcons and other birds of prey. This, the 483,000-acre **Snake River Birds of Prey National Conservation Area**, has been set aside for the protection of these graceful raptors. Scan the sky to catch glimpses of eagles and falcons coasting the thermals.

To access the BLM-administered area, you must cross the Snake via Idaho 45 and proceed to Melba. Take the Southside Road to the Kuna Road and hang a right. From Kuna, the Swan Falls Road leads to a grassy picnic area at **Swan Falls Dam**. The best way to really see the Birds of Prey Area is by boat. (See *On Water*.)

Murphy, 10 miles farther down Idaho 78, takes pride in being the Owyhee County seat, albeit a laid-back one. Only a one-parking-meter courthouse indicates Murphy's status. Out in front, a monument erected by the Sons and Daughters of Idaho Pioneers honors 44 whites killed by Shoshoni in 1860. The full story is not apparent. The town's other most prominent structures are the inevitable **Wagon Wheel Café** and a general store distinguished by a tattered windmill. The US Post Office rivals an outhouse for size.

The **Owyhee County Historical Museum** sits a half-block from the courthouse. Wander among the flotsam of over 100 years of down-and-dirty homesteading, sheep and cattle ranching and gold mining. A sod-roofed log cabin moldering in the yard, complete with dinner bell and woodpile, resembles countless others that housed entire families in a time when folks were hardscrabble poor and didn't know it. What stories it could tell! The museum is open year-round, Wed-Fri, 10-4. ☎ 208-495-2319 for summer weekend hours.

At Grand View, 31 miles southeast of Murphy, you can cross the Snake and proceed past the Mountain Home Air Force Base to Mountain

Home, or head south on the Owyhee Uplands National Backcountry Byway. More about the Byway in due time. For now, continue on Idaho 78 to the hamlet of Bruneau, gateway to **Bruneau Dunes State Park**.

Less extensive than St. Anthony Dunes (about 600 acres), Bruneau claims the tallest free-standing sand dune (470 feet) in North America. We'll take their word for it. A small lake adds visual relief to all that sand. Be warned: swimmers fall victim to a vicious itching referred to by the locals as "swimmers' itch." The dunes area includes an abundant cross-section of the desert wildlife, including scorpions, lizards and slithery rattlesnakes.

Near Bruneau, the Bruneau River feeds into the Snake at C.J. Strike Reservoir. South of Bruneau, this river with an attitude thrashes through **Bruneau Canyon**, whose sheer walls rise upwards of 1,200 feet above the river bed. The Bruneau-Jarbidge river system offers some of the most challenging river running in North America. (See *On Water*.) A paved road parallels the canyon for some eight miles before dwindling to unimproved status and striking out into the desert badlands.

North of Bruneau Dunes State Park, Idaho 78 follows the Snake, and the route of the Oregon Trail's South Alternate, until it crosses the Snake, butts up against I-84 and fizzles out. There's no way to avoid driving I-84 for 26 miles before picking up US 30 and the Thousand Springs Scenic Byway at Bliss. **Three Island Crossing State Park** and the town of **Glenns Ferry** afford a timely respite from the roar of the interstate.

Three Island Crossing

Emigrants faced one of the most harrowing challenges of the entire route at Three Island Crossing. It took great courage to hopscotch over three islands in a effort to across the deep, swiftly flowing Snake. The emigrants had crossed the Snake some miles back, preferring the comparatively agreeable route along the south side of the river. From here, the more direct route lay north of the river. Some chose the South Alternate, but this dry, rough route offered scant water and scanter grass for their stock.

Most emigrants attempted the treacherous crossing. Wagons had to be floated across. Stock swam against the swift current. Untold numbers of lives, wagons and livestock were lost. Exhibits at Three Island Crossing State Park describe the harrowing crossing. A re-enactment of the crossing is staged every August.

Southern Idaho

Glenns Ferry, population 1,300, is a drowsy town typifying small-town America. Some residents have capitalized on the proximity to the historic site, with delightful results. Watch for **Carmela Vineyards** as you approach Three Island Crossing State Park. The winery is open year-round, 9-9. A restaurant and a nine-hole golf course (☎ 208-366-2313) round out the attractions. Nearby **Cunningham's Bed and Breakfast** (see *Lodgings*) has river-view guest rooms named for the ferrys that crossed the Snake here before roads bridged the river.

Thousand Springs Scenic Byway

The Thousand Springs Scenic Byway follows the Snake for 67.8 miles. Beginning at Bliss, it looks in on numerous scenic and historic attractions before pulling up at Twin Falls. The Byway owes its name to springs gushing from sheer canyon walls and cascading into the river below. The springs are fed by the Snake River Plains Aquifer's thousands of square miles of porous volcanic rock. Some waterfalls were diverted by hydroelectric projects, thus reducing the impact of the springs that so impressed Oregon Trail emigrants. However, the remaining falls are still spectacular, especially in spring.

Lava also breeds hot springs. Three thermal hot springs along the Byway offer soothing soaks. **Silger's Thousand Springs Resort** at Hagerman has private hydrojet pools complete with views of Snake River waterfalls. Open year-round, ☎ 208-837-4987. **Miracle Hot Springs** at Buhl bills itself as a health spa offering massages, soaks in private hot baths, and two swimming pools. Open year-round. ☎ 208-543-6002. **Banbury Hot Springs**, across the highway from Miracle Hot Springs, has similar facilities. ☎ 208-543-4098.

Thousand Springs Scenic Byway

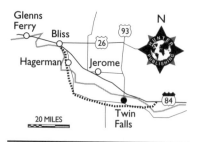

Look for a directional sign to nearby **Malad Gorge State Park** as you head down a steep decline from Bliss. The park's sheer rock walls, quite hidden from the road, force the Malad River into a slender torrent. Stand on the footbridge spanning the gorge to feel and hear the impact of the foaming, plunging river. Trails lead to rock-rimmed "fingers" where you can dip your toes in springs pattering into ponds.

Kelton Road wagon ruts are visible in the park, as are traces of the Kelton Stage Stop. The Kelton Road was once a heavily traveled stage and wagon road linking Boise with Kelton, Utah.

Hagerman is situated at the bottom of the decline beginning at Bliss. Hagerman's claim to fame is the fossil dig bearing its name. It is also the home of the **Rose Creek Winery**, in the basement of a historic stone bank building on State Street, south of town. Open 11:30-5:30. Tours are offered daily. ☎ 208-837-4413.

A temporary **Hagerman Fossil Beds visitor center** is in the middle of town, at 221 North State Street. (A new center is planned, but with National Park Service coffers low, there's no telling when it will be completed.) A slide show explains the geologic history behind the fossil beds. Exhibits include a skeltal Hagerman Horse, which just happens to be Idaho's official state fossil. Free ranger-led field programs include fossil beds tours, fossil identification, Oregon Trail living history and more. ☎ 208-837-4793 for current visitor center hours.

You can visit the fossil beds on your own, though you're more likely to see Oregon Trail wagon ruts than fossils. The boardwalk overlooking the beds offers a graphic fix on this harsh country, with sweeping views of the Snake to boot. White stakes mark Oregon Trail ruts. This is sagebrush desert; beware of rattlesnakes and scorpions, both of which can sour your vacation. The Fossil Beds are surrounded by private land; be respectful of that fact.

To reach the fossil beds, follow US 30 across the Snake and turn right on Bell Rapids Road, at the south end of the bridge. There are no signs.

A bit farther down US 30, watch for Sportsmen's Access signs on roads leading to boat ramps. Many of these offer good views of the **Thousand Springs Preserve**'s waterfalls gushing from the cliffs across the river.

Backtrack to the north side of the Snake to visit **Niagara Springs State Park**, a place boasting such magnificent glacier-blue cascades that the site is a National Natural Landmark. The access road is extremely narrow and steep; driving a large RV or pulling a trailer is strongly discouraged. To reach the park, return to I-84, get off at Exit 157, and head south.

Just before recrossing the river, watch for directional signs to the **Clear Springs Trout Farm Visitor Center**. The hatchery is one of several Hagerman Valley facilities raising and processing some 70% of North America's commercial trout. Watch enormous sturgeon luxuriating in a pond while you are picnicking among colorful flowerbeds. The visitor center is open daily, 9-5:30.

Southern Idaho

I took a detour at Buhl, one hot September day. Following signs beside roads scraping through hayfields, I pulled up near **Balanced Rock**, one of the many natural landmarks that wowed Oregon Trail emigrants. A short, steep climb leads to this hunk of stone, measuring 48 feet high and 40 feet wide, balancing delicately on a three-foot-thick base. As I pondered this curiosity, an old man with a face as seamed as the rocky landscape slip-slid downhill from the rock. He allowed as how he'd been climbing this rock every Monday for 30 years. Saying his wife likely had dinner ready, he climbed into a flivvery pickup and rumbled off down the road. I ate my lunch at a grassy oasis where Devil Creek passes under the road.

Twin Falls, a not inconsiderable city of over 27,000 on the south side of the Snake, is home to the College of Southern Idaho. At **Centennial Waterfront Park**, you can hop a boat for a tour of the Snake River Canyon (see *On Water*). Twin Falls is best known for **Shoshone Falls**, often dubbed "the Niagara of the West." Shoshone Falls' plunge of 212 feet outfalls Niagara by 52 feet. See the massive flow in spring, before irrigation canals tap upstream waters. If Evel Kneivel's derring-do exploits are of interest, you can see the very spot where he failed to jump the Snake River. Check it out from the Parrine Bridge approach to town, near the Twin Falls Visitor Center on US 93.

The **Herrett Museum**, part of the complex bearing that name on the College of Southern Idaho campus (315 Falls Ave. W.), has rotating exhibits featuring Idaho archaeology, as well as a galley of contemporary art. Open all year, Tues, 9:30-8, Wed-Fri, 9:30-4:30, Sat, 1-4:30. ☎ 208-733-9554.

The **Herret Center**'s pride is the Northwest's newest and largest planetarium, equipped with a Sutherland Digistar II computer-graphic projection system, Sony projector with a Conic pan-tilt video head, 49 Kodak EKTA-Pro 7000 slide projectors, laser disk players wrapped in a five-channel digital audio system, and a 50-foot dome whose 40 million-plus perforations allow air and sound movement through the theater. The experience compares to that of an IMAX movie theater. Shows, many reflecting Idaho's unique qualities, change periodically. For current information, contact The Herrett Center for Arts and Science, College of Southern Idaho, 315 Falls Ave., Twin Falls, ID 83301. ☎ 208-733-9554, ext. 2655.

Twin Falls County Historical Society Museum, 144 Taylor St., features a furnished pioneer house, plus antique machinery and clothing and 19th-century photographs. Open May 1-Sept 15, Mon-Fri, noon-5. ☎ 208-734-5547.

The Scenic Byway ends at Kimberly, a pleasant Idaho Falls bedroom community. You'll find **South Hills Winery** tucked in the hills four miles south of Kimberly. The small winery is owned and operated by the Hegy family. Oenophiles will be interested in an antique Italian press that is still used for pressing grapes. Visiting hours are by appointment only. ☎ 208-734-6369.

US 30 continues tracking the Snake to Murtaugh, then travels through extensive farmland to Burley and Declo, where it ends.

Caldron, Caribou & Grasslands

Murtaugh might escape note except for **Caldron Linn**, two miles north of town. Here, a mile below Milner Dam, the Snake boils between escarpments a mere 40 feet apart, forming caldron-like whirlpools. You can still make out the place where, in 1810, a party of Pacific Fur Company "Astorians" left off floating the Snake River in favor of overland travel. The change in plans came about after the Caldron swallowed a raft, drowning steersman Antoine Clappine and scaring the starch out of the rest of the party. Rusty traps and guns recovered two miles below Milner Dam in 1938 are believed to have belonged to the trappers. They repose in the State Historical Society Museum in Boise.

To reach Caldron Linn, drive north at the Y in Murtaugh, then proceed east 0.6 miles to a T, where you take the south fork (3425 North Road) to a trail leading to the rim above the Caldron.

At **Declo**, you can take Idaho 77 to City of Rocks National Reserve. Or head east on I-84 to Idaho 37, which accesses the **Curlew National Grassland** and a slice of the **Caribou National Forest**. Much of this high-desert country wedged between I-86, I-84 and I-15 is taken up by ranchlands and the **Fort Hall Indian Reservation**. Pockets of land, including the Grasslands, are administered by the Caribou National Forest. Touring this country is pointless, unless expanses of grazing land and dry farms chasing the horizon speak to your soul. Here and there, creeks and streamlets trickling from low mountain ranges form oases. The weathered ranch buildings huddled in many of these patches of green define lonely. More about this terrain in *Adventures*, below.

Rocking Through History

For a place so remote, **City of Rocks National Reserve** has an astonishing number of access routes. You can get there from I-84 by

Southern Idaho

exiting onto an Idaho 77 spur at Sublett, from Declo by heading south on Idaho 77, or from Burley via Idaho 27. The most interesting choice is via Idaho 77 heading south from Declo, looping westward past City of Rocks, then returning via Idaho 27 to Burley and I-84. This route trails through towns where history reaches out and grabs you.

Albion's 300 or so residents recall the saga of Diamondfield Jack as though it happened last week, not last century. A park features a historical sign commemorating the events that put the town on the map in the wild old days before the Cassia County seat was moved to Burley.

Diamondfield Jack

In the 1870s and '80s, Albion was surrounded by lush rangeland supporting large herds of cattle. By the 1890s, harsh winters and overgrazing had rendered the range inhospitable to cattle, but hospitable to sheep. Hard feelings between cattlemen and sheepmen resulted in a mutually agreed upon "Deadline," which sheep were not to cross. But in 1895 some sheep herders expanded their range across the Deadline. Jackson Lee Davis, aka Diamondfield Jack, was hired by cattleman John Sparks to serve as a nightrider on the lookout for overstepping sheep. When two sheepherders were found murdered, Jack was presumed guilty, tried, convicted and sentenced to hang. A labyrinthine appeals process ensued, during which Jack dodged the noose eight times.

This real life Wild West saga wrapped up as neatly as a penny dreadful. Jack finally went free. He hit gold near Tonopah, Nevada, highrolling it for a time, but died a pauper in 1949. James Hawley, Jack's defending lawyer, later became mayor of Boise and governor of Idaho. William Borah, counsel for the prosecution, was the US Senator from Idaho for whom Mount Borah, the state's highest peak, is named. John Sparks lived to became governor of Nevada.

There's not much to see here. The derelict Magic Christian College, formerly the Albion State Normal School, sits amid impossibly green lawns on the approach to town. Two attractive lodgings, Mountain Manor B&B and Marsh Creek Inn, a log motel, attest to the pull of this historic town straddling the road to City of Rocks.

You'll know you're in **Almo** when you see a mural depicting a horse and cowboy and sporting a sign proudly announcing that Almo was settled in 1878. Another sign informs you that Tracy's General Store has been in business since 1894. Yet another announces that Old Homestead B&B lies down a road thataway. A look at this old ranching and dryland farming town almost convinces you that it still is 1894. Tumbledown houses, abandoned when their owners were able to afford better ones, stand watch over the past.

The City of Rocks Administration Headquarters stands on a rise at the far end of town, where the pavement deteriorates to gravel. The Reserve is administered jointly by the National Park Service and the Idaho Department of Parks and Recreation.

Shoshone-Bannock Indians hunted and gathered pinyon nuts near City of Rocks. In 1826, Peter Skene Ogden noted the rock formations, but was more interested in trapping beaver. Oregon Trail emigrants, likening these upthrusting, fractured and eroded pinnacles to a city, gave City of Rocks its name.

The formations began as molten matter in the Earth's crust. Some of them are among the oldest rocks in the Lower 48 states. Erosion has created numerous caves, bath tubs and hollow boulders. Frost wedging occurs continually on the sides of spires, creating cracks and sloughing off huge slabs of rock, thereby destroying some of the signatures left by awed Oregon Trail emigrants.

City of Rocks saw as much traffic in the mid-19th century as it does today; maybe more. It stood on the route to Granite Pass, a route through the mountains to Utah, California and Oregon. The Salt Lake Cutoff and the California Trail (Oregon-bound emigrants knew it as the Applegate Trail) intersected at this place, and Hudspeth's Cutoff joined the California Trail here. In 1852, some 52,000 persons oohed and aahed over City of Rocks en route to California gold fields.

Emigrants were enthralled by City of Rocks. They wrote their names on the rocks in axel grease; a popular one came to be called Register Rock. Some wanted to record their passage as a stab at immortality in an all too mortal age. Others wrote messages for friends and family members yet to follow.

A stage station was apparently located at the junction of the California Trail and the Salt Lake Cutoff, 1½ miles south of the inaccurately named Twin Sisters peaks (the two granite pinnacles are, respectively, 2½ billion and 25 million years old).

The lumpy dirt road in the vicinity of City of Rocks becomes gravel, then pavement, as it turns north to Oakley, closely following the route of the Kelton Stage Road.

Oakley, settled by Mormon colonists in 1878, contains enough interesting historic structures to earn it a place on the National Register of Historic Places. The Oakley Co-op is typical of numerous similar struc-

Southern Idaho

tures, formerly church-run co-ops, gracing small towns throughout Utah and Southeastern Idaho. Other notable landmarks include the old opera house and an extravagant turreted Queen Anne brick house seeming better suited to Boise than to this outpost. This, and several more modest houses, reflect the presence of a town brickyard. The remains of the sheepherders Diamondfield Jack was accused of shooting are buried in the town cemetery.

Follow the **Warm Springs** sign from the Oakley High School to yet another of the mineral water spas sprinkling Southern Idaho. Warm Springs has an outdoor pool, two indoor pools and three private baths. Open in summer, Mon-Sat, 1-9. The rest of the year it's open Mon, Wed, Fri, Sat, 1-8. ☎ 208-862-3372.

Nearby Oakley Dam and Lower Goose Creek Reservoir are typical of high deser irrigation water "catch basins." These "lakes," lapping sagebrush hills, surprise visitors accustomed to forest-rimmed lakes.

Watering the Desert

Twin Falls residents' favorite playground is the **South Hills**, an area of low mountains, reservoirs and aspen stands between Twin Falls and the Utah line.

Magic Mountain Ski Area, at the top of steep, twisting County Route G3, exerts little magic in summer, but the drive along burbling Rock Creek through stands of aspen and juniper accesses several trailheads and campgrounds. Catch Route G3 at Hansen.

A gravel and dirt road extends from Magic Mountain and the Diamondfield Jack Recreation Area to Rogerson, on US 93. The road offers a pleasant summer shortcut to the Salmon Creek Reservoir area, but is closed in winter.

US 93 accesses the Salmon and Cedar Creek Reservoir areas from Twin Falls. Hiking, boating, fishing, cross-country skiing, snowmobiling, camping... you name it, the South Hills have it.

Three and a half miles east of Hollister you'll come upon yet another of Idaho's felicitous hot springs resorts. **Nat-Soo-Pah Hot Springs** (Shoshoni for "magic mineral water") has a large swimming pool fed by an artesian spring pumping out 99° water. A big slide and two diving boards add to the fun. A waterslide graces a 25-person hot-soak pool. A shady picnic area, plus RV and tent sites, complete this popular resort. Open May 1 through Labor Day, 10-10 on weekends, noon-10 on weekdays. ☎ 208-655-4337.

At Rogerson, 10 miles south of Hollister, you can pick up the Three Creek Highway for a 40-mile desert jaunt to **Murphy's Hot Springs** (open year-round, ☎ 208-857-2233) and the **Jarbridge River put-in**. Murphy's pool and bathhouse are situated in the most rugged canyon that ever seeped a hot spring. Rental cabins and a café are nearby.

The Owyhees: Rising to the Challenge

Silver City slumbers in the heart of the Owyhee Mountains, at the end of a dusty track that begins off Idaho 78, a couple of miles east of Murphy. A no-nonsense sign at the turnoff discourages driving in anything other than a high-clearance 4WD vehicle. At this point, the road looks as innocuous as a garter snake, but it turns into a rattler as it takes the climb up 6,676-foot New York Summit, the gateway to the queen of Idaho's ghost towns. The road is passable only in summer, usually after May 1. Attempting it in wet weather begs for trouble.

Silver City occupies a draw between 7,784-foot Florida Mountain and 8,065-foot War Eagle Mountain. It was on the slopes of the latter that Michael Jordan made the 1864 silver and gold strike that prompted the founding, though that's too fancy a term, of Silver City. In its heyday from 1866 until roughly the 1920s, Silver City boasted hotels, stores, saloons, churches, houses of ill repute, a brewery, a school, a miner's union hospital, Idaho Territory's first daily newspaper and a Wells Fargo office. The houses and shacks of both the respectable and the socially suspect lined dusty streets teeming with mining town excesses.

In 1934, voters moved the Owyhee County seat from Silver City to Murphy. World War II mining restrictions shut the last door on the city, whose residents had mined $40 million in gold and silver. Numerous buildings were dismantled for their lumber. Others were left to their memories.

Some 40 frame structures remain. Restoration is an unknown concept in Silver City. Arrested decay, often simple decay, is a better description. The 1866 **Idaho Hotel**, once as grand as any in the Territory with 50 rooms and attendant amenities, is not only interesting, it's open for business. If you don't mind sharing a bath, you can sleep in one of 20 guest rooms and pretend it's 1880, with the stamp mills still crushing rock, and flush miners bellying up to the bar downstairs. Not too far-fetched: the bar and café are still in business as well.

The circa 1892 **Old Schoolhouse Museum** will fill you in on the entire Silver Creek saga, the rowdy and the ribald, the risque and the righteous.

From Silver City, you can dirt track it cross-country to the western end of the **Owyhee Uplands National backcountry Byway**. The locals refer to it as the Mud Flat Road. They should know. The roughly 100-mile, mostly 1½-lane, sometimes-gravel, sometimes-dirt road extends from a point just east of Jordan Valley, Oregon to Grand View, Idaho on Idaho 78. Wrapping around the Owyhee Mountains like a snake with an attitude, the storied road slithers and crawls across one of the country's most remote chunks of desert ranching country.

Most passenger cars can take the drive in summer, but a high-clearance 4WD vehicle makes more sense, considering grades of up to 12% and an east-to-west elevation gain of some 2,700 feet. "Mud Flat" is no idle appellation. Sudden showers turn portions of this dusty road goopy slick. Locals refer to the mud as Owyhee gumbo. Freezes occur nearly every night in fall and spring, the seasons when rain is most likely. Ergo: if you become stuck, say in the afternoon, and sunshine fails to dry out the road (it usually will in a hour or so), unroll your sleeping bag and wait it out. Morning should bring freeze-dried road surfaces. Snow usually renders the road impassable from October to May. See pages 23, 255, 291 for vital driving caveats.

As long as you remain on the Mud Flat Road, you should be okay. But off-the-Byway exploring is tempting. You'll notice occasional hard-scrabble roads intersecting the Byway – tracks apparently leading no-where. But they all lead somewhere, or did 100 years ago when blazed by pack strings or wagons. They haven't changed much.

This is ranching country; has been for generations. Hard to believe, but people still live out here. Some tracks lead to lonely graves or to old ranch buildings desiccated by wind and time. Others lead to working ranches whose lands blend seamelssly with BLM lands. These tracks range from bad to badder; obstacle courses strewn with rocks, ruts, dips and dives. Cowboys ride pickups over them like bucking broncos held together with baling wire and cusswords. Private property signs posted on some roads may seem incongrous out here, but courtesy dictates that you respect them.

Much of this land traces private ownership back to the 1862 Homestead Act, the 1877 Desert Land Entry Act, and the 1916 Stock Raising Act. However, private ownership is limited by scarce water and rugged terrain, leaving much of Owyhee County in the public domain. The BLM administers over 3.6 million acres of Owyhee County land.

This is forbidding country, quixotically fascinating country for those who would see beyond canyon-crossed vistas rubbing up against the biggest sky west of Montana. The occasional green-fringed creek or spring, the wildflower-strewn draw, the aspen stand, the slope decorated with spring-greened mountain mahogany, seem the more remarkable in contrast.

If in the harsh light of midday the only living creature you see is a side-blotched lizard trying to blend into a rock, wait until dusk brings out the animals and birds preferring the cool of evening. No doubt you would expect the Owyhees' expanses of sagebrush and "rock gardens" to be teeming with cold blooded desert denizens, but you may be surprised at the number and diversity of warm-blooded animals and birds taking advantage of meadows, stream beds, trees, tree cavities and other hospitable habitats. Birds bring flashes of color to the monochromatic landscape. Deer, antelope, elk and pronghorn sheep live here in considerable numbers. It's a good idea to check with Idaho Fish & Game to determine current hunting seasons if you're traveling the Owyhees in the fall.

Mountain bluebirds, Idaho's state bird, can occasionally be seen at **North Fork Campground**, on the North Fork of the Owyhee River. This, the Byway's only improved campground, offers river access. "Improved" translates to mean the campground has pit toilets, grills and camper pads, but no running water. Measuring from Grand View, the campground is at Mile 70.4. There is an airfield at Cliffs, a once-upon-a-time town at Mile 73. The only other sign of 20th-century life is the **Poison Creek Picnic Area** at Mile 19.8. This shady BLM picnic area has tables, grills and running water. As the name implies, the water is not potable.

In concert with many of the West's seemingly empty spaces, the Owyhee Badlands hug a history teeming with folk who homesteaded, birthed, quarreled, sweated and died on this land. They were good folk, bad folk, and in-between folk; ranchers, women raising children, horse thieves, make-doers. You can see traces of their presence in a pile of stones, a cellar hole near a spring, a jumble of scrap metal, a track in the desert. You have only to look.

Adventures

On Foot

Hiking & Backpacking

 Southern Idaho's hiking and backpacking choices are less interconnected than in most other parts of Idaho. The Owyhee Badlands appeal to bushwhacking backpackers. The South Hills are ideal for day hikes from BLM campgrounds. The Curlew

National Grassland is rewarding for day-hiking bird lovers. The two chunks of Caribou National Forest west of I-15 appeal to both backpackers and day hikers. The Idaho State Centennial Trail is recommended for experienced desert backpackers. The City of Rocks National Reserve appeals mostly to day hikers, though backpacking is an option. Malad Gorge and Bruneau Dunes State Parks trails offer pleasant day hikes.

! TAKE
• CARE

This is high desert. Expect extreme temperature fluctuations, air that's been wrung out and left to dry, blazing hot sunshine and miles of open spaces. Take the same sensible backcountry precautions you would take elsewhere in Idaho.

Pack plenty of water on day hikes, twice or more what you would expect to consume. If backpacking, pack a water purifier and/or water purification tablets. Never drink untreated water, no matter how pure it might look. Giardia, the coliform bacteria parasite, is no joke even if the name does remind you of a flower. Pack enough food to last an extra couple of days.

Bring a high-rated sun screen and wear lightweight clothing that covers as much skin as possible. Pack something warm to put on after the sun goes down. Air temperatures can fluctuate as much as 50° in a 24-hour period. Wear stout hiking boots; sandals don't cut it. Desert terrain is strewn with unfriendly scorpions and other nasty critters, plus sharp stones and prickers.

Check road restrictions and conditions with the applicable Forest Service office or the district BLM office in Boise. If backpacking, check if a permit is necessary for a given area. Obtain a map. The BLM sells maps showing federal, state and private land ownership in Owyhee County. The Idaho Department of Fish & Game sells topographical maps showing hunting unit boundaries. Both agencies have copies of the "Triangle" map covering the Mud Flat Road and vicinity.

Let someone know where you are going and when you plan to return. It's a good idea to leave a note on the dashboard of your parked car stating your proposed route, expected time of return, and who to contact in the event of a mishap. Carry a compass. It's easy to lose your sense of direction in the trackless Owyhee Badlands.

Except for the South Hills area, which tends to fill up on weekends, southern Idaho's high desert offers plenty of solitude. Hiking here isn't for everyone. If forests are your thing, you may not enjoy this country. If you're into desert environments, you'll find some fantastic adventures here.

FS Road 020, intersecting with Idaho 38 out of Malad City, slices through the **Curlew National Grassland**. Administered by the Caribou National Forest, the Grassland is an area of grasses preserved in its native state. It serves as a reminder of what much of Southern Idaho looked like before over-grazing peeled back the fragile soil structure. Use the 12-unit primitive campground as a base for pleasant walks through this habitat of numerous upland game birds.

The chunk of **Caribou National Forest** just north and east of the Grassland has a labyrinth of trails looking in on numerous springs. A primitive campground is at the trailhead for **Wright's Creek National Recreation Trail**. This trail tracks through varied topography that includes both timbered and open settings. There's a nature trail in conjunction with the trail complex. The *Caribou National Forest Travel Map* delineates the trails in this section of the Forest. Stop in at the Malad Ranger District office for updated trail conditions.

The Pocatello Ranger District oversees the Caribou National Forest area bordered by I-15 and the Fort Hall Indian Reservation. A tangled network of trails through varied terrain can be accessed via the following Forest Service roads: 014 from Inkom and 280, 289, 010 and 008 from Pocatello.

Most people connect the **City of Rocks National Reserve** with technical rock climbing and the Oregon Trail. But don't rule out hiking and backpacking in this giant's rock garden. You can hike where California-bound emigrants once trod. In spring and early summer, meadows vibrant with wildflowers and Rocky Mountain bluebirds soften the austere landscape. There are several primitive campgrounds within the Reserve. Stop at the headquarters in Almo to obtain a map and an overnight backpacking permit.

The **Rock Creek Canyon-Magic Mountain Scenic Area** south of Kimberly has many primitive campgrounds and trailheads along gurgling Rock Creek. It's hard to lose your way on these popular trails. The good news: trails winding through grassy meadows, shimmering stands of aspen and scattered pine look in on beaver dams and trickling streams. The bad news: most trails are multi-use, meaning hikers must share with horses and mountain bikes.

Harrington Fork Picnic Area and **Third Fork Trailhead** access several multi-use trails offering fine views of the Snake River country. The **Ross**

Southern Idaho

Falls Trail, leading to a pretty fern glade enlivened by a small waterfall, is disappointingly brief.

This area is administered by the Sawtooth National Forest. Stop at the Kimberly Ranger Station to obtain an area map and current trail information.

Malad Gorge and **Bruneau Dunes State Parks** have hiking trails through sharply contrasting terrain. Malad Gorge trails meander through a cool, damp stream habitat. Bruneau Dunes trails define arid. Hiking these parks' trails on consecutive days brings Idaho's fantastic topographical variety into focus.

The southern lap of the **Idaho State Centennial Trail** originates at Three Creek, a non-town south of Murphy Hot Springs (see *Touring*, page 355). The trail follows the Jarbridge and Bruneau River Canyons before angling north to Three Island Crossing at Glenns Ferry. Backpack this desert section of the trail in spring or fall in order to beat summer's extreme heat. The BLM district office in Boise sells maps delineating this section of the trail.

Backpacking in the **Owyhee Badlands** is the ultimate do-it-yourself adventure. Unless you stick to roads tracking off the Mud Flat Road (see *Touring*), you won't find marked trails. Don't strike off into these mazes of canyons and upland desert alone; bring a friend or two. One of you should be an experienced orienteer/bushwacker.

Following a creek or river canyon makes sense. The going is often cooler, you can find some shade, and it's easier to retrace your steps. You're likely to see animals, usually in evening or early morning when they come to drink. Following side streams and canyons heightens the adventure. You may discover petroglyphs and other indicators that humans once passed this way long ago.

Sections of the Owyhee River System sprawling across southwestern Idaho figure among the state's most remote and rewarding backpacking adventures. **Battle Creek**, off the East Fork of the Owyhee, and the **West Little Owyhee River** offer Idaho's best high desert stream bed trekking, plus all the solitude you'll ever want. (See *Whitewater Rafting/Kayaking*, below.)

Purchase topographical and other area maps from the BLM office in Boise well ahead of your trip. Study them before heading for Idaho. Upon your arrival, stop in at the BLM office to discuss route options. Ask questions. You'll leave with some interesting, possibly daunting, insight into hiking the Owyhee Uplands.

Don't overestimate your ability to survive in hostile country. Don't underestimate the potential for adventure inherent in these splendid badlands. Go prepared on both counts, and you'll have the adventure of your life. There's no other place like it.

Rock Climbing

Technical rock climbers rate **City of Rocks** on a par with, or better than, Yosemite National Park and Utah's American Fork Canyon. Rabbit Rock, Morning Glory Spire, Bread Loaves and others offer experienced technical climbers a high degree of challenge. The degree of difficulty scale ranges from 5.0 to 5.14. There is a considerable number and variety of 5.13 and better climbs.

Do not attempt to climb here unless you are a trained, experienced rock climber and have the necessary safety equipment. Quash any temptation to go rock scrambling unless you know what you're doing. Rock climbers should stop at the Reserve headquarters in Almo for regulations and current conditions.

Travel with Horses

Southern Idaho playgrounds are popular with local horse owners. Horse-owning families living in Twin Falls, Boise and other Snake River Plain towns and environs often trailer their steeds to the **South Hills** of a weekend. Most trails here and in the **Caribou National Forest** are multi-use for all save motorized off-road vehicles. Some restrictions are in force. If you will be trailering your horse and want to ride here, be sure to contact the applicable ranger district or BLM office to obtain a map and learn about current trail restrictions.

Unlike more highly hyped regions, Southern Idaho has been slow to jump on the horse rental/trail ride chuck wagon. The following have come to my attention in time to be included in this book, but that doesn't mean others aren't out there. You might inquire about horse rentals at a local ranger district, BLM office or chamber of commerce.

- City of Rocks National Reserve, on the other hand, is popular enough to prompt Base Ward, owner of **Indian Grove Outfitters** in Almo, to offer horseback tours in the City of Rocks area. ☎ Ward at 208-824-5766 to reserve your horses.

- Ken Jafek, owner of **War Eagle Outfitters and Guides** and a member of the Idaho Outfitter and Guides Association, offers trail rides in Raft River country from his spread at Malta.

Jafek also offers five-day Massacre Rocks to City of Rocks covered wagon jaunts over the Oregon and California Trails. Participants walk or ride in mule-powered covered wagons, camp along the trail, eat trailside grub and receive you-were-there insights into the trail as experienced by thousands of emigrants. Ken Jafek, Malta, ID 83342. ☎ 208-645-2455.

- Jim Bass, owner of **Whiskey Mountain Outfitters**, offers trail rides, dinner rides and that ultimate Western adventure: cattle drives. Based in Murphy, he operates in the Owyhees. HC 88, Box 1050, Murphy, ID 83650. ☎ 208-495-2563.

- If you picture yourself in Silver City during its heyday, **Owyhee Expeditions** will hand you into a stagecoach for a three-day trip to the famed mining town. Even your duds and digs will be authentic to the period. You'll be outfitted in the latest 19th-century travel garb and lodge in a Silver City home.

Owyhee Expeditions also arranges visits to Owyhee Uplands working cattle ranches where you can ride with the cowboys, herd cattle and participate in other ranch activities. These are dude ranches, but they are the real item. Owyhee Expeditions, 10732 Cranberry, Boise, ID 83704. ☎ 208-322-4242.

On Wheels

Mountain Biking

The two sections of the **Caribou National Forest** between I-15 and I-84 include trails accommodating both hikers and mountain bikers. The **South Hills'** long slopes, high rims and sun-splotched trails offer great mountain biking. See *On Foot* for trail descriptions.

You can bike the roads in the **C.J. Strike Wildlife Management Area** while watching for birds and deer. (See *Wildlife Viewing*, below, for directions.)

The high desert's incised canyon country is ill-suited to mountain biking, but you might make a stab at biking the **Mud Flat Road.**

Check in with the local ranger district or BLM office for a travel map, current trail information and restrictions.

ATVs

Desert country looks tough, but is actually extremely fragile. Once disturbed, the crust is tortoise-slow to recover. The process is measured in decades. So ATVs are about as welcome as snakes in a sleeping bag.

Some trails in the **Caribou National Forest** are open to ATVs, but most prohibit them. Contact the applicable ranger station or BLM office for current restrictions. Better yet, head for Wallace, where ATVs are welcomed with boundless enthusiasm (see *Region 2*, page 128).

On Water

Southern Idaho's water comes in two guises: high desert rivers and man-made reservoirs.

The former are the Owyhee and Bruneau/Jarbridge Rivers, beloved by whitewater thrill seekers and respected by those who know their tricks. Visually, these rivers, alternately rampaging and slouching through canyons deeply incised by time and water, will knock your socks off. Experientially, they're playgrounds for big girls and boys.

Southern Idaho's reservoirs are banked by sagebrush desert and offer little to recommend them from a visual standpoint. However, they are wildly popular with those who equate fun with power boating, water-skiing, wind surfing and personal watercrafting. Anglers like them, too. If you live in such an arid climate, any blue water pool looks good.

Whitewater Rafting/Kayaking

The north-running **Bruneau/Jarbridge River System** slips through narrow, straight-up canyons of volcanic rock laid down eight to 12 million years ago. Over time, rivers cut through fractures in the rock, creating canyon walls rising 100 to 1,200 feet above the river beds. Mostly sunless, often only two boat lengths wide, the canyons are habitat to a wide variety of plants and animals. There are no signs of civilization on these rivers. Only the melody of the hustling river interrupts the solitude.

This river system drains the mountains of northern Nevada, emptying into the Snake River some 70 miles later. The Jarbridge and the West Fork of the Bruneau join forces 24 miles north of the Nevada border, becoming the Bruneau River.

The **Bruneau** has frequent or sustained Class II to IV rapids. Gnarly **Five Mile Rapids** is just that: five miles of stairstep Class III and IV drops. The several portages depend on the water level. Varying water levels determine this river's character at any given time. Flows of 1,000 cubic feet per second (cfs) mean watch out for rocks. At flows above 2,000 cfs, most rocks are hidden beneath rampaging water. Logjams caused by wind-downed Western juniper trees pose a serious problem at all water levels. Floating logs and flood debris present hazards in high water. The normal floating season is during spring runoff, from about April 1 to June 15. From June 15 well into July, the water flow drops to 200 to 500 cfs, bringing out the inflatable kayak crowd. After July, the water flow is negligible.

The Jarbridge and Bruneau Rivers can be run by raft or kayak, but the West Fork of the Bruneau should be run only by expert kayakers. Hard rapids and numerous portages characterize the more constricted West Fork. Careful timing linked to water levels is crucial to a successful adventure on any of these rivers.

The Jarbridge launch site is two miles north of Murphy Hot Springs, accessed via the Three Creek Road off US 93 at Rogerson.

You'll need a 4WD vehicle to reach the Bruneau put-in. The best route is via a rough dirt road off the Bruneau-Three Creek Road, reached on Idaho 51. The most convenient way to reach the West Fork put-in is via the Grasmere-Rowland Road off Idaho 51. Contact the Boise BLM office to obtain an area map.

Unless you or members of your party are experienced whitewater rafters and/or kayakers, don't even think about rafting or kayaking the Bruneau/Jarbridge River System in spring spate. Extreme caution should be exercised even at summer water levels. These river canyons are other-worldly isolated. The environment is hostile in the extreme. Prior registration with the BLM is required for all launches. Prior perusal of the BLM's Owyhee & Bruneau River Systems Boating Guide is a must if you should decide to go it on your own. The book includes river descriptions, mile-by-mile maps, registration forms, river ethics advice and other vital information. Don't think about tackling these rivers without a copy of the guide in hand. See page 29 for BLM addresses and phone numbers.

The **Owyhee River System** splotches across extreme southwest Idaho and portions of Nevada and Oregon, carving deep, narrow canyons that occasionally widen to grassy verges. Streams meander in a mostly

Idaho offers some of the best river running in the country.

westerly and northwesterly direction, allowing sunlight to penetrate the canyons. Thus, the environment is extremely arid and hostile to all save desert wildlife.

The Owyhee tributaries lying within Idaho include all of the East Fork, Battle Creek, Deep Creek, the northern half of the South Fork and the eastern porton of the North Fork. The main Owyhee runs through southeastern Oregon.

The **Upper Owyhee's East** and **South Forks** are boatable in rafts, canoes and kayaks. Two difficult portages make hard work of rafting the East Fork. Portaging kayaks or canoes is sometimes necessary on the South Fork. Except for a few Class IV and V rapids, most of the Upper Owyhee is Class I, II and III whitewater. Nonetheless, these waterways can be hazardous for the inexperienced.

Deep Creek, a tributary of the East Fork, is boatable in kayaks or canoes early in the float season. No difficult rapids, but this stream calls for skill in negotiating narrow channels, overhanging vegetation, gravel bars and cliffs that seem to grow straight up from the stream bed.

The Upper Owyhee and its tributaries are accessed from a rough unimproved road off Idaho 51 at the Idaho-Nevada state line. If you find yourself in Owyhee, Nevada you've gone too far. The East Fork's main put-in is at Garat Crossing, accessed by branching off the above-mentioned road. The South Fork's Idaho put-in is at the "45" Ranch, at

Southern Idaho

the end of the above-mentioned road. Request the landowner's permission to proceed to the put-in. A 4WD vehicle is a must over roads that have been pummelled and beat up by wind, snow, rain and hard use for decades.

 Don't attempt the North Fork of the Owyhee unless you are a world-class expert kayaker or cata-rafter. The put-in is at the North Fork Campground on the Mud Flat Road.

The caveats applying to the Bruneau/Jarbridge River System also apply to the Owyhee. Study a copy of the BLM's Owyhee and Bruneau River Systems Boating Guide well in advance of setting out.

Experiencing these river systems is not a pleasure available only to expert rafters and kayakers. Adventurers innocent of the rivers' ways can put themselves in the hands of experienced guides licensed for these particular rivers. The following outfitters' memberships in the Idaho Outfitters and Guides Association assures their guests of the utmost in reliability and skill.

Because of the interconnectedness of the Owyhee River System, and because these river trips usually begin and end in Boise, outfitters offering floats on Oregon's Middle and Main Owyhee are also listed below. These rivers vary in character and challenge, the Middle offering the most intense experience, the Main being more laid-back, with opportunities for hiking and exploring.

- **Northwest Voyageurs** owner Jeff Peavey offers multi-day spring floats on the Middle and Main Owyhee. PO Box 373, Lucile, ID 83542. ☎ 800-727-9977 or 208-628-3021. Fax 208-628-3780.

- **River Odysseys West** (ROW), with Peter Grubb and Betsy Bowen, has five- and six-day April and May floats on the Lower Owyhee. They will arrange a seven-day April or May Upper Owyhee trip or a four-day May Middle Owyhee trip on request. PO Box 579, Coeur d'Alene, ID 83816. ☎ 800-451-6034. Fax 208-667-6506.

- **Salmon River Experience** owners Chuck and Linda Boyd offer five-day Lower Owyhee, Rome to Owyhee Reservoir, trips in April, May and June. 812 Truman, Moscow, ID 83843. ☎ 800-892-9223 or 208-882-2385.

- **Wilderness River Outfitters**, specializing in small groups of 12 or less, in keeping with these rivers' wilderness character, runs four-day Bruneau River floats and six-day

Bruneau/Jarbridge River System trips. Both floats are scheduled for May. Also on offer are five- and six-day trips on the Owyhee River System: choose between Middle, Lower or Upper Owyhee trips scheduled for April into May. Some excursions feature naturalists offering insight into desert flora and fauna. PO Box 72, Lemhi, ID 83465. ☎ 800-252-6581.

Canoeing

You can experience incredibly challenging early season canoeing on the **Upper Owyhee River System** (see *Whitewater Rafting/Kayaking*). Like most desert rivers and streams innocent of dams and reservoirs, these tributaries offer quieter canoeing later in the season, after spring runoff. The flip side is that water levels may fall too low for canoeing. Check water levels with the Boise District BLM office before making the elaborate plans mandated by desert travel.

By way of contrast, the **Thousand Springs Preserve** and other Hagerman Valley portions of the Snake River offer delightful, leisurely canoeing. The famed springs and the myriad wildlife enjoying their congenial habitat here assume a whole new dimension when seen from the river. Sportsmen's Access signs on US 30 between Hagerman and Buhl indicate boat ramp and launch locations. The Thousand Springs Preserve's canoe put-in is at the south end of West Point Road. Take-out is at the Idaho Power Plant Picnic Area (see *Wildlife Watching,* page 374).

The **Snake River Birds of Prey National Conservation Area**, comprising a mostly quiet stretch of the Snake accessed from I-84's Meridian Exit (watch for signs at Kuna), is a great place to canoe or float. The cliffs and canyon walls lining some 80 miles of river are pocked and scored by countless cracks, crevices and ledges offering ideal spring nesting conditions for over 800 pairs of falcons, eagles, hawks and owls. Gliding over the deep-flowing river while watching these raptors hang-gliding the warm air currents rising from the canyon is an unforgettable experience.

The water is slack above **Swan Falls Dam**. A shady park here offers pleasant picnicking. You can portage around the dam before continuing downriver to Celebration Point. This portion of the river contains two Class II rapids that might cause some difficulty for inexperienced canoers, but otherwise offers a leisurely day trip. Be sure to bring along plenty of water to slake high desert thirsts.

Salmon Falls Creek Reservoir and **Cedar Creek Reservoir**, both in the South Hills area west of Rogerson, offer canoeing as well as boating and fishing. You can also canoe on **Lower Goose Creek Reservoir**, south of

Southern Idaho

Oakley. **Milner Reservoir,** west of Burley, is a good place to canoe while watching waterfowl (see *Wildlife Watching,* page 374).

Power Boating & Other Water Adventures

Slack water reservoirs behind Snake River dams are popular with local power boaters, waterskiers and owners of personal watercraft. These include the **C.J. Strike Reservoir** south of Mountain Home, accessed via Idaho 51, and slackwater above **Milner Dam,** in the vicinity of Burley. Contact the Southcentral Idaho Travel Association for a current list of businesses renting boats and personal watercraft (858 Blue Lakes Blvd. North, Twin Falls, ID 83301. ☎ 800-255-8946 or 208-733-3974. Fax 208-733-9216. E-mail: tfidcham@cybernethighway.net).

Snake River Tours

The **Snake River's Thousand Springs** and **Birds of Prey National Conservation Area** are best seen from the river. Two tour companies will assist you in seeing these areas as they were meant to be seen.

- **Snake River Canyon Scenic Cruises** offers two-hour pontoon boat floats past Thousand Springs waterfalls and over Blue Heart Springs. Minerals in these springs bubbling up from the riverbed lend the water an azure hue. Dinner and cocktail cruises are also available. PO Box 449, Hagerman, ID 83332. ☎ 800-838-1096 or 208-837-9006. Fax 208-837-4832.

- **Whitewater Shop River Tours** offers half-day February through November jetboat tours inside the Snake River Birds of Prey National Conservation Area. Ask about February and March raptor courtship tours. 252 N. Meridian Rd., Kuna, ID 83634. ☎ 208-922-5285. Fax 208-922-5286.

Fishing

The **Snake River** offers some of the West's best sturgeon fishing. These catch and release prehistoric fish can measure over six feet and weigh in at several hundred pounds. Before throwing your catch back, snap a picture to prove the veracity of the fish story you'll tell the folks back home.

In addition to sturgeon, **C.J. Strike Reservoir** has a good stock of wild whitefish, under-utilized gamefish that are often caught where trout thrive. Other than rainbow trout, which are stocked in most reservoirs and some creeks, Southern Idaho's fish population comes down heavily on the wild side.

Niagara Springs Wildlife Management Area is known for an abundance of wild rainbow. **Hagerman Wildlife Management Area** is a good place to catch largemouth bass, bluegill, bullhead catfish and pumpkinseed. Ice fishing for perch and trout is big in **Magic Valley reservoirs.**

 Before unpacking your tackle, obtain copies of two Idaho Department of Fish & Game publications: General Fishing Rules *and* The Official Guide to Fishing in Idaho. *These booklets contain vital fishing information, including state fishing rules and licensing regulations, which species of fish you can expect to catch and where to catch them, catch and release regulations, fishing seasons and exceptions, and much more.*

On Snow

Downhill Skiing

 Magic Mountain Ski Area, at the top of Rock Creek Canyon south of Twin Falls, has 20 runs with a vertical drop of only 700 feet, but is incredibly popular with local skiers. There is one double lift, a Poma, and a rope tow. 3367 N. 3600 East, Kimberly, ID 83341. ☎ 800-255-8946 or 208-733-3974. Fax 208-734-6557.

Pomerelle Ski Area, off Idaho 77 near Albion, is where Burley residents go to ski. The small area has 17 runs with a vertical drop of 1,000 feet accessed by triple and double lifts and a rope tow. PO Box 158, Albion, ID 83311. ☎ 208-638-5599.

Cross-Country Skiing

Southern Idaho offers a few outstanding Nordic skiing venues. The most rewarding is **City of Rocks National Reserve**, four miles west of Almo. Idaho 77 is paved as far as Almo, but the road continuing on to City of Rocks may be snowed in. However, most skiers enjoy skiing the four miles. Skiing among these silent sentinels, now shrouded by winter, is an otherworldly experience. Contact City of Rocks National Reserve Headquarters at 208-824-5519 for current conditions.

The **Diamondfield Jack Snowplay Area** in the South Hills has groomed snowmobile trails. You can ski these trails if sharing with snowmobiles isn't a problem for you. Several cross-country ski trails branch from the Magic Mountain ski area.

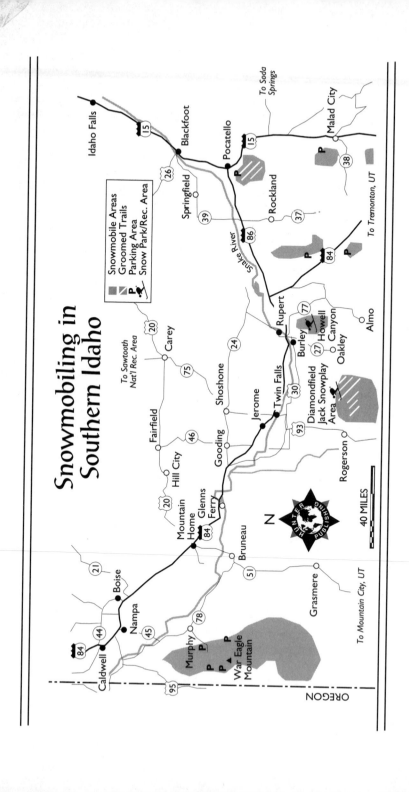

Snowmobiling in Southern Idaho

Snowmobiling

The aforementioned **Diamondfield Jack Snowplay Area** is one of two southern Idaho areas having groomed snowmobile trails (the other is in the **Caribou National Forest south of Pocatello**). Both form the nuclei of more extensive ungroomed areas.

Lands bordering the **Owyhee Uplands National Scenic Byway**, or Mud Flat Road, are accessible to snowmobiles from four designated parking areas along the road. To reach them, you must trailer your machine behind a high-clearance 4WD vehicle and pack survival gear, supplies and tools for extreme winter conditions. It's not that you'll need these **if** you get stuck; you'll need them **when** you get stuck.

Contact the Idaho Department of Parks and Recreation to obtain a copy of *Idaho Snowmobiling Registration Laws and Riding Information* and a snowmobiling map and guide.

Kid Stuff

 Southern Idaho's numerous **hot springs**, many including water slides and other fun stuff, (see *Touring* and *Camping*) make it easy to keep eight-to-teens happy. Ditto: **horseback riding** opportunities. If your kids are like mine, the desert heat will elicit loud complaints, but water fun time-outs can go far toward saving your trip.

If you wish to really wow your tagalongs, treat them to a show at Idaho Falls' **Herret Center's new planetarium** (see *Touring*).

Eco-Travel & Cultural Excursions

 Three cultural excursions, each highlighting a distinct facet of this desert environment, are available to those whose curiosity leads them to out-of-the-ordinary adventures.

- **Owyhee Expeditions** offers customized interpretive dawn-to-dark trips on the Owyhee Plateau. Air conditioned Suburbans make the heat bearable. Guests explore ancient Indian sites, see vivid petroglyphs, and partake of pre-Columbian Shoshone-Paiute foods such as wasnah, maise, pumpkin stew and buffalo jerky. Owyhee Expeditions Outfitters, 10732 Cranberry, Boise, ID 83704. ☎ 208-322-4242.

- **Snake River Expeditions** owner Steve Guinn offers one-day interpretive trips in the Birds of Prey National Conservation Area that include a land tour of the raptor habitat and a boat tour spotting eagle, peregrine falcon and other raptor nesting sites in the Snake River Canyon above Swan Falls Dam. A special three-day deluxe tour is offered every May featuring interpretive talks by Morlan Nelson, the naturalist who was instrumental in establishing the Birds of Prey Area. Nelson knows the area as well as he does his own dooryard; maybe better. He has filmed movies in the area for Wild Kingdom, Disney, and Nature Conservancy. Listening to him reminisce is a trip in itself. Nelson sometimes interprets on day trips. Ask for him. 252 N. Meridian road, Kuna, ID 83634. ☎ 208-922-5285. Fax 208-922-5286.

- **Wapiti River Guides** owner Gary Lane continually comes up with the new and unique. This time, he's offering a six-day Owyhee River trip whereon Jim Riggs, an advisor for the movie *Clan of the Cave Bear*, teaches guests how to make fires by hand, to make arrowheads and primitive tools, build traps and snares and identify native plants. Riggs has claimed that he can walk naked into the woods and survive. Box 1125, Riggins, ID 83549. ☎ 208-628-3523.

Wildlife Viewing

Southern Idaho is no slouch where wildlife viewing is concerned. You may not see a bear or a moose, but catching sight of a bobcat, a coyote or a red fox is a distinct possibility. Riparian areas support mink and river otter, while craggy cliffs are the domain of raptors. Shorebirds live here, too, congregating in the spotty stream bottoms. Numerous species of songbirds attract birders. So it's not all desert reptiles, though they do make their presence known.

It may require some effort to reach most of the following wildlife viewing areas, but you'll be glad you did. Leslie Benjamin Carpenter's *Idaho Wildlife Viewing Guide*, available at area bookstores or by sending a check for $6.25, made out to the Nongame Wildlife Program, to Idaho Department of Fish & Game (see *Getting Around*), is an indispensable handbook

If you are into wildlife watching, you won't be visiting the **Fort Boise Wildlife Management Area and Preserve** just to see the site of Old Fort Boise. Situated at the confluence of the Snake, Boise and Owyhee Rivers, this wildlife area provides a natural haven for some of the West's most spectacular wildfowl, raptors and songbirds. You're most likely to spot a ring-necked pheasant, turkey, Anerican avocet, great blue heron, black-crowned night heron, Swainson's hawk, great egret or a yellow-headed blackbird. Bald eagles, merlin and Copper's hawks are often seen in winter. Migrating birds, including white-fronted geese, can be seen in March and April. Marsh areas are closed during the nesting season. Maps and area guides are available at WMA headquarters. The WMA is on the Old Fort Boise Road, three miles north of Parma off US 95.

Deer Flat National Wildlife Refuge at Lake Lowell, off Idaho 55 between Caldwell and Nampa, is a convenient birding spot. Over 200 species have been recorded here. Sighting is seasonal. During peak migration periods, you can view large concentrations of birds on the lake. Numerous shorebirds are visible in August. In fall, mallard, pintail, Canada geese, wood duck, American widgeon and green-winged teal congregate on refuge fields. In fall and winter, raptors, including bald and golden eagles, rough-legged hawks and peregrine falcons are attracted by the abundance of prey. April and May bring migrating songbirds. In spring and summer, you may spot nesting western and Clark's grebes, Caspian terns, barn owls and more.

Snake River Birds of Prey National Conservation Area is best seen by boat (see *Touring, Canoeing, Snake River Tours and Cultural Excursions*). However, the access drive to Swan Falls Dam will doubtless produce sightings of birds of prey soaring overhead or perched on electrical poles fitted with safety barriers designed to protect raptors from electrical hazards. The Area's 14 documented breeding species include prairie falcon, golden eagle, red-tailed hawk, northern harrier, great horned owl, turkey vulture, Swainson's and ferruginous hawk and American kestral. Riparian bottomlands provide nesting habitat for songbirds and cover for reptiles and rodents. The SRBOPA is habitat for several lizard and snake species found nowhere else in Idaho. Mid-March to the end of June is the best time to see raptors.

C.J. Strike Wildlife Management Area, fed by the Snake and Bruneau Rivers, is bordered by marshy terrain that attracts thousands of migrating ducks, geese, shorebirds and wading birds. See white-tailed and mule deer at dawn or dusk. The WMA headquarters is west of Bruneau on Idaho 78.

Bruneau Dunes State Park abounds with migratory waterfowl that includes Canada geese and tundra swans. Assorted mammals, reptiles and amphibians include Ord's kangaroo rat, gopher snakes, coyote, short-horned and western whiptail lizards. A five-mile hiking trail circles the park. An interpretive center has wildlife displays.

Hagerman Wildlife Management Area's marshy ponds, surrounded by emergent aquatic vegetation, provide ideal habitat for waterfowl and wading birds that include ring-necked duck, lesser scaup, pied-billed and western grebe and black-crowned night heron. You can walk the wide, dry dikes from July 15 to October 31.

View rainbow and steelhead trout at the nearby **Hagerman National Fish Hatchery**, offering interpretive displays and self-guided tours. Follow US 30 for 3.3 miles south of Hagerman; turn left onto a gravel road just past the rest area. Turn right after one mile.

You will find the Nature Conservancy's **Thousand Springs Preserve** three miles beyond the Hagerman National Fish Hatchery, across the bridge from the Idaho Power Plant Picnic Area. The preserve includes over two miles of springs and creeks and three miles of Snake River frontage. The canyon walls are scored by spectacular springs representing the last unaltered wall springs in a system that once continued along the Snake for miles. The 400-foot-tall **Sand Springs Falls** and two spring creeks are home to the rare Shoshone sculpin. Heron rookeries line the cliffs. Canoeing is a good way to see the Preserve. Launch your canoe at the boat launch area at the south end of West Point Road; take it out at the power plant. Tours of the Preserve are arranged by appointment only. ☎ 208-536-2242.

The **Niagara Springs Area** is a major waterfowl over-wintering site where you may observe over 5,000 birds. Spring and summer wildlife include canyon wren, yellow-breasted chat, white pelican, northern oriole, yellow warbler, double-crested cormorant, golden eagle and mule deer. Take Wendell Exit 157 off I-84 and drive south for seven miles to the signed entrance road.

Rock Creek Canyon sometimes yields a porcupine or a long-tailed weasel. A 25-acre marsh near Electric Spring is fenced to protect nesting waterfowl and wading birds. Look for yellow warblers, American goldfinches, belted kingfishers, brown-headed cowbirds and northern flickers along Rock Creek.

Sagebrush-grassland surrounds **Milner Reservoir**, creating habitat for ring-necked pheasant, black-tailed jackrabbit, Nutall's cottontail, Townsend's ground squirrel and wintering mule deer. Tundra swan winter on the reservoir. Canada geese nest in area junipers. You can see American white pelicans in spring and summer. Take US 30 west from Burley for seven miles, turn north and drive one mile, then head west for about three miles to the parking area and nearby boat ramp. Walk the shoreline or boat on the lake.

Songbirds abound at **City of Rocks National Reserve**. An extensive stand of pinyon pine, juniper and mountain mahogany attract pinyon and scrub jays, green-tailed towhees, Virginia's warblers, Townsend's solitaires and mountain bluebirds. Black-chinned hummingbirds and house, canyon and rock wrens, plain titmice, red-naped sapsuckers, common bushtits and gray flycatchers also like it here.

Festivals & Special Events

June

 Twin Falls' Western Days whoops it up for a full week of activities that include a shoot-out, a barbecue, dances, chili cook-off and parade. Held the first weekend in June. For further information, ☎ 208-736-2271.

July

Buhl throws a down-home **4th of July Sagebrush Days** celebration featuring fireworks and more. Buhl Chamber of Commerce, ☎ 208-543-6682.

Kimberly Good Neighbor Days, taking place in late July, features a parade and crafts. ☎ 208-423-6401.

Oakley's Pioneer Days, also held in late July, features a pony express ride, Dutch oven cook-off, barbecue and rodeo. ☎ 208-678-1575 or 208-862-9255.

Twin Falls' Art in the Park, featuring homespun crafts and other works of art, occurs the last weekend in July. ☎ 208-733-8458.

August

The annual **Three Island Crossing re-enactment** takes place at Three Island Crossing State Park near Glenns Ferry the second weekend in August. Glenns Ferry Chamber of Commerce, ☎ 208-366-2002.

Burley's Cassia County Fair and Rodeo extends over six days in the second week of August. Enjoy daring cowboy riding, agricultural exhibits, carnival rides, and plenty of food. Burley Chamber of commerce, ☎ 208-678-7230.

September

Mountain Home's Air Force Appreciation Day falls on the first Saturday after Labor Day. A parade, free barbecue and entertainment follow an opening Air force "fly by." Mountain Home Chamber of Commerce, ☎ 208-587-4334.

Southern Idaho

The **Twin Falls County Fair** is held at Filer the first week in September. The rodeo is a P.C.R.A. points gathering event at which Miss Rodeo Idaho is crowned. There's top name entertainment, in addition to an agricultural exposition, exhibits and carnival. Twin Falls Chamber of Commerce, ☎ 208-733-3974.

October

Twin Falls' Oktoberfest is a two-day early October extravaganza. Twin Falls Chamber of Commerce, ☎ 208-733-3974.

Where to Stay & Eat

A s you might expect, southern Idaho's lodging and dining choices are limited. That's a generous assessment. Here, the tourism-B&B connection is full-blown, making family-run B&Bs your best lodging choices. Chain motels run a distant second.

Except for a couple of notable exceptions, "dining" is a foreign term. Chowing down might be more accurate. The best advice, unless you find yourself in the vicinity of one of the restaurants listed below, or unless you really go for indifferent steaks, burgers and fries, is to pack a camp stove and prepare your own meals, al fresco.

Motels, other than the occasional better-than-average chain or small town motel, are listed only when there are no alternatives. As for chowing down, we'll list the best and forget the rest.

Lodgings

Albion

Marsh Creek Inn is a pleasant 12-unit in-town log motel. PO Box 545, Albion, ID 83311. ☎ 208-673-6259.

Mountain Manor Bed and Breakfast's three guest rooms have saved many a trip to City of Rocks. Located in the center of Albion. PO Box 128, Albion, ID 83311. ☎ 208-673-6642.

Almo

Old Homestead, a three-room B&B, is Almo's only lodging. PO Box 186, Almo, ID 83312. ☎ 208-824-5521.

Bruneau

Pleasant Hill Country Inn is just that: a small, pleasant B&B outside town. Call for reservations and directions. HC 85, Box 179A, Bruneau, ID 83604. ☎ 208-845-2018.

Buhl

Amsterdam Inn is a three-room B&B outside town. Rt. 4 Box 55, Buhl, ID 83316. ☎ 208-543-6754.

Grammy Willow Inn, a half-mile east of Buhl, offers six guest rooms with breakfast. Rt.4, Buhl, ID 83316. ☎ 208-543-4782.

Burley

Best Western Burley Inn is an oasis in a desert of ho-hum lodgings. Families enjoy the swimming pool and volleyball court. 800 N. Overland Ave., Burley, ID 83318. ☎ 800-599-1849 or 208-678-3501. Fax 208-678-9532.

Glenns Ferry

Cunningham's Bed & Breakfast, on the road to Three Island State Park, is one of those gems that travelers encounter all too seldom. Each of the five guest rooms, and the charming log cabin at river's edge, all named for ferrys that once plied the river near here, have views of the Snake River and parts of the Oregon Trail across the Snake. Elaine and Bob Cunningham, PO Box 760, Glenns Ferry, ID 83623. ☎ 208-366-7342.

Hagerman

Sportsman River Resort, seven miles south of Hagerman off US 30, is a B&B, campground and motel all in one. 5 Gilhooley Lane, Hagerman, ID 83332. ☎ 208-837-6202. Fax 208-837-6575.

Malta

Connor Creek Cowboy Cabins is neither one-night-stand lodging nor guest ranch, but a mix of both. Guests can enjoy horseback riding, buggy rides, fishing and steak pit barbecues. Harvey Wickel and Jeanne Crane, HC 61, Box 1288, Malta, ID 83342. ☎ 208-638-5515 or 678-5518.

Southern Idaho

Mountain Home

Rose Stone Inn is a charming five-room B&B in a historic home. 495 N. 3 East, Mountain Home, ID 83647. ☎ 800-717-ROSE.

Oakley

Poulton's Bed & Breakfast's four guest rooms comprise the only pad in town. 200 E. Main St., Oakley, ID 83346. ☎ 208-862-3649.

Silver City

The **Idaho Hotel**, a remnant of Silver City's mining heyday, has 20 guest rooms with shared baths and a ghost town restaurant. Jordan St., Silver City, ID 83650. ☎ 208-495-2520.

Silver City Lodgings offers rental properties ranging from rustic miner's cabins, to a Victorian home, to a group hostel. PO Box 56, Murphy, ID 83650. ☎ 208-583-4111.

Twin Falls

Best Western Canyon Springs Inn is a big, comfortable full-service facility near the Snake River Canyon. 1357 Blue Lakes Blvd., Twin Falls, ID 83301. ☎ 800-727-5003 or 208-734-5000. Fax 208-734-5000.

Where to Eat

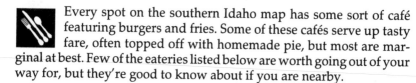

Every spot on the southern Idaho map has some sort of café featuring burgers and fries. Some of these cafés serve up tasty fare, often topped off with homemade pie, but most are marginal at best. Few of the eateries listed below are worth going out of your way for, but they're good to know about if you are nearby.

Burley

Price's Café is a tradition hereabouts. All-you-can-eat lunch and dinner buffets assure that no one goes away hungry. 2444 S. Overland Ave. ☎ 208-678-5149.

Hagerman

Snake River Grill, at State Street and Hagerman Ave., will satisfy your appetite for local farm-raised rainbow trout. ☎ 208-837-6227.

Marsing

Sandbar River House offers well-prepared steaks and local trout served on a pleasant deck above the river. Worth going out of your way for. 18 First Avenue. ☎ 208-896-4124.

Melba-Murphy

The Blue Canoe is another restaurant that's worth driving the extra mile to reach. You'll fine it on Idaho 78 between Melba and Murphy. This culinary oddball, for these parts that is, serves up creative continental cuisine. ☎ 208-495-2269.

Twin Falls

La Casita reflects the area's Mormon influence by eschewing alcoholic beverages (what's a Mexican dinner without beer?), but the food is as authentic as the track-side house at 111 S. Park Ave. West. ☎ 208-734-7974.

Uptown Bistro takes a fling at traditional bistro ambience and cuisine, a daring departure in this bland-is-safe city. 117 Main Ave. East. ☎ 208-733-0900.

Camping

The national forest campgrounds hereabouts are in the South Hills, along Rock Creek and in the Diamondfield Jack Recreatonal Area. You'll find a few on Caribou National Forest lands west of I-15, especially immediately south of Pocatello. The North Fork BLM Campground, on the Mud Flat Road, can be a welcome sight for Owyhee Uplands adventurers. So are the campsites at City of Rocks. All of the above are primitive campgrounds. Don't count on finding drinking water; pack in water or a good water purifier. Some of the best camping bets for tents and RVs are found at the several hot springs flecking the area like so many gold nuggets. Most are developed campgrounds with tent pads and RV hookups.

Bruneau Dunes and Three Island Crossing State Parks offer very different camping experiences. If you enjoy a desert ambience, you'll love Bruneau Dunes. Three Island Crossing is pleasantly situated among mature trees on a grassy hill overlooking the Snake. Both are first-come, first-served.

Bruneau Dunes State Park, HC 85, Box 41, Mountain Home, ID 83647. ☎ 208-366-7919.

Southern Idaho

Three Island Crossing State Park, PO Box 609, Glenns Ferry, ID 83623. ☎ 208-366-2394.

Some of the following campgrounds are situated at or near hot springs. Most are open only in the summer months. Call for current dates. Others are included because they enjoy a good location or have some other recommendable feature.

Buhl

Banbury Hot Springs, 10 miles west of Buhl on Hwy 30, then 1½ miles east on Banbury Road. Rt. 3, Box 408, Buhl, ID 83316. ☎ 208-543-4098.

Miracle Hot Springs is on US 30. PO Box 171, Buhl, ID 83316. ☎ 208-543-6002. Fax 208-543-6091.

Declo

Snake River RV Park, at Exit 216 off I-84, is handy if night catches you short of your destination. Rt. 1 Box 33, Declo, ID 83323. ☎ 208-654-2133.

Hagerman

Sligars 1000 Springs Resort is a largish park convenient to Hagerman Fossil Beds and other Magic Valley attractions. 18734 Highway 30, Hagerman, ID 83332. ☎ 208-837-4987.

Melba

Given's Hot Springs, 11 miles south of Marsing on US 30, has a campground shaded by mature trees. HC 79,Box 103, Melba, ID 83641. ☎ 800-874-6046 or 208-495-2000. Fax 208-286-0925.

Rogerson

Desert Hot Springs is just as it sounds. It's 50 miles west of Rogerson (see *Touring*). General Delivery, Rogerson, ID 83302. ☎ 208-857-2233.

Twin Falls

Nat-Soo-Pah Hot Springs & RV Park, 16 miles south of Twin Falls on Blue Lakes Road, is a fun family campground. 2738 E. 2400 North, Twin Falls, ID 83301. ☎ 208-655-4337.

Index